DNS on Windows Server 2003

Matt Larson, Cricket Liu, and Robbie Allen

O'REILLY®

Beijing · Cambridge · Farnham · Köln · Paris · Sebastopol · Taipei · Tokyo

DNS on Windows Server 2003

by Matt Larson, Cricket Liu, and Robbie Allen

Portions of this book previously appeared in *DNS and BIND*, Fourth Edition, Copyright © 2001 O'Reilly Media, Inc.

Published by O'Reilly Media, Inc., 1005 Gravenstein Highway North, Sebastopol, CA 95472.

O'Reilly Media, Inc. books may be purchased for educational, business, or sales promotional use. Online editions are also available for most titles (*safari.oreilly.com*). For more information, contact our corporate/institutional sales department: (800) 998-9938 or *corporate@oreilly.com*.

Editors:	Mike Loukides and Debra Cameron
Production Editor:	Matt Hutchinson
Production Services:	Octal Publishing, Inc.
Cover Designer:	Edie Freedman
Interior Designer:	David Futato

Printing History:

October 1998:	First Edition.
September 2001:	Second Edition.
December 2003:	Third Edition.

 This book uses RepKover™, a durable and flexible lay-flat binding.

ISBN: 0-596-00562-8

[M]

[4/05]

Table of Contents

Preface vii

1. **Background** 1
   A (Very) Brief History of the Internet   1
   On the Internet and Internets   2
   The Domain Name System in a Nutshell   4
   The History of the Microsoft DNS Server   8
   Must I Use DNS?   9

2. **How Does DNS Work?** 11
   The Domain Namespace   11
   The Internet Domain Namespace   17
   Delegation   21
   Name Servers and Zones   22
   Resolvers   26
   Resolution   26
   Caching   33

3. **Where Do I Start?** 36
   Which Name Server?   36
   Choosing a Domain Name   39

4. **Setting Up the Microsoft DNS Server** 50
   Our Zone   50
   Installing the Microsoft DNS Server   51
   The DNS Console   55
   Setting Up DNS Data   58
   Running a Primary Master Name Server   82

Running a Secondary Name Server   86
Adding More Zones   92
DNS Properties   92
What Next?   95

5. DNS and Electronic Mail **96**
MX Records   97
Adding MX Records with the DNS Console   99
What's a Mail Exchanger, Again?   99
The MX Algorithm   102
DNS and Exchange   104

6. Configuring Hosts **106**
The Resolver   106
Resolver Configuration   107
Advanced Resolver Features   118
Other Windows Resolvers   120
Sample Resolver Configurations   124

7. Maintaining the Microsoft DNS Server **127**
What About Signals?   127
Logging   129
Updating Zone Data   129
Zone Datafile Controls   136
Aging and Scavenging   141

8. Integrating with Active Directory **146**
Active Directory Domains   147
Storing Zones in Active Directory   152
DNS as a Service Location Broker   155

9. Growing Your Domain **164**
How Many Name Servers?   164
Adding More Name Servers   171
Registering Name Servers   174
Changing TTLs   177
Planning for Disasters   180
Coping with Disaster   182

10. Parenting **185**

When to Become a Parent   186

How Many Children?   186

What to Name Your Children   187

How to Become a Parent: Creating Subdomains   188

Subdomains of in-addr.arpa Domains   198

Good Parenting   206

Managing the Transition to Subdomains   212

The Life of a Parent   214

11. Advanced Features and Security **215**

New Ways to Make Changes   215

WINS Linkage   224

Building Up a Large, Sitewide Cache with Forwarders   229

Load Sharing Between Mirrored Servers   232

The ABCs of IPv6 Addressing   233

Securing Your Name Server   234

12. nslookup and dig **237**

Is nslookup a Good Tool?   237

Interactive Versus Noninteractive   239

Option Settings   239

Avoiding the Search List   242

Common Tasks   243

Less Common Tasks   246

Troubleshooting nslookup Problems   252

Best of the Net   255

Using dig   256

13. Managing DNS from the Command Line **261**

Installing the DNS Server   262

Stopping and Starting the DNS Server Service   262

Managing the DNS Server Configuration   265

An Installation and Configuration Batch Script   278

Other Command-Line Utilities   279

14. Managing DNS Programmatically **282**

WMI and the DNS Provider   282

WMI Scripting with VBScript and Perl   284

Server Classes 289
Zone Classes 299
Resource Record Classes 304

15. Troubleshooting DNS **308**
Is DNS Really Your Problem? 308
Checking the Cache 309
Using DNSLint 311
Potential Problem List 313
Interoperability Problems 324
Problem Symptoms 325

16. Miscellaneous **329**
Using CNAME Records 329
Wildcards 332
A Limitation of MX Records 333
DNS and Internet Firewalls 333
Dial-up Connections 351

A. DNS Message Format and Resource Records **355**

B. Converting from BIND to the Microsoft DNS Server **372**

C. Top-Level Domains **376**

Index **385**

Preface

You may not know much about the Domain Name System—yet—but whenever you use the Internet, you use DNS. Every time you send electronic mail or surf the Web, you rely on the Domain Name System.

You see, while you, as a human being, prefer to remember the *names* of computers, computers like to address each other by number. On an internet, that number is 32 bits long, or between zero and four billion or so.* That's easy for a computer to remember because computers have lots of memory ideal for storing numbers, but it isn't nearly as easy for us humans. Pick 10 phone numbers out of the phone book at random, and then try to recall them. Not easy? Now flip to the front of the book and attach random area codes to the phone numbers. That's about how difficult it would be to remember 10 arbitrary Internet addresses.

This is part of the reason we need the Domain Name System. DNS handles mapping between hostnames, which we humans find convenient, and Internet addresses, which computers deal with. In fact, DNS is the standard mechanism on the Internet for advertising and accessing all kinds of information about hosts, not just addresses. And DNS is used by virtually all internetworking software, including electronic mail, remote terminal programs such as *telnet*, file transfer programs such as *ftp*, and web browsers such as Netscape Navigator and Microsoft Internet Explorer.

Another important feature of DNS is that it makes host information available *all over* the Internet. Keeping information about hosts in a formatted file on a single computer helps only users on that computer. DNS provides a means of retrieving information remotely from anywhere on the network.

More than that, DNS lets you distribute the management of host information among many sites and organizations. You don't need to submit your data to some central site or periodically retrieve copies of the "master" database. You simply make sure

---

* And, with IP Version 6, it's soon to be a whopping 128 bits long, or between 0 and a 39-digit decimal number.

your section, called a *zone*, is up to date on your name servers. Your name servers make your zone's data available to all the other name servers on the network.

Because the database is distributed, the system also needs to be able to locate the data you're looking for by searching a number of possible locations. The Domain Name System gives name servers the intelligence to navigate through the database and find data in any zone.

Of course, DNS does have a few problems. For example, the system allows more than one name server to store data about a zone for redundancy's sake, but inconsistencies can crop up between copies of the zone data.

But the *worst* problem with DNS is that despite its widespread use on the Internet, there's really very little documentation about managing and maintaining it. Most administrators on the Internet make do with the documentation their vendors see fit to provide and with whatever they can glean from following Internet mailing lists and Usenet newsgroups on the subject.

This lack of documentation means that the understanding of an enormously important Internet service—one of the linchpins of today's Internet—is either handed down from administrator to administrator like a closely guarded family recipe or relearned repeatedly by isolated programmers and engineers. New zone administrators suffer through the same mistakes made by countless others.

Our aim with this book is to help remedy this situation. We realize that not all of you have the time or the desire to become DNS experts. Most of you, after all, have plenty to do besides managing your zones and name servers: system administration, network engineering, or software development. It takes an awfully big institution to devote a whole person to DNS. We'll try to give you enough information to allow you to do what you need to do, whether that's running a small zone or managing a multinational monstrosity, tending a single name server or shepherding a hundred of them. Read as much as you need to know now, and come back later if you need to know more.

DNS is a big topic—big enough to require three authors, anyway—but we've tried to present it as sensibly and understandably as possible. The first two chapters give you a good theoretical overview and enough practical information to get by, and later chapters fill in the nitty-gritty details. We provide a roadmap up front to suggest a path through the book appropriate for your job or interest.

When we talk about actual DNS software, we'll concentrate on the Microsoft DNS Server, which is a popular implementation of the DNS specs included in Windows Server 2003 (and in Windows 2000 Server and Windows NT Server 4.0 before that). We've tried to distill our experience in managing and maintaining zones into this book. (One of our zones, incidentally, was once one of the largest on the Internet, but that was a long time ago.)

We hope that this book will help you get acquainted with DNS on Windows Server 2003 if you're just starting out, refine your understanding if you're already familiar with it, and provide valuable insight and experience even if you know it like the back of your hand.

Versions

This book deals with name servers that run on Windows Server 2003, particularly the Microsoft DNS Server. We will also occasionally mention other name servers that run on Windows Server 2003, especially ports of BIND, a popular implementation of the DNS specifications. However, if you need a book on BIND, we suggest this book's sister edition, *DNS and BIND* by Paul Albitz and Cricket Liu (O'Reilly). This book is essentially a Windows Server 2003 edition of *DNS and BIND*.

We use *nslookup*, a name server utility program, a great deal in our examples. The version of *nslookup* we use is the one shipped with Windows Server 2003. Other versions of *nslookup* provide similar functionality to that in the Windows *nslookup*. We have tried to use commands common to most *nslookups* in our examples; when this was not possible, we tried to note it.

What's New in This Edition

The first two editions of this book were called *DNS on Windows NT* and *DNS on Windows 2000*, and they dealt with Microsoft's DNS implementation for those operating systems. This new edition has been updated to document the many changes to DNS, large and small, found in Windows Server 2003. In particular, this edition documents use of the *dnscmd* program to manage the Microsoft DNS Server from the command line and development using the WMI DNS provider to manage the name server programmatically. The book also covers new features of the Microsoft DNS Server in Windows Server 2003, including conditional forwarding and zone storage in Active Directory (AD) application partitions.

Organization

This book is organized, more or less, to follow the evolution of a zone and its administrator. Chapters 1 and 2 discuss Domain Name System theory. Chapters 3–6 help you decide whether to set up your own zones, then describe how to go about it, should you choose to. Chapters 7–11 describe how to maintain your zones, integrate zone data with Active Directory, configure hosts to use your name servers, plan for the growth of your zones, create subdomains, and secure your name servers. Chapters 12–16 deal with common problems, management tools, and troubleshooting tools.

Here's a more detailed, chapter-by-chapter breakdown:

- Chapter 1, *Background*, provides a little historical perspective and discusses the problems that motivated the development of DNS. It presents an overview of DNS theory.

- Chapter 2, *How Does DNS Work?*, goes over DNS theory in more detail, including the DNS namespace, domains, and name servers. We also introduce important concepts such as name resolution and caching.

- Chapter 3, *Where Do I Start?*, covers how to choose and acquire your DNS software if you don't already have it and what to do with it once you've got it; that is, how to figure out what your domain name should be and how to contact the organization that can delegate your domain to you.

- Chapter 4, *Setting Up the Microsoft DNS Server*, details how to set up your first two name servers, including creating your name server database, starting up your name servers, and checking their operation.

- Chapter 5, *DNS and Electronic Mail*, deals with DNS's MX record, which allows administrators to specify alternate hosts to handle a given destination's mail. The chapter covers mail-routing strategies for a variety of networks and hosts, including networks with firewalls and hosts without direct Internet connectivity.

- Chapter 6, *Configuring Hosts*, explains how to configure a Windows resolver.

- Chapter 7, *Maintaining the Microsoft DNS Server*, describes the periodic maintenance administrators must perform to keep their domains running smoothly, such as checking name server health and authority.

- Chapter 8, *Integrating with Active Directory*, covers how to design the namespace for your Active Directory forest, how to use application partitions for zone storage, and how to enable secure dynamic updates. The chapter ends with a description of the various resource records used by domain controllers.

- Chapter 9, *Growing Your Domain*, covers how to plan for the growth and evolution of your domain, including how to get big and how to plan for moves and outages.

- Chapter 10, *Parenting*, explores the joys of becoming a parent domain. We explain when to become a parent (i.e., create subdomains), what to call your children, how to create them (!), and how to watch over them.

- Chapter 11, *Advanced Features and Security*, goes over name server configuration options that can help you tune your name server's performance, secure your name server, and ease administration.

- Chapter 12, *nslookup and dig*, shows the ins and outs of the most popular tools for doing DNS debugging, including techniques for digging obscure information out of remote name servers.

- Chapter 13, *Managing DNS from the Command Line*, examines *dnscmd* and other command-line utilities that can be used for configuring, managing, and updating the Microsoft DNS Server.

- Chapter 14, *Managing DNS Programmatically*, details how to program with Microsoft's WMI DNS provider. This chapter includes examples of reading and modifying name server configurations and updating zone data using scripts written in VBScript and Perl.

- Chapter 15, *Troubleshooting DNS*, covers many common DNS problems and their solutions and then describes a number of less common, harder-to-diagnose scenarios.

- Chapter 16, *Miscellaneous*, ties up all the loose ends. We cover DNS wildcards, special configurations for networks that connect to the Internet through firewalls, and hosts and networks with intermittent Internet connectivity via dial-up.

- Appendix A, *DNS Message Format and Resource Records*, contains a byte-by-byte breakdown of the formats used in DNS queries and responses as well as a list of commonly used resource record types.

- Appendix B, *Converting from BIND to the Microsoft DNS Server*, covers migrating from an existing BIND 4 name server to the Microsoft DNS Server.

- Appendix C, *Top-Level Domains*, lists the current top-level domains in the Internet domain namespace.

Audience

This book is intended primarily for Windows Server 2003 system administrators who manage zones and one or more name servers, but it also includes material for network engineers, postmasters, and others. Not all the book's chapters will be equally interesting to a diverse audience, though, and you don't want to wade through 16 chapters to find the information pertinent to your job. We hope this roadmap will help you plot your way through the book.

System administrators setting up their first zones
Should read Chapters 1 and 2 for DNS theory, Chapter 3 for information on getting started and selecting a good domain name, then Chapters 4 and 5 to learn how to set up a zone for the first time. Chapter 6 explains how to configure hosts to use the new name servers. Soon after, they should read Chapter 7, which explains how to "flesh out" their implementation by setting up additional name servers and adding additional zone data, and Chapter 8, if they plan on using the Active Directory–integration features of the Microsoft DNS Server. Chapters 12 and 15 describe useful troubleshooting tools and techniques.

Experienced administrators
May benefit from reading Chapter 6 to learn how to configure DNS resolvers on different hosts and Chapter 7 for information on maintaining their zones.

Chapter 8 deals with Active Directory integration, which may be useful to administrators new to the Microsoft DNS Server. Chapter 9 contains instructions on how to plan for a zone's growth and evolution, which should be especially valuable to administrators of large zones. Chapter 10 explains parenting— creating subdomains—which is essential reading for those considering the big move. Chapter 11 covers security features of the Microsoft DNS Server, many of which may be useful for experienced administrators. Chapters 12 and 15 describe tools and techniques for troubleshooting, which even advanced administrators may find worth reading.

System administrators on networks without full Internet connectivity
Should read Chapter 5 to learn how to configure mail on such networks and Chapter 16 to learn how to set up an independent DNS infrastructure.

Network administrators not directly responsible for any zones
Should still read Chapters 1 and 2 for DNS theory, Chapter 12 to learn how to use *nslookup* and *dig*, then Chapter 15 for troubleshooting tactics.

Postmasters
Should read Chapters 1 and 2 for DNS theory, then Chapter 5 to find out how DNS and electronic mail coexist. Chapter 12, which describes *nslookup* and *dig*, will also help postmasters dig mail routing information out of the domain namespace.

Interested users
Can read Chapters 1 and 2 for DNS theory, and then whatever else they like!

Note that we assume you're familiar with basic Windows Server 2003 system administration and TCP/IP networking. We don't assume you have any other specialized knowledge, though. When we introduce a new term or concept, we'll do our best to define or explain it. Whenever possible, we'll use analogies from Windows (and from the real world) to help you understand.

Obtaining the Example Programs

The example programs in this book are available from this URL:

http://www.oreilly.com/catalog/dnswin3/

Viewing Microsoft Knowledge Base Articles

You can access a Microsoft Knowledge Base (KB) Article by appending the KB number to the end of the following URL:

http://support.microsoft.com/?kbid=

For example, this URL references KB article 810733:

http://support.microsoft.com/?kbid=810733

You can search the Microsoft Knowledge Base by visiting the Microsoft Support web site:

http://support.microsoft.com/

Conventions Used in This Book

We use the following font and format conventions:

Italic

Used for new terms where first defined, Registry values, domain names, filenames, and commands when they appear in the body of a paragraph exactly as a user would type them (for example, run *dir* to list the files in a directory). Italic is also used for Windows commands when they are mentioned in passing and not as part of a command line (for example, to find more information on *nslookup*, a user could consult the Windows help system).

Bold

Used for menu names and for text appearing in windows and dialog boxes, such as names of fields, buttons, and menu options. For example, enter a domain name in the **Server name** field and then click the **OK** button.

Constant width

Used for method, class, and object names. Also used for excerpts from scripts or configuration files. For example, a snippet of Perl:

```
if ( -x "$ENV{systemroot}/system23/dns.exe"){
    print "DNS is installed!\n";
}
```

Sample interactive sessions showing command-line input and corresponding output are also shown in a constant width font, with user-supplied input in **constant width bold**:

```
C:\> more %systemroot%\system32\drivers\etc\hosts
# Copyright (c) 1993-1999 Microsoft Corp.
#
# This is a sample HOSTS file used by Microsoft TCP/IP for Windows.
#
```

When a line of code is continued on a second line, we insert a bent arrow to indicate it, like this:

```
ec4caf62-31b2-4773-bcce-7b1e31c04d25._msdcs.movie.edu. 600 IN CNAME↵
terminator.movie.edu.
```

 Indicates a tip, suggestion, or general note.

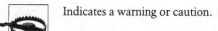 Indicates a warning or caution.

Using Code Examples

This book is here to help you get your job done. In general, you may use the code in this book in your programs and documentation. You do not need to contact us for permission unless you're reproducing a significant portion of the code. For example, writing a program that uses several chunks of code from this book does not require permission. Selling or distributing a CD-ROM of examples from O'Reilly books *does* require permission. Answering a question by citing this book and quoting example code does not require permission. Incorporating a significant amount of example code from this book into your product's documentation *does* require permission.

We appreciate, but do not require, attribution. An attribution usually includes the title, author, publisher, and ISBN. For example: *"ActionScript: The Definitive Guide, Second Edition*, by Colin Moock. Copyright 2001 O'Reilly & Associates, Inc., 0-596-00369-X."

How to Contact Us

We at O'Reilly have tested and verified the information in this book to the best of our ability, but mistakes and oversights do occur. Please let us know about errors you may find, as well as your suggestions for future editions, by writing to:

> O'Reilly & Associates
> 1005 Gravenstein Highway North
> Sebastopol, CA 95472
> (800) 998-9938 (in the U.S. or Canada)
> (707) 829-0515 (international or local)
> (707) 829-0104 (fax)

To ask technical questions or comment on the book, send email to:

> *bookquestions@oreilly.com*

We have a web site for this book where examples, errata, and any plans for future editions are listed. You can access this site at:

> *http://www.oreilly.com/catalog/dnswinsvr/*

For more information about this book and others, see the O'Reilly web site:

> *http://www.oreilly.com*

Quotations

The quotations that begin each chapter are from the Millennium Fulcrum Edition 2.9 of the Project Gutenberg electronic text of Lewis Carroll's *Alice's Adventures in Wonderland* (Chapters 1, 2, 5, 6, 9, 11, and 16) and *Through the Looking-Glass* (Chapters 4, 7, 8, 10, and 11–15).

Acknowledgments

The authors would like to thank their technical reviewers for this edition, Alain Lissoir, Roger Abell, Gil Kirkpatrick, and Jeff Westhead as well as the technical reviewers for previous editions, Levon Esibov, Jon Forrest, and David Blank-Edelman, for their invaluable contributions to this book. Paul Robichaux provided assistance from his wealth of Exchange knowledge for Chapter 5, and John Peterson offered helpful suggestions based on his production Windows 2000 environment.

Robbie would like to thank Cricket and Matt for giving him the opportunity to work on this book. He'd also like to thank his wife, Janet, for being supportive even though she thinks he needs a break.

Matt would like to thank his wife, Sonja, for her support and unflagging patience, and Cricket for asking him to help with the book in the first place. He'd also like to thank his current and former managers at VeriSign, Manoj Srivastava and Aristotle Balogh, for their support.

Cricket owes a debt of gratitude to his wife, Paige, for running the show while he wrote this book. (And when he's not writing, for that matter.) Additional thanks are due Walt, Dakota, and Annie, for their many sacrifices while Papa was working, always working. Finally, love and thanks to his grandparents for their support, guidance, and company over many years.

We would also like to thank the folks at O'Reilly & Associates for their hard work and patience. Credit is especially due to our editors, Mike Loukides and Deb Cameron.

## CHAPTER 1

Background

> *The White Rabbit put on his spectacles. "Where shall I*
> *begin, please your Majesty?" he asked.*
> *"Begin at the beginning," the King said, very gravely,*
> *"and go on till you come to the end: then stop."*

It's important to know a little ARPAnet history to understand the Domain Name System (DNS). DNS was developed to address particular problems on the ARPAnet, and the Internet—a descendant of the ARPAnet—is still its main user.

If you've been using the Internet for years, you can probably skip this chapter. If you haven't, we hope it'll give you enough background to understand what motivated the development of DNS.

A (Very) Brief History of the Internet

In the late 1960s, the U.S. Department of Defense's Advanced Research Projects Agency, ARPA (later DARPA), began funding the *ARPAnet*, an experimental wide area computer network that connected important research organizations in the U.S. The original goal of the ARPAnet was to allow government contractors to share expensive or scarce computing resources. From the beginning, however, users of the ARPAnet also used the network for collaboration. This collaboration ranged from sharing files and software and exchanging electronic mail—now commonplace—to joint development and research using shared remote computers.

The Transmission Control Protocol/Internet Protocol (TCP/IP) protocol suite was developed in the early 1980s and quickly became the standard host-networking protocol on the ARPAnet. The inclusion of the protocol suite in the University of California at Berkeley's popular BSD Unix operating system was instrumental in democratizing internetworking. BSD Unix was virtually free to universities. This meant that internetworking—and ARPAnet connectivity—were suddenly available cheaply to many more organizations than were previously attached to the ARPAnet. Many of the computers being connected to the ARPAnet were being connected to local area networks (LANs), too, and very shortly the other computers on the LANs were communicating via the ARPAnet as well.

The network grew from a handful of hosts to tens of thousands of hosts. The original ARPAnet became the backbone of a confederation of local and regional networks based on TCP/IP, called the Internet.

In 1988, however, DARPA decided the experiment was over. The Department of Defense began dismantling the ARPAnet. Another network, the NSFNET, funded by the National Science Foundation, replaced the ARPAnet as the backbone of the Internet.

In the spring of 1995, the Internet made a transition from using the publicly funded NSFNET as a backbone to using multiple commercial backbones, run by telecommunications companies, such as SBC and Sprint, and long-time commercial internetworking players, such as MFS and UUNET.

Today, the Internet connects millions of hosts around the world. In fact, a significant proportion of the non-PC computers in the world are connected to the Internet. Some commercial backbones carry a volume of several gigabits per second, tens of thousands of times the bandwidth of the original ARPAnet. Tens of millions of people use the network for communication and collaboration daily.

On the Internet and Internets

A word on "the Internet," and on "internets" in general, is in order. In print, the difference between the two seems slight: one is always capitalized, one isn't. The distinction between their meanings, however, *is* significant. The Internet, with a capital "I," refers to the network that began its life as the ARPAnet and continues today as, roughly, the confederation of all TCP/IP networks directly or indirectly connected to commercial U.S. backbones. Seen up close, it's actually quite a few different networks—commercial TCP/IP backbones, corporate and U.S. government TCP/IP networks, and TCP/IP networks in other countries—interconnected by high-speed digital circuits.

A lowercase internet, on the other hand, is simply any network made up of multiple smaller networks using the same internetworking protocols. An internet (little "i") isn't necessarily connected to the Internet (big "I"), nor does it necessarily use TCP/IP as its internetworking protocol. There are isolated corporate internets, for example.

An intranet is really just a TCP/IP-based "little i" internet, used to emphasize the use of technologies developed and introduced on the Internet on a company's internal corporate network. An "extranet," on the other hand, is a TCP/IP-based internet that connects partner companies, or a company to its distributors, suppliers, and customers.

The History of the Domain Name System

Through the 1970s, the ARPAnet was a small, friendly community of a few hundred hosts. A single file, *HOSTS.TXT*, contained a name-to-address mapping for every host connected to the ARPAnet. The familiar Unix host table, */etc/hosts*, was compiled from *HOSTS.TXT* (mostly by deleting fields Unix didn't use).

HOSTS.TXT was maintained by SRI's Network Information Center (dubbed "the NIC") and distributed from a single host, *SRI-NIC*.* ARPAnet administrators typically emailed their changes to the NIC and periodically *ftp*ed to *SRI-NIC* and grabbed the current *HOSTS.TXT* file. Their changes were compiled into a new *HOSTS.TXT* file once or twice a week. As the ARPAnet grew, however, this scheme became unworkable. The size of *HOSTS.TXT* grew in proportion to the growth in the number of ARPAnet hosts. Moreover, the traffic generated by the update process increased even faster: every additional host meant not only another line in *HOSTS. TXT*, but potentially another host updating from *SRI-NIC*.

When the ARPAnet moved to TCP/IP, the population of the network exploded. Now there was a host of problems with *HOSTS.TXT* (no pun intended):

Traffic and load
> The toll on *SRI-NIC*, in terms of the network traffic and processor load involved in distributing the file, was becoming unbearable.

Name collisions
> No two hosts in *HOSTS.TXT* could have the same name. However, while the NIC could assign addresses in a way that guaranteed uniqueness, it had no authority over hostnames. There was nothing to prevent someone from adding a host with a conflicting name and breaking the whole scheme. Adding a host with the same name as a major mail hub, for example, could disrupt mail service to much of the ARPAnet.

Consistency
> Maintaining consistency of the file across an expanding network became harder and harder. By the time a new *HOSTS.TXT* file could reach the farthest shores of the enlarged ARPAnet, a host across the network may have changed addresses or a new host may have sprung up.

The essential problem was that the *HOSTS.TXT* mechanism didn't scale well. Ironically, the success of the ARPAnet as an experiment led to the failure and obsolescence of *HOSTS.TXT*.

The ARPAnet's governing bodies chartered an investigation into a successor for *HOSTS.TXT*. Their goal was to create a system that solved the problems inherent in

---

* SRI is the former Stanford Research Institute in Menlo Park, California. SRI conducts research into many different areas, including computer networking.

a unified host table system. The new system should allow local administration of data, yet make that data globally available. The decentralization of administration would eliminate the single-host bottleneck and relieve the traffic problem. And local management would make the task of keeping data up-to-date much easier. The new system should use a hierarchical namespace to name hosts. This would ensure the uniqueness of names.

Paul Mockapetris, then of USC's Information Sciences Institute, was responsible for designing the architecture of the new system. In 1984, he released RFCs* 882 and 883, which describe the Domain Name System. These RFCs were superseded by RFCs 1034 and 1035, the current specifications of the Domain Name System. RFCs 1034 and 1035 have since been augmented by many other RFCs, which describe potential DNS security problems, implementation problems, administrative gotchas, mechanisms for dynamically updating name servers and for securing zone data, and more.

The Domain Name System in a Nutshell

The Domain Name System is a distributed database. This structure allows local control of the segments of the overall database, yet data in each segment is available across the entire network through a client/server scheme. Robustness and adequate performance are achieved through replication and caching.

Programs called *name servers* constitute the server half of DNS's client/server mechanism. Name servers contain information about some segments of the database and make that information available to clients, called *resolvers*. Resolvers are often just library routines that create queries and send them across a network to a name server.

The structure of the DNS database, shown in Figure 1-1, is similar to the structure of the Windows filesystem. The whole database (or filesystem) is pictured as an inverted tree, with the root node at the top. Each node in the tree has a text label, which identifies the node relative to its parent. This is roughly analogous to a "relative pathname" in a filesystem, like *Temp*. One label—the null label, or " "—is reserved for the root node. In text, the root node is written as a single dot (.). In the Windows filesystem, the root is written as a backslash (\ ).

Each node is also the root of a new subtree of the overall tree. Each of these subtrees represents a partition of the overall database—a "directory" or "folder" in the Windows filesystem, or a *domain* in the Domain Name System. Each domain or directory can be further divided into additional partitions, called *subdomains* in DNS, like

---

* RFCs are Request for Comments documents, part of the relatively informal procedure for introducing new technology on the Internet. RFCs are usually freely distributed and contain fairly technical descriptions of the technology, often intended for implementers.

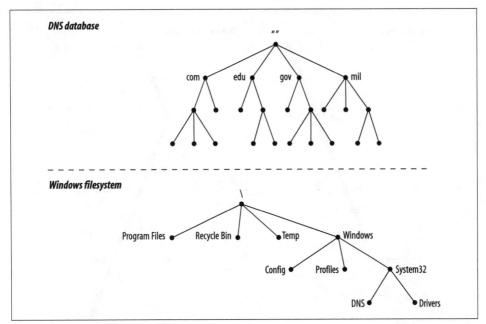

Figure 1-1. The DNS database versus a Windows filesystem

a filesystem's subdirectories. Subdomains, like subdirectories, are drawn as children of their parent domains.

Every domain has a unique name, like every directory. A domain's *domain name* identifies its position in the database, much as a directory's "absolute pathname" specifies its place in the filesystem. In DNS, the domain name is the sequence of labels from the node at the root of the domain to the root of the whole tree, with dots (.) separating the labels. In the Windows filesystem, a directory's absolute pathname is the list of relative names read from root to leaf (the opposite direction from DNS, as shown in Figure 1-2), using a slash to separate the names.

In DNS, each domain can be broken into a number of subdomains, and responsibility for those subdomains can be doled out to different organizations. For example, an organization called EDUCAUSE manages the *edu* (educational) domain, but delegates responsibility for the *berkeley.edu* subdomain to U.C. Berkeley (see Figure 1-3). This is similar to remotely mounting a filesystem: certain directories in a filesystem may actually be filesystems on other hosts, mounted from remote hosts. The administrator on host *winken*, for example (again, Figure 1-3), is responsible for the filesystem that appears on the local host as the directory */usr/nfs/winken*.

Delegating authority for *berkeley.edu* to U.C. Berkeley creates a new *zone*, an autonomously administered piece of the namespace. The zone *berkeley.edu* is now independent from *edu*, and contains all domain names that end in *berkeley.edu*. The zone *edu*, on the other hand, contains only domain names that end in *edu* but aren't in

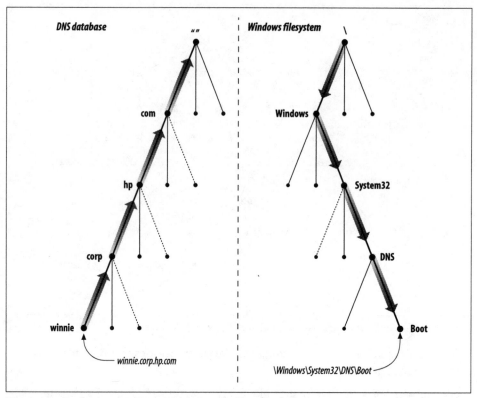

Figure 1-2. Reading names in DNS and in a Windows filesystem

delegated zones like *berkeley.edu*. *berkeley.edu* may be further divided into subdomains, like *cs.berkeley.edu*, and some of these subdomains may themselves be separate zones, if the *berkeley.edu* administrators delegate responsibility for them to other organizations. If *cs.berkeley.edu* is a separate zone, the *berkeley.edu* zone doesn't contain domain names that end in *cs.berkeley.edu* (see Figure 1-4).

Domain names are used as indexes into the DNS database. You might think of data in DNS as "attached" to a domain name. In a filesystem, directories contain files and subdirectories. Likewise, domains can contain both hosts and subdomains. A domain contains those hosts and subdomains whose domain names are within the domain's subtree of the namespace.

Each host on a network has a domain name, which points to information about the host (see Figure 1-5). This information may include IP addresses, information about mail routing, etc. Hosts may also have one or more *domain name aliases*, which are simply pointers from one domain name (the alias) to another (the official or canonical domain name). In Figure 1-5, *mailhub.nv...* is an alias for the canonical name *rincon.ba.ca....*

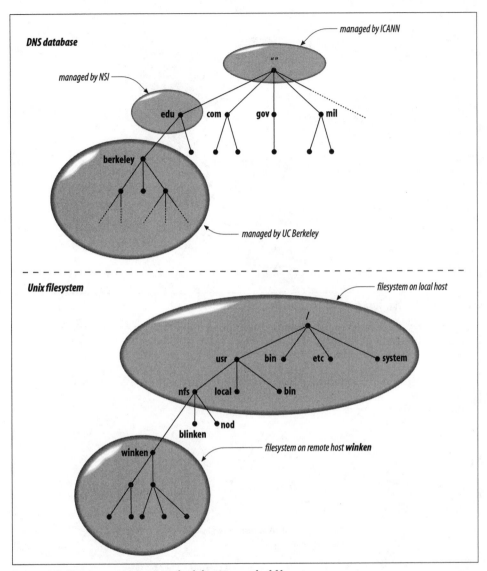

Figure 1-3. Remote management of subdomains and of filesystems

Why all the complicated structure? To solve the problems that *HOSTS.TXT* had. For example, making domain names hierarchical eliminates the pitfall of name collisions. Each domain has a unique domain name, so the organization that runs the domain is free to name hosts and subdomains within its domain. Whatever name they choose for a host or subdomain won't conflict with other organizations' domain names, since it will end in their unique domain name. For example, the organization that runs *hic.com* can name a host *puella* (as shown in Figure 1-6), since it knows that the host's domain name will end in *hic.com*, a unique domain name.

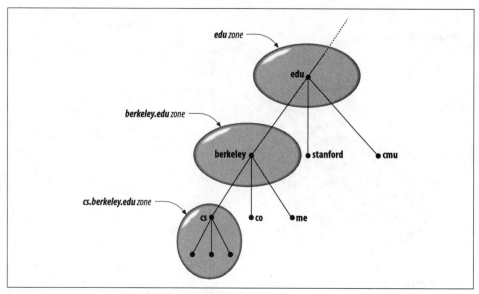

Figure 1-4. The edu, berkeley.edu, and cs.berkeley.edu zones

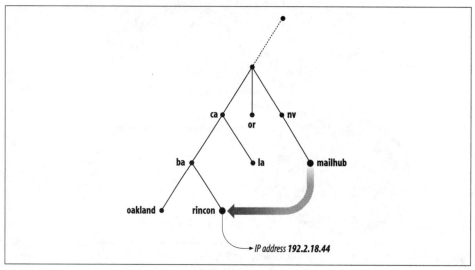

Figure 1-5. An alias in DNS pointing to a canonical name

The History of the Microsoft DNS Server

The first implementation of the Domain Name System was called JEEVES, written by
Paul Mockapetris himself. A later implementation was BIND, an acronym for Berkeley

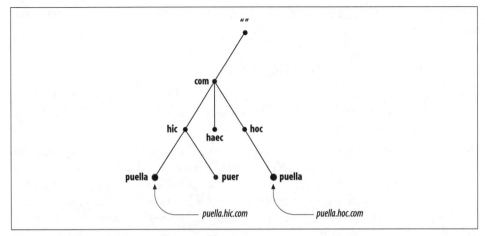

Figure 1-6. Solving the name collision problem

Internet Name Domain, written by Kevin Dunlap for BSD 4.3 Unix. BIND is now maintained by the Internet Software Consortium.[*]

Although the Microsoft DNS Server can read BIND's configuration and datafiles, it is not BIND. Microsoft wrote its server from scratch, according to the DNS specifications. The first version of the Microsoft DNS Server was a beta version that ran on Windows NT 3.51. Microsoft made it available for some time from one of its FTP servers. The first product version of the DNS Server was shipped with Microsoft Windows NT Server 4.0 (but not with NT Workstation 4.0). The DNS server shipped with Windows 2000 Server and Windows Server 2003 comes from the same code base as the Windows NT DNS server—it's really just a later version.

There are other name servers that run on Windows. For example, the Internet Software Consortium distributes free ports of BIND, including 9.2.2 (the latest released version as of this writing), which run on Windows NT, Windows 2000, and Windows Server 2003 (see *ftp://ftp.isc.org/isc/bind/contrib/*).

Must I Use DNS?

Despite the usefulness of the Domain Name System, there are some situations in which it doesn't pay to use it. There are other name-resolution mechanisms besides DNS, some of which may be a standard part of your operating system. Sometimes the overhead involved in managing zones and their name servers outweighs the benefits. On the other hand, there are circumstances in which you have no other choice

---

[*] For more information on the Internet Software Consortium and its work on BIND, see *http://www.isc.org/bind.html*.

but to set up and manage name servers. Here are some guidelines to help you make that decision.

If You're Connected to the Internet…

…DNS is a must. Think of DNS as the *lingua franca* of the Internet: nearly all of the Internet's network services use DNS. That includes the Web, electronic mail, remote terminal access, and file transfer.

On the other hand, this doesn't necessarily mean that you have to set up and run zones *by* yourself *for* yourself. If you've got only a handful of hosts, you may be able to join an existing zone (see Chapter 3) or find someone else to host your zones for you. If you pay an Internet service provider for your Internet connectivity, ask if they'll host your zone for you, too. Even if you aren't already a customer, there are companies who will help out, for a price.

If you have a little more than a handful of hosts, or a lot more, you'll probably want your own zone. And if you want direct control over your zone and your name servers, you'll want to manage it yourself. Read on!

If You Have Your Own TCP/IP-Based Internet…

…you probably want DNS. By an internet, we don't mean just a single Ethernet of workstations using TCP/IP (see the next section if you thought that was what we meant); we mean a fairly complex "network of networks." Maybe you have several dozen Ethernet segments connected via routers, for example.

If your internet is basically homogeneous and your hosts don't need DNS (say they don't run TCP/IP at all), you may be able to do without it. But if you've got a variety of hosts, especially if some of those run some variety of Unix, you'll want DNS. It'll simplify the distribution of host information and rid you of any kludgy host-table distribution schemes you may have cooked up.

If You Have Your Own Local Area Network or Site Network…

…and that network isn't connected to a larger network, you can probably get away without using DNS. You might consider using Microsoft's Windows Internet Name Service (WINS), host tables, or Sun's Network Information Service (NIS) product.

But if you need distributed administration or have trouble maintaining the consistency of data on your network, DNS may be for you. And if your network is likely to soon be connected to another network, such as your corporate internet or the Internet, it would be wise to start up your zones now.

## CHAPTER 2

How Does DNS Work?

"…and what is the use of a book," thought Alice,
"without pictures or conversations?"

The Domain Name System is basically a database of host information. Admittedly, you get a lot with that: funny dotted names, networked name servers, a shadowy "namespace." But keep in mind that, in the end, the service DNS provides is information about internet hosts.

We've already covered some important aspects of DNS, including its client/server architecture and the structure of the DNS database. However, we haven't gone into much detail, and we haven't explained the nuts and bolts of DNS's operation.

In this chapter, we'll explain and illustrate the mechanisms that make DNS work. We'll also introduce the terms you'll need to know to read the rest of the book (and to converse intelligently with your fellow zone administrators).

First, though, let's take a more detailed look at the concepts introduced in the previous chapter. We'll try to add enough detail to spice it up a little.

The Domain Namespace

DNS's distributed database is indexed by domain names. Each domain name is essentially just a path in a large inverted tree, called the domain namespace. The tree's hierarchical structure, shown in Figure 2-1, is similar to the structure of the Windows filesystem. The tree has a single root at the top.* In the Windows filesystem, this is called the root directory and is represented by a backslash (\ ). DNS simply calls it "the root." Like a filesystem, DNS's tree can branch any number of ways at each intersection point, or node. The depth of the tree is limited to 127 levels (a limit you're not likely to reach).

---

* Clearly this is a computer scientist's tree, not a botanist's.

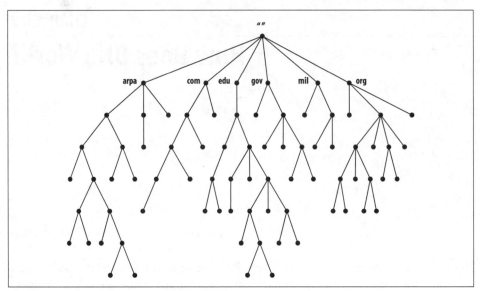

Figure 2-1. The structure of the DNS namespace

Domain Names

Each node in the tree has a text label (without dots) that can be up to 63 characters long. A null (zero-length) label is reserved for the root. The full domain name of any node in the tree is the sequence of labels on the path from that node to the root. Domain names are always read from the node toward the root ("up" the tree), with dots separating the names in the path.

If the root node's label actually appears in a node's domain name, the name looks as though it ends in a dot, as in "www.oreilly.com.". (It actually ends with a dot—the separator—and the root's null label.) When the root node's label appears by itself, it is written as a single dot, ".", for convenience. Consequently, some software interprets a trailing dot in a domain name to indicate that the domain name is *absolute*. An absolute domain name is written relative to the root and unambiguously specifies a node's location in the hierarchy. An absolute domain name is also referred to as a *fully qualified domain name*, often abbreviated FQDN. Names without trailing dots are sometimes interpreted as relative to some domain name other than the root, just as directory names without a leading slash are often interpreted as relative to the current directory.

DNS requires that sibling nodes—nodes that are children of the same parent—have different labels. This restriction guarantees that a domain name uniquely identifies a single node in the tree. The restriction really isn't a limitation, because the labels need to be unique only among the children, not among all the nodes in the tree. The same restriction applies to the Windows filesystem: you can't give two sibling directories or two files in the same directory the same name. As illustrated in Figure 2-2, just as you can't have two *hobbes.pa.ca.us* nodes in the namespace, you can't have two *\Temp* directories. You can, however, have both a *hobbes.pa.ca.us* node and a *hobbes.lg.ca.us* node, as you can have both a *\Temp* directory and a *\Windows\Temp* directory.

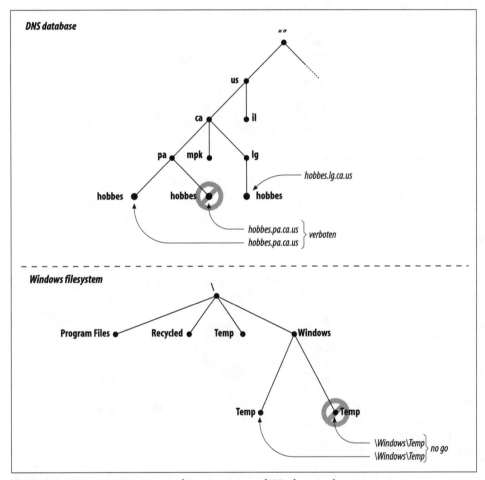

Figure 2-2. Ensuring uniqueness in domain names and Windows pathnames

Domains

A *domain* is simply a subtree of the domain namespace. The domain name of a domain is the same as the domain name of the node at the very top of the domain. So, for example, the top of the *purdue.edu* domain is a node named *purdue.edu*, as shown in Figure 2-3.

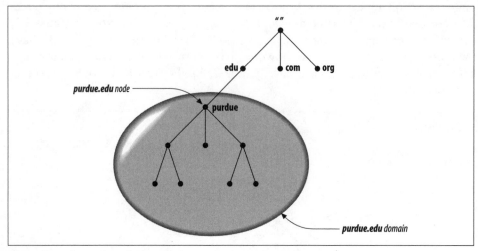

Figure 2-3. The purdue.edu domain

Likewise, in a filesystem, at the top of the \Program Files directory you'd expect to find a node called \Program Files, as shown in Figure 2-4.

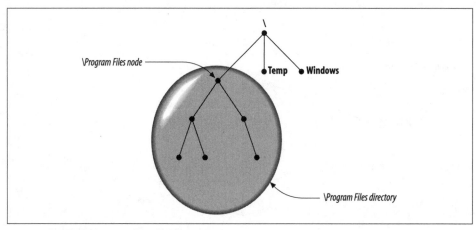

Figure 2-4. The \Program Files directory

Any domain name in the subtree is considered a part of the domain. Because a domain name can be in many subtrees, a domain name can also be in many domains. For example, the domain name *pa.ca.us* is part of the *ca.us* domain and also part of the *us* domain, as shown in Figure 2-5.

So in the abstract, a domain is just a subtree of the domain namespace. But if a domain is simply made up of domain names and other domains, where are all the hosts? Domains are groups of hosts, right?

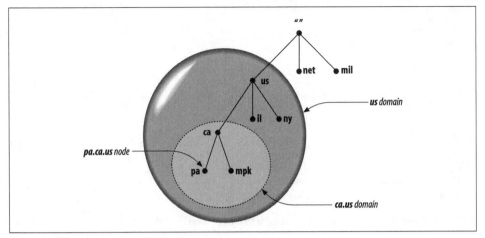

Figure 2-5. A node in multiple domains

The hosts are there, represented by domain names. Remember, domain names are just indexes into the DNS database. The "hosts" are the domain names that point to information about individual hosts, and a domain contains all the hosts whose domain names are within the domain. The hosts are related *logically*, often by geography or organizational affiliation, and not necessarily by network or address or hardware type. You might have 10 different hosts, each of them on a different network and perhaps even in a different country, all in the same domain.

One note of caution: don't confuse domains in DNS with domains in NIS. Though an NIS domain also refers to a group of hosts and both types of domains have similarly structured names, the concepts are quite different. NIS uses hierarchical names, but the hierarchy ends there: hosts in the same NIS domain share certain data about hosts and users, but they can't navigate the NIS namespace to find data in other NIS domains. NT domains, which provide account-management and security services, also don't have any relationship to DNS domains. Active Directory domains, however, are closely related to DNS. We discuss that relationship in Chapter 8.

Domain names at the leaves of the tree generally represent individual hosts, and they may point to network addresses, hardware information, and mail-routing information. Domain names in the interior of the tree can name a host *and* point to information about the domain; they aren't restricted to one or the other. Interior domain names can represent both the domain they correspond to and a particular host on the network. For example, *hp.com* is both the name of the Hewlett-Packard Company's domain and a domain name that refers to the hosts that run HP's main web server.

The type of information retrieved when you use a domain name depends on the context in which you use it. Sending mail to someone at *hp.com* would return mail-routing information, while *telnet*ing to the domain name would look up the host information (in Figure 2-6 (for example, *hp.com*'s IP address).

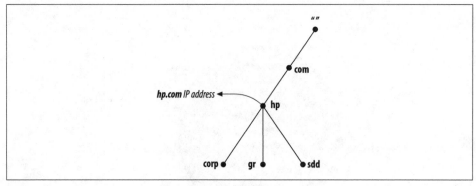

Figure 2-6. An interior node with both host and domain data

A domain may have several subtrees of its own, called *subdomains*.*

A simple way of determining if a domain is a subdomain of another domain is to compare their domain names. A subdomain's domain name ends with the domain name of its parent domain. For example, the domain *la.tyrell.com* must be a subdomain of *tyrell.com*, because *la.tyrell.com* ends with *tyrell.com*. It's also a subdomain of *com*, as is *tyrell.com*.

Besides being referred to in relative terms, as subdomains of other domains, domains are often referred to by *level*. On mailing lists and in Usenet newsgroups, you may see the terms *top-level domain* or *second-level domain* bandied about. These terms simply refer to a domain's position in the domain namespace:

- A top-level domain is a child of the root.
- A first-level domain is a child of the root (a top-level domain).
- A second-level domain is a child of a first-level domain, and so on.

Resource Records

The data associated with domain names is contained in *resource records*, or RRs. Records are divided into classes, each of which pertains to a type of network or software. Currently, there are classes for internets (any TCP/IP-based internet), networks based on the Chaosnet protocols, and networks that use Hesiod software. (Chaosnet is an old network of largely historic significance.) The internet class is by far the most popular. (We're not really sure if anyone still uses the Chaosnet class, and use of the Hesiod class is mostly confined to MIT.) In this book, we concentrate on the internet class.

---

* The terms "domain" and "subdomain" are often used interchangeably, or nearly so, in DNS documentation. Here, we use "subdomain" only as a relative term: a domain is a subdomain of another domain if the root of the subdomain is within the domain.

Within a class, records come in several types, which correspond to the different varieties of data that may be stored in the domain namespace. Different classes may define different record types, though some types are common to more than one class. For example, almost every class defines an *address* type. Each record type in a given class defines a particular record syntax to which all resource records of that class and type must adhere. (For details on resource record types and their syntaxes, see Appendix A.)

If this information seems sketchy, don't worry—we'll cover the records in the internet class in more detail later. The common records are described in Chapter 4, and a more comprehensive list is included as part of Appendix A.

The Internet Domain Namespace

So far, we've talked about the theoretical structure of the domain namespace and what sort of data is stored in it, and we've even hinted at the types of names you might find in it with our (sometimes fictional) examples. But this won't help you decode the domain names you see on a daily basis on the Internet.

The Domain Name System doesn't impose many rules on the labels in domain names, and it doesn't attach any *particular* meaning to the labels at a given level of the namespace. When you manage a part of the domain namespace, you can decide on your own semantics for your domain names. Heck, you could name your subdomains A through Z and no one would stop you (though they might strongly recommend against it).

The existing Internet domain namespace, however, has some self-imposed structure to it. Especially in the upper-level domains, the domain names follow certain traditions (not rules, really, as they can be and have been broken). These traditions help to keep domain names from appearing totally chaotic. Understanding these traditions is an enormous asset if you're trying to decipher a domain name.

Top-Level Domains

The original top-level domains divided the Internet domain namespace organizationally into seven domains:

com
> Commercial organizations, such as Hewlett-Packard (*hp.com*), Sun Microsystems (*sun.com*), and IBM (*ibm.com*).

edu
> Educational organizations, such as U.C. Berkeley (*berkeley.edu*) and Purdue University (*purdue.edu*).

gov

Government organizations, such as NASA (*nasa.gov*) and the National Science Foundation (*nsf.gov*).

mil

Military organizations, such as the U.S. Army (*army.mil*) and Navy (*navy.mil*).

net

Formerly organizations providing network infrastructure, such as NSFNET (*nsf.net*) and UUNET (*uu.net*). Since 1996, however, *net* has been open to any commercial organization, like *com* is.

org

Formerly noncommercial organizations, such as the Electronic Frontier Foundation (*eff.org*). Like *net,* though, restrictions on *org* were removed in 1996.

int

International organizations, such as NATO (*nato.int*).

Another top-level domain called *arpa* was originally used during the ARPAnet's transition from host tables to DNS. All ARPAnet hosts originally had hostnames under *arpa* so they were easy to find. Later, they moved into various subdomains of the organizational top-level domains. However, the *arpa* domain remains in use in a way you'll read about later.

You may notice a certain nationalistic prejudice in our examples: we've used primarily U.S.-based organizations. That's easier to understand—and forgive—when you remember that the Internet began as the ARPAnet, a U.S.-funded research project. No one anticipated the success of the ARPAnet, or that it would eventually become as international as the Internet is today.

Today, these original seven domains are called *generic top-level domains* or gTLDs. The "generic" contrasts them with the country-code top-level domains, which are specific to a particular country.

Country-code top-level domains

To accommodate the increasing internationalization of the Internet, the implementers of the Internet namespace compromised. Instead of insisting that all top-level domains describe organizational affiliation, they decided to allow geographical designations, too. New top-level domains were reserved (but not necessarily created) to correspond to individual countries. Their domain names followed an existing international standard called ISO 3166.* ISO 3166 establishes official, two-letter abbrevia-

---

* Except for Great Britain. According to ISO 3166 and Internet tradition, Great Britain's top-level domain name should be *gb*. Instead, most organizations in Great Britain and Northern Ireland (i.e., the United Kingdom) use the top-level domain name *uk*. They drive on the wrong side of the road, too.

tions for every country in the world. We've included the current list of top-level domains as Appendix C.

New top-level domains

Then, in late 2000, the organization responsible for the management of the Domain Name System, the Internet Corporation for Assigned Names and Numbers, or ICANN, created seven new generic top-level domains to accommodate the rapid expansion of the Internet and the need for more domain name "space." A few of these were truly generic top-level domains, like *com*, *net*, and *org*, while others were closer in purpose to *gov* and *mil*: reserved for use by a specific (and sometimes surprisingly small) community.* These new gTLDs are:

aero
> For the aeronautical industry

biz
> Generic

coop
> For cooperatives

info
> Generic

museum
> For museums

name
> For individuals

pro
> For professionals

Further Down

Within these top-level domains, the traditions and the extent to which they are followed vary. Some of the ISO 3166 top-level domains closely follow the U.S.'s original organizational scheme. For example, Australia's top-level domain, *au*, has subdomains such as *edu.au* and *com.au*. Some other ISO 3166 top-level domains follow the *uk* domain's lead and have organizationally oriented subdomains such as *co. uk* for corporations and *ac.uk* for the academic community. In most cases, however, even these geographically oriented top-level domains are divided up organizationally.

That wasn't originally true of the *us* top-level domain, though. In the beginning, the *us* domain had 50 subdomains that correspond to—guess what?—the 50 U.S. states.†

---

* ICANN refers to this latter variety as a "sponsored gTLD," and the former as an "unsponsored gTLD."
† Actually, there are a few more domains under *us*: one for Washington, D.C., one for Guam, and so on.

Each was named according to the standard two-letter abbreviation for the state—the same abbreviation standardized by the U.S. Postal Service. Within each state's domain, the organization was still largely geographical: most subdomains corresponded to individual cities. Beneath the cities, the subdomains usually corresponded to individual hosts.

As with so many namespace rules, though, this structure was abandoned when a new company, Neustar, began managing *us* in 2002. Now *us*—like *com* and *net*—is open to all comers.

Reading Domain Names

Now that you know what most top-level domains represent and how their namespaces are structured, you'll probably find it much easier to make sense of most domain names. Let's dissect a few for practice:

lithium.cchem.berkeley.edu

> You've got a head start on this one, as we've already told you that *berkeley.edu* is U.C. Berkeley's domain. (Even if you didn't already know that, though, you could have inferred that the name probably belongs to a U.S. university because it's in the top-level *edu* domain.) *cchem* is the College of Chemistry's subdomain of *berkeley.edu*. Finally, *lithium* is the name of a particular host in the domain—and probably one of about a hundred or so, if they've got one for every element.

winnie.corp.hp.com

> This example is a bit harder, but not much. The *hp.com* domain in all likelihood belongs to the Hewlett-Packard Company (in fact, we gave you this earlier, too). Their *corp* subdomain is undoubtedly their corporate headquarters. And *winnie* is probably just some silly name someone thought up for a host.

fernwood.mpk.ca.us

> Here you'll need to use your understanding of the *us* domain. *ca.us* is obviously California's domain, but *mpk* is anybody's guess. In this case, it would be hard to know that it's Menlo Park's domain unless you knew your San Francisco Bay Area geography. (And no, it's not the same Menlo Park that Edison lived in—that one's in New Jersey.)

daphne.ch.apollo.hp.com

> We've included this example just so you don't start thinking that all domain names have only four labels. *apollo.hp.com* is the former Apollo Computer subdomain of the *hp.com* domain. (When HP acquired Apollo, it also acquired Apollo's Internet domain, *apollo.com*, which became *apollo.hp.com*.) *ch.apollo.hp.com* is Apollo's Chelmsford, Massachusetts site. *daphne* is a host at Chelmsford.

Delegation

Remember that one of the main goals of the design of the Domain Name System was to decentralize administration? This is achieved through *delegation*. Delegating domains works a lot like delegating tasks at work. A manager may break up a large project into smaller tasks and delegate responsibility for each of these tasks to different employees.

Likewise, an organization administering a domain can divide it into subdomains. Each of those subdomains can be delegated to other organizations. This means that an organization becomes responsible for maintaining all the data in that subdomain. It can freely change the data and even divide its subdomain into more subdomains and delegate those. The parent domain retains only pointers to sources of the subdomain's data, so that it can refer queriers there. The domain *stanford.edu*, for example, is delegated to the folks at Stanford who run the university's networks (see Figure 2-7).

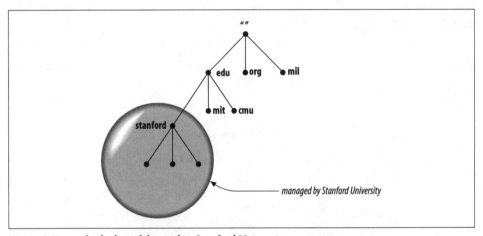

Figure 2-7. stanford.edu is delegated to Stanford University

Not all organizations delegate away their whole domain, just as not all managers delegate all their work. A domain may have several delegated subdomains and also contain hosts that don't belong in the subdomains. For example, the Acme Corporation (it supplies a certain coyote with most of his gadgets), which has a division in Rockaway and its headquarters in Kalamazoo, might have a *rockaway.acme.com* subdomain and a *kalamazoo.acme.com* subdomain. However, the few hosts in the Acme sales offices scattered throughout the U.S. would fit better under *acme.com* than under either subdomain.

We'll explain how to create and delegate subdomains later. For now, it's important only that you understand that the term delegation refers to assigning responsibility for a subdomain to another organization.

Name Servers and Zones

The programs that store information about the domain namespace are called *name servers*. Name servers generally have complete information about some part of the domain namespace, called a *zone*, which they load from a file or from another name server. The name server is then said to have *authority* for that zone. Name servers can be authoritative for multiple zones, too.

The difference between a zone and a domain is important, but subtle. All top-level domains and many domains at the second level and lower, such as *berkeley.edu* and *hp.com*, are broken into smaller, more manageable units by delegation. These units are called zones. The *edu* domain, shown in Figure 2-8, is divided into many zones, including the *berkeley.edu* zone, the *purdue.edu* zone, and the *nwu.edu* zone. At the top of the domain, there's also an *edu* zone. It's natural that the folks who run *edu* would break up the *edu* domain: otherwise, they'd have to manage the *berkeley.edu* subdomain themselves. It makes much more sense to delegate *berkeley.edu* to Berkeley. What's left for the folks who run *edu*? The *edu* zone, which contains mostly delegation information for the subdomains of *edu*.

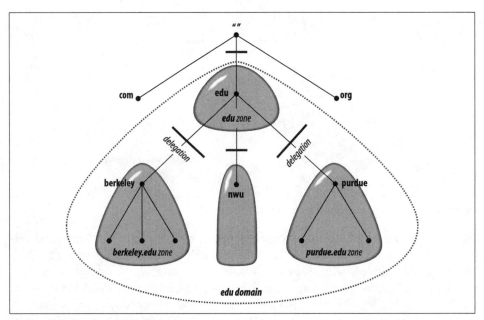

Figure 2-8. The edu domain broken into zones

The *berkeley.edu* subdomain is, in turn, broken up into multiple zones by delegation, as shown in Figure 2-9. There are delegated subdomains called *cc*, *cs*, *ce*, *me*, and more. Each of these subdomains is delegated to a set of name servers, some of which are also authoritative for *berkeley.edu*. However, the zones are still separate and may have totally different groups of authoritative name servers.

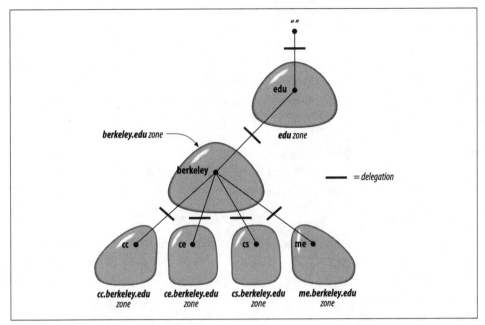

Figure 2-9. The berkeley.edu domain broken into zones

A zone contains all the domain names the domain with the same domain name contains, except for domain names in delegated subdomains. For example, the top-level domain *ca* (for Canada) has subdomains called *ab.ca*, *on.ca*, and *qc.ca*, for the provinces Alberta, Ontario, and Quebec. Authority for the *ab.ca*, *on.ca*, and *qc.ca* domains may be delegated to name servers in each of the provinces. The *domain ca* contains all the data in *ca* plus all the data in *ab.ca*, *on.ca*, and *qc.ca*. However, the *zone ca* contains only the data in *ca* (see Figure 2-10), which is probably mostly pointers to the delegated subdomains. *ab.ca*, *on.ca*, and *qc.ca* are separate zones from the *ca* zone.

The zone also contains the domain names and data in any subdomains that aren't delegated away. For example, the *bc.ca* and *sk.ca* (British Columbia and Saskatchewan) subdomains of the *ca* domain may exist but not be delegated. (Perhaps the provincial authorities in B.C. and Saskatchewan aren't yet ready to manage their subdomains, but the authorities running the top-level *ca* domain want to preserve the consistency of the namespace and implement subdomains for all of the Canadian provinces right away.) In this case, the zone *ca* has a ragged bottom edge, containing *bc.ca* and *sk.ca*, but not the other *ca* subdomains, as shown in Figure 2-11.

Now it's clear why name servers load zones instead of domains: a domain may contain more information than the name server needs, since it can contain data delegated

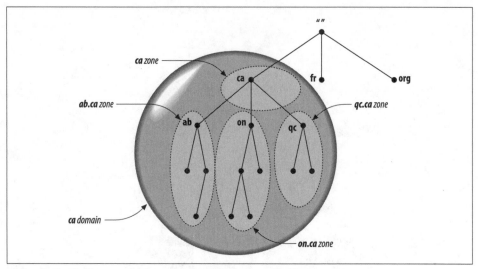

Figure 2-10. The domain ca...

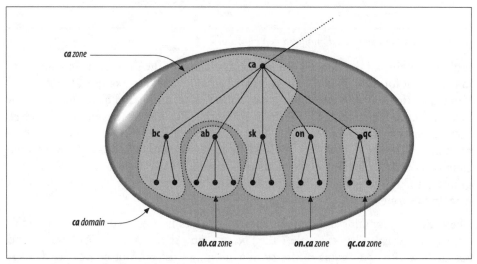

Figure 2-11. versus the zone ca...

to other name servers.* Since a zone is bounded by delegation, it will never include delegated data.

---

* Imagine if a root name server loaded the root domain instead of the root zone: it would be loading the entire namespace!

If you're just starting out, your domain probably won't have any subdomains. In this case, since there's no delegation going on, your domain and your zone will contain the same data.

Delegating Subdomains

Even though you may not need to delegate parts of your domain just yet, it's helpful to understand a little more about how the process of delegating a subdomain works. Delegation, in the abstract, involves assigning responsibility for some part of your domain to another organization. What really happens, however, is the assignment of authority for a subdomain to different name servers. (Note that we said "name servers," not just "name server.")

Your zone's data, instead of containing information in the subdomain you've delegated, includes pointers to the name servers that are authoritative for that subdomain. Now if one of your name servers is asked for data in the subdomain, it can reply with a list of the right name servers to contact.

Types of Name Servers

The DNS specs define two types of name servers: primary masters and secondaries. A *primary master* name server for a zone reads the data for the zone from a file on its host. A *secondary* name server for a zone gets the zone data from another name server authoritative for the zone, called its master server. Quite often, the master server is the zone's primary master, but that's not required: a secondary can load zone data from another secondary. When a secondary starts up, it contacts its master name server and, if necessary, pulls the zone data over. This is referred to as a *zone transfer*. Nowadays, the preferred term for a secondary name server is a *slave*, though many people (and some software, including Microsoft's DNS console) still use the old term.

Both the primary master and secondary name servers for a zone are authoritative for that zone. Despite the somewhat disparaging name, secondaries aren't second-class name servers. DNS provides these two types of name servers to make administration easier. Once you've created the data for your zone and set up a primary master name server, you don't need to copy that data from host to host to create new name servers for the zone. You simply set up secondary name servers that load their data from the primary master for the zone. The secondaries you set up will transfer new zone data when necessary.

Secondary name servers are important because it's a good idea to set up more than one authoritative name server for any given zone. You'll want more than one for redundancy, to spread the load around, and to make sure that all the hosts in the zone have a name server close by. Using secondary name servers makes this administratively workable.

Calling a *particular* name server a primary master name server or a secondary name server is a little imprecise, though. We mentioned earlier that a name server can be authoritative for more than one zone. Similarly, a name server can be a primary master for one zone and a secondary for another. Most name servers, however, are either primary for most of the zones they load or secondary for most of the zones they load. So if we call a particular name server a primary or a secondary, we mean that it's the primary master or a secondary for *most* of the zones for which it's authoritative.

Datafiles

The files from which primary master name servers load their zone data are called, simply enough, *zone datafiles*. We often refer to them as *datafiles*. Secondary name servers can also load their zone data from datafiles. Secondaries are usually configured to back up the zone data they transfer from a master name server to datafiles. If the secondary is later killed and restarted, it will read the backup datafiles first, then check to see whether its zone data is current. This both obviates the need to transfer the zone data if it hasn't changed and provides a source of the data if the master is down.

Resolvers

Resolvers are the clients that access name servers. Programs running on a host that need information from the domain namespace use the resolver. The resolver handles:

- Querying a name server
- Interpreting responses (which may be resource records or an error)
- Returning the information to the programs that requested it

In Windows Server 2003, the resolver is a set of library routines, linked into programs such as *telnet* and *ftp*, and a system service called the DNS Client, which is responsible for caching records that applications have requested. The resolver relies almost entirely upon the name servers it queries. It has the smarts to put together a query, to send it and wait for an answer, and to resend the query if it isn't answered, but that's about all. Most of the burden of finding an answer to the query is placed on the name server. The DNS specs call this kind of resolver a *stub resolver*.

Other implementations of DNS have had smarter resolvers that could do more sophisticated things, such as follow referrals to locate the name servers authoritative for a particular zone.

Resolution

Name servers are adept at retrieving data from the domain namespace. They have to be, given the limited intelligence of most resolvers. Not only can they give you data about zones for which they're authoritative, they can also search through the domain namespace to find data for which they're not authoritative. This process is called *name resolution* or simply *resolution*.

Because the namespace is structured as an inverted tree, a name server needs only the domain names and addresses of the root name servers to find its way to any point in the tree. A name server can issue a query to a root name server for any domain name in the domain namespace, and the root name server will start the name server on its way.

Root Name Servers

The root name servers know where the authoritative name servers for each of the top-level zones are. (In fact, some of the root name servers are authoritative for some of the generic top-level zones.) Given a query about any domain name, the root name servers can at least provide the names and addresses of the name servers that are authoritative for the top-level zone the domain name ends in. In turn, the top-level name servers can provide the list of authoritative name servers for the second-level zone that the domain name ends in. Each name server queried either gives the querier information about how to get "closer" to the answer it's seeking or provides the answer itself.

The root name servers are clearly important to resolution. Because they're so important, DNS provides mechanisms—such as caching, which we'll discuss a little later—to help offload the root name servers. But in the absence of other information, resolution has to start at the root name servers. This makes the root name servers crucial to the operation of DNS; if all the Internet root name servers were unreachable for an extended period, all resolution on the Internet would fail. To protect against this, the Internet has 13 root name servers (as of this writing) spread across different parts of the network. One is on PSINet, a commercial Internet backbone; one is on the NASA Science Internet; two are in Europe; and one is in Japan.

Being the focal point for so many queries keeps the roots busy; even with 13, the traffic to each root name server is very high. A recent informal poll of root name server administrators showed each root receiving thousands of queries per second.

Despite the load placed on root name servers, resolution on the Internet works quite well. Figure 2-12 shows the resolution process for the address of a real host in a real domain, including how the process corresponds to traversing the domain namespace tree.

The local name server queries a root name server for the address of *girigiri.gbrmpa. gov.au* and is referred to the *au* name servers. The local name server asks an *au* name server the same question, and is referred to the *gov.au* name servers. The *gov.au* name server refers the local name server to the *gbrmpa.gov.au* name servers. Finally,

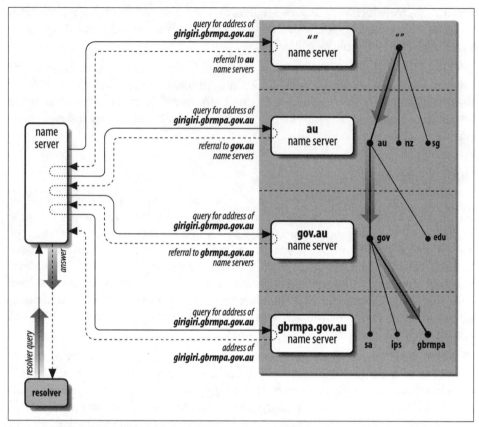

Figure 2-12. Resolution of girigiri.gbrmpa.gov.au on the Internet

the local name server asks a *gbrmpa.gov.au* name server for the address and gets the answer.

Recursion

You may have noticed a big difference in the amount of work done by the name servers in the previous example. Four of the name servers simply returned the best answer they already had—mostly referrals to other name servers—to the queries they received. They didn't have to send their own queries to find the data requested. But one name server—the one queried by the resolver—had to follow successive referrals until it received an answer.

Why couldn't the local name server simply have referred the resolver to another name server? Because a stub resolver wouldn't have had the intelligence to follow a referral. And how did the name server know not to answer with a referral? Because the resolver issued a *recursive* query.

Queries come in two flavors, *recursive* and *iterative*, also called *nonrecursive*. Recursive queries place most of the burden of resolution on a single name server. *Recursion*, or *recursive resolution*, is just a name for the resolution process used by a name server when it receives recursive queries. As with recursive algorithms in programming, the name server repeats the same basic process (querying a remote name server and following any referrals) until it receives an answer.

Iteration, or *iterative resolution*, on the other hand, refers to the resolution process used by a name server when it receives iterative queries.

In recursion, a resolver sends a recursive query to a name server for information about a particular domain name. The queried name server is then obliged to respond with the requested data or with an error stating either that data of the requested type doesn't exist or that the domain name specified doesn't exist.* The name server can't just refer the querier to a different name server, because the query was recursive.

If the queried name server isn't authoritative for the data requested, it will have to query other name servers to find the answer. It could send recursive queries to those name servers, thereby obliging them to find the answer and return it (and passing the buck), or it could send iterative queries and possibly be referred to other name servers "closer" to the domain name it's seeking. Current implementations are polite and by default do the latter, following the referrals until an answer is found.†

A name server that receives a recursive query that it can't answer itself will query the "closest known" name servers. The closest known name servers are the servers authoritative for the zone closest to the domain name being looked up. For example, if the name server receives a recursive query for the address of the domain name *giri-giri.gbrmpa.gov.au*, it will first check whether it knows which name servers are authoritative for *girigiri.gbrmpa.gov.au*. If it does, it will send the query to one of them. If not, it will check whether it knows the name servers for *gbrmpa.gov.au*, and after that *gov.au*, and then *au*. The default, where the check is guaranteed to stop, is the root zone, since every name server knows the domain names and addresses of the root name servers.

Using the closest known name servers ensures that the resolution process is as short as possible. A *berkeley.edu* name server receiving a recursive query for the address of *waxwing.ce.berkeley.edu* shouldn't have to consult the root name servers; it can simply follow delegation information directly to the *ce.berkeley.edu* name servers. Likewise, a name server that has just looked up a domain name in *ce.berkeley.edu* shouldn't have to start resolution at the root to look up another *ce.berkeley.edu* (or

---

* The Microsoft DNS Server can be configured to ignore recursive queries. See Chapter 11 for how and why you'd want to do this.

† The exception is a name server configured to forward all unresolved queries to a designated name server, called a *forwarder*. See Chapter 11 for more information on using forwarders.

berkeley.edu) domain name; we'll show how this works in the upcoming section on caching.

The name server that receives the recursive query always sends the same query that the resolver sent it; for example, for the address of *waxwing.ce.berkeley.edu*. It never sends explicit queries for the name servers for *ce.berkeley.edu* or *berkeley.edu*, though this information is also stored in the namespace. Sending explicit queries could cause problems: there may be no *ce.berkeley.edu* name servers (that is, *ce.berkeley.edu* may be part of the *berkeley.edu* zone). Also, it's always possible that an *edu* or *berkeley. edu* name server would know *waxwing.ce.berkeley.edu*'s address. An explicit query for the *berkeley.edu* or *ce.berkeley.edu* name servers would miss this information.

Iteration

Iterative resolution doesn't require nearly as much work on the part of the queried name server. In iterative resolution, a name server simply gives the best answer *it already knows* back to the querier. No additional querying is required. The queried name server consults its local data (including its cache, which we'll talk about shortly), looking for the data requested. If it doesn't find the answer there, it finds the names and addresses of the name servers closest to the domain name in the query in its local data and returns that as a referral to help the querier continue the resolution process. Note that the referral includes *all* of the name servers listed in the local data; it's up to the querier to choose which one to query next.

Choosing Between Authoritative Name Servers

Some of the card-carrying Mensa members in our reading audience may be wondering how the name server that receives the recursive query chooses between the name servers authoritative for the zone. For example, we said that there are 13 root name servers on the Internet today. Does the name server simply query the one that appears first in the referral? Does it choose randomly?

The Microsoft DNS Server uses *roundtrip time* (RTT) to choose between name servers authoritative for the same zone. Roundtrip time is a measurement of how long a remote name server takes to respond to queries. Each time a Microsoft DNS Server sends a query to a remote name server, it starts an internal stopwatch. When it receives a response, it stops the stopwatch and makes a note of how long that remote name server took to respond. When the name server must choose which of a group of authoritative name servers to query, it simply chooses the one with the lowest roundtrip time.

Before a Microsoft DNS Server has queried a name server, it ranks it according to how many octets its IP address has in common with the local host's. This is designed to favor remote name servers on the same or nearby networks.

On the whole, this simple but elegant algorithm allows Microsoft DNS Servers to "lock on" to the closest name servers quickly and without the overhead of an out-of-band mechanism to measure performance.

The Whole Enchilada

What this amounts to is a resolution process that, taken as a whole, looks like Figure 2-13.

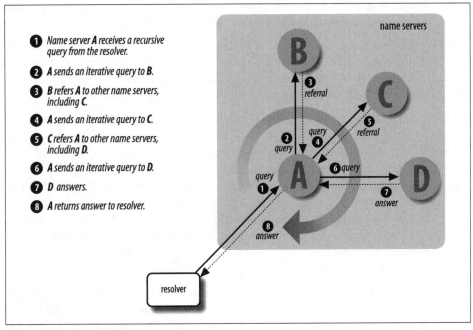

1. Name server **A** receives a recursive query from the resolver.
2. **A** sends an iterative query to **B**.
3. **B** refers **A** to other name servers, including **C**.
4. **A** sends an iterative query to **C**.
5. **C** refers **A** to other name servers, including **D**.
6. **A** sends an iterative query to **D**.
7. **D** answers.
8. **A** returns answer to resolver.

Figure 2-13. The resolution process

A resolver queries a local name server, which then sends iterative queries to a number of other name servers in pursuit of an answer for the resolver. Each name server it queries refers it to another name server that is authoritative for a zone further down in the namespace and closer to the domain name sought. Finally, the local name server queries the authoritative name server, which returns an answer. All the while, the local name server uses each response it receives—whether a referral or the answer—to update the RTT of the responding name server, which will help it decide which name servers to query to resolve domain names in the future.

Mapping Addresses to Names

One major piece of functionality missing from the resolution process as explained so far is how addresses get mapped back to domain names. Address-to-name mapping is used to produce output that is easier for humans to read and interpret (in log files, for instance). It's also used in some authorization checks. Unix hosts map addresses to domain names to compare against entries in *.rhosts* and *hosts.equiv* files, for example. When using host tables, address-to-name mapping is trivial. It requires a straightforward sequential search through the host table for an address. The search returns the official hostname listed. In DNS, however, address-to-name mapping isn't so simple. Data, including addresses, in the domain namespace is indexed by name. Given a domain name, finding an address is relatively easy. But finding the domain name that maps to a given address would seem to require an exhaustive search of the data attached to every domain name in the tree.

Actually, there's a better solution that's both clever and effective. Because it's easy to find data once you're given the domain name that indexes that data, why not create a part of the domain namespace that uses addresses as labels? In the Internet's domain namespace, this portion of the namespace is the *in-addr.arpa* domain.

Nodes in the *in-addr.arpa* domain are labeled after the numbers in the dotted-octet representation of IP addresses. (Dotted-octet representation refers to the common method of expressing 32-bit IP addresses as four numbers in the range 0 to 255, separated by dots.) The *in-addr.arpa* domain, for example, could have up to 256 subdomains, one corresponding to each possible value in the first octet of an IP address. Each of these subdomains could have up to 256 subdomains of its own, corresponding to the possible values of the second octet. Finally, at the fourth level down, there are resource records attached to the final octet giving the full domain name of the host at that IP address. That makes for an awfully big domain: *in-addr.arpa*, shown in Figure 2-14, is roomy enough for every IP address on the Internet.

Note that when read in a domain name, the IP address appears backward because the name is read from leaf to root. For example, if *winnie.corp.hp.com*'s IP address is 15.16.192.152, the corresponding node in the *in-addr.arpa* domain is *152.192.16.15. in-addr.arpa*, which maps back to the domain name *winnie.corp.hp.com*.

IP addresses could have been represented the opposite way in the namespace, with the first octet of the IP address at the bottom of the *in-addr.arpa* domain. That way, the IP address would have read correctly (forward) in the domain name. IP addresses are hierarchical, however, just like domain names. Network numbers are doled out much as domain names are, and administrators can then subnet their address space and further delegate numbering. The difference is that IP addresses get more specific from left to right, while domain names get less specific from left to right. Figure 2-15 shows what we mean.

Making the first octets in the IP address appear highest in the tree gives administrators the ability to delegate authority for *in-addr.arpa* zones along network lines. For example, the *15.in-addr.arpa* zone, which contains the reverse-mapping information for all hosts whose IP addresses start with 15, can be delegated to the administrators of network 15/8. This would be impossible if the octets appeared in the opposite

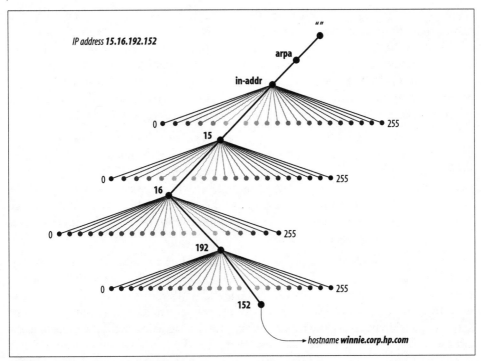

Figure 2-14. The in-addr.arpa domain

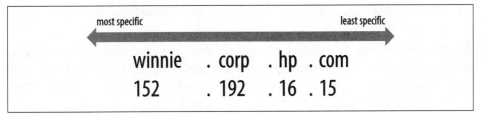

Figure 2-15. Hierarchical names and addresses

order. If the IP addresses were represented the other way around, *15.in-addr.arpa* would consist of every host whose IP address ended with 15—not a practical zone to try to delegate.

Caching

The whole resolution process may seem awfully convoluted and cumbersome to someone accustomed to simple searches through the host table. Actually, though, it's usually quite fast. One of the features that speeds it up considerably is *caching*.

A name server processing a recursive query may have to send out quite a few queries to find an answer. However, it discovers a lot of information about the domain namespace as it does so. Each time it's referred to another list of name servers, it learns that those name servers are authoritative for some zone, and it learns the addresses of those servers. At the end of the resolution process, when it finally finds the data the original querier sought, it can store that data for future reference, too. The Microsoft DNS Server even implements *negative caching*: if a name server responds to a query with an answer that says the domain name or data type in the query doesn't exist, the local name server will also temporarily cache that information.

Name servers cache all this data to help speed up successive queries. The next time a resolver queries the name server for data about a domain name the name server knows something about, the process is shortened quite a bit. The name server may have cached the answer, positive or negative, in which case it simply returns the answer to the resolver. Even if it doesn't have the answer cached, it may have learned the identities of the name servers that are authoritative for the zone the domain name is in and be able to query them directly.

For example, say our name server has already looked up the address of *eecs.berkeley. edu*. In the process, it cached the names and addresses of the *eecs.berkeley.edu* and *berkeley.edu* name servers (plus *eecs.berkeley.edu*'s IP address). Now if a resolver were to query our name server for the address of *baobab.cs.berkeley.edu*, our name server could skip querying the root name servers. Recognizing that *berkeley.edu* is the closest ancestor of *baobab.cs.berkeley.edu* that it knows about, our name server would start by querying a *berkeley.edu* name server, as shown in Figure 2-16. On the other hand, if our name server discovered that there was no address for *eecs.berkeley. edu*, the next time it received a query for the address, it could simply respond appropriately from its cache.

In addition to speeding up resolution, caching obviates a name server's need to query the root name servers to answer any queries it can't answer locally. This means it's not as dependent on the roots, and the roots won't suffer as much from all its queries.

Time to Live

Name servers can't cache data forever, of course. If they did, changes to that data on the authoritative name servers would never reach the rest of the network; remote name servers would just continue to use cached data. Consequently, the administrator of the zone that contains the data decides on a *time to live* (TTL) for the data. The time to live is the amount of time that any name server is allowed to cache the data. After the time to live expires, the name server must discard the cached data and get new data from the authoritative name servers. This also applies to negatively cached data: a name server must time out a negative answer after a period in case new data has been added on the authoritative name servers.

Deciding on a time to live for your data is essentially deciding on a trade-off between performance and consistency. A small TTL will help ensure that data in your zones is

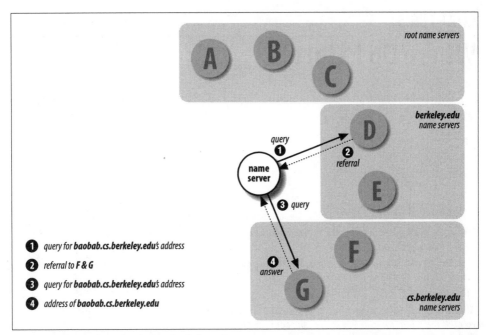

(1) query for **baobab.cs.berkeley.edu**'s address

(2) referral to **F & G**

(3) query for **baobab.cs.berkeley.edu**'s address

(4) address of **baobab.cs.berkeley.edu**

Figure 2-16. Resolving baobab.cs.berkeley.edu

consistent across the network, because remote name servers will time it out more quickly and be forced to query your authoritative name servers more often for new data. On the other hand, this will increase the load on your name servers and lengthen the average resolution time for information in your zones.

A large TTL reduces the average time it takes to resolve information in your zones because the data can be cached longer. The drawback is that your information will be inconsistent longer if you make changes to the data on your name servers.

But enough of this theory—I'll bet you're antsy to get on with things. You have some homework to do before you can set up your zones and your name servers, though, and we'll assign it in the next chapter.

CHAPTER 3
Where Do I Start?

"What do you call yourself?" the Fawn said at last.
Such a soft sweet voice it had!

"I wish I knew!" thought poor Alice. She answered,
rather sadly, "Nothing, just now."

"Think again," it said: "that won't do."

Alice thought, but nothing came of it. "Please, would
you tell me what you call yourself?" she said timidly.
"I think that might help a little."

"I'll tell you, if you come a little further on," the Fawn
said. "I can't remember here."

Now that you understand the theory behind the Domain Name System, we can attend to more practical matters. Before you set up your zones, you may need to get name server software. While a name server is included as a standard part of Windows Server 2003, you may want to look at alternatives. Once you've got the software to run your name server, you need to decide on a domain name for your main zone—which may not be quite as easy as it sounds, because it entails finding an appropriate place in the Internet namespace. With that decided, you need to contact the administrators of the parent of the zone whose domain name you've chosen.

One thing at a time, though. Let's talk about how to decide on name server software and where to get it.

Which Name Server?

If you plan to set up your own zones and run name servers for them, you'll need name server software first. Even if you're planning on having someone else run the name servers for your zones, it's helpful to have the software around. For example, you can use a local name server to test your zone datafiles before giving them to your remote name server administrator.

Microsoft ships a name server on the Windows Server 2003 CD-ROM, but you have to install it separately from the OS. This server, which we call the Microsoft DNS Server, is the server we cover in this book. It's notable because it sports a nice graphical front-end for configuring the server. This isn't the only name server available for Windows Server 2003, however. There are several others. Many are ports of BIND, which has traditionally been a Unix-based name server. If you're more comfortable configuring BIND than learning to configure a new name server (even with a GUI), you might consider running the latest version of BIND (9.2.2 as of this writing) on Windows Server 2003.

BIND 9.2.2 compiles on Windows Server 2003 without any modification of the source code. However, since many people lack the software necessary to compile it, the Internet Software Consortium distributes a compiled version from its web site at *http://www.isc.org/products/BIND/bind9.html*.

If you decide to run BIND on Windows Server 2003, we suggest you pick up a copy of *DNS and BIND*. That book concentrates on the BIND implementation; this book emphasizes the Microsoft DNS Server.

Getting the DNS Server

If you've read to this section, we'll assume you've decided to use the Microsoft DNS Server. Before proceeding, you'll need to install the name server and its configuration front-end from the Windows Server 2003 CD-ROM. For detailed instructions on this process, see Chapter 4.

Handy Mailing Lists and Usenet Newsgroups

Now that you've installed your name server, it's important to keep abreast of DNS and name server developments. Three Usenet newsgroups are helpful for this: *microsoft. public.windows.server.dns*, *microsoft.public.win2000.dns* and *comp.protocols.dns.bind*. The new *microsoft.public.windows.server.dns* focuses on the Windows Server 2003 version of the Microsoft DNS Server, but includes discussion of older versions, too. *microsoft.public.win2000.dns* concentrates on the Windows 2000 version of the Microsoft DNS Server. *comp.protocols.dns.bind* is more BIND-centric (as the name indicates) but is an excellent source of information about the art and practice of running domains and name servers. It arguably has a better signal-to-noise ratio than the

Microsoft newsgroups and is also available as a mailing list, *bind-users@isc.org.*[*] A searchable archive of the list can be found at *http://www.isc.org/ml-archives/bind-users/*.

Microsoft's online support site, at *http://support.microsoft.com/*, is a valuable source of information about known bugs in the name server and updates to the code. Also, be sure to checkout Andras Salamon's "DNS Resource Directory" at *http://www.dns. net/dnsrd/* for pointers to online DNS resources and documentation.

Another mailing list you might be interested in is the *namedroppers* list. Folks on the *namedroppers* mailing list are involved in the IETF working group that develops extensions to the DNS specifications, DNSEXT. For example, the discussion of a new, proposed DNS record type would probably take place on *namedroppers* instead of the BIND users mailing list. For more information on DNSEXT's charter, see *http:// www.ietf.org/html.charters/dnsext-charter.html*.

The address for the *namedroppers* mailing list is *namedroppers@ops.ietf.org*, and it is gatewayed into the Internet newsgroup *comp.protocols.dns.std*. To join the *name-droppers* mailing list, send mail to *namedroppers-request@ops.ietf.org* with the text "subscribe namedroppers" as the body of the message.

Finding IP Addresses

You'll notice that we gave you a number of domain names of hosts that have *ftp*able software, and the mailing lists we mentioned include domain names. This should underscore the importance of DNS: see what valuable software and advice you can get with the help of DNS? Unfortunately, it's also something of a chicken-and-egg problem: you can't send email to an address with a domain name in it unless you've got DNS set up, so how can you ask someone on the list how to set up DNS?

Well, we could give you the IP addresses for all the hosts we mentioned, but since IP addresses change often (in publishing timescales, anyway), we'll show you how you can *temporarily* use someone else's name server to find the information instead. As long as your host has Internet connectivity and the *nslookup* program, you can retrieve information from the Internet namespace.

To look up the IP address for *ftp.microsoft.com*, for example, you could use:

```
C:\> nslookup ftp.microsoft.com. 207.69.188.185
```

---

[*] To ask a question on an Internet mailing list, all you need to do is send a message to the mailing list's address. If you'd like to join the list, however, you have to send a message to the list's maintainer first, requesting that he or she add your email address to the list. Don't send this message to the list itself; that's considered rude. You can reach the maintainer of a mailing list by sending mail to *list-request@domain*, where *list@domain* is the address of the mailing list. So, for example, you can reach the BIND users mailing list's administrator by sending mail to *bind-users-request@isc.org*.

This instructs *nslookup* to query the name server running on the host at the IP address 207.69.188.185 to find the IP address for *ftp.microsoft.com* and should produce output such as:

```
Server:  ns1.mindspring.com
Address:  207.69.188.185


Name:    ftp.microsoft.com
Address: 207.46.133.140
```

Now you can *ftp* to *ftp.microsoft.com*'s IP address, 207.46.133.140.

How did we know that the host at IP address 207.69.188.185 runs a name server? Our ISP, Mindspring, told us—it's one of their name servers. If your ISP provides name servers for its customers' use (and most do), use one of them. If your ISP doesn't provide name servers (shame on them!), you can *temporarily* use one of the name servers listed in this book. As long as you only use it to look up a few IP addresses or other data, the administrators probably won't mind. It's considered very rude, however, to point your resolver or query tool at someone else's name server permanently.

Of course, if you already have access to a host with Internet connectivity *and* have DNS configured, you can use it to *ftp* what you need.

Once you've got a working version of the Microsoft DNS Server, you're ready to start thinking about your domain name.

Choosing a Domain Name

Choosing a domain name is more involved than it may sound because it entails both choosing a name *and* finding out who runs the parent zone. In other words, you need to find out where you fit in the Internet domain namespace, then find out who runs that particular corner of the namespace.

The first step in picking a domain name is finding where in the existing domain namespace you belong. It's easiest to start at the top and work your way down: decide which top-level domain you belong in, then which of that top-level domain's subdomains you fit into.

Note that in order to find out what the Internet domain namespace looks like (beyond what we've already told you), you'll need access to the Internet. You don't need access to a host that already has name service configured, but it would help a little. If you don't have access to a host with DNS configured, you'll have to "borrow" name service from other name servers (as in our previous *ftp.microsoft.com* example) to get you going.

On Registrars and Registries

Before we go any further, we need to define a few terms: registry, registrar, and registration. These terms aren't defined anywhere in the DNS specs. Instead, they apply to the way the Internet namespace is managed today.

A *registry* is an organization responsible for maintaining a top-level domain's (well, zone's, really) datafiles, which contain the delegation to each subdomain of that top-level domain. Under the current structure of the Internet, a given top-level domain can have no more than one registry.

A *registrar* acts as an interface between customers and the registry, providing registration and value-added services. It submits to the registry the zone data and other data (including contact information) for each of its customers in a single top-level domain.

Registration is the process by which a customer tells a registrar which name servers to delegate a subdomain to and provides the registrar with contact and billing information. The registrar makes these changes through the registry.

To give you some concrete examples of how this works in the real world, Public Interest Registry runs the *org* registry. VeriSign, Inc. currently acts as the registry for the *com* and *net* top-level domains. There are dozens of registrars for *com*, *net*, and *org*, including Network Solutions—a former subsidiary of VeriSign. An organization called EDUCAUSE runs the *edu* registry and is its only registrar. But before we get too off-track, let's get back to our story.

Where in the World Do I Fit?

If your organization is attached to the Internet outside of the United States, you first need to decide whether you'd rather request a subdomain of one of the generic top-level domains, such as *com*, *net*, and *org*, or a subdomain of your country's top-level domain. The generic top-level domains aren't exclusively for U.S. organizations. If your company is a multi- or transnational company that doesn't fit in any one country's top-level domain, or if you'd simply prefer a generic top-level to your country's top-level domain, you're welcome to register in one. If you choose this route, skip to "The generic top-level domains" later in this chapter.

If you opt for a subdomain under your country's top level, you should check whether your country's top-level domain is registered and, if it is, what kind of structure it has. Consult our list of the current top-level domains (Appendix C) if you're not sure what the name of your country's top-level domain would be.

Some countries' top-level domains, such as New Zealand's *nz*, Australia's *au*, and the United Kingdom's *uk*, are divided organizationally into second-level domains. The names of their second-level domains, such as *co* or *com* for commercial entities, reflect organizational affiliation. Others, like France's *fr* domain and Denmark's *dk* domain, are divided into a multitude of subdomains managed by individual universities and companies, such as the University of St. Etienne's domain, *univ-st-etienne.fr*, and the Danish Unix Users Group's *dkuug.dk*. Many top-level domains have their own web sites that describe their structure. If you're not sure of the URL for your country's top-level domain's web site, start at *http://www.allwhois.com*, a directory of links to such web sites.

If your country's top-level domain doesn't have a web site explaining how it's organized, but you have some idea of which subdomain you belong in, you can use a DNS query tool such as *nslookup* to find the email address of the technical contact for the subdomain. (If you're uncomfortable with our rushing headlong into *nslookup* without giving it a proper introduction, you might want to skim Chapter 12.)

To find out whom to ask about a particular subdomain, you'll have to look up the corresponding zone's start of authority (SOA) record. In each zone's SOA record, there's a field that contains the electronic mail address of the zone's technical contact.* (The other fields in the SOA record provide general information about the zone—we'll discuss them in more detail later.)

For example, if you're curious about the purpose of the *csiro.au* subdomain, you can find out who runs it by looking up *csiro.au*'s SOA record:

```
C:\> nslookup - 207.69.188.185
Default Server: ns1.mindspring.com
Address:  207.69.188.185

> set type=soa      Look for start of authority data
> csiro.au.         for csiro.au.
Server:  ns1.mindspring.com
Address: 207.69.188.185

csiro.au
        origin = zas.csiro.au
        mail addr = hostmaster.csiro.au
        serial = 2003071501
        refresh = 10800 (3H)
        retry   = 3600 (1H)
        expire  = 3600000 (5w6d16h)
        minimum ttl = 3600 (1H)
```

---

* The subdomain and the zone have the same domain name, but the SOA record really belongs to the zone, not the subdomain. The person at the zone's technical contact email address may not manage the whole subdomain (there may be additional delegated subdomains beneath), but he should certainly know the purpose of the subdomain.

The *mail addr* field is the Internet address of *csiro.au*'s contact. To convert the address into Internet email address format, you'll need to change the first "." in the address to an "@". So *hostmaster.csiro.au* becomes *hostmaster@csiro.au*.[*]

whois

The *whois* service can also help you figure out the purpose of a given domain. Unfortunately, there are many *whois* servers—most good administrators of top-level domains run one—and they don't talk to each other, like name servers do. Consequently, the first step to using *whois* is finding the right *whois* server.

One of the easiest places to start your search for the right *whois* server is at *http://www.allwhois.com* (see Figure 3-1). We mentioned earlier that this site has a list of the web sites for each country code's top-level domain; it also sports a unified *whois* search facility.

Figure 3-1. The www.allwhois.com web site

---

[*] This form of Internet mail address is a vestige of two former DNS records, MB and MG. MB (mailbox) and MG (mail group) were to be DNS records specifying Internet mailboxes and mail groups (mailing lists) as subdomains of the appropriate domain. MB and MG never took off, but the address format they would have dictated is used in the SOA record, maybe for sentimental reasons.

Say you were wondering what the *ad.jp* domain was for. You can enter *ad.jp* in the text box at the top of *http://www.allwhois.com/* and the web site will query the right *whois* server and show you the results, as in Figure 3-2.

Figure 3-2. Information about ad.jp from the jp whois server

Obviously, this is a useful web site if you're looking for information about a domain outside of the U.S.

Once you've found the right web site or the right contact, you may have found the registrar. Outside the U.S., many domains have a single registrar. A few, though, such as Denmark's *dk* and Great Britain's *co.uk* and *org.uk*, have multiple registrars. However, the process we've described will still lead you to them.

Back in the U.S.A.

In true cosmopolitan spirit, we covered international domains first. But what if you're from the good ol' U.S. of A.?

If you're in the U.S., where you belong depends mainly upon what your organization does, how you'd like your domain names to look, and how much you're willing to pay. If your organization falls into one of the following categories, you may want to consider joining *us*:

- K–12 (kindergarten through twelfth grade) schools
- Community colleges and technical vocational schools
- State and local government agencies

That's because these organizations have historically registered under *us*, according to the namespace design documented in RFC 1480. In that design, a high school, for example, would register under *k12.<state>.us*, where *<state>* is the two-letter postal abbreviation for the state in which the school is located.

However, even these organizations don't need to follow this rigid structure. Many K-12 schools, community colleges, and government agencies register subdomains of *org* or even *com*. The registry that runs *us* has relaxed the restrictions placed on *us* registrants, too: now you can register in either the "locality space" (*<state>.us*) or the "expanded space." In the "expanded space," you could register (for example) *acme.us* rather than *acme.co.us*.

Many people, however, prefer the better-known generic top-level domains. For information on registering in one of those, read on.

The generic top-level domains

As we said, there are many reasons why you might want to ask for a subdomain of one of the generic top-level domains, such as *com*, *net*, and *org*: you work for a multi- or transnational company, you like the fact that they're better-known, or you just prefer the sound of your domain name with "com" on the end. Let's go through a short example of choosing a domain name under a generic top-level domain.

Imagine you're the network administrator for a think tank in Hopkins, Minnesota. You've just gotten a connection to the Internet through a commercial ISP. Your company has never had so much as a dialup link, so you're not currently registered in the Internet namespace.

Since you're in the United States, you have the choice of joining either *us* or one of the generic top-level domains. Your think tank is world-renowned, though, so you feel *us* wouldn't be a good choice. A subdomain of a generic top-level domain would be best.

But which one? As of this writing, there are five open to anyone:

biz
> A new generic top-level domain

com
> The original generic top-level domain, and the best known

info

> A new generic top-level domain

net

> Originally used by networking organizations, but now open to anyone

org

> Originally used by nonprofit and other noncommercial organizations, but now open to anyone

The think tank is known as The Gizmonic Institute, so you decide *gizmonics.com* might be an appropriate domain name. Now you've got to check whether the name *gizmonics.com* has been taken by anyone, so you use an account you have at the University of Minnesota:

```
C:\> nslookup
Default Server: ns.unet.umn.edu
Address:  128.101.101.101

> set type=any          Look for any records
> gizmonics.com.        for gizmonics.com.
Server:  ns.unet.umn.edu
Address:  128.101.101.101

gizmonics.com    nameserver = ns1.111.net
gizmonics.com    nameserver = ns2.111.net
```

Whoops! Look like *gizmonics.com* is already taken (who would have thought?). Well, *gizmonic-institute.com* is a little longer, but still intuitive:[*]

```
C:\> nslookup
Default Server: ns.unet.umn.edu
Address:  128.101.101.101

> set type=any              Look for any records
> gizmonic-institute.com.   for gizmonic-institute.com.
Server:  ns.unet.umn.edu
Address:  128.101.101.101

*** ns.unet.umn.edu can't find gizmonic-institute.com.: Non-existent host/domain
```

gizmonic-institute.com is free, so you can go on to the next step: picking a registrar.

Choosing a registrar

Choose a registrar? Welcome to the brave new world of competition! Before the spring of 1999, a single company, Network Solutions, Inc., was both the registry and

---

[*] If you're having a hard time figuring out a good domain name, many registrars' web sites provide suggestions for free. For example, *www.nameboy.com* will recommend various combinations of "gizmonic" and "institute," even using rhyming words.

sole registrar for *com*, *net*, and *org*, as well as *edu*. To register a subdomain of any of these generic top-level domains, you had to go to Network Solutions.

In June 1999, ICANN, the organization that manages the domain namespace (we mentioned them in the last chapter) introduced competition to the registrar function of *com*, *net*, and *org*. There are now dozens of *com*, *net*, and *org* registrars from which you can choose (see *http://www.internic.net/regist.html*).

We won't presume to tell you how to pick a registrar, but take a look at the price and any other services the registrar provides that interest you. See if you can get a nice package deal on registration and aluminum siding, for example.

Checking That Your Network Is Registered

Before proceeding, you should check whether or not your IP network or networks are registered. Some registrars won't delegate a subdomain to name servers on unregistered networks, and network registries (we'll talk about them shortly) won't delegate an *in-addr.arpa* zone that corresponds to an unregistered network.

An IP network defines a range of IP addresses. For example, the network 15/8 is made up of all IP addresses in the range 15.0.0.0 to 15.255.255.255. The network 199.10.25/24 starts at 199.10.25.0 and ends at 199.10.25.255.

The InterNIC was once the official source of all IP networks; they assigned all IP networks to Internet-connected networks and made sure no two address ranges overlapped. Nowadays, the InterNIC's old role has been largely assumed by Internet service providers (ISPs), who allocate space from their own networks for customers to use. If you know your network came from your ISP, the larger network from which your network was carved is probably registered (to your ISP). You may still want to double-check that your ISP took care of registering their network, but you don't have to (and probably can't) do anything yourself, except nag your ISP if they didn't register their network. Once you've verified their registration, you can skip the rest of this section and move on.

 It's not necessary to register RFC 1918 address space (e.g., the networks 10/8, 192.168/16). In fact, you can't since these networks are used by so many different organizations.

If your network was assigned by the InterNIC, way back when, or you *are* an ISP, you should check to see whether your network is registered. Where do you go to check whether your network is registered? Why, to the same organizations that register networks, of course. These organizations, called *regional Internet registries*, or *RIRs*, each handle network registration in some part of the world. In North America, ARIN, the American Registry of Internet Numbers (*http://www.arin.net*), hands out IP address space and registers networks. In Asia and the Pacific, APNIC, the Asia

A Sidebar on CIDR

Once upon a time, when we wrote the first edition of this book, the Internet's 32-bit address space was divided up into three main classes of networks: Class A, Class B, and Class C. Class A networks were networks in which the first octet (the first eight bits) of the IP address identified the network, and the remaining bits were used by the organization that was assigned the network to differentiate hosts on the network. Most organizations with Class A networks also subdivided their networks into subnetworks, or subnets, adding another level of hierarchy to the addressing scheme. Class B networks devoted two octets to the network identifier and two to the host; Class C networks gave three octets to the network identifier and one to the host.

Unfortunately, this small/medium/large system of networks didn't work well for everyone. Many organizations were large enough to require more than a Class C network, which could accommodate at most 254 hosts, but too small to warrant a full Class B network, which could serve 65,534 hosts. Many of these organizations were allocated Class B networks anyway. Consequently, Class B networks quickly became scarce.

To help solve this problem and create networks that were just the right size for all sorts of organizations, Classless Inter-Domain Routing, or CIDR (pronounced "cider"), was developed. As the name implies, CIDR does away with the old Class A, Class B, and Class C network designations. Instead of allocating either one, two, or three octets to the network identifier, the allocator could assign any number of contiguous bits of the IP address to the network identifier. So, for example, if an organization needed an address space roughly four times as large as a Class B network, the powers-that-be could assign it a network identifier of 14 bits, leaving 18 bits (four Class B's worth) of space to use.

Naturally, the advent of CIDR made the "classful" terminology outdated—although it's still used a good deal in casual conversation. Now, to designate a particular CIDR network, we specify the particular high-order bit value assigned to an organization, expressed in dotted octet notation, and how many bits identify the network. The two terms are separated by a slash. So 15/8 is the old, Class A-sized network that begins with the eight-bit pattern 00001111. The old, Class B-sized network 128.32.0.0 is now 128.32/16. And the network 192.168.0.128/25 consists of the 128 IP addresses from 192.168.0.128 to 192.168.0.255.

Pacific Network Information Center (*http://www.apnic.net*), serves the same function. In Europe, it's the RIPE Network Coordination Centre (*http://www.ripe.net*). And Latin America and the Caribbean are served by LACNIC, the Latin America and Caribbean Internet Addresses Registry (*http://www.lacnic.net*). Each RIR may also delegate registration authority for a region; for example, ARIN delegates registration authority for Mexico to a registry in that country. Be sure to check for a network registry local to your country.

If you're not sure your network is registered, the best way to find out is to use the *whois* services provided by the various network registries to look for your network. Here are the URLs for each registry's *whois* web page:

ARIN
> *http://www.arin.net/whois/index.html*

APNIC
> *http://www.apnic.net/search/index.html*

RIPE
> *http://www.ripe.net/perl/whois/*

LACNIC
> *http://lacnic.net/cgi-bin/lacnic/whois?lg=EN*

If you find out your network isn't registered, you'll need to get it registered before setting up your *in-addr.arpa* zones. Each registry has a different process for registering networks, but most involve money changing hands (from your hands to theirs, unfortunately).

You may find out that your network is already assigned to your ISP. If this is the case, you don't need to register independently with the RIR.

Once all your Internet-connected hosts are on registered networks, you can register your zones.

Registering Your Zones

Different registrars have different registration policies and procedures, but most, at this point, handle registration online, through their web sites. Since you found or chose your registrar earlier in the chapter, we'll assume you know which web site to use.

The registrar will need to know the domain names and addresses of your name servers and enough information about you to send you a bill or charge your credit card. If you're not connected to the Internet, give them the IP addresses of the Internet hosts that will act as your name servers. Some registrars also require that you already have operational name servers for your zone. (Those that don't may ask for an estimate of when the name servers will be fully operational.) If that's the case with your registrar, skip ahead to Chapter 4 and set up your name servers. Then contact your registrar with the requisite information.

Most registrars will also ask for some information about your organization, including an administrative contact and a technical contact for your zone (who can be the same person). If your contacts aren't already registered in the registrar's *whois* database, you'll also need to provide information to register them in *whois*. This includes their names, surface mail addresses, phone numbers, and electronic mail addresses.

If they are already registered in *whois*, just specify their *whois* "handles" (unique alphanumeric IDs) in the registration.

There's one more aspect of registering a new zone that we should mention: cost. Most registrars are commercial enterprises and charge money for registering domain names. Network Solutions, the original registrar for *com*, *net*, and *org*, charges $35 per year to register subdomains under the generic top-level domains. (If you've already registered a subdomain under *com*, *net*, or *org* and haven't received a bill recently, it'd be a good idea to check your contact information with *whois* to make sure they've got a current address and phone number for you.)

If you're directly connected to the Internet, you should also have the *in-addr.arpa* zones corresponding to your IP networks delegated to you. (For information on IPv6 reverse-mapping, see Chapter 11.) For example, if your company was allocated the network 192.201.44/24, you should manage the *44.201.192.in-addr.arpa* zone. This will let you control the IP address-to-name mappings for hosts on your network. Chapter 4 also explains how to set up your *in-addr.arpa* zones.

Earlier in this chapter, we asked you to find the answers to several questions: is your network a slice of an ISP's network? Is your network, or the ISP network that your network is part of, registered? If so, with which RIR? You'll need these answers to have your *in-addr.arpa* zones delegated to you.

If your network is part of a larger network registered to an ISP, you should contact the ISP to have the appropriate subdomains of their *in-addr.arpa* zone delegated to you. Each ISP uses a different process for setting up *in-addr.arpa* delegation. Your ISP's web page is a good place to research that process. If you can't find the information there, try looking up the SOA record for the *in-addr.arpa* zone that corresponds to your ISP's network. For example, if your network is part of UUNET's 153.35/16 network, you could look up the SOA record of *35.153.in-addr.arpa* to find the email address of the technical contact for the zone.

If your network is registered directly with one of the regional Internet registries, contact them to get your *in-addr.arpa* zone registered. Each network registry makes information on its delegation process available on its web site.

Now that you've registered your zones, you'd better take some time to get your house in order. You've got some name servers to set up, and in the next chapter, we'll show you how.

## CHAPTER 4

Setting Up the Microsoft DNS Server

"It seems very pretty," she said when she had finished it, "but it's rather hard to understand!" (You see she didn't like to confess, even to herself, that she couldn't make it out at all.) "Somehow it seems to fill my head with ideas—only I don't exactly know what they are!"

If you have been diligently reading each chapter of this book, you're probably anxious to get a name server running. This chapter is for you. Let's set up a couple of name servers. Some of you may have read the table of contents and skipped directly to this chapter. (Shame on you!) If you are one of those people who cuts corners, be aware that we may use concepts from earlier chapters and expect you to understand them.

Several factors influence how you should set up your name servers. The biggest factor is what sort of access you have to the Internet: complete access (for example, you can *ftp* to *ftp.uu.net*), limited access (limited by a security firewall), or no access at all. This chapter assumes you have complete access. We'll discuss the other cases in Chapter 16.

In this chapter, we'll set up two name servers for a fictitious domain as an example for you to follow in setting up your own domain. We'll cover the topics in this chapter in enough detail for you to get your first two name servers running. Subsequent chapters will fill in the holes and go into greater depth. If you already have your name servers running, skim through this chapter to familiarize yourself with the terms we use or just to verify that you didn't miss something when you set up your servers.

Our Zone

Our fictitious zone serves a college. Movie University studies all aspects of the film industry and researches novel ways to distribute films. One of our most promising projects is research into using IP as a distribution medium. After visiting our registrar's web site, we have decided on the domain name *movie.edu*. A recent grant has enabled us to connect to the Internet.

Movie U. currently has two Ethernets, and we have plans for another network or two. The Ethernets have network addresses 192.249.249/24 and 192.253.253/24. A portion of our host table contains the following entries:

```
127.0.0.1     localhost

# These are our killer machines.

192.249.249.2  robocop.movie.edu robocop
192.249.249.3  terminator.movie.edu terminator bigt
192.249.249.4  diehard.movie.edu diehard dh

# These machines are in horror(ible) shape and will be replaced
# soon.

192.253.253.2  misery.movie.edu misery
192.253.253.3  shining.movie.edu shining
192.253.253.4  carrie.movie.edu carrie

# A wormhole is a fictitious phenomenon that instantly transports
# space travelers over long distances and is not known to be
# stable. The only difference between wormholes and routers is
# that routers don't transport packets as instantly--especially
# ours.

192.249.249.1  wormhole.movie.edu wormhole wh wh249
192.253.253.1  wormhole.movie.edu wormhole wh wh253
```

The network is pictured in Figure 4-1.

Installing the Microsoft DNS Server

Our plan for the Movie U. network is to run name servers on two hosts: *terminator* and *wormhole*. But a fresh installation of Windows Server 2003 doesn't include the DNS server by default, so we need to install it on these hosts.*

Start by selecting **Start → Manage Your Server**. This brings up the administrator's one-stop-shopping application, **Manage Your Server**, as shown in Figure 4-2.

Choose **Add or remove a role**. The next window is titled **Preliminary Steps** and we don't show it, but it just admonishes you to have the computer connected to the network and any peripherals and to have your installation media handy. After clicking **Next** on this screen, you might (or might not)† see the **Configuration Options**

---

* We cover one method for installation here, but you could also install the DNS server using Active Directory, as described later in this section.

† The Configuration Options screen is apparently displayed only when you add the first role. After that, Windows assumes you know what you're doing and doesn't offer this shortcut to install multiple roles at once.

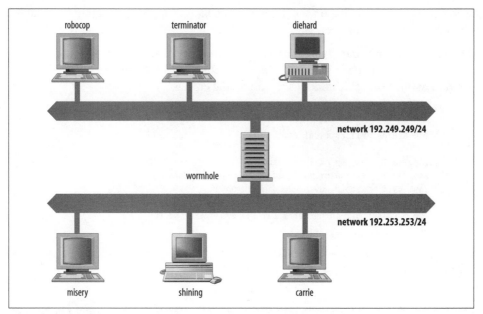

Figure 4-1. The Movie University network

Figure 4-2. Manage Your Server

screen, which gives you the option to install several common services all at once or pick and choose a custom configuration. We don't show this screen either, but choose **Custom configuration** and click **Next**.

Now you're presented with the **Server Role** window, shown in Figure 4-3. Select **DNS server** as shown in the figure and click **Next**.

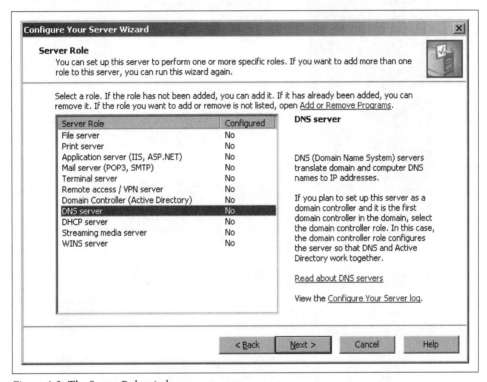

Figure 4-3. The Server Role window

The resulting window, **Summary of Selections**, describes the actions about to be taken. Click **Next** to install the DNS server and do some preliminary configuration. After the installation from the media completes, the Configure Your Server Wizard starts the Configure a DNS Server Wizard, which is shown in Figure 4-4.

If you want to, at this point you can review the checklists, but since we're walking you through this process, select **Next** and you'll see the **Select Configuration Action** window shown in Figure 4-5.

The wizard can helpfully create both forward- and reverse-mapping zones for you, but we're going to show you how to do that outside the wizard. That's why we suggest you select the third option, **Configure root hints only**. Don't be scared off by the warning that this step is for advanced users only. Here's what's happening: after the wizard completes, your newly installed name server will not be authoritative for any

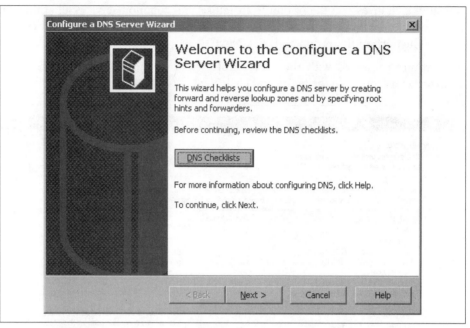

Figure 4-4. Configure a DNS Server Wizard

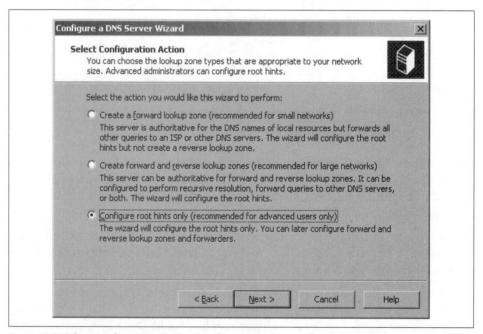

Figure 4-5. Select Configuration Action Window

zones and it will know only about the Internet's root name servers. So it will know how to contact other name servers (starting with the root name servers) to resolve domain names, but it won't know anything in particular about your organization's zones—yet.* Click **Next** and the wizard shows one more window telling you that it's done. After clicking **Finish** on that window, you're back to the **Configure Your Server** Wizard's last window. Click **Finish** and, congratulations—you've installed the DNS server.

Active Directory

We should point out that there's another way to install the DNS server and it has to do with Active Directory. You can promote a server to be a domain controller by running **Manage Your Server** and selecting the **Domain Controller** role. Active Directory requires that certain information about Active Directory domains be present in DNS. When you create the first domain controller for an Active Directory domain, the domain controller installation process tries to add this necessary information to the appropriate DNS zone. If this process fails, the Installation Wizard offers to install the DNS Server on the domain controller and create the appropriate zones so the critical information related to Active Directory can be added and will be present in DNS.

If your organization already has a domain controller or two set up, it's possible that those domain controllers are running the DNS server and that some zones have already been created. If that's the case, you won't need to follow all the steps in the rest of the chapter: you won't need to create your zones, but you'll still need to add information about your hosts to DNS. Just be aware that as you take a look at what's in your zones, you might find that extra information related to Active Directory.

We're going to talk a lot more about Active Directory and how it uses DNS in Chapter 8, but it's not too early to highlight the close relationship between Active Directory and DNS.

The DNS Console

To manage a Microsoft DNS Server and maintain your DNS data, you'll use a tool called the *DNS console*, a snap-in for the Microsoft Management Console (MMC). MMC is a general-purpose program that hosts administrative tools. Introduced in Windows 2000, MMC replaced the "one-off" administrative tools found in Windows NT 4.0, such as DNS Manager, WINS Manager, DHCP Manager, and the like. The DNS console has a graphical user interface and is capable of managing multiple

---

* A name server that isn't authoritative for any zones is called a *caching-only server*. We describe this in more detail in Chapter 9.

name servers. The DNS console is located on the **Administrative Tools** menu, provided you've already installed the DNS Server. The DNS console communicates with the Microsoft DNS Server using a proprietary management protocol built on Microsoft's RPC (remote procedure call) mechanism. That means the DNS console is able to manage only Microsoft DNS Servers and not other name servers, such as BIND.

The main DNS console window looks like Figure 4-6 (or will look like it, after we've set everything up in the course of this chapter).

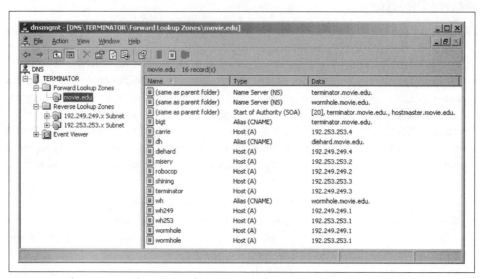

Figure 4-6. The DNS console main window

The left pane is called the *console tree*. It shows name servers, zones, and domains. The right pane shows either informational messages or resource records.

This particular DNS console knows about only one name server, *terminator*. That name server is authoritative for three zones: *movie.edu*, *249.249.192.in-addr.arpa*, and *253.253.192.in-addr.arpa*. The DNS console segregates *forward-lookup zones* (which hold primarily address records) and *reverse-lookup zones* (which hold primarily pointer records). If any of these zones had subdomains, they would show up as subfolders under the appropriate zone. For example, *comedies.movie.edu* would be represented as a folder called *comedies* under *movie.edu*.

Let's take a look at the menus at the top of the window. The **File**, **Window**, and **Help** menus control the MMC application itself and, to be honest, they're not that interesting. The **File** menu has just two choices: **Options** and **Exit**. **Options** has a single window that lets you reset any changes you've made to the DNS console's configuration. This window has no effect on the settings of any name servers managed by the DNS console, however; name server configuration is stored separately from DNS console configuration. The **Window** menu has the expected options to manage MMC subwindows, but you'll find that all the DNS administrative action happens in a single window for the DNS console. Choosing **New Window** produces another DNS console window; we haven't found a need to have more than one DNS console window open, but you might find multiple windows useful. Finally, the **Help** menu has the usual suspects: **Help Topics** brings up the MMC help system, which offers quick jumps to help with the MMC application and the DNS console.

The **Action** and **View** menus are included in all MMC snap-ins. The really important commands are in the **Action** menu: add new name servers, create zones and domains, and create resource records. You can also delete objects and view object properties. We'll explain the various commands throughout this chapter.

But let's take a moment to go over the choices on the **View** menu. Since this is a standard MMC menu, not all the options are useful with the DNS console. For example, **Choose Columns** allows you to customize the columns in the right pane. That's nice, except that they don't need customization. In our opinion, you'll always want to see all available columns in whatever DNS console view you're looking at. The next set of choices is **Large Icons**, **Small Icons**, **List**, and **Detail**, and the selection determines the display format in the right pane. We recommend choosing **Detail** when you first start the DNS console and leaving the view that way forever; otherwise, you don't necessarily see all the columns and the useful information displayed in them.

Next is **Advanced**, which toggles between a more basic, or beginner's, view and an advanced view more suitable for you DNS experts out there. Windows Server 2003 has fewer differences between advanced and nonadvanced views. The main difference is whether or not the DNS console displays some additional information in the console tree on the left. Advanced mode shows an icon allowing access to the name server's cache of records from previous lookups. We'll talk more about the name server's cache later in this chapter.

The **Filter** selection brings up a dialog box like the one shown in Figure 4-7. Filtering is handy when you've got a really large zone with hundreds or even thousands of resource records. Rather than displaying them all in the righthand pane, you can limit the display with this option.

Customize is another standard choice on the **View** menu. It controls which MMC menus and toolbars appear. We recommend leaving these options at their default settings, as shown in Figure 4-8, since those settings are optimal.

But enough about the DNS console's generic knobs and switches. Let's move on to some DNS administrative tasks.

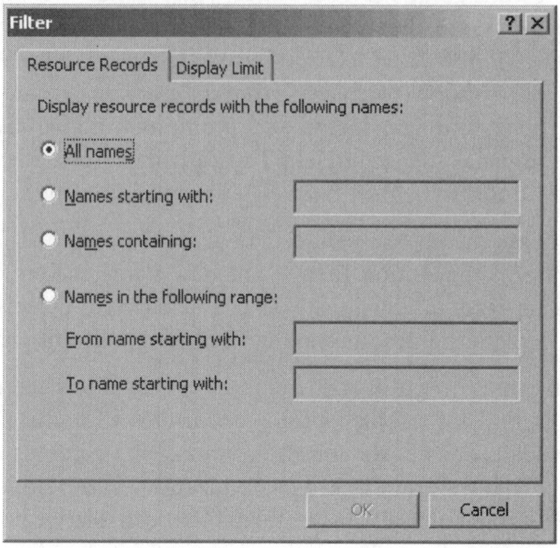

Figure 4-7. Filter dialog box

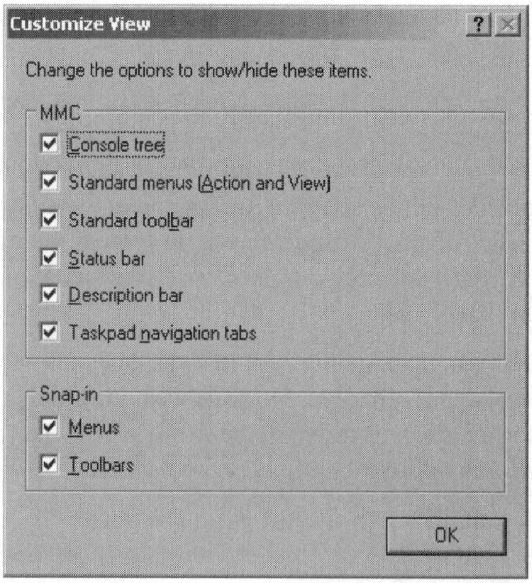

Figure 4-8. Customize dialog box

Setting Up DNS Data

Let's configure the first of Movie U.'s name servers. We'll use the DNS console for most of this process, so start it up if you haven't already done so. You don't have to run the DNS console on the machine running the name server, but for now it's easier if you do. You'll also need to have Administrator privileges to use the DNS console; otherwise, you'll only be able to start the application, not manage any name servers with it.

Adding a New Server to the DNS Console

The first step is configuring the DNS console to manage the *primary master name server* for your zone. The primary master for a zone—also called just the *primary*—stores information about the zone on its disk. You make all changes to your zone on the primary master.

Select **Action → Connect To DNS Server** and specify where the name server you want to manage—the primary master—is running. As you can see in Figure 4-9, you can choose either the local machine or specify a name server running somewhere else. If the name server isn't local, enter its name or IP address. Leave the box checked, which causes the DNS console to immediately contact the server to obtain its status and a list of any zones it might already be authoritative for.

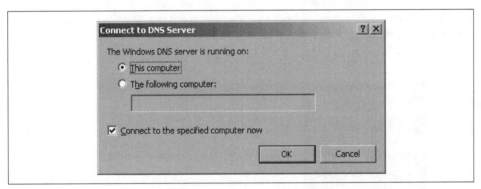

Figure 4-9. Specifying the location of a name server to manage

The DNS console adds an icon in the left pane for that name server, as in Figure 4-10.

It's important to understand what we just did here. We told the DNS console about a name server for it to manage and it added that name server to its configuration. The DNS console did *not* start the name server on the target machine. If the name server isn't already installed and running, the DNS console can't manage it and will complain with the message, "The server is unavailable. Would you like to add it anyway?"

Selecting **Connect to DNS Server** adds that name server to the list of servers the DNS console knows about. As you might expect, selecting the server and choosing **Action → Delete** (or just pressing the **Delete** key) removes the server from the DNS console's configuration but doesn't change anything on the name server itself. The

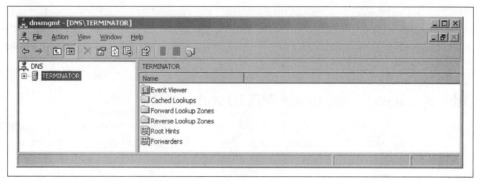

Figure 4-10. The DNS console with a new server

server will still be running—you can use **Connect to DNS Server** to add it, and you'll be right back where you started.

Creating a New Zone

Now it's time to create the *movie.edu* zone. Select the name server on the left where you want to create the zone. (There's only one server now, *terminator*, but the DNS console could know about multiple servers.) Choose **Action → New Zone**. You'll see the New Zone Wizard, as in Figure 4-11.

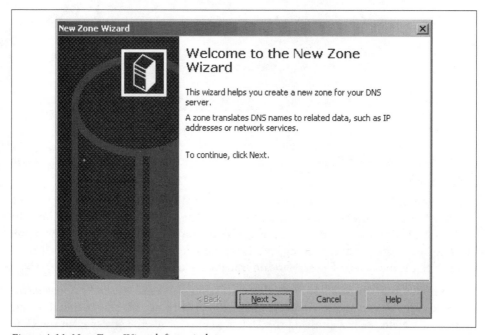

Figure 4-11. New Zone Wizard, first window

To continue, click **Next**. In the next window (see Figure 4-12), you have three choices for the type of zone: **Primary zone**, **Secondary zone**, and **Stub zone**. For now, choose **Primary zone** and click **Next**. Notice that the option to store this zone's data in Active Directory is greyed out. Microsoft calls this feature *Active Directory integration* and we'll talk about it more in Chapter 8.

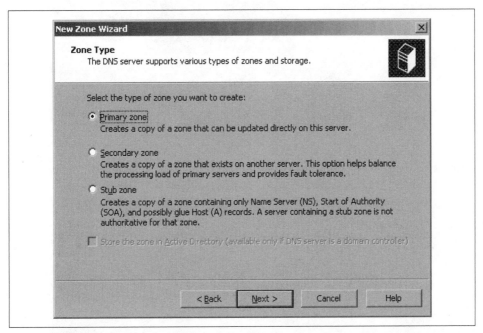

Figure 4-12. New Zone Wizard, second window

Now you need to choose whether this is a forward- or reverse-mapping zone, as shown in Figure 4-13. *movie.edu* is, of course, a forward-mapping zone, so make that selection and click **Next**.

Getting tired of all these windows yet? In the next one, shown in Figure 4-14, type the domain name of the zone, which is *movie.edu*. Click **Next**.

Now you need to specify the file that will hold all the zone information, as shown in Figure 4-15.

The zone file, also called a *zone datafile*, is the zone's permanent storage location. It's the file on the name server's disk where all the information about the zone is stored: it contains all the zone's resource records. Other name servers require you to edit the zone datafile to make changes to the zone, but the DNS console allows you to avoid editing the file by hand. As a result, you probably won't see the zone datafiles very much. We'll talk about their format later in this chapter.

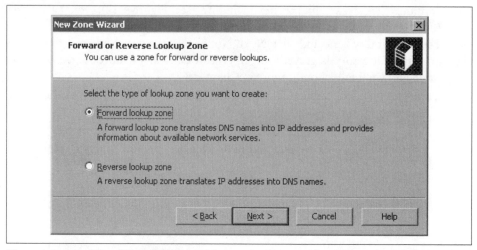

Figure 4-13. New Zone Wizard, third window

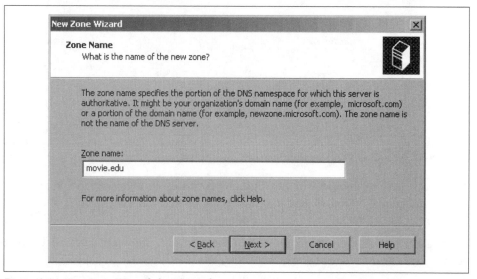

Figure 4-14. New Zone Wizard, fourth window

Even if you won't be looking at it often, you need to specify a zone datafile name when you create a zone. The server expects these files to be in *%SystemRoot%\System32\ DNS*. Microsoft's suggested naming convention uses the domain name of the zone followed by the *.dns* extension. (Notice that the DNS console has filled in the filename based on the zone name.) You can name the zone file whatever you want, but as long as the DNS console fills in the field for you, we recommend sticking with its suggestion. You may be familiar with other naming conventions, such as *db.* followed by the zone's domain name (e.g., *db.movie.edu*). In fact, that's the recommendation in our

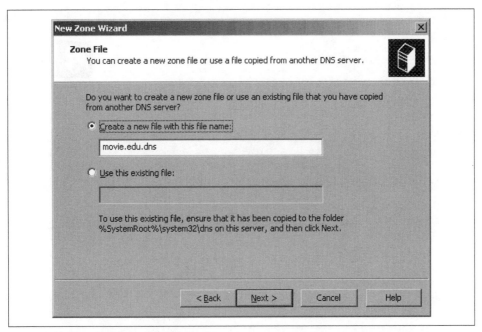

Figure 4-15. New Zone Wizard, fifth window

sister book, *DNS and BIND*. In the case of the DNS console, however, it's best to go along with Microsoft's default *.dns* extension.

When you've entered a filename (or left the automatically chosen name alone), click **Next** to display the window shown in Figure 4-16, which asks you to choose this zone's policy for dynamic updates. Dynamic updates are a relatively recent extension to the DNS protocol that we describe in detail in Chapter 11. Briefly, they allow another entity—such as a domain controller or a DHCP server—to update the contents of a zone by sending a message to the name server over the network. The alternative (and traditional) way to make changes to the zone involves using the DNS console as we're about to describe. As you might guess, allowing just anyone to send messages to your name server to change your zone is a significant security risk! That's why the DNS console asks you up front, when creating the zone, how you want to handle dynamic updates. Some Windows components, such as domain controllers and DHCP servers, use dynamic updates to keep DNS information up to date, so it's possible you'll want to enable this feature eventually. But for now, check the third option, **Do not allow dynamic updates**, to leave dynamic update disabled while we set things up.

Click **Next** and you'll see the confirmation window shown in Figure 4-17.

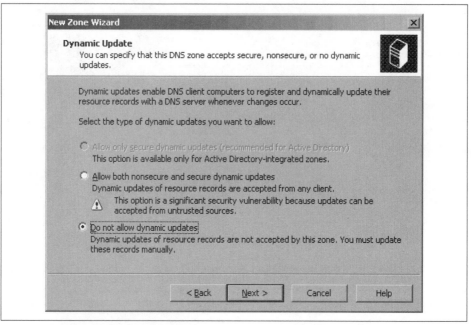

Figure 4-16. New Zone Wizard, sixth window

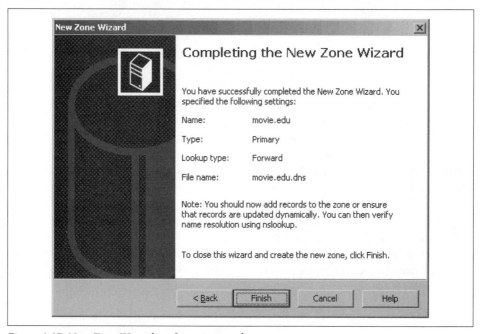

Figure 4-17. New Zone Wizard confirmation window

Click **Finish** to create the zone. If we double-click on *terminator* in the left pane, then double-click on **Forward Lookup Zones** and select the *movie.edu* zone, we see a window like the one pictured in Figure 4-18. The DNS console has created the zone and a few resource records. Let's talk about them one by one.

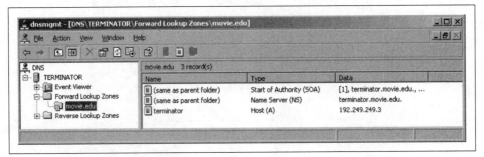

Figure 4-18. The DNS console with a new zone

The SOA record

The first record displayed is the start of authority, or SOA, resource record for the *movie.edu* zone. It's a little tricky to see that the name of this record is really *movie.edu*, since the DNS console displays (**same as parent folder**) in the **Name** column. You need to look at the domain name selected in the left pane to know the domain name of this resource record.

The SOA record indicates that this name server is the best source of information for the data within this zone. Our name server is authoritative for the *movie.edu* zone because of the SOA record. An SOA record is required in each zone, and there can be one, and only one, SOA record in a zone.

Double-click the SOA record to view its details. You'll see a window like the one in Figure 4-19.

Let's skip that first field, **Serial number**, for now—don't worry, we'll cover it later in the chapter—and go on to the next field. The second field is the name of the primary master name server for this zone. (You may hear it called the MNAME field, which is its official name.) The third field contains the email address of the person in charge of the zone (to turn this field into an email address, you replace the first dot with an at sign, @). The DNS console defaults to a username of *hostmaster*, but in other zones you might see *root*, *postmaster*, or *administrator* as the email address. Name servers won't use these names—they are meant for human consumption. If you notice a problem in someone's zone, you can send an email message to the listed email address.

Most of the remaining fields are for use by secondary name servers (also known as slave name servers) and are discussed when we introduce secondary name servers later in this chapter. For now, assume these are reasonable values.

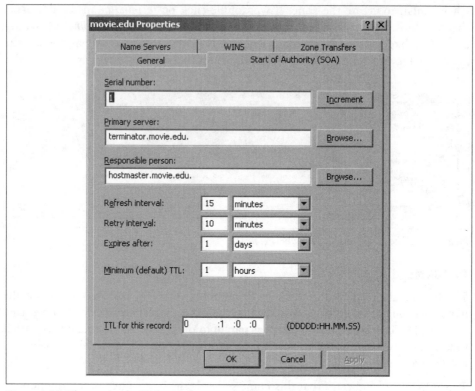

Figure 4-19. The movie.edu SOA record

The NS record

The next record is an NS (name server) resource record. There should be one NS record for each name server authoritative for the zone. Like the SOA record, NS records are attached to the zone's domain name. In our example, the NS records are attached to *movie.edu*. Right now there's only one name server (the primary master), but as we configure secondary name servers, we'll add NS records. The DNS console created an NS record for *terminator* because it's a name server—the primary master name server—for *movie.edu*.

The A record

The final automatically created record is an address record or A record. Address records fulfill the main purpose of DNS: they provide name-to-address mapping. Each A record maps a domain name, like *terminator.movie.edu*, to an IP address, like 192.249.249.3.

Every NS record needs a corresponding A record in some zone. Think about it: an NS record says, "To find out information about this zone, go to this name server." To use the NS record, you need the IP address of the name server it specifies. In this case, the name of the name server, *terminator.movie.edu*, is contained in the *movie.edu* zone we just created, so the DNS console automatically created the A record for *terminator.movie.edu* to specify its IP address. When you create a new zone, the DNS console creates an address record for the primary name server. It uses the hostname configured in the primary master's DNS configuration.

Note that some abbreviating is going on in the DNS console's display. The DNS console displays only *terminator*, but the fully qualified domain name of this host is *terminator.movie.edu*. The DNS console normally displays a relative (that is, abbreviated) domain name on the right, so you have to look at what zone or domain is selected on the left to construct the fully qualified domain name. And recall that when records are attached to the name of the zone (which is the case for the SOA and NS records here), the DNS console displays the somewhat cryptic phrase (**same as parent folder**) in the **Name** column.

You're probably anxious to add resource records for the rest of your zone, but it's best to create the reverse-mapping (*in-addr.arpa*) zones first.

Creating a New Reverse-Mapping Zone

Zones like *movie.edu* handle mapping names to addresses using A records. But mapping addresses back to names—reverse mapping—is just as important. As you may recall from Chapter 2, a special portion of the namespace, the *in-addr.arpa* domain, is designated for reverse mapping. There's one domain name in *in-addr.arpa* for every possible IP address, and PTR (pointer) records attached to a domain name provide the actual reverse mapping. Just think of a PTR record as the opposite of an A record.

So after we create *movie.edu*, we're not done. Movie U. has two /24 networks, 192.249.249/24 and 192.253.253/24. We need to create the corresponding *in-addr.arpa* zones for reverse mapping with the DNS console: *249.249.192.in-addr.arpa* and *253.253.192.in-addr.arpa*.

The process for creating an *in-addr.arpa* zone is the same as that for creating any other zone. Select *terminator* in the left pane and choose **Action → New Zone**. Follow the prompts in the New Zone Wizard as we did earlier, except this time choose **Reverse lookup zone** in the third window. Figure 4-20 shows the fourth window of the New Zone Wizard when creating a reverse-mapping zone.

We specified the network number (see the selected field), and the DNS console automatically calculated the zone name (see the grayed-out field). Click **Next** and the wizard concludes as shown earlier.

Select the newly created zone in the left pane to see its contents in the right pane. Note that, just as it did with the *movie.edu* zone, the DNS console automatically creates the SOA record and an NS record.

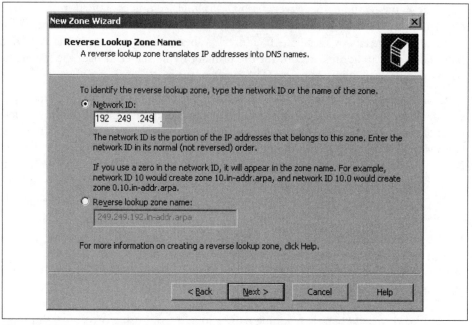

Figure 4-20. Specifying the network number or name of a reverse-mapping zone

For Movie U., we'll repeat this process to create the *253.253.192.in-addr.arpa* zone. You create *in-addr.arpa* zones according to the networks you have. Usually there's one *in-addr.arpa* zone per /24 (or smaller) network. Larger networks are often broken into several *in-addr.arpa* zones to make management easier. The zones usually correspond to subnets. This topic is covered in more detail in Chapter 10.

Adding Resource Records

Now that we've created Movie U.'s zones, we can add information about all its machines. Each machine requires two resource records: an A record in the *movie.edu* zone to provide name-to-address mapping and a PTR record in the appropriate *in-addr.arpa* zone to provide address-to-name mapping. Adding the A record is intuitive, but it's easy to forget about the PTR record. The DNS console makes the job easier with the **New Host** command, which creates an A record and a PTR record in one pass.

Select a forward-mapping zone (like *movie.edu*) and choose **Action → New Host (A)**. Enter the name of the host and its IP address. To create the PTR record as well, you also need to check the **Create associated pointer (PTR) record** box. The window looks like the one in Figure 4-21.

You'll notice that we typed a relative domain name (*robocop*) and not a fully qualified domain name (*robocop.movie.edu*). The DNS console is being helpful here and

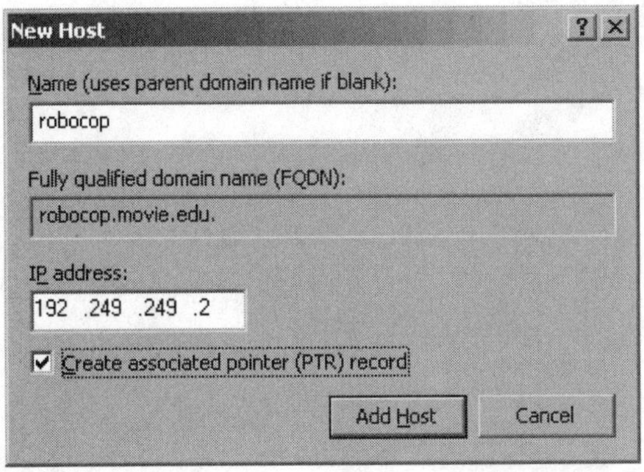

Figure 4-21. The New Host window

saving you some typing: it appends the domain name of the zone selected in the left pane (i.e., the zone that you're adding the new host to) to create a fully qualified domain name as shown.

Aliases

Looking back at Movie U.'s host table in the beginning of the chapter, you'll see that some hosts have aliases. (The aliases are any additional names after the first one listed.) For example, *terminator* is also known as *bigt*. A special resource record called the CNAME record is used to make an alias. The name of this record is confusing because CNAME is short for canonical name, which means the "real" name of the host. But a CNAME record doesn't make a canonical name; it makes an alias. All other types of records make a canonical name. We recommend thinking of it this way: CNAME records *point* to canonical names while other record types *make* canonical names.

To create an alias, select the zone to which you want to add the record on the left, and choose **Action → New Alias (CNAME)**. You'll see a window that looks like the one in Figure 4-22.

The input shown in Figure 4-22 will generate an alias from *bigt.movie.edu* to *terminator.movie.edu*. The **Fully qualified domain name (FQDN)** field shows the full name of the alias, which resides in the current zone. But the name that the alias points to (labeled **Fully qualified name (FQDN) for target host**) can point anywhere, to any domain name. We could alias *bigt.movie.edu* to *www.whitehouse.gov* if we wanted to. An important note, however: if you leave off the domain in the canonical name field, the zone's domain name is *not* appended automatically. You should always enter a fully qualified domain name in the last field.

It's important to know that the name server handles CNAME records in a different manner than aliases are handled in the host table. When a name server looks up a

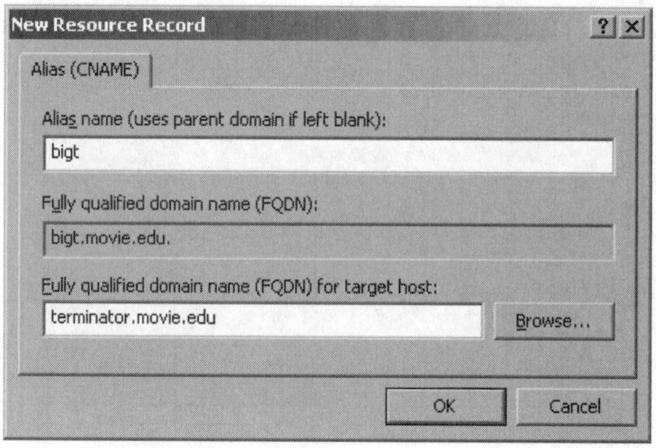

Figure 4-22. Creating a CNAME record

name and finds a CNAME record, it replaces the alias with the canonical name and looks up the new name. For example, when the name server looks up *bigt.movie.edu*, it finds a CNAME record pointing to *terminator.movie.edu*. Then it looks up *terminator.movie.edu*, and its address is returned.

One thing you must remember about aliases like *bigt* is that they should never appear in the data portion (that is, on the right side) of a resource record. Stated differently, always use the canonical name (*terminator*) in the data portion of the resource record. Notice that the NS records use the canonical name.

Sometimes you can use an A record to get the effect of an alias. Suppose you have a router, like *wormhole*, and you want to check one of the interfaces. One common troubleshooting technique is to *ping* the interface to verify that it is responding. If you *ping* the name *wormhole*, the name server returns the addresses of both interfaces. *ping* uses the first address in the list. But which address is first?

The solution is to create two A records for *wormhole*. We could use the **New Host** command to create them as we did earlier in this chapter, but we'll show you another way. The **Other New Records** command lets you choose from 22 different resource records to create. Choose **Action → Other New Records** and you'll see a window like Figure 4-23. Select a record type to see its description. We've selected **Host (A)**, and after we select **Create Record** we'll see the same **New Host** window that we showed earlier, which we'll use to add an A record for *wh249.movie.edu*.

With the host table, we chose the address we wanted by using either *wh249* or *wh253*—each name referred to *one* of the host's addresses. To provide equivalent capability with DNS, we didn't make *wh249* and *wh253* into aliases (CNAME records). That would result in both addresses for *wormhole* being returned when we looked up the alias. Instead, we used address records. Now, to check the operation

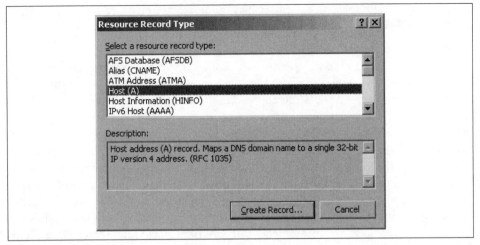

Figure 4-23. Other new records window

of the 192.253.253.1 interface on *wormhole*, we *ping wh253* since it refers to only one address. The same applies to *wh249*.

 As a general rule, if a host is multihomed (i.e., has more than one network interface), create an address (A) record for each alias unique to one address. Create a CNAME record for each alias common to all the addresses.

One more note about PTR records

We now have two A records, *wormhole.movie.edu* and *wh249.movie.edu*, pointing to the same address, 192.249.249.1. We also have a PTR record pointing from *1.249.249.192.in-addr.arpa* to *wormhole.movie.edu*. (This record was added automatically to the *249.249.192.in-addr.arpa* zone by the **New Host** option. Remember that addresses are looked up as names: the IP address is reversed, and *in-addr.arpa* is appended.) Thus, 192.249.249.1 maps to *wormhole.movie.edu* and not to *wh249.movie.edu*. Should you create another PTR record that maps 192.249.249.1 to *wh249.movie.edu*? You *can* create two PTR records—it's perfectly legal—but most systems are not prepared to see more than one name for an address. We recommend that you don't bother with multiple PTR records since so few systems can use them.

Where Is All This Information Stored?

You may be wondering what's happened to all the resource records we've been entering. Where are they being stored? The answer is: in the memory of the DNS server process. We mentioned earlier that the DNS console communicates with the DNS server using an RPC mechanism. As you add records to a zone with the DNS console, they are added "on the fly" to the name server's memory. Of course, the name server's memory is transient—when the name server process stops, its memory is lost. Obviously it needs a permanent storage location, too.

This is where the zone datafiles specified when we created the zones come in. The zone datafiles are the zones' permanent storage location, holding all the zones' resource records. If you use the DNS console to make a change to a zone, the copy of the zone in the name server's memory is changed, and a flag is set to update that zone's datafile. The name server updates the zone datafile when it exits, unless you tell it to update the file sooner. Choosing **Action → Update Server Data Files** (available when a name server is selected in the left pane) causes the name server to update the zone datafiles of all the zones for which it's a primary (if the version of a zone in the server's memory is more recent than the version on disk). There's also a per-zone version of this command: with a primary zone selected in the left pane, selecting **Action → Update Server Data File** causes the server to update only that zone's file. To avoid losing data, we recommend using **Action → Update Server Data File(s)** after a batch of changes—use it like you use the **Save** command in other applications. Of course, the difference here is that the server *will* save your data if it exits gracefully. You don't have to use **Action → Update Server Data File(s)** after a batch of changes, but it doesn't hurt anything and you'll sleep better.

As you've probably guessed, when the name server starts up, it reads the zone datafiles into memory. When you select **Action → Refresh** or press **F5**, the DNS console queries the name server and updates the console's display.

If you've been keeping track, you'll realize that DNS information exists in three places: zone datafiles, the name server's memory, and the DNS console's window. The diagram in Figure 4-24 helps explain how the information flows.

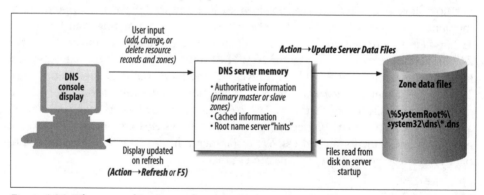

Figure 4-24. Where everything is stored

The Zone Datafiles

Let's take a look at the zone datafiles for Movie U. After inputting the remaining host table entries, we end up with the display shown in Figure 4-2. (Of course, this view shows only the contents of *movie.edu*. The *249.249.192.in-addr.arpa* and *253.253.192.in-addr.arpa* zones are populated with PTR records.)

Next we select **Action → Update Server Data Files**, and the server generates three files in *%SystemRoot%\System32\DNS*: *movie.edu.dns*, *249.249.192.in-addr.arpa.dns*, and *253.253.192.in-addr.arpa.dns*. We include them here.

Contents of movie.edu.dns

```
;
;  Database file movie.edu.dns for movie.edu zone.
;      Zone version:  17
;

@                      IN  SOA terminator.movie.edu.  hostmaster.movie.edu. (
                       17            ; serial number
                       900           ; refresh
                       600           ; retry
                       86400         ; expire
                       3600       )  ; default TTL


;
;  Zone NS records
;

@                      NS      terminator.movie.edu.


;
;  Zone records
;

bigt                   CNAME   terminator.movie.edu.
carrie                 A 192.253.253.4
dh                     CNAME   diehard.movie.edu.
diehard                A 192.249.249.4
misery                 A 192.253.253.2
robocop                A 192.249.249.2
shining                A 192.253.253.3
terminator             A 192.249.249.3
wh                     CNAME   wormhole.movie.edu.
wh249                  A 192.249.249.1
wh253                  A 192.253.253.1
wormhole               A 192.253.253.1
                       A 192.249.249.1
```

Contents of 249.249.192.in-addr.arpa.dns

```
;
;  Database file 249.249.192.in-addr.arpa.dns for 249.249.192.in-addr.arpa zone.
;      Zone version:  7
;
```

```
@                           IN  SOA terminator.movie.edu.  hostmaster.movie.edu. (
                            7               ; serial number
                            900             ; refresh
                            600             ; retry
                            86400           ; expire
                            3600        ) ; default TTL


;
;   Zone NS records
;

@                           NS      terminator.movie.edu.


;
;   Zone records
;

1                           PTR     wormhole.movie.edu.
2                           PTR     robocop.movie.edu.
3                           PTR     terminator.movie.edu.
4                           PTR     diehard.movie.edu.
```

Contents of 253.253.192.in-addr.arpa.dns

```
;
;   Database file 253.253.192.in-addr.arpa.dns for 253.253.192.in-addr.arpa zone.
;       Zone version:   7
;

@                           IN  SOA terminator.movie.edu.  hostmaster.movie.edu. (
                            7               ; serial number
                            900             ; refresh
                            600             ; retry
                            86400           ; expire
                            3600        ) ; default TTL


;
;   Zone NS records
;

@                           NS      terminator.movie.edu.


;
;   Zone records
;

1                           PTR     wormhole.movie.edu.
2                           PTR     misery.movie.edu.
3                           PTR     shining.movie.edu.
4                           PTR     carrie.movie.edu.
```

Zone Datafile Format

The format of zone datafiles is specified in the DNS standards. That means all name servers, whether Microsoft DNS Server or the BIND name server, can read each other's zone datafiles.

You've probably already guessed that the semicolon is the comment character. It can appear anywhere on a line, and anything to the right is considered a comment and is ignored by the name server. Blank lines are okay, too.

Each resource record must start in the first column of the file—no preceding whitespace. (Don't be confused by the examples in this book, which are indented because of the way the book is formatted.) Resource records are case-insensitive—you can use uppercase or lowercase. The name server doesn't preserve the case, though. It matches the case of the reply to the case of the query. For example, if a record is written as *terminator* in the zone datafile but you query for *Terminator*, the server responds with *Terminator*.

Resource records are broken up into fields, with any amount of whitespace (tabs or spaces) separating the fields.

The first field, called the owner, is the domain name of the record. Put another way, it's the node in the namespace to which the resource record is attached. You've seen the domain name on the *left* side of the *right* pane of the DNS console.

The next field in our examples is the class, IN, which stands for Internet. Other classes exist, but none of them are currently in widespread use. Our examples use only the IN class.

The field after that is the record type. We've already discussed the SOA, NS, A, PTR, and CNAME record types, and you've probably browsed through the list of other record types in the DNS console's **Other New Records** window. The type simply specifies what type of data is associated with the domain name on the right: A means IP address, NS means the name of an authoritative name server, and so on.

That's a good lead-in to the final field, the RDATA or resource record data field. This field holds the kind of data specified by the record type. It can be divided into multiple subfields, depending on the type. For example, A records specify only one parameter, an IP address, but the SOA record specifies seven parameters (remember all those fields in Figure 4-19?).

Speaking of the SOA record, you'll notice in the examples that it's the only record spanning multiple lines. If you ever have to edit zone datafiles by hand, you can use parentheses to allow a resource record to span multiple lines. This trick works for all record types, not just SOA.

Domain names appear a lot in resource records. The left side of every resource record is a domain name, and the right side (RDATA field) of many record types also contains domain names (for example, NS and SOA records). Using a fully qualified domain name in each case is perfectly legal, but it would be a lot of work: imagine having to type *movie.edu* at the end of every hostname if you were entering these files by hand. Fortunately, abbreviations are allowed. You need to understand the abbreviations because the Microsoft DNS Server uses them in records it generates.

Appending domains

Every zone has a domain name: it's just the name of the zone. (This probably strikes you as pretty obvious.) This domain name is the key to the most useful shortcut. This domain name is the *origin* of all the data in the datafile. The origin is appended to all domain names in the file not ending in a dot. The origin is different for each file because each file is associated with a different zone, each of which has a different domain name.

Since the origin is appended to names, instead of entering *robocop*'s address in *movie.edu.dns* as this:

```
robocop.movie.edu.    IN A    192.249.249.2
```

the server generated it like this:

```
robocop               A       192.249.249.2
```

The server also used another shortcut and omitted the class, IN. If you omit the class on a record, the previous record's class is used. Since this file uses only the IN class, it makes sense to specify it once on the first record in the file and leave it off the subsequent records. In that case, the first record's class applies to all the other records.

In *192.249.249.in-addr.arpa.dns*, this is the long way to write this record:

```
2.249.249.192.in-addr.arpa.  IN PTR robocop.movie.edu.
```

But since *249.249.192.in-addr.arpa* is the origin, the server generated:

```
2                            PTR robocop.movie.edu.
```

Notice that all the fully qualified domain names in the file end in a dot. That tells the server that this domain name is complete and should be left alone. Suppose you forgot the trailing dot. An entry like this:

```
robocop.movie.edu    A    192.249.249.2
```

turns into an entry for *robocop.movie.edu.movie.edu*, not what you intended at all.

@ notation

If the domain name is the *same* as the origin, the name can be specified with an at sign (@). This is most often seen in the SOA record in datafiles generated by hand, but the Microsoft DNS Server also uses the @ notation in NS records. In the *movie.edu.dns* file in the previous example, the @ stands for *movie.edu*. Of course, in the *249.249.192.in-addr.arpa.dns* file, the @ stands for *249.249.192.in-addr.arpa*, and in the *253.253.192.in-addr.arpa.dns* file...well, you get the idea.

Repeat last name

If there is a space or a tab in column one, the name from the last resource record is used. This shortcut gets used when a name has multiple resource records. This example shows two address records for one name:

```
wormhole    A    192.253.253.1
            A    192.249.249.1
```

In the second address record, the name *wormhole* is implied. You can use this short-cut even if the resource records are of different types—for example, if *wormhole* also had a TXT (arbitrary text) record.

The Loopback Address

Those of you familiar with the BIND name server may be wondering if we forgot about the loopback address. If we were setting up a BIND name server, it would need one additional zone datafile to cover the *loopback* network: the special address that hosts use to direct traffic to themselves. This network is (almost) always 127.0.0.0, and the host number is (almost) always 127.0.0.1. Therefore, the name of this file would be *0.0.127.in-addr.arpa.dns*, and it would look like the other *in-addr.arpa.dns* files.

The following would be the contents of the *0.0.127.in-addr.arpa.dns* file:

```
@               IN    SOA terminator.movie.edu.  administrator.movie.edu.  (
                      1            ; serial number
                      3600         ; refresh
                      600          ; retry
                      86400        ; expire
                      3600      )  ; minimum TTL

;
; Zone NS records
;

@                     NS terminator.movie.edu.

;
; Zone records
;

1                     PTR localhost.
```

Why do name servers need this file? Think about it for a second. No one was given responsibility for network 127.0.0.0, yet systems use it for a loopback address. Since no one has direct responsibility, everyone who uses it is responsible for it individually. If you omit this file on a name server, it will still operate. However, a lookup of 127.0.0.1 might fail: the name server will send the query to a root name server that might not be configured to map 127.0.0.1 to a name.

With the Microsoft DNS Server, you don't have to worry about creating this file and making your name server authoritative for the *in-addr.arpa* zone corresponding to network 127.0.0.0. The server is authoritative for this zone by default. It's called an *automatically created zone* and is visible in the DNS console only in advanced mode. Select **View** → **Advanced** and you can see the three automatically created zones shown in Figure 4-25.

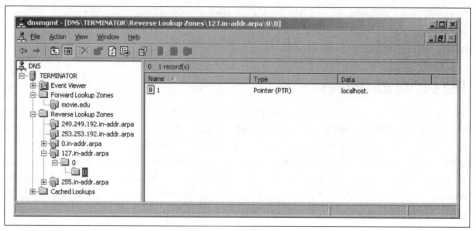

Figure 4-25. The DNS console showing automatically created zones

We've drilled down into the *127.in-addr.arpa* zone to show that there's a PTR record for *1.0.0.127.in-addr.arpa* pointing to the domain name *localhost*. In other words, the Microsoft DNS Server reverse-maps the IP address 127.0.0.1 to the domain name *localhost* "out of the box" without any work on your part.

The *0.in-addr.arpa* and *255.in-addr.arpa* zones are empty, save for NS and A records. Some hosts attempt to reverse-map the IP addresses 0.0.0.0 and 255.255.255.255, and these zones cause the local server to return an immediate Name Error (also known as NXDOMAIN, which is short for nonexistent domain) for those queries rather than asking a root name server.

The Root Hints Data

Besides your local information, the name server also needs to know where the name servers for the root zone are. (Remember that the resolution process starts at the root zone, so knowing which name servers are authoritative for the root zone is critical.) This information is stored in a file called the *root name server hints file*, which is named *%SystemRoot%\System32\DNS\cache.dns* on your name server. The Microsoft DNS Server ships with a version of this file that looks like this (or at least it did when this book was published):

```
;
;   cache.dns -- DNS CACHE FILE
```

```
;
;    Initial cache data for root domain servers.
;
;    YOU SHOULD CHANGE:
;    -> Nothing if connected to the Internet.  Edit this file only when
;       updated root name server list is released.
;          OR
;    -> If NOT connected to the Internet, remove these records and replace
;       with NS and A records for the DNS server authoritative for the
;       root domain at your site.
;
;    Note, if you are a root domain server, for your own private intranet,
;    no cache is required, and you may edit your boot file to remove
;    it.
;

;        This file holds the information on root name servers needed to
;        initialize cache of Internet domain name servers
;        (e.g. reference this file in the "cache  .  <file>"
;        configuration file of BIND domain name servers).
;
;        This file is made available by InterNIC
;        under anonymous FTP as
;            file                /domain/named.root
;            on server           FTP.INTERNIC.NET
;
;        last update:    Nov 5, 2002
;        related version of root zone:    2002110501
;
;
; formerly NS.INTERNIC.NET
;
.                             3600000  IN  NS   A.ROOT-SERVERS.NET.
A.ROOT-SERVERS.NET.           3600000      A    198.41.0.4
;
; formerly NS1.ISI.EDU
;
.                             3600000      NS   B.ROOT-SERVERS.NET.
B.ROOT-SERVERS.NET.           3600000      A    128.9.0.107
;
; formerly C.PSI.NET
;
.                             3600000      NS   C.ROOT-SERVERS.NET.
C.ROOT-SERVERS.NET.           3600000      A    192.33.4.12
;
; formerly TERP.UMD.EDU
;
.                             3600000      NS   D.ROOT-SERVERS.NET.
D.ROOT-SERVERS.NET.           3600000      A    128.8.10.90
;
; formerly NS.NASA.GOV
;
.                             3600000      NS   E.ROOT-SERVERS.NET.
E.ROOT-SERVERS.NET.           3600000      A    192.203.230.10
```

```
;
; formerly NS.ISC.ORG
;
.                       3600000     NS      F.ROOT-SERVERS.NET.
F.ROOT-SERVERS.NET.     3600000     A       192.5.5.241
;
; formerly NS.NIC.DDN.MIL
;
.                       3600000     NS      G.ROOT-SERVERS.NET.
G.ROOT-SERVERS.NET.     3600000     A       192.112.36.4
;
; formerly AOS.ARL.ARMY.MIL
;
.                       3600000     NS      H.ROOT-SERVERS.NET.
H.ROOT-SERVERS.NET.     3600000     A       128.63.2.53
;
; formerly NIC.NORDU.NET
;
.                       3600000     NS      I.ROOT-SERVERS.NET.
I.ROOT-SERVERS.NET.     3600000     A       192.36.148.17
;
; operated by VeriSign, Inc.
;
.                       3600000     NS      J.ROOT-SERVERS.NET.
J.ROOT-SERVERS.NET.     3600000     A       192.58.128.30
;
; housed in LINX, operated by RIPE NCC
;
.                       3600000     NS      K.ROOT-SERVERS.NET.
K.ROOT-SERVERS.NET.     3600000     A       193.0.14.129
;
; operated by IANA
;
.                       3600000     NS      L.ROOT-SERVERS.NET.
L.ROOT-SERVERS.NET.     3600000     A       198.32.64.12
;
; housed in Japan, operated by WIDE
;
.                       3600000     NS      M.ROOT-SERVERS.NET.
M.ROOT-SERVERS.NET.     3600000     A       202.12.27.33
; End of File
```

The domain name "." refers to the root zone.

This information can also be retrieved from the Internet host *ftp.rs.internic.net* (198.41.0.7). Use anonymous FTP to retrieve the file *named.root* from the *domain* subdirectory. However, you probably won't ever need to update your server's *cache.dns* file. Because the ability to reach the root name servers is so important, the Microsoft DNS Server goes out of its way to make sure its list of root name servers is always up to date. It views the contents of *cache.dns* somewhat suspiciously and doesn't use that list of name servers directly. (That's why this file is called the root *hints*.) Rather, when the server starts up, it chooses a root name server from *cache.dns* at random and asks it for the current list of root name servers. After all, who would know the current list of root name servers better than one of the root name servers? The list returned is the one used by the name server to start the resolution process and is the list you see when you drill down in the left pane of the DNS console. The DNS server also overwrites the contents of *cache.dns* with the updated list. As a result, if you've started the DNS server even just once, your *cache.dns* will look different than the one shown here because the server doesn't preserve the comments when it overwrites the file.

You can also view this information from within the DNS console. Select a name server in the left pane and choose **Action** → **Properties** → **Root Hints** tab to see a window like the one shown in Figure 4-26.

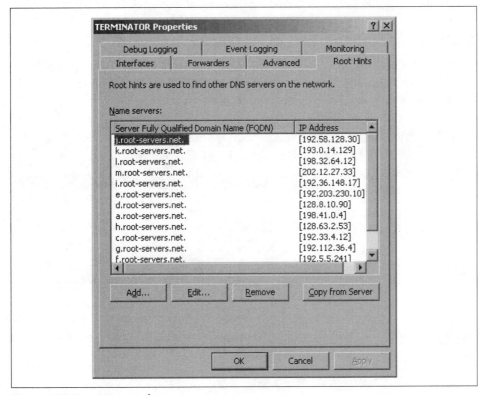

Figure 4-26. Root Hints window

Finally, you may be wondering what the *3600000*s in the file are for. In older versions of this file, this number was *99999999*. It dates back to the behavior of early versions of BIND. The BIND name server used to put the contents of the root hints file directly into its cache, and it had to know how long to keep these records active. The *99999999*s meant a *very long time*. The root name server data was to be kept active for as long as the server ran. Since both BIND and the Microsoft DNS Server now store the root hints data in a special place and don't discard it if it times out, the TTL is unnecessary. But it's not harmful to have the *3600000*s, and it makes for interesting DNS folklore when you pass responsibility to the next name server administrator.

Running a Primary Master Name Server

Your primary name server is already up and running; you've been talking to it via the DNS console. You've created a zone and populated it with information. You directed the server to write out zone datafiles with the **Action** → **Update Server Data Files** command. In the interest of completeness, next we'll show you how to stop and restart the server and then check the Event Log for any messages or errors.

Starting and Stopping the DNS Server

You can start and stop the DNS server in several ways. First, you can control it just like any other Windows Server 2003 service: with the Services MMC snap-in. Select **Start** → **Administrative Tools** → **Services**. You'll see a window like Figure 4-27.

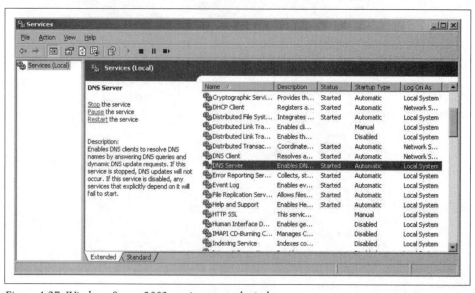

Figure 4-27. Windows Server 2003 services control window

Your system should look like this: the server should be running (that is, it should be started). Select the server as we've done by clicking anywhere on the **DNS Server** line. Select **Action** → **Stop**. After the server stops, select **Action** → **Start**. In a few seconds, the server should be running again. You can also use the handy links in the upper left of the right pane to stop and start the service.

While you've got this window open, check to make sure that the DNS server is being started automatically when the system is booted. You want to see **Automatic** in the **Startup Type** column (and not **Manual** or **Disabled**). To change the startup behavior, double-click on the service and choose the appropriate behavior in the **Startup Type** field of the resulting window.

You can also start and stop the DNS server from within the DNS console. With the server selected in the left pane, select **Action** → **All Tasks**. You'll see a menu with choices that include **Start**, **Stop**, and **Restart**. (The latter does just what you'd expect: stops, then starts, the server.)

Finally, you can start and stop the DNS server from the command line: *net start dns* starts the server, and *net stop dns* stops it. Of course, this command must be run on the system on which the DNS server is running, which is not necessarily the same system on which the DNS console is running. See Chapter 13 for more information on managing DNS from the command line.

Check the Event Log for Messages and Errors

Now you need to check the Event Log. In previous versions of Windows, you had to start the Event Viewer (by selecting **Start** → **Administrative Tools** → **Event Viewer**) separately, but in Windows Server 2003, events for the DNS server can be viewed right from within the DNS console. Expand the **Event Viewer** tab under a name server in DNS console's left pane. Click on **DNS Events** and you'll see a window like the one shown in Figure 4-28.

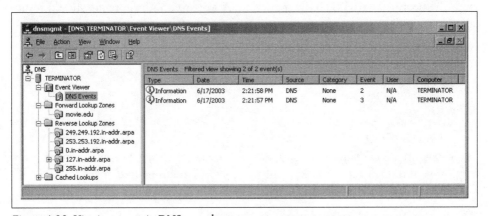

Figure 4-28. Viewing events in DNS console

DNS Server Event ID 3 is "The DNS server has shutdown," and Event ID 2 is "The DNS server has started." (More events are listed in Chapter 7.) These first two events are just what you want to see: a normal server shutdown and startup. We're reading from bottom to top since the default view shows newest events first. We also cleared the Event Log before we stopped and started the server—that's why only these two events are showing.

If there were any other messages or errors, we'd take steps to correct them now. To be honest, we didn't expect any problems because we entered all the data via the DNS console. Since it performs syntax and sanity checking, it's hard to enter bad data that will make the name server upset enough to complain in the Event Log. Still, it doesn't hurt to check. If you ever start editing zone datafiles by hand (which we don't recommend), you'll definitely need to check the Event Log.

Testing Your Setup with nslookup

If you have correctly set up your local domain and your connection to the Internet is up, you should be able to look up a local and a remote domain name. We'll step you through the lookups with *nslookup*. This book contains an entire chapter on this topic (Chapter 12), but we will cover *nslookup* in enough detail here to do basic name-server testing.

Look up a local name

You can use *nslookup* to look up any type of resource record, and it can be directed to query any name server. By default, it looks up A (address) records using the name server on the local system. To look up a host's address with *nslookup*, run *nslookup* with the host's name as the only argument. A lookup of a local name should return almost instantly.

We ran *nslookup* to look up *carrie*:

```
C:\> nslookup carrie
Server:  terminator.movie.edu
Address:  192.249.249.3

Name:    carrie.movie.edu
Address:  192.253.253.4
```

If looking up a local name works, your local name server has been configured properly for your domain. If the lookup fails, you'll see something like this:

```
*** terminator.movie.edu can't find carrie: Non-existent domain
```

This means that either *carrie* is not in your zone—check the DNS console or the zone datafile—or some name server error occurred (but you should have caught the error when you checked the Event Log).

Look up a local address

When *nslookup* is given an address to look up, it knows to send a PTR query instead of an address query. We ran *nslookup* to look up *carrie*'s address:

```
C:\> nslookup 192.253.253.4
Server:  terminator.movie.edu
Address:  192.249.249.3

Name:    carrie.movie.edu
Address:  192.253.253.4
```

If looking up an address works, your local name server has been configured properly for your *in-addr.arpa* domain. If the lookup fails, you'll see the same error message as when you looked up a name.

Look up a remote name

The next step is to use the local name server to look up a remote name, such as *ftp.uu.net* or another system you know on the Internet. Don't forget to add a period at the end of your input so the system doesn't automatically append the domain name, *movie.edu*.

This command may not return as quickly as the last one. If *nslookup* fails to get a response from your name server, it will wait a few seconds before giving up.

```
C:\> nslookup ftp.uu.net.
Server:  terminator.movie.edu
Address:  192.249.249.3

Name:    ftp.uu.net
Address:  192.48.96.9
```

If this lookup works, your name server knows where the root name servers are and how to contact them to find information about domains other than your own. If it fails, there is a problem with the root hints file or the network. The root hints file might be empty or missing address records for the root name servers. Or perhaps the network is broken somewhere and you can't reach the name servers for the remote domain. Try a different remote domain name.

If these first three lookups succeeded, congratulations! You have a primary master name server up and running. At this point, you are ready to start configuring your secondary name server.

One more test

While you are testing, though, run one more test. Try having a remote name server look up a name in your zone. This will work only if your parent name servers have already delegated your zone to the name server you just set up. If your parent required you to have your two name servers running before delegating your zone, skip ahead to the next section.

To make *nslookup* use a remote name server to look up a local name, give the local host's name as the first argument and the remote server's name as the second argument. Again, if this doesn't work, it may take 30 seconds or so before *nslookup* gives you an error message. For instance, to have *vnsc-pri.sys.gtei.net* look up *carrie,* we'd enter:

```
C:\> nslookup carrie vnsc-pri.sys.gtei.net.
Server:  vnsc-pri.sys.gtei.net.
Address:  4.2.2.1

Name:    carrie.movie.edu
Address:  192.253.253.4
```

If the first two lookups worked but using a remote name server to look up a local name failed, you may not be registered with your parent name server. That is not a problem at first because systems within your zone can look up the names of other systems within and outside your zone. You'll be able to send email and *ftp* to local and remote systems. Some systems won't allow FTP connections if they can't map your host's address back to a name. But not being registered will shortly become a problem. Hosts outside of your zone cannot look up names within your zone. You will be able to send email to friends in remote domains, but you won't get their responses. To fix this problem, contact someone responsible for your parent zone and have them check the delegation of your zone.

Running a Secondary Name Server

You need to set up another name server for robustness. You can (and probably will) set up more than two name servers. Two servers are the minimum. If you have only one name server and it goes down, no one can look up names in your zone. A second name server splits the load with the first server or handles the whole load if the first server is down. You *could* set up another primary master name server, but we don't recommend it. Set up a secondary name server instead.

How does a server know if it is a primary master or a secondary for a zone? The DNS server configuration information in the Registry tells the server it is a primary master or a secondary on a per zone basis. The NS records don't tell us which server is the primary master for a zone and which servers are secondaries for a zone—they only say who the servers are. (Globally, DNS doesn't care; as far as the actual name resolution goes, secondary servers are as good as primary master servers.)

What is different between a primary master name server and a secondary name server? The crucial difference is where the server gets its data. A primary master name server reads its data from files. A secondary name server loads its data over the network from another name server. This process is called a *zone transfer*.

A secondary name server is not limited to loading zones from a primary master name server; a secondary can load from another secondary. The big advantage of secondary name servers is that you maintain only one set of zone datafiles: the ones on the primary master name server. You don't have to worry about synchronizing the files among name servers; the secondaries do that for you.

A secondary name server doesn't need to retrieve *all* of its datafiles over the network; the *cache.dns* file is the same as on a primary master, so you'll need a local copy on the secondary. Fortunately, the DNS server installation process includes this file.

Add a New Server to the DNS Console

The first step in configuring a secondary server is to add the server to the DNS console's world view. Just as we did when configuring the primary master, select **Action →**
Connect to DNS Server, then enter the name or IP address of the secondary. In this case our secondary will be *wormhole* with IP address 192.249.249.1. Of course, the DNS server has to be installed and running on the secondary-to-be for the DNS console to be able to manage it.

Create a New Zone

This new server will be a secondary for every zone on the primary, so we'll have to go through the new zone process for each zone. Let's start with *movie.edu*. Select **Action → New Zone**. This time, select **Secondary zone** in the second window of the wizard. In the third window, select **Forward lookup zone**. The fourth window is shown in Figure 4-29.

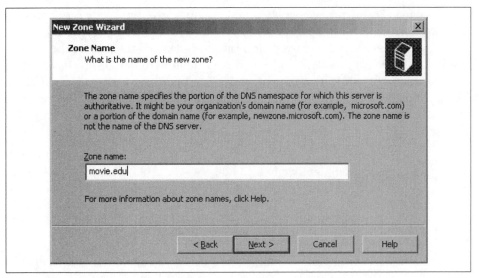

Figure 4-29. Creating a new secondary zone: specifying the zone's domain name

In the **Zone name** field, enter the domain name of the zone (in this case, *movie.edu*). Click **Next** to move to the next window, shown in Figure 4-30.

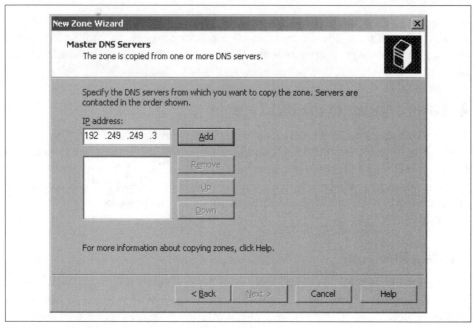

Figure 4-30. Creating a new secondary zone: specifying master servers

At this point, the processes of creating a primary master zone and a secondary zone really diverge. This is the screen where you specify where this name server will get the zone data. In this example, we're making *wormhole* a secondary for the *movie. edu* zone. We need to tell *wormhole* to load the zone from *terminator*, the primary master. In fact, on this screen you can specify multiple IP addresses. In advanced (and complicated) configurations, a secondary can sometimes get the zone information from multiple primaries or multiple sources. The DNS console supports those configurations. You could also just specify the IP address of another secondary after that of the primary: in case the primary is down, this secondary can load from another secondary. Of course, Movie U. doesn't have another secondary (yet).

For now, we just specify *terminator*'s IP address, 192.249.249.3, then click **Next**. The final window in the process is the same as when creating a primary zone: it just tells you that you're done now and asks you to click **Finish**. We'll omit showing it to you.

When you're done, the new secondary immediately initiates a zone transfer to the primary to download the zone. Within a few seconds you should be able to double-click the secondary's icon for the zone and see the records in the zone.

Add an NS Record for the New Secondary Name Server

Your new secondary won't be much good if the rest of the world doesn't know about it. As a general rule, when you add another name server for a zone, you also need to add an NS record for it. (We'll discuss the exceptions to this in Chapter 9.)

You need to add an NS record for the secondary on the zone's primary. (Remember that all changes to a zone are made on the primary and propagate automatically to the secondaries. Don't get confused by the fact that the DNS console lets you see all your name servers—you make the changes only to the zone's primary.) In our case, we need to add an NS record for *wormhole* to the *movie.edu* zone. So we click on *movie.edu* under *terminator* and select **Action** → **Properties**. Click on the **Name Servers** tab and you'll see a window like the one in Figure 4-31.

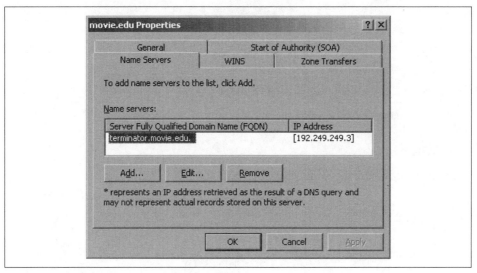

Figure 4-31. NS records for the movie.edu zone

This window shows that right now there's only one NS record for the *movie.edu* zone, which specifies *terminator.movie.edu* as an authoritative name server. To add another, click **Add** and you'll see the window shown in Figure 4-32.

Enter the name and IP address of the secondary name server and click **OK**.

Don't Forget the in-addr.arpa Zones!

Now repeat this secondary zone creation process with the *249.249.192.in-addr.arpa* and *253. 253.192.in-addr.arpa* zones.

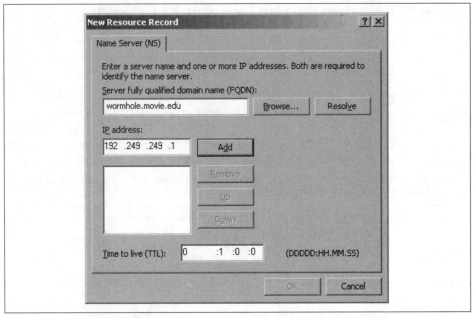

Figure 4-32. Adding an NS record

SOA Values

Remember this SOA record for the *movie.edu* zone?

```
@                        IN  SOA terminator.movie.edu.  hostmaster.movie.edu. (
                         17        ; serial number
                         900       ; refresh
                         600       ; retry
                         86400     ; expire
                         3600      ) ; default TTL
```

We never explained what the values in between the parentheses were for.

The serial number applies to all the data within the zone. Think of it as a version number for the zone. When we created this zone with the DNS console, the serial number began at 1. The DNS console automatically increments the serial number in a zone's SOA record whenever you make a change to the zone. The current serial number of 17 shows we've made a few changes since creating the zone. If you look at SOA records from other zones, you might see the date encoded in the serial number—for example, 2000102301. This format is YYYYMMDDNN, where YYYY is the year, MM is the month, DD is the day, and NN is a count of how many times the zone data was modified that day. Note that you can't use this convention with the DNS console. It just increments the serial number by one each time a change is made and doesn't understand the date encoding.

When a secondary name server contacts a primary master server for zone data, it first asks for the serial number of the data. If the secondary's serial number is lower than the primary's, the secondary's zone data is out of date. In this case, the secondary pulls a new copy of the zone. As you might guess, if you ever modify the zone datafiles on the primary master by hand, you must increment the serial number, too. Updating zone datafiles is covered in Chapter 7.

The next four fields specify various time intervals in seconds:

refresh

> The refresh interval tells the secondary how often to check that its data is up to date. To give you an idea of the system load this feature causes, a secondary will make one SOA query per zone per refresh interval. The default value generated by the DNS console when the zone was created, one hour, is reasonably aggressive. Most users will tolerate a delay of half a working day for things like name server data to propagate when they are waiting for their new workstation to be operational. If you provide one-day service for your site, consider raising this value to eight hours. If your data doesn't change very often, or if all your secondaries are spread over long distances (as the root name servers are), consider a longer value, such as 24 hours.

retry

> If a secondary fails to reach the primary name server(s) after the refresh period (the hosts or hosts could be down), it starts trying to connect every *retry* seconds. The retry interval is usually shorter than the refresh interval, but it doesn't have to be.

expire

> If a secondary fails to contact the primary server(s) for *expire* seconds, the secondary expires its data. Expiring the data means the secondary stops giving out answers about the data because the data is too old to be useful. Essentially, this field says: at some point, the data is so old that having no data is better than having stale data. We think Microsoft's default expire time of 86,400 seconds (24 hours) is awfully short. Expire times on the order of a week are common, and the interval can be longer (up to a month) if you frequently have problems reaching your updating source. The expiration time should always be much larger than the retry and refresh intervals; if the expire time is smaller than the refresh interval, your secondaries will expire their data before trying to load new data.

default TTL

> TTL stands for time to live. This value applies to all the resource records in the zone datafile. The name server supplies this TTL in query responses, allowing other servers to cache the data for the TTL interval. If your data doesn't change much, you might consider using a minimum TTL of several days. One week is about the longest value that makes sense. The default value of 3,600 seconds

(one hour) is very short, which we don't recommend because of the amount of DNS traffic it causes.

What values you choose for your SOA record will depend upon the needs of your site. In general, longer times cause less loading on your systems and lengthen the propagation of changes; shorter times increase the load on your systems and speed up the propagation of changes. We find the following values work well for most sites; they're also a good starting point if you're not sure what values to use:

```
  10800 ;  Refresh       3 hours
   3600 ;  Retry         1 hour
2592000 ;  Expire        30 days
  86400 ;  Minimum TTL   1 day
```

Some final notes about TTL values. First, the DNS console only displays TTL values on individual records if you're in advanced mode. Check out the setting on the **View** menu. Second, the DNS console displays TTLs in a somewhat cryptic fashion. Take a look back at the NS record we added in Figure 4-32. Notice the TTL specified as **0: 1: 0: 0**. "What the heck is that?" you ask. Well, the first field is days, then hours, minutes, and seconds. So rather than display a value in seconds and make you do the math, the DNS console lets you specify a TTL in a more convenient way.

Adding More Zones

Now that you have your name servers running, you might want to handle more zones. What needs to be done? Nothing special, really. Just use the DNS console to select the appropriate server in the left pane, then choose **Action → New Zone**. Follow the instructions earlier in this chapter according to whether you are creating a primary or a secondary zone.

At this point, it's useful to repeat something we said in an earlier chapter. Calling a *given* name server a primary master name server or secondary name server is a little silly. Name servers can be authoritative for more than one zone (and almost always are). A name server can be a primary master for one zone and a secondary for another. Most name servers, however, are either primary masters for most of the zones they load or secondaries for most of the zones they load. So if we call a particular name server a primary master or a secondary, we mean that it's the primary master or a secondary for *most* of the zones it loads.

DNS Properties

Let's finish this chapter with an explanation of the **Action → Properties** selection. The **Properties** selection on the **Action** menu is context-sensitive. When selected, the DNS console displays the properties of the highlighted resource record, zone, or server.

Resource Record Properties

Select a resource record on the right by single-clicking it. Then choose **Action** → **Properties**. The window should look familiar: it's the same one you used to add the record. You can get the same effect by simply double-clicking the record, too.

Zone Properties

The zone properties window is viewed by selecting a zone on the left and choosing **Action** → **Properties**. Unlike resource record properties, some zone information can be changed only from this window. It has five tabs:

General
> This window shows the name of the zone's datafile as well as indicating whether it's a primary or secondary zone. The type of the zone can be changed from primary to secondary or vice versa. (Dynamic updates and aging/scavenging are advanced topics that we'll cover in Chapters 11 and 7, respectively.) The window for the *movie.edu* zone is shown in Figure 4-33.

Start of Authority (SOA)
> This window shows the zone's SOA record. The display is the same as the window shown way back in Figure 4-19 and is no different than if you double-click the SOA record in the right panel.

Name Servers
> We've already seen this window—see Figure 4-31.

WINS
> The **WINS** tab is covered in Chapter 11.

Zone Transfers
> The **Zone Transfers** tab and settings are also covered in Chapter 11.

Server Properties

You can view the server properties by selecting a server on the left and choosing **Action** → **Properties**. It has seven tabs:

Interfaces
> This window allows you to specify the interfaces on which the server will listen for queries. If you have multiple interfaces (as for virtual web hosting), you might not need them all to be listed here. The default behavior is for the server to listen on all interfaces. The window is shown in Figure 4-34.

Forwarders, Advanced, Debug Logging, Event Logging, and Monitoring
> These tabs are all covered in Chapter 11.

Root Hints
> We discussed this window earlier (see Figure 4-26).

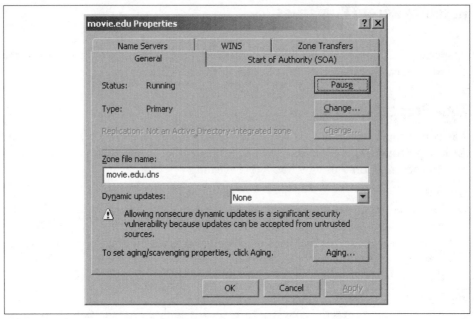

Figure 4-33. Zone properties window, General tab

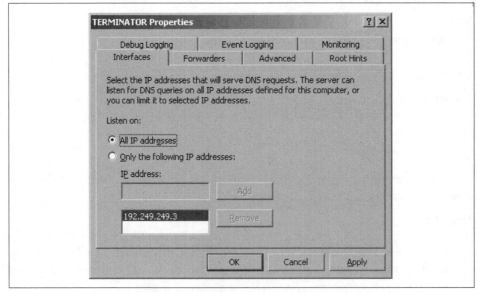

Figure 4-34. Server properties, Interfaces tab

What Next?

In this chapter, we showed you how to set up a primary master and a secondary name server. There is more work to do to complete setting up your local domain: you need to modify your DNS data for email, configure the other hosts in your domain to use name servers, and possibly start up more name servers. These topics are covered in the following chapters.

## CHAPTER 5

DNS and Electronic Mail

And here Alice began to get rather sleepy, and went on saying to herself, in a dreamy sort of way, "Do cats eat bats? Do cats eat bats?" and sometimes "Do bats eat cats?" for, you see, as she couldn't answer either question, it didn't much matter which way she put it.

I'll bet you're drowsy too, after that looong chapter. Thankfully, this chapter discusses a topic that will probably be very interesting to you system administrators and postmasters: how DNS affects electronic mail. And even if it isn't interesting to you, at least it's shorter than the last chapter.

One of the advantages of the Domain Name System over host tables is its support for advanced mail routing. When mailers had only the *HOSTS.TXT* file (and its derivatives, */etc/hosts* in the Unix world and *%SYSTEMROOT%\system32\drivers\etc\ HOSTS* under Windows) to work with, the best they could do was to attempt delivery to a host's IP address. If that failed, they could either defer delivery of the message and try again later or bounce the message back to the sender.

DNS offers a mechanism for specifying backup hosts for mail delivery. The mechanism also allows hosts to assume mail-handling responsibilities for other hosts. This lets diskless hosts that don't run mailers, for example, have mail addressed to them processed by their servers.

DNS, unlike host tables, allows arbitrary names to represent electronic mail destinations. You can—and most organizations on the Internet do—use the domain name of your main forward-mapping zone as an email destination. Or you can add domain names to your zone that are purely email destinations and don't represent any particular host. A single logical email destination may also represent several mail servers. With host tables, mail destinations were hosts, period.

Together, these features give administrators much more flexibility in configuring electronic mail on their networks.

MX Records

DNS uses a single type of resource record to implement enhanced mail routing, the MX record. Originally, the MX record's function was split between two records, the MD (mail destination) and MF (mail forwarder) records. MD specified the final destination to which a message addressed to a given domain name should be delivered. MF specified a host that would forward mail on to the eventual destination, should that destination be unreachable.

Early experience with DNS on the Internet showed that separating the functions didn't work very well. A mailer needed both the MD and MF records attached to a domain name (if both existed) to decide where to send mail—one or the other alone wouldn't do. But an explicit lookup of one type or another (either MD or MF) would cause a name server to cache just that record type. So mailers either had to do two queries, one for MD and one for MF records, or they could no longer accept cached answers. This meant that the overhead of running mail was higher than that of running other services, which was eventually deemed unacceptable.

The two records were integrated into a single record type, MX, to solve this problem. Now a mailer just needed all the MX records for a particular domain name destination to make a mail-routing decision. Using cached MX records was fine, as long as the TTLs matched.

MX records specify a *mail exchanger* for a domain name: a host that will *either* process *or* forward mail for the domain name (through a firewall, for example). "Processing" the mail means either delivering it to the individual to whom it's addressed or gatewaying it to another mail transport, such as X.400. "Forwarding" means sending it to its final destination or to another mail exchanger "closer" to the destination via SMTP, the Internet's Simple Mail Transfer Protocol. Sometimes forwarding the mail involves queuing it for some amount of time, too.

In order to prevent mail routing loops, the MX record has an extra parameter, besides the domain name of the mail exchanger: a *preference value*. The preference value is an unsigned 16-bit number (between 0 and 65535) that indicates the mail exchanger's priority. For example, the MX record:

```
peets.mpk.ca.us.   IN   MX   10 relay.hp.com.
```

specifies that *relay.hp.com* is a mail exchanger for *peets.mpk.ca.us* at preference value 10.

Taken together, the preference values of a destination's mail exchangers determine the order in which a mailer should use them. The preference value itself isn't important, only its relationship to the values of other mail exchangers. Is it higher or lower than the values of this destination's other mail exchangers? Unless other records are involved, this:

```
plange.puntacana.dr.  IN  MX  1 listo.puntacana.dr.
plange.puntacana.dr.  IN  MX  2 hep.puntacana.dr.
```

does exactly the same thing as:

```
plange.puntacana.dr.  IN  MX  50  listo.puntacana.dr.
plange.puntacana.dr.  IN  MX  100 hep.puntacana.dr.
```

Mailers should attempt delivery to the mail exchangers with the *lowest* preference values first. This may seem a little counterintuitive—the *most* preferred mail exchanger has the *lowest* preference value. But since the preference value is an unsigned quantity, this lets you specify a "best" mail exchanger at preference value 0.

If delivery to the most-preferred mail exchanger(s) fails, mailers should attempt delivery to less-preferred mail exchangers (those with *higher* preference values), in order of increasing preference value. That is, mailers should try more-preferred mail exchangers before they try less-preferred mail exchangers. More than one mail exchanger may share the same preference value, too. This gives the mailer its choice of which to send to first. The mailer must try all the mail exchangers at a given preference value before proceeding to the next higher value, though.

For example, the MX records for *oreilly.com* might be:

```
oreilly.com.    IN    MX    0 ora.oreilly.com.
oreilly.com.    IN    MX    10 ruby.oreilly.com.
oreilly.com.    IN    MX    10 opal.oreilly.com.
```

Interpreted together, these MX records instruct mailers to attempt delivery to *oreilly.com* by sending to:

1. *ora.oreilly.com* first

2. Either *ruby.oreilly.com* or *opal.oreilly.com* next

3. The remaining preference 10 mail exchanger (the one not used in step 2)

Of course, once the mailer successfully delivers the mail to one of *oreilly.com*'s mail exchangers, it can stop. A mailer successfully delivering *oreilly.com* mail to *ora.oreilly.com* doesn't need to try *ruby.oreilly.com* or *opal.oreilly.com*.

Note that *oreilly.com* isn't a particular host; it's the domain name of O'Reilly & Associates' main forward-mapping zone. O'Reilly & Associates uses the domain name as the email destination for everyone who works there. It's much easier for correspondents to remember the single email destination *oreilly.com* than to remember which host—*ruby.oreilly.com*? *amber.oreilly.com*?—each employee has an email account on.

This requires, of course, that the administrator of the mailer on *ora.oreilly.com* maintain a file of aliases for all email users at O'Reilly, forwarding their mail to the hosts on which they read it, or run a server that offers users remote access to their mail stores, such as a POP or IMAP server. What if a destination doesn't have any MX records, but has one or more A records? Will a mailer simply not deliver mail to that destination? Well, it depends on the mail server. Both Microsoft Exchange and the SMTP servers provided with Windows Server 2003 require the presence of a valid

MX record for any domain name to which you want to deliver mail. However, *Sendmail*, a popular mail transport agent from the Unix world, is different. Recent versions of *Sendmail* can be compiled to deliver mail to a destination with no MX records but at least one A record. Most vendors have compiled their *Sendmail*s this way. *Sendmail* Version 8, compiled "out of the box," will try the address of a mail destination without MX records. Check your vendor's documentation if you're not sure whether your mail server will send mail to destinations with only address records.

Even though nearly all mailers will deliver mail to a destination with just an address record and no MX records, it's still a good idea to have at least one MX record for each legitimate mail destination. Most mailers, including *Sendmail*, will always look up the MX records for a destination first when there is mail to deliver. If the destination doesn't have any MX records, a name server—usually one of your authoritative name servers—still must answer that query, and then *Sendmail* will go on to look up A records. That takes extra time, slows mail delivery, and adds a little load to your zone's authoritative name servers. If you simply add an MX record for each mail destination pointing to a domain name that maps to the same address that an address lookup would return, the mailer will have to send only one query, and the mailer's local name server will cache the MX record for future use.

Adding MX Records with the DNS Console

Now that you're familiar with MX records as they appear in zone datafiles, let's cover how to add them with the DNS console. First, right-click on the domain name of the zone to which you'd like to add the MX record. You'll see the drop-down menu shown in Figure 5-1.

Choose **New Mail Exchanger** from the pop-up menu. A small window, shown in Figure 5-2, is displayed.

In Figure 5-2, we're adding an MX record for *terminator.movie.edu* at preference 10, pointing to *terminator.movie.edu* itself. The record that's added to the zone datafile looks like this:

```
terminator    IN MX 10 terminator.movie.edu.
```

What's a Mail Exchanger, Again?

The idea of a mail exchanger is probably new to many of you, so let's go over it in a little more detail. A simple analogy should help here: imagine that a mail exchanger is an airport, and instead of setting up MX records to instruct mailers where to send messages, you're advising your in-laws about which airport to fly into when they come to visit you.

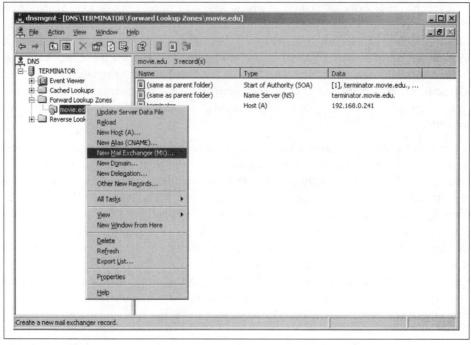

Figure 5-1. Adding an MX record to a zone

Say you live in Los Gatos, California. The closest airport for your in-laws to fly into is San Jose, the second closest is San Francisco, and the third Oakland. (We'll ignore other factors such as price of the ticket, Bay Area traffic, etc.) Don't see the parallel? Then picture it like this:

```
los-gatos.ca.us.    IN    MX    1 san-jose.ca.us.
los-gatos.ca.us.    IN    MX    2 san-francisco.ca.us.
los-gatos.ca.us.    IN    MX    3 oakland.ca.us.
```

The MX list is just an ordered list of destinations that tells mailers (your in-laws) where to send messages (fly) if they want to reach a given email destination (your house). The preference value tells them how desirable it is to use that destination—you can think of it as a logical "distance" from the eventual destination (in any units you choose), or simply as a "top ten"–style ranking of the proximity of those mail exchangers to the final destination.

With this list, you're saying, "Try to fly into San Jose, and if you can't get there, try San Francisco and Oakland, in that order." It *also* says that if you reach San Francisco, you should take a commuter flight to San Jose. If you wind up in Oakland, you should try to get a commuter to San Jose or at least to San Francisco.

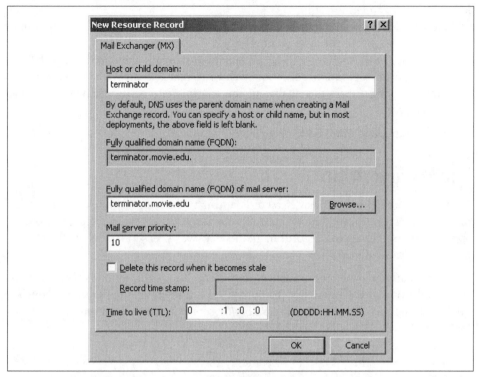

Figure 5-2. Adding an MX record for terminator.movie.edu

What makes a good mail exchanger, then? The same qualities that make a good airport:

Size

> You wouldn't want to fly into tiny Reid-Hillview Airport to get to Los Gatos because the airport's not equipped to handle large planes or many people. (You'd probably be better off landing a big jet on Interstate 280 than at Reid-Hillview.) Likewise, you don't want to use an emaciated, underpowered host as a mail exchanger; it won't be able to handle the load.

Uptime

> You know better than to fly through Denver International Airport in the winter, right? Then you should know better than to use a host that's rarely up or available as a mail exchanger.

Connectivity

> If your relatives are flying in from far away, you've got to make sure they can get a direct flight to at least one of the airports in the list you give them. You can't tell them their only choices are San Jose and Oakland if they're flying in from Helsinki. Similarly, you've got to make sure that at least one of your hosts' mail exchangers is reachable to anyone who might conceivably send you mail.

Management and administration

How well an airport is managed has a bearing on your safety while flying into or just through the airport and on how easy it is to use. Think of these factors when choosing a mail exchanger. The privacy of your mail, the speed of its delivery during normal operations, and how well your mail is treated when your hosts go down all hinge upon the quality of the administrators who manage your mail exchangers.

Keep this example in mind because we'll refer to it again later.

The MX Algorithm

That's the basic idea behind MX records and mail exchangers, but there are a few more wrinkles you should know about. To avoid routing loops, mailers need to use a slightly more complicated algorithm than what we've described when they determine where to send mail.[*]

Imagine what would happen if mailers didn't check for routing loops. Let's say you send mail from your workstation to *nuts@oreilly.com*, raving (or raging) about the quality of this book. Unfortunately, *ora.oreilly.com* is down at the moment. No problem! Recall *oreilly.com*'s MX records:

```
oreilly.com.    IN    MX    0  ora.oreilly.com.
oreilly.com.    IN    MX    10 ruby.oreilly.com.
oreilly.com.    IN    MX    10 opal.oreilly.com.
```

Your mailer falls back and sends your message to *ruby.oreilly.com*, which is up. *ruby.oreilly.com*'s mailer then tries to forward the mail on to *ora.reilly.com* but can't because *ora.oreilly.com* is down. Now what? Unless *ruby.oreilly.com* checks the sanity of what she is doing, she'll try to forward the message to *opal.oreilly.com* or maybe even to herself. That's certainly not going to help get the mail delivered. If *ruby.oreilly.com* sends the message to herself, we have a mail routing loop. If *ruby.oreilly.com* sends the message to *opal.oreilly.com*, *opal.oreilly.com* will either send it back to *ruby.oreilly.com* or send it to herself, and we again have a mail routing loop.

To prevent this from happening, mailers discard certain MX records before they decide where to send a message. A mailer sorts the list of MX records by preference value and looks in the list for the canonical domain name of the host on which it's running. If the local host appears as a mail exchanger, the mailer discards that MX record and all MX records in which the preference value is equal or higher (that is, equally or less-preferred mail exchangers). That prevents the mailer from sending messages to itself or to mailers "farther" from the eventual destination.

---

[*] This algorithm is based on RFC 974, which describes how Internet mail routing works.

Let's think about this in the context of our airport analogy. This time, imagine you're an airline passenger (a message) trying to get to Greeley, Colorado. You can't get a direct flight to Greeley, but you can fly to either Fort Collins or Denver (the two next-highest mail exchangers). Since Fort Collins is closer to Greeley, you opt to fly to Fort Collins.

Now, once you've arrived in Fort Collins, there's no sense in flying to Denver, away from your destination (a lower-preference mail exchanger). (And flying from Fort Collins to Fort Collins would be silly, too.) So the only acceptable flight to get you to your destination is now a Fort Collins-Greeley flight. You eliminate flights to less-preferred destinations to prevent frequent-flyer looping and wasteful travel time.

One caveat: most mailers will look *only* for their local host's *canonical* domain name in the list of MX records. They don't check for aliases (domain names on the left side of CNAME records). Unless you always use canonical names in your MX records, there's no guarantee that a mailer will be able to find itself in the MX list, and you'll run the risk of having your mail loop.

If you do list a mail exchanger by an alias and it unwittingly tries to deliver mail to itself, most mailers will detect the loop and bounce the mail with an error. Here's the error message from recent versions of *sendmail*:

```
554 MX list for movie.edu points back to relay.isp.com
554 <root@movie.edu>... Local configuration error
```

The moral: in an MX record, always use the mail exchanger's canonical name.

One more caveat: the hosts you list as mail exchangers *must* have address records. A mailer needs to find an address for each mail exchanger you name or else it can't attempt delivery there.

To go back to our *oreilly.com* example, when *ruby.oreilly.com* received the message from your workstation, her mailer would have checked the list of MX records:

```
oreilly.com.    IN    MX    0 ora.oreilly.com.
oreilly.com.    IN    MX    10 ruby.oreilly.com.
oreilly.com.    IN    MX    10 opal.oreilly.com.
```

Finding the local host's domain name in the list at preference value 10, *ruby.oreilly. com*'s mailer would discard all the records at preference value 10 or higher (the records in bold):

```
oreilly.com.    IN    MX    0 ora.oreilly.com.
oreilly.com.    IN    MX    10 ruby.oreilly.com.
oreilly.com.    IN    MX    10 opal.oreilly.com.
```

leaving only:

```
oreilly.com.    IN    MX    0 ora.oreilly.com.
```

Since *ora.oreilly.com* is down, *ruby.oreilly.com* would defer delivery until later and queue the message.

What happens if a mailer finds *itself* at the highest preference (lowest preference value) and has to discard the whole MX list? Some mailers attempt delivery directly to the destination host's IP address as a last-ditch effort. In most mailers, however, it's an error. It may indicate that DNS thinks the mailer should be processing (not just forwarding) mail for the destination, but the mailer hasn't been configured to know that. Or it may indicate that the administrator has ordered the MX records incorrectly by using the wrong preference values.

Say, for example, the folks who run *acme.com* add an MX record to direct mail addressed to *acme.com* to a mailer at their Internet service provider:

```
acme.com.   IN   MX   10 mail.isp.net.
```

Most mailers need to be configured to identify their aliases and the names of other hosts for which they process mail. Unless the mailer on *mail.isp.net* is configured to recognize email addressed to *acme.com* as local mail, it will assume it's being asked to relay the mail and attempt to forward the mail to a mail exchanger closer to the final destination.* When it looks up the MX records for *acme.com*, it will find itself as the most-preferred mail exchanger and will bounce the mail back to the sender.

You may have noticed that we tend to use multiples of 10 for our preference values. Ten is convenient because it allows you to insert other MX records temporarily at intermediate values without changing the other weights, but otherwise there's nothing magical about it. We could just as easily have used increments of 1 or 100—the effect would have been the same.

DNS and Exchange

If you're running Microsoft Exchange Server, you need to know how it interoperates with DNS, whether or not you're using the Microsoft DNS Server. Here are some subtle differences between the various versions of Exchange that run on Windows NT, Windows 2000, and Windows Server 2003:

- If you're using Exchange 4.x or 5.x on Windows NT, you can run Exchange without DNS. However, before you can install the Internet Mail Service (IMS, which is what Microsoft calls its SMTP server), you must have A and MX records defined for the host and domain on which you're installing the IMS. You also need to make sure that the Exchange server's DNS settings are set correctly so it can look up mail forwarders for outgoing mail.

- If you're using the SMTP server that comes with the Windows NT Option Pack, Internet Information Server 4.x, Windows 2000, or Windows Server 2003, you

---

* Unless, of course, *mail.isp.net*'s mailer is configured not to relay mail for unknown domains. In this case, it would simply reject the mail.

need an MX record if you want to receive mail; to send mail you only need access to a name server.

- If you're using Active Directory, you'll find that your need for DNS is pervasive: Active Directory depends on DNS to find domain controllers, global catalog servers, and other services. We'll cover the DNS needs of Active Directory in Chapter 8.

- Exchange 2000 uses Active Directory as its directory service, so it is totally dependent on the underlying OS's DNS setup. In particular, Exchange 2000 needs access to SRV records so it can find global catalog servers, instant messaging hosts, and domain controllers. Don't worry—SRV records are also covered in Chapter 8.

## CHAPTER 6

Configuring Hosts

*They were indeed a queer-looking party that
assembled on the bank—the birds with draggled
feathers, the animals with their fur clinging close to
them, and all dripping wet, cross, and uncomfortable.*

Now that you or someone else in your organization has set up name servers for your zones, you'll want to configure the hosts on your network to use them. That involves configuring those hosts' resolvers, which you can do by telling the resolvers which name servers to query and which domain names to search. This chapter covers these topics and focuses on the Windows 2000, Windows XP, and Windows Server 2003 resolvers (which are basically the same). It also briefly describes configuring the resolver in Windows 95, Windows 98, and Windows NT.

The Resolver

We introduced resolvers way back in Chapter 2, but we didn't say much more about them. The resolver, you'll remember, is the client half of the Domain Name System. It's responsible for translating a program's request for host information into a query to a name server and for translating the response into an answer for the program.

We haven't done any resolver configuration yet because the occasion for it hasn't arisen. When we set up our name servers in Chapter 4, the resolver's default behavior worked just fine for our purposes. But if we'd needed the resolver to do more than or behave differently from the default, we would have had to configure the resolver.

There's one thing we should mention up front: what we describe in the next few sections is the behavior of the Windows 2000, Windows XP, and Windows Server 2003 resolvers. There are lots of other resolvers, though. Every version of Windows has its

own resolver, and the configuration and behavior of each one is slightly different.*
Unix hosts normally use some variant of the BIND resolver, discussed in O'Reilly's
DNS and BIND, and many Unix vendors have extended their resolvers' functionality. Still, the basic concepts behind the operation of each resolver are quite common.

Resolver Configuration

So, what exactly does the resolver allow you to configure? Most resolvers let you configure at least three aspects of their behavior: the DNS suffix,† the search list, and the
name server(s) that the resolver queries.

DNS Suffix

The DNS suffix is the DNS domain in which a system resides. Under certain circumstances, the resolver uses the DNS suffix to generate the search list (which we discuss next). Don't confuse the DNS suffix, which is obviously a DNS domain name,
with the name of the Active Directory domain of which the system is a member. The
two values are usually the same because the DNS suffix defaults to a host's Active
Directory domain, but they don't have to be. As we'll see in a moment, you can configure a host's DNS suffix to be different from the Active Directory domain of which
it's a member. We're going to talk much more about domain names—both DNS and
Active Directory—in Chapter 8. But for now, it's not necessary to know anything
more about Active Directory domains to understand resolver configuration.

All configuration options for the Windows NT 4.0 resolver were found in a single
window. The Windows 2000, Windows XP, and Windows Server 2003 resolvers'
configuration settings, however, are located on three separate windows. The first of
these windows is where you change a host's DNS suffix. To get there in Windows
2000, open the **Control Panel**, double-click on **System**, then click the **Network Identification** tab. In Windows XP, open the **Control Panel**, click on **Switch to Classic
View**, double-click **System**, and finally click the **Computer Name** tab. In Windows
Server 2003, open the **Control Panel** and choose **System**, then click the tab labeled
Computer Name. In any case, a window very much like the one in Figure 6-1
appears. (This is the version from Windows Server 2003.)

Here you see the host's fully qualified domain name, which Windows refers to as the
Full computer name. It's the concatenation of the host's single-label computer name

---

* Installing a Service Pack can also change resolver behavior.

† We're using the Windows term here for clarity. You may know the DNS suffix as the default domain if
you've configured the BIND resolver before.

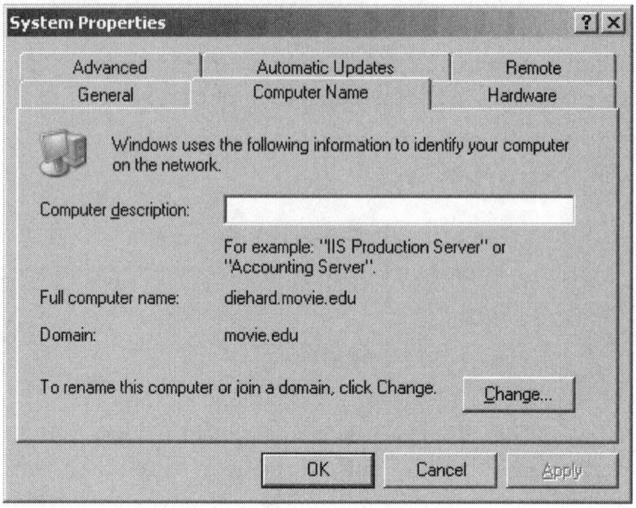

Figure 6-1. Computer Name tab

and its primary DNS suffix. The value listed as **Domain** is not the DNS suffix; it's the host's Active Directory domain. To change the primary DNS suffix, click **Change** (**Properties** in Windows 2000), and you'll see a window like the one shown in Figure 6-2.

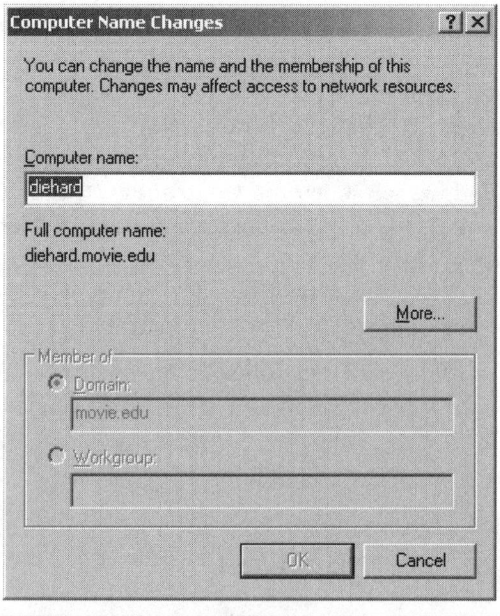

Figure 6-2. Computer Name Changes window

You can change the computer name—the first label of the host's name—only from this window. The **Member of** box again refers to Active Directory domain membership, which, strictly speaking, doesn't affect resolver behavior. To change the DNS suffix, click on **More** to display the window shown in Figure 6-3.

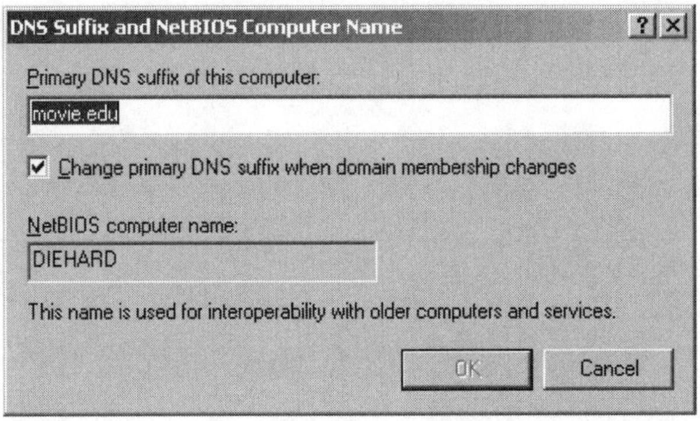

Figure 6-3. DNS Suffix window

Here—finally!—is where you can change the DNS suffix. This window also shows the only linkage between Active Directory and DNS resolver behavior. A host's DNS suffix stays the same as its Active Directory domain as long as the **Change primary DNS suffix when domain membership changes** box is checked, which is the default setting. By unchecking this box and changing the **Primary DNS suffix of this computer** setting, you can decouple the DNS default domain and Active Directory domain. You do this only if you want your hosts to reside in (that is, be named in) a different domain than your Active Directory domain. Few organizations who set up Active Directory want to do this, and Microsoft does not recommend setting the primary DNS suffix to any value other than the DNS name of an Active Directory domain to which the computer is joined. But enough about Active Directory until Chapter 8.

The Windows 2000 and Windows Server 2003 resolvers also support a different DNS suffix for each network interface on the system. In fact, each network interface (or *adapter* in Windows parlance) has its own resolver configuration. Getting to the connection-specific resolver configuration windows is a little involved, though: in Windows Server 2003, click on **Start**, then **Control Panel**, then **Network Connections**. This brings up the window shown in Figure 6-4.

This particular host has one LAN network interface. Right-click on the local area network adapter and choose **Properties**. This brings up a window like the one shown in Figure 6-5.

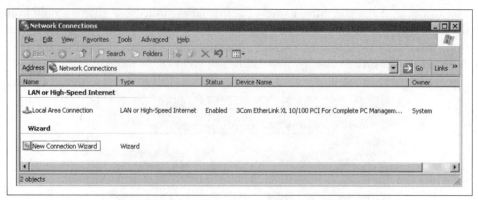

Figure 6-4. Network Connections window

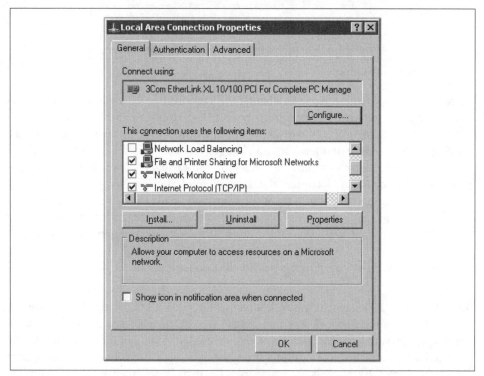

Figure 6-5. Local Area Connection Properties window

(If you know which network interface you want to configure, Windows Server 2003 lets you skip this last step by choosing the name of the network adapter from the menu that cascades from the right of **Network Connections**.)

Double-click on **Internet Protocol (TCP/IP)**. This displays the second of the three windows used for resolver configuration, which is shown in Figure 6-6.

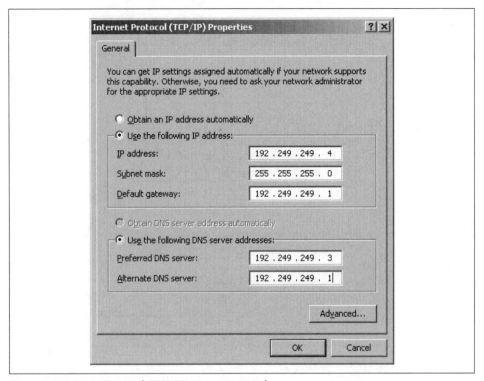

Figure 6-6. Internet Protocol (TCP/IP) Properties window

Further resolver configuration options are available by clicking the **Advanced** button and selecting the **DNS** tab, which produces the third and final window with resolver settings; it's shown in Figure 6-7.

The connection-specific DNS suffix is set in the field on the screen in Figure 6-7. Connection-specific DNS suffixes do affect resolver behavior (as we'll talk about in the next section, which discusses the search list), but their primary purpose is to assist with DNS registration. As we discuss in Chapter 8, hosts running Windows 2000, Windows XP, and Windows Server 2003 automatically register their names in DNS. You'd specify a connection-specific suffix if your host connects to multiple networks and needs a different fully qualified domain name on each network. For example, perhaps one interface is connected to a network in which the host is named *diehard.movie.edu* and another interface is connected to a network in which the host has a different fully qualified domain name, such as *diehard.fx.movie.edu*.

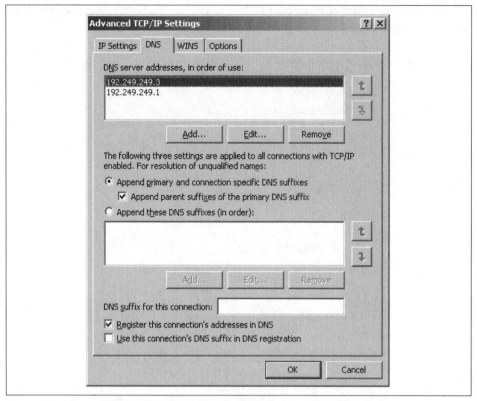

Figure 6-7. Advanced TCP/IP Settings window, DNS tab

Search List

The primary DNS suffix and any connection-specific suffixes determine the default *search list*. The search list was designed to make users' lives a little easier by saving them some typing. The idea is to search one or more domains for incomplete names—that is, names that might not be fully qualified domain names.

Most Windows networking commands that take a domain name as an argument, such as *ftp* and *ping*, apply the search list to those arguments.

With the Windows resolver, a user can indicate that a domain name is fully qualified by adding a trailing dot to it.* For example, the trailing dot in the command:

```
C:\> ftp ftp.oreilly.com.
```

---

* Note that we said the resolver can handle a trailing dot. Some programs, particularly mail user agents, don't deal correctly with a trailing dot in email addresses. They cough even before they hand the domain name in the address to the resolver.

means "don't bother searching any other domains; this domain name is fully qualified." This is analogous to the leading backslash in full pathnames in the Windows filesystem. Pathnames without a leading backslash are interpreted as relative to the current working directory while pathnames with a leading backslash are absolute, anchored at the root.

The default search list includes the primary DNS suffix and any connection-specific suffixes. If the **Append parent suffixes of the primary DNS suffix** box is checked (see Figure 6-7), each of the primary DNS suffix's parent domains with two or more labels is also included in the default search list. So on a Windows 2000, Windows XP, or Windows Server 2003 host configured with a primary DNS suffix of *cv.hp.com* and the **Append parent suffixes of the primary DNS suffix** box checked, the default search list would contain first *cv.hp.com*, the primary DNS suffix, then *hp.com* (the primary DNS suffix's parent), but not *com*, as it has only one label.[*]

The search list is usually applied after the name is tried as-is. As long as the argument you type has at least one dot in it, it's looked up exactly as you typed it before any element of the search list is appended. If that lookup fails, the search list is applied.

Why is it better to try the argument first if it contains one or more dots? From experience, people who wrote resolvers found that, more often than not, if a user bothered to type in a name with even a single dot in it, he was probably typing in a fully qualified domain name without the trailing dot. Better to see right away whether the name was a fully qualified domain name than to create nonsense domain names unnecessarily by appending the elements of the search list to it.

Thus, a user typing:

```
C:\> telnet pronto.cv.hp.com
```

causes a lookup of *pronto.cv.hp.com* first since the name contains three dots, which is certainly more than one. If the resolver doesn't find an address for *pronto.cv.hp.com*, it then tries *pronto.cv.hp.com.cv.hp.com*, and, if necessary, *pronto.cv.hp.com.hp.com*.

A user typing:

```
C:\> telnet asap
```

on the same host causes the resolver to look up first *asap.cv.hp.com* and then *asap.hp.com*, if necessary, but not just *asap*.

---

[*] One reason resolvers don't append just the top-level domain is that there are few hosts at the second level of the Internet's namespace, so just tacking on *com* or *edu* to *foo* is unlikely to result in the domain name of a real host. Also, looking up the address of *foo.com* or *foo.edu* might well require sending a query to a root name server, which taxes the roots and can be time-consuming.

Note that application of the search list stops as soon as a prospective domain name finds the needed data. In the *asap* example, the search list would never get around to appending *hp.com* if *asap.cv.hp.com* resolved to an address.

Setting the search list manually

What if you don't like the default search list you get when you set your local domain? Windows lets you set the search list explicitly, domain name by domain name, in the order in which you want the domains searched. You do this with the **Append these DNS suffixes (in order)** field on the main resolver configuration window (see Figure 6-8).

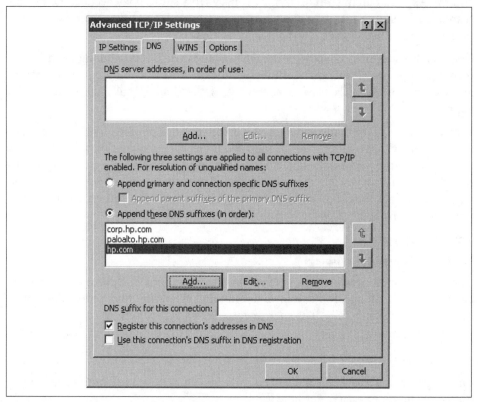

Figure 6-8. A search order example

You can add as many domain names as you like to this field,* in the order in which you want them appended, and this becomes the host's search list. Setting the search list with **Append these DNS suffixes (in order)** overrides the default search list.

---

* Or so it appears; we stopped after adding 10.

The user interface is simple to use: click **Add** to add a domain name to the list, select a domain name and click **Remove** to remove it from the list or click **Edit** to change the domain name. You can also use the **Up** and **Down** arrow buttons to reorder the list. The basic search algorithm still applies: the resolver looks up domain name arguments as-is if they contain at least one dot.

The settings shown in Figure 6-8, for example, instruct the resolver to search the *corp.hp.com* domain first, then *paloalto.hp.com*, then both domains' parent, *hp.com*.

This setup might be useful on a host whose users frequently access hosts in both *corp.hp.com* and *paloalto.hp.com*. On the other hand, the configuration shown in Figure 6-9 has the resolver search only *corp.hp.com* (and not that domain's parent, *hp.com*) when the search list is applied.

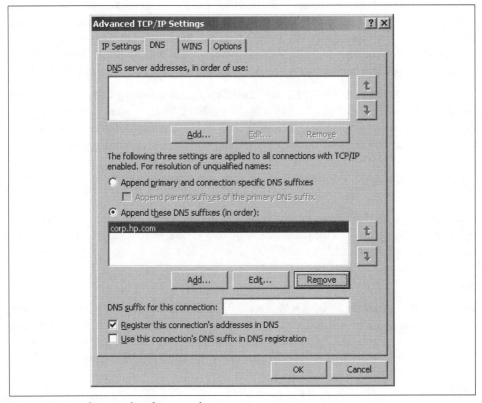

Figure 6-9. Another search order example

This might be useful if the host's users access hosts only in the local domain or if connectivity to the parent name servers isn't good, because the configuration minimizes unnecessary queries to the parent name servers.

Name Servers to Query

This section discusses how to tell your resolver which name servers to query. By default, the resolver looks for a name server running on the local host, which is why we could use *nslookup* on *terminator* and *wormhole* right after we configured their name servers. You can, however, instruct the resolver to look to another host for name service. This configuration is sometimes called a *DNS client*.

The **DNS server addresses, in order of use** field (see Figure 6-7) tells the resolver the IP addresses of the name server(s) to query. What's potentially confusing is that the information in this field is linked to the **Use the following DNS server addresses** field in the main TCP/IP properties window (see Figure 6-6). You can specify as many name servers as you want* in the **DNS server addresses, in order of use** field. As with the list of DNS suffixes in Figure 6-8, the **Add**, **Edit**, and **Remove** buttons have the expected effect. You can also use the **Up** and **Down** arrows to reorder the list of addresses. The first two addresses show up as the **Preferred DNS server** and **Alternate DNS server**† on the main TCP/IP properties window. Likewise, changes made to the **Preferred DNS server** and **Alternate DNS server** fields are reflected in this list.

The settings in Figure 6-7 instruct the resolver to send queries to the name servers running at IP addresses 192.249.249.3 and 192.249.249.1. Typically, you configure the resolvers on your hosts to query your own name servers, but you can configure your resolver to query almost anyone's name server. Of course, configuring your host to use someone else's name server without first asking permission is presumptuous, if not downright rude, and using one of your own usually gives you better performance, so we'll consider this only an emergency option.

If you want the resolver to query the name server running on the local host, you have two choices: you can specify the address of one of the host's adapters, or you can specify the loopback IP address of 127.0.0.1.

Query behavior

The way the Windows 2000, Windows XP, and Windows Server 2003 resolvers determine which of the name servers you specify to query is significantly different than in other versions of Windows. Older versions of Windows send a query to the first name server specified. If that name server doesn't respond—say it's down or

---

* As with the DNS suffix list, we stopped after entering 10 values.

† Kudos to Microsoft for clarifying their labels. In previous versions of Windows, name servers were sometimes labeled *Primary DNS* and *Secondary DNS*. This sometimes misled users into listing the primary master and secondary name servers for some zone or another in those fields. Besides, "DNS" is an abbreviation for "Domain Name System," not "domain name server."

there's a network problem—the resolver tries subsequent name servers in the order configured, waiting a few seconds between each query. If it queries all configured name servers without getting a response, it cycles through the list again—six more times on some Windows resolvers! In the case of Windows NT 4.0 SP3, if three name servers are configured and none of them are responding, the resolver tries for 75 seconds before finally giving up.

Microsoft's customers must have complained about this long resolver timeout, because things changed drastically with the release of Service Pack 4 for Windows NT 4.0. The resolver retransmission algorithm became much more aggressive. The Windows 2000, Windows XP, and Windows Server 2003 resolvers exhibit the same behavior.

Here's how these resolvers behave after applying the search list to determine the name to look up:

1. The resolver first checks its local cache, which is systemwide (and therefore shared by all applications calling the resolver). If the desired record is not in the cache, the resolver has to send at least one query to a name server.

2. The resolver queries the first name server of the preferred network adapter and waits just one second.

3. If no answer is received, the resolver resends the query simultaneously to the first name server configured for each network adapter and waits two seconds. If the host has only one network adapter, this step is skipped.

4. If no answer is received, the resolver resends the query simultaneously to all name servers configured for all adapters and waits two seconds.

5. If no answer is received, the resolver resends the query simultaneously to all name servers configured for all adapters and waits four seconds.

6. If no answer is received, the resolver resends the query simultaneously to all name servers configured for all adapters and waits eight seconds.

7. If after all this time no name server has returned an answer, the resolver gives up.

What does the resolver do after it gives up? It times out and returns an error to the calling application. Typically this results in an error like:

```
C:\> ping tootsie
Bad IP address tootsie.
```

Adding up all the waiting time, you can see that the maximum timeout is much less than in older resolvers: 17 seconds (1+2+2+4+8), as opposed to 75 seconds for Windows NT 4.0 SP3—quite a difference!

As soon as the resolver receives a positive answer during this process, it stops and returns that answer to the calling application. A positive answer is a list of resource records answering the query. If the resolver receives a negative answer (indicating that a domain name doesn't exist or that the particular type of record queried doesn't exist for a domain name), it doesn't immediately halt and return that answer. Instead, it just removes from consideration all name servers configured on the network adapter from which it received a negative answer for the duration of that query round. Only if it receives a negative answer from a name server configured for each adapter does it return a negative answer. If the resolver receives even a single positive answer from a name server, it returns that. The net effect of this mechanism is that if the resolver is configured to query name servers on multiple adapters that have different "views" of the namespace, the resolver sees the aggregate view.

The resolver also tracks the response time of individual name servers and shuffles the fastest-responding one to the top of the list. In other words, it adaptively changes the order of the name servers you specify (although these changes are not permanent, nor are they reflected in the resolver configuration windows). As you can see from the retransmission algorithm, the first name server gets only two or three seconds to reply before the resolver begins blasting queries to all configured name servers. By tracking how fast individual name servers respond and favoring the best performer, the resolver tries to minimize simultaneous querying.

The newer resolvers add another twist: if no name servers from a particular adapter respond during a query round, all name servers from that adapter are ignored—that is, not queried—for 30 seconds. This penalty-box treatment cuts down on unnecessary retransmission: if a network connection appears to be dead, there's no sense trying its name servers for every query.

Advanced Resolver Features

The Windows 2000, Windows XP, and Windows Server 2003 resolvers have some advanced features that are worth describing here.

Caching

The Windows 2000, Windows XP, and Windows Server 2003 resolvers store every record they receive in a shared cache available to all programs on the system. The Windows NT 4.0 resolver caches, but only on a per-process basis. For example, if you have two different web browsers running (say, Internet Explorer and Netscape Navigator), each has its own copy of the resolver with a separate cache. Windows 98, 95, and 3.1 resolvers don't do any caching.

The Windows 2000, Windows XP, and Windows Server 2003 resolvers obey the TTL (time to live) field on resource records they cache, up to a maximum of 24 hours by default. So if a record specifies a TTL longer than that, the resolver rounds down to 24 hours. This maximum TTL is configurable with a Registry setting:

```
MaxCacheTtl
HKEY_LOCAL_MACHINE\SYSTEM\CurrentControlSet\Services\DNSCache\Parameters
Data type: REG_DWORD
Default value: 86,400 seconds (= 24 hours)
```

(On Windows 2000, this Registry value is called MaxCacheEntryTtlLimit.)

The Windows 2000 and Windows Server 2003 resolvers also support negative caching. Windows Server 2003 caches negative responses for fifteen minutes by default, while Windows 2000 caches them for only five. This negative caching timeout is also configurable with a Registry setting:

```
MaxNegativeCacheTtl
HKEY_LOCAL_MACHINE\SYSTEM\CurrentControlSet\Services\DNSCache\Parameters
Data type: REG_DWORD
Default value: 900 seconds (= 15 minutes)
```

(On Windows 2000, this Registry value is called NegativeCacheTime.) To disable negative caching altogether, set this value to zero.

To view the resolver's cache, use *ipconfig /displaydns*. To clear the cache, type *ipconfig /flushdns*. To disable caching on Windows XP or Windows Server 2003, you can use the command:

```
C:\> net stop dnscache
```

However, this only lasts until the next reboot. To disable caching permanently, go to **Services** (in the **Administrative Tools** program group) and set the DNS Client service's **Startup type** to **Disabled**.

Subnet Prioritization

Subnet prioritization is analogous to the BIND resolver's address-sorting feature. When the resolver receives multiple address records for the same domain name, it examines the IP address in each record and adjusts the order of the records before returning the list to the calling application: any records with IP addresses on the same subnets as the host on which the resolver is running are moved to the top of the list. Since most applications use addresses in the order returned by the resolver, this behavior causes traffic to remain on local networks.

For example, Movie University has two mirrored web servers on two different subnets:

```
www.movie.edu.   IN  A  192.253.253.101
www.movie.edu.   IN  A  192.249.249.101
```

Let's say the resolver on *terminator.movie.edu* (192.249.249.3) sends a query and receives these records. It sorts the record with address 192.249.249.101 to the top of the list because *terminator* shares a network with that address.

Note that this behavior defeats the round-robin feature implemented by most name servers. *Round robin* refers to the name server behavior of rotating the order of multiple address records in successive responses to distribute the load among the servers (again taking advantage of the behavior of most applications to use the first address in the list returned by the resolver). With subnet prioritization enabled, the order of the records is subject to shuffling by the resolver. You can disable subnet prioritization with a Registry setting:

```
PrioritizeRecordData
HKEY_LOCAL_MACHINE\SYSTEM\CurrentControlSet\Services\DNSCache\Parameters
Data type: REG_DWORD
Range: 0 - 1
Default value: 1 (Subnet prioritization enabled)
```

Other Windows Resolvers

Since you probably have hosts running other versions of Windows on your network, it's helpful to know how these resolvers behave, too.

Windows 95

Windows 95 includes its own TCP/IP stack with a DNS resolver. In fact, Windows 95 actually includes two TCP/IP stacks: one for TCP/IP over LANs and another for TCP/IP over dial-up connections. To get to the main DNS configuration panel, go to the **Control Panel**, then select **Network**. Select **TCP/IP**, then click the **Properties** button. This brings up a new dialog, which looks similar to the one in Figure 6-10. Choose the tab labeled **DNS Configuration**.

Configuration using this panel is fairly self-explanatory: first select **Enable DNS** to turn on DNS resolution, then fill in the PC's hostname (in this case, the first label of its domain name) in the **Host** field and the local domain name (everything after the first dot) in the **Domain** field. Add the IP addresses of up to three name servers you want to query, in the order in which you want to query them, under **DNS Server Search Order**. Finally, fill in the domain names in the search list under **Domain Suffix Search Order** in the order in which you want them appended. If you leave out the **Domain Suffix Search Order**, the Windows 95 resolver derives one from the local domain name in the same way a Windows 2000 resolver does: appending successive parent domains with at least two labels.

One interesting note about Windows 95: you can configure a different set of name servers for each dial-up connection you might have to an ISP in the Dial-Up Networking

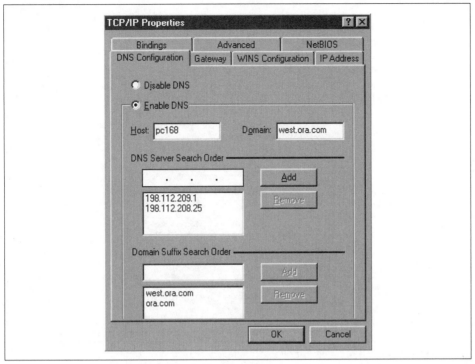

Figure 6-10. Resolver configuration under Windows 95

(DUN) configuration. To configure DUN-specific resolver settings, double-click on the **My Computer** icon on your desktop, then double-click on **Dial-Up Networking**, right-click on the name of the connection whose resolver settings you'd like to configure, and select **Properties**. Select the **Server Types** tab and click on **TCP/IP Settings**. You'll see the window shown in Figure 6-11.

If you leave the **Server assigned name server addresses** radio button checked, the resolver retrieves the name servers it should query from the server you dial into. If you check **Specify name server addresses** and specify the addresses of one or two name servers, Windows 95 tries to use those name servers when the DUN connection is active.

This is really useful if you use multiple ISPs and each has its own name servers. However, configuring name servers in the **TCP/IP Properties** panel overrides the DUN-specific name servers. To use the DUN-specific name server feature, you must leave the **TCP/IP Properties** panel blank except for enabling DNS and specifying the local hostname. This limitation is due to a lack of integration between the dial-up and LAN TCP/IP stacks and is corrected in DUN 1.3. See Knowledge Base article 191494 for details.

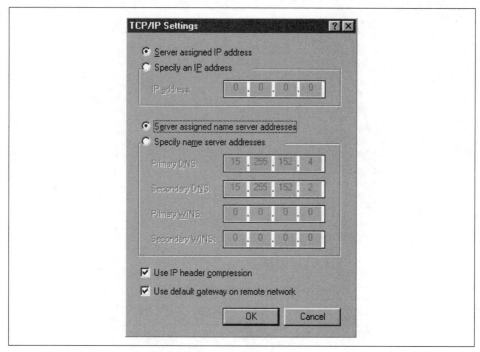

Figure 6-11. DUN resolver configuration under Windows 95

Windows 98

The resolver in Windows 98 is almost identical to Windows 95's resolver. (Graphically, in fact, it *is* identical, so we won't show you any screenshots.) The major differences between the two resolvers are due to the fact that Windows 98 ships with Winsock 2.0.* Winsock 2.0, for example, sorts responses as we described in the previous section on subnet prioritization. For details, see Knowledge Base article 182644.

Configuring DUN-specific name servers also works with Windows 98. The resolver queries the name servers listed in the **TCP/IP Properties** panel and the DUN-specific name servers simultaneously and takes the first positive answer it receives from either set. If the resolver receives only negative answers, it returns a negative answer.

Windows NT 4.0

In Windows NT, LAN resolver configuration is done from a single panel that looks remarkably similar to Windows 95's, since NT 4.0 incorporated the Windows 95

---

* The version of Winsock in Windows 95 can be upgraded to 2.0; see Knowledge Base article 182108.

"shell." In fact, other than the presence of the new **Edit** button and the handy little arrows that allow you to reorder name servers and elements of the search list, there's really no semantic difference between them, as shown in Figure 6-12.

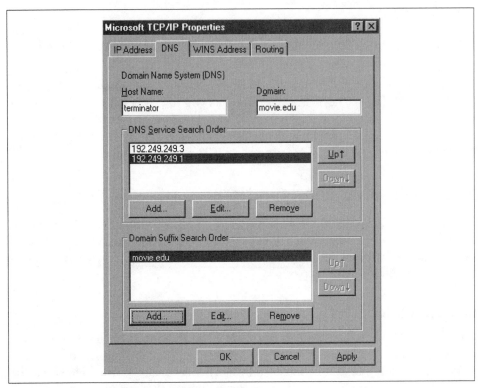

Figure 6-12. Resolver configuration under Windows NT

To get to the **DNS Configuration** panel, go to the **Control Panel,** click on **Network,** and select the **Protocols** tab. Double-click on **TCP/IP Protocol,** then select the **DNS** tab.

Windows NT also allows users to configure resolver settings specific to particular dial-up networking connections. To configure these, click on the **My Computer** icon, select **Dial-Up Networking,** pull down the top selection box, and choose the name of the DUN connection whose resolver you'd like to configure. Then click on the **More** pull-down and select **Edit Entry** then **Modem Properties.** Select the **Server** tab on the resulting window, and click on the **TCP/IP Settings** button. You'll see the same window you'd see in Windows 95 (shown earlier).

If you leave the **Server assigned name server addresses** radio button checked, the resolver retrieves the name servers it should query from the server you dial into. If you check **Specify name server addresses** and specify the addresses of one or two name servers, Windows NT uses those name servers when the DUN connection is active. When you drop the DUN connection, NT reverts to using the LAN resolver's settings.

The Windows NT 4.0 resolver caches name-to-address mappings on a per-process basis, according to the TTL on the returned address records, as mentioned earlier.

Microsoft updated the resolver fairly extensively in Windows NT 4.0, Service Pack 4. The SP4 resolver supports subnet prioritization. See Microsoft Knowledge Base article 196500 for details. The SP4 resolver also lets you turn off caching in the resolver using a Registry value. For details, see Knowledge Base article 187709. The SP4 resolver uses the same, more aggressive retransmission algorithm as the Windows 2000 resolver. See Knowledge Base article 198550 for more information.

Sample Resolver Configurations

Let's go over what some Windows Server 2003 resolver configurations look like on real hosts. Resolver configuration needs vary depending on whether or not a host runs a local name server, so we'll cover both cases: hosts using remote name servers and hosts running name servers locally.

Remote Name Server

We, as the administrators of *movie.edu*, have been asked to configure a professor's new workstation, which doesn't run a name server. Deciding which domain the workstation belongs in is easy: there's only *movie.edu* to choose from. However, the professor *is* working with researchers at Pixar on new shading algorithms, so perhaps it'd be wise to put *pixar.com* in her workstation's list of DNS suffixes to append.

The new workstation is on the 192.249.249.0 network, so the closest name servers are *wormhole.movie.edu* (192.249.249.1) and *terminator.movie.edu* (192.249.249.3). As a rule, you should configure hosts to first use the closest name server available. (The closest possible name server is a name server on the local host; the next closest is a name server on the same subnet or network.) In this case, both name servers are equally close, but we know that *wormhole* is bigger (it's a faster host, with more capacity).

Since this particular professor is known to get awfully vocal when she has problems with her computer, we'll also add *terminator.movie.edu* (192.249.249.3) as a backup name server. That way, if *wormhole* is down for any reason, the professor's workstation can still get name service (assuming *terminator* and the rest of the network are up).

Figure 6-13 shows what her workstation's resolver configuration will look like.

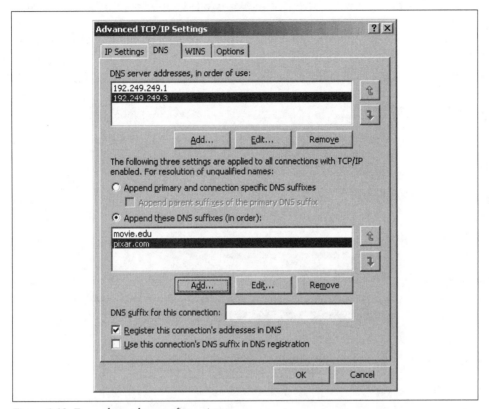

Figure 6-13. Example resolver configuration

Local Name Server

Next, we have to configure the university mail hub, *postmanrings2x*, to use DNS. *postmanrings2x* is shared by all groups in the *movie.edu* domain. We've recently configured a name server on the host to help cut down the load on the other name servers, so we should make sure the resolver queries the name server on the local host first.

If we decide we need a backup name server—a prudent decision—we can add a name server to the **DNS server addresses, in order of use** field. Whether or not we configure a backup name server depends largely on the reliability of the local name server. A robust name server implementation will keep running for longer than some operating systems, so there may be no need for a backup. If the local name server has a history of problems, though—say it hangs occasionally and stops responding to queries—it's prudent to add a backup name server.

To add a backup name server, we just list the local name server first in the list of DNS suffixes to append and then list one or two backup name servers. Since we'd rather be safe than sorry, we're going to add two backup name servers. *postmanrings2x* is on the 192.249.249.0 network, too, so *terminator* and *wormhole* are the closest name servers to it (besides its own). The final configuration is shown in Figure 6-14.

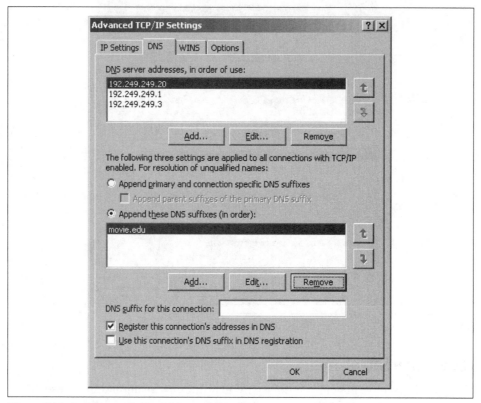

Figure 6-14. Another example resolver configuration

## CHAPTER 7

Maintaining the Microsoft DNS Server

*"Well, in our country," said Alice, still panting a little,
"you'd generally get to somewhere else—if you ran
very fast for a long time as we've been doing."*

*"A slow sort of country!" said the Queen. "Now, here,
you see, it takes all the running you can do, to keep in
the same place. If you want to get somewhere else, you
must run at least twice as fast as that!"*

This chapter discusses a number of related topics pertaining to name server maintenance. We'll talk about commands you can (and can't) send to a running name server, modifying the zone datafiles, and keeping the root name server cache file up to date. We'll also list common Event Log messages.

This chapter doesn't cover troubleshooting problems. Maintenance involves keeping your data current and watching over your name servers as they operate. Troubleshooting involves putting out fires—those little DNS emergencies that flare up periodically. Firefighting is covered in Chapter 15.

What About Signals?

Those of you familiar with the BIND name server know that it's possible to signal a running name server to perform certain tasks, such as rereading its configuration file or turning on debugging information. The Microsoft DNS Server has no exact analog to a BIND name server's signals, but you can still make it perform certain tasks while running. We'll go over the tasks possible using signals on a BIND name server and show how to accomplish the same thing (if possible) with the Microsoft DNS Server:

Restart the name server. You can signal a BIND name server to reread its configuration file and zone datafiles. There's no comparable Microsoft DNS Server command. If the server obtains its configuration information from the Registry (the default mode), this command isn't necessary: as you make configuration changes with the DNS console, they take effect immediately in the running name server. If the server is using a BIND-style boot file, you must stop and restart the server after making a change to the boot file. For more information on the server "boot method," see Appendix B.

Dump a copy of the name server's internal database to a file. A BIND server can dump its entire memory database of authoritative data, cached data, and root name server "hints" to a file. There's no direct Microsoft DNS Server equivalent, but you can come close—all this information is visible in the DNS console. To see authoritative data, just select the appropriate zone. By selecting the **Cached Lookups** folder, you can see the contents of the name server's cache as well as the list of root name servers it's using.[*]

Dump name server statistics to a file. You can't dump the Microsoft DNS Server's usage statistics to a file, but you can view them from Performance Monitor, a Microsoft Management Console snap-in. Statistics are covered in detail at the end of this chapter.

Start/stop writing debugging information to a file. The Microsoft DNS Server can log several different kinds of debugging-related information to a file. This behavior is controlled from the **Debug Logging** tab of the server properties window, where you can select the types of debugging information that should be logged.

Log all queries. As with a BIND server, you can also direct the Microsoft DNS Server to log individual queries processed. The default options on the **Debug Logging** tab cause the server to record all queries received (and responses sent) when debug logging is turned on.

The main thing you can do to a running Microsoft DNS Server is stop it and start it again. What happens when you stop and start the server? Remember that the name server answers queries from its in-memory database. This database includes three kinds of information: authoritative data (zones for which the server is a primary or secondary), cached data (answers from other name servers), and root name server "hints" (the list of root name servers from the root name server cache file, *cache.dns*). When you stop the name server, this data is lost.

When you restart the server, it reloads the authoritative data from the zone datafiles on its disk. Zones for which the server is a primary are loaded and not read again for the lifetime of the server process. (Of course, you can make a change to a primary zone with the DNS console and direct the server to *write* to the zone datafile with **Action → Update Server Data Files**, but the server *reads* the zone datafile only at startup.) Zones for which the server is a secondary are also loaded from the zone datafiles. But for each zone, the server queries its master (usually the zone's primary)

---

[*] You can see the *Cached Lookups* folder only if the DNS console is showing the advanced view: select **View → Advanced**.

for the SOA record to compare serial numbers. If the master's serial number is larger than the serial number in the zone just loaded from disk, the server performs a zone transfer.

The server also reads *cache.dns* at startup. In Chapter 4, we described how root name server information is used not directly, but as a "hint" to find the current list of root name servers: the server queries a root name server from *cache.dns* for the current list of root name servers, and the results are the first records in the cache. Remember, the cache is empty when the server starts up.

Logging

The Windows Server 2003 Microsoft DNS Server is much improved over its predecessors when it comes to logging and debugging. Previous versions of the server were like a "black box" you couldn't see inside of. But now you can direct the server to write several different kinds of helpful logging and debugging information while it's running.

To enable this feature, right-click on a server in the left pane of the DNS console, choose **Properties**, then select the **Debug Logging** tab. The window looks like the one shown in Figure 7-1.

Updating Zone Data

For nearly all changes to your zones, you'll use the DNS console. In Chapter 4 we described how to add a name server to the DNS console, create zones, and create resource records. Deleting these objects is easy: just select the object by left-clicking it, then press **Delete** (or select **Action** → **Delete**). Modifying objects is also straightforward. Name server names and zone names cannot be changed but must be deleted and added with the new name. For example, if the name of a name server you're managing changes, you have to delete the name server within the DNS console and replace it with the new name. The same thing goes if you change the name of a zone, say from *movie.edu* to *movie.net*.

Changing resource record data is easy, too. Just double-click the record in the right pane (or select it with a single click and choose **Action** → **Properties**). You'll see the same window as when you added the record. Note that you can change resource record data (also called *RDATA*) but not the name of the record (the owner). In other words, you can change the right side of the record but not the left side (as viewed in the DNS console's righthand pane or in the zone datafile). So you can change the IP address of *terminator*'s A record, but you can't change *terminator* to *terminator2*. If you need to change the owner, you'll have to delete the record and replace it with the new owner.

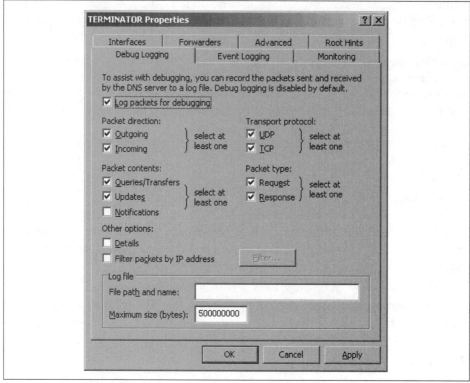

Figure 7-1. Server properties, Debug Logging tab

Adding and Deleting Resource Records by Hand

Most of the time, you really should use the DNS console to make changes to your zones. However, the DNS console isn't suited for some tasks—sometimes you might want to edit the zone datafiles by hand. For example, adding, deleting, or changing a lot of records at once is tough with the DNS console but easy with a little Perl code or a good text editor. If you run a name server for long enough, you'll eventually want to make a change outside the DNS console.

Editing by hand is a little complicated because you have to manually perform some steps that the DNS console does for you automatically. The following list describes what to do:

1. Remember that all changes must be made on a zone's primary name server. This is the case whether you're using the DNS console or editing by hand. If you make changes to the zone datafile on a secondary, the next zone transfer from the primary will overwrite your work.

2. If you've made any changes using the DNS console since you started the name server (that usually means since the last reboot), stop the name server. Here's

why: when you change a zone with the DNS console, the change takes effect in the primary name server's memory right away, but the zone datafile on disk is not updated immediately. The name server sets an internal "update pending" flag to remind itself that that zone's datafile needs updating. If you select **Action → Update Server Data Files**, all the zone datafiles of changed zones are updated and any flags are cleared. But if the server stops (whether it's halted by you or by a system reboot—or for any other reason) and some zones have their update pending flags set, the server updates the corresponding zone datafiles before terminating. So you can see what happens if you make a change by hand but forget about a recent change made with the DNS console: when you stop and restart the server to put the manual change into effect, the zone datafile gets updated, and your manual editing is lost.

3. Find the zone datafile of the zone you want to change. Recall from Chapter 4 that the zone datafiles are stored in *%SystemRoot%\system32\dns* and the default naming convention is the name of the zone followed by the *.dns* extension—for example, *movie.edu.dns*.

4. Bring up the zone datafile in your favorite text editor. Notepad is a good choice; Microsoft Word isn't. Whatever you use, make sure you eventually save the file in plain text format. That's why we like Notepad—you can't save a file as anything but plain text.

5. Increment the serial number in the SOA record at the top of the file. (See the next section for more information on SOA serial numbers.) Since the SOA record is at the top of the file, it's a good idea to update it first so you won't forget to do it later.

6. Make whatever changes you need to make. If you're adding a host, you might need MX records in addition to the A record. For example, we added the following resource records to *movie.edu.dns* when we added the new host *cujo* to our network:

   ```
   cujo  IN A  192.253.253.5
         IN MX  10 cujo
         IN MX  20 terminator
   ```

7. When you're done, don't forget to save the file!

8. Don't forget to add PTR records! If you're adding a host, you should add a PTR record to the appropriate *in-addr.arpa* zone for each of its IP addresses. This step is easy to forget because the DNS console adds PTR records for you automatically. And remember—if you change an *in-addr.arpa* zone, don't forget to increment the serial number in its SOA record. Our new host *cujo* has only one IP address, 192.253.253.5, so we added one PTR record to the *253.253.192.in-addr.arpa.dns* file:

   ```
   5 IN PTR cujo.movie.edu.
   ```

Your changes won't take effect until you restart the primary name server: stop it, and then start it again. This is another task handled by the DNS console. When you make changes with the DNS console, the changes take effect immediately in the name server's memory and are written to disk later. Editing by hand reverses the process: you make the changes first on disk and have to restart the name server to get the changes into its memory.

Secondary name servers load the new data after some length of time within the time interval defined in the SOA record for refreshing their data. Sometimes your users won't want to wait for the secondaries to pick up the new data—they'll want it available right away. Can you force a secondary to load the new information right away? If you've enabled zone change notification, the secondaries will pick up the new data quickly because the primary notifies the secondary of changes within 15 minutes of the change. (See Chapter 11 for more information on zone change notification.) If you don't have notification set up, you should! But you can get the same effect the hard way by restarting the name server on each of the secondaries. When the name server starts up, it does a serial number compare with its master for every zone for which it's a secondary. If it discovers an out-of-date zone, it immediately performs a zone transfer.

To delete a host, remove all the resource records pertaining to it from the appropriate zone datafiles. Make sure you remove the A record, any MX records, and the PTR record. Also be sure to increment the serial number in each zone datafile you modify and restart your primary name server. (But, realistically, deleting hosts is best done with the DNS console.)

SOA Serial Numbers

Every zone has a serial number. Every time the data in a file is changed, the zone's serial number must be incremented. If the serial number is not incremented, secondary name servers for the zone will not pick up the updated data. The change is simple. If the original datafile had the following SOA record:

```
@                       IN  SOA terminator.movie.edu.  hostmaster.movie.edu. (
                        24              ; serial number
                        900             ; refresh
                        600             ; retry
                        86400           ; expire
                        3600        ) ; default TTL
```

the updated datafile would have the following SOA record:

```
@                       IN  SOA terminator.movie.edu.  hostmaster.movie.edu. (
                        25              ; serial number
                        900             ; refresh
                        600             ; retry
                        86400           ; expire
                        3600        ) ; default TTL
```

(Recall from Chapter 4 that "@" expands to the current origin of the zone datafile, which is usually the name of the zone. In this example, the "@" stands for *movie. edu.*) This simple change is the key to distributing the data to all of your secondaries. Failing to increment the serial number is the most common mistake made when updating by hand. The first few times you make a change manually, you'll remember to update the serial number because this process is new and you are paying close attention. After modifying zone datafiles becomes second nature (we bet you can't wait for *that*), you'll make some quick little change, forget to update the serial number...and none of the secondaries will pick up the new data. Eternal vigilance is the price of modifying zone datafiles by hand.

There are several good ways to manage serial numbers, which are just integers. The obvious way is just to use a counter: increment the serial number by one each time the file is modified. That's what the DNS console does. Every time it updates a zone, it increments the zone's serial number. If you make changes with the DNS console, you're locked into this method. If you modify the zone datafiles only by hand, you have other options, such as deriving the serial number from the date. For example, you could use the eight-digit number formed by *<year><month><day>*. Suppose today is March 5, 2004. In this form, your serial number would be 20040305. This scheme allows only one update per day, though, and that may not be enough. Add another two digits to this number to indicate how many times the file has been updated that day. The first number for March 5, 2004, would then be 2004030500. The next modification that day would change the serial number to 2004030501. This scheme allows 100 updates per day. Whatever scheme you choose (or are forced to go along with), the serial number must be less than or equal to 2,147,483,647.* And since you probably want to use the DNS console at least some of the time, you may just want to follow its numbering scheme.

Additional Records

After you've been running a name server for a while, you may want to add data to your name server to help you manage your domain. Have you ever been stumped when someone asked you *where* one of your hosts is? Maybe you don't even remember what kind of host it is. Administrators have to manage larger and larger populations of hosts these days, making it easy to lose track of this information. The name server can help you out. And if one of your hosts is acting up and someone notices remotely, the name server can help them get in touch with you.

So far, we've covered records critical to everyday operation: SOA, NS, A, CNAME, MX, and PTR. Name servers need these records to operate, and applications look up

---

* For the curious, that value is $2^{31} - 1$. Serial numbers are unsigned 32-bit integers, but for complicated historical reasons, serial numbers in the bottom half of the space are equivalent to serial numbers in the top half. For more information on serial numbers, see RFC 1982.

data of these types. Two other useful resource record types are TXT (text) and RP (Responsible Person); these can be used to tell you the machine's location and who is responsible for it. But DNS defines still more data types. For a list of the most useful resource records, see Appendix A.

General text information

TXT stands for TeXT. These records contain simply a list of strings. The Microsoft DNS Server supports one string of up to 255 characters per TXT record. TXT records can be used for anything you want; a common use is to list a host's location. Creating a TXT record is easy: just highlight the zone or domain in the DNS console's left pane and select **Action → Other New Records**. In the **Resource Record Type** window, choose **Text (TXT)**, select **Create Record**, and fill in the fields as shown in Figure 7-2.

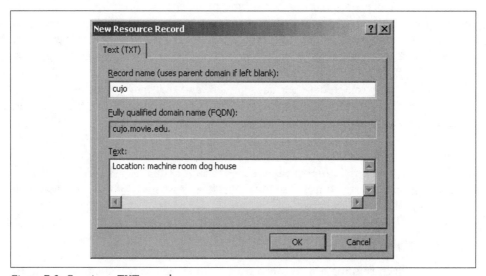

Figure 7-2. Creating a TXT record

The TXT record shown in Figure 7-2 looks like this in a zone datafile:

```
cujo  IN  TXT  "Location: machine room dog house"
```

Responsible Person

Domain administrators will undoubtedly develop a love/hate relationship with the Responsible Person (RP) record. The RP record can be attached to any domain name, internal or leaf, and indicates who is responsible for that host or domain. This enables you to locate the miscreant responsible for the host peppering you with DNS queries, for example. But it also leads people to you when one of your hosts acts up.

The record takes two arguments as its record-specific data: an electronic mail address in domain name format and a domain name, which points to additional data about the contact. The electronic mail address is in the same format the SOA record uses: it substitutes a dot (.) for the at sign (@). The next argument is a domain name, which must have a TXT record associated with it. The TXT record contains free-format information about the contact, such as a full name and phone number. You can omit either field and specify the root (.) as a placeholder instead. For example, let's say that the Movie U. Network Hotline is responsible for the host *robocop*. It also happens that the Movie U. hotline reads all mail sent to *root@movie.edu*. You'd add the RP record shown in Figure 7-3 with **Action → Other New Records**.

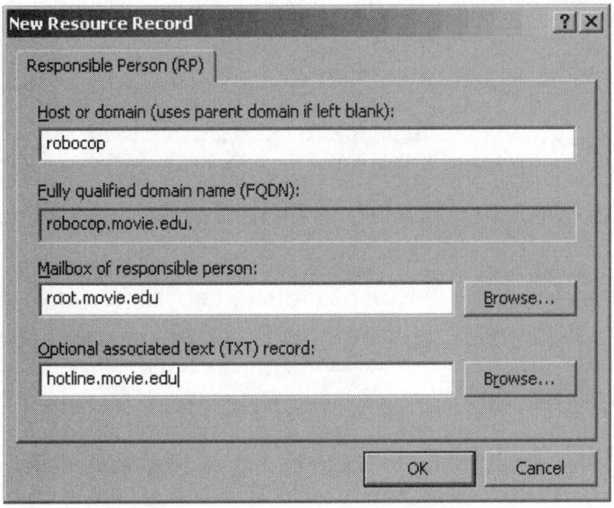

Figure 7-3. Creating an RP record

You'd also add the TXT record shown in Figure 7-4 for *hotline.movie.edu*.

Here's what these records would look like in a zone datafile:

```
robocop     IN  RP   root.movie.edu.  hotline.movie.edu.
hotline     IN  TXT  "Movie U. Network Hotline, (415) 555-4111"
```

Note that a TXT record for *root.movie.edu* isn't necessary since it's only the domain name encoding of an electronic mail address (i.e., *root@movie.edu*), not a real domain name.

Keeping cache.dns Current

As we explained in Chapter 4, the *cache.dns* file tells your server where the servers for the root zone are. We also explained that, unlike a BIND name server (which never

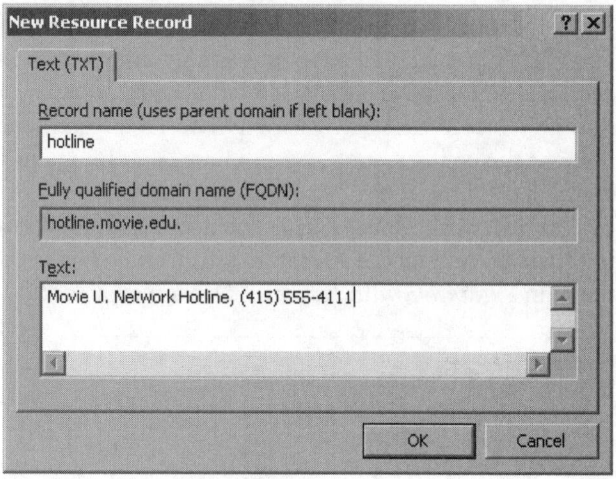

Figure 7-4. Creating an associated TXT record

modifies the cache file), a Microsoft DNS Server updates *cache.dns* with its current notion of the root name servers every time it exits.

The root name servers don't change very often, but they do change. A Microsoft DNS Server that starts with a proper cache file should, in theory, always have the current list of root name servers in its cache file. A good practice and a part of maintaining your name server is to check your *cache.dns* file a couple times a year. In Chapter 4, we told you to get the current cache file by *ftp*ing to *ftp.rs.internic.net*. That's probably the best method to keep the file current. Remember that you must stop the name server before updating *cache.dns*! If you don't, the cache file you install will be overwritten the next time the server does stop.

You can use *dig*, a utility that works like nslookup, to retrieve the current list of roots just by running:

```
C:\> dig @a.root-servers.net  .  ns > cache.dns
```

See Chapter 12 for more details about using *dig*.

Zone Datafile Controls

The datafiles for all name servers, whether Microsoft or BIND, can include two control entries: $ORIGIN and $INCLUDE. $ORIGIN changes the origin, and $INCLUDE inserts a new file into the current file. These control entries are not resource records; they facilitate the maintenance of DNS data. They were designed back in the "good old days" as a shortcut for people who had to edit zone datafiles by hand. If you make changes to your zones with the DNS console only, you won't encounter these controls: the Microsoft DNS Server doesn't use them in the zone datafiles it generates. However, some day you might need to work with zone datafiles created by hand, so it's important that you understand these controls.

Changing the Origin in a Datafile

The default origin for a DNS datafile is just the domain name of the zone. The origin is a domain name that is appended automatically to all names not ending in a dot. This origin can be changed within the zone datafile using $ORIGIN, which must be followed by a domain name. (Don't forget the trailing dot if you give the full domain name!) From that point in the file on, the new origin will be appended to all names not ending in a dot.

If we didn't have the DNS console to make changes and had to edit files by hand, we'd run into times when $ORIGIN would save us some work. For example, if your name server were responsible for a number of subdomains, you could use the $ORIGIN entry to reset the origin and simplify the files. For example, from the *movie.edu* zone datafile:

```
$ORIGIN classics.movie.edu.
maltese      IN  A  192.253.253.100
casablanca   IN  A  192.253.253.101

$ORIGIN comedy.movie.edu.
mash         IN  A  192.253.253.200
twins        IN  A  192.253.253.201
```

We'll discuss creating subdomains in Chapter 10.

Including Other Datafiles

To continue our example of editing zone datafiles by hand: once you've subdivided your domain like this, you might find it more convenient to keep the subdomain records in separate files. The $INCLUDE statement would let you do this:

```
$ORIGIN classics.movie.edu.
$INCLUDE classics.dns

$ORIGIN comedy.movie.edu.
$INCLUDE comedy.dns
```

To simplify the file even further, the new origin can be specified on the $INCLUDE line:

```
$INCLUDE classics.dns classics.movie.edu.
$INCLUDE comedy.dns   comedy.movie.edu.
```

When you specify the origin on the $INCLUDE line, it applies only to the particular file that you're including. For example, the *comedy.movie.edu* origin applies only to the names in *comedy.dns*. After *comedy.dns* has been included, the origin returns to what it was before $INCLUDE, even if *comedy.dns* contained an $ORIGIN entry.

Remember that, strictly speaking, you don't need to know anything about these directives to create subdomains with the DNS console, and the Microsoft DNS Server doesn't generate zone datafiles using these shortcuts. But you do need to know about them to complete your knowledge of zone datafiles.

Keeping Everything Running Smoothly

A significant part of maintenance is being aware when something has gone wrong—before it becomes a real problem. If you catch a problem early, chances are it'll be that much easier to fix. As the adage says, an ounce of prevention is worth a pound of cure.

This isn't quite troubleshooting—we'll devote an entire chapter to troubleshooting (Chapter 15)—but you can think of it as "pre-troubleshooting." Troubleshooting (the pound of cure) is what you have to do if you ignore maintenance, after your problem has developed complications, when you need to identify the problem by its symptoms.

The next two sections deal with preventive maintenance: looking periodically at the Event Log and the name server statistics to see whether any problems are developing. Consider this a name server's medical checkup.

Common Event Log Messages

The Microsoft DNS Server logs events to the System Log. To view the events, you can either use the Event Viewer (which you start with **Start → Administrative Tools → Event Viewer**) or click on the *Event Viewer* folder for a given server in the DNS console's left pane. The DNS server logs to a special category called, appropriately enough, DNS Server. If you use the Event Viewer, make sure you're looking at the correct log messages by selecting **DNS Server** in the left pane. To save space, when we describe an event we won't show a screenshot of the complete event. Instead, we'll list just the description from the event detail. (Double-click an event to see its details.) We'll also list the Event ID in parentheses after the text of the event.

When the server starts up (either at boot time or because you restarted it) and is ready to answer queries, you'll see this event:

```
The DNS Server has started. (ID 2)
```

For a healthy server, you should see this event after booting. If you stop the server manually, you'll see this event:

```
The DNS Server has shutdown. (ID 3)
```

If a server is a secondary for a zone, it will notify you every time it performs a zone transfer:

```
A more recent version, version 2000120500 of zone movie.edu was found at DNS server
at 192.249.249.3. Zone transfer is in progress.  (ID 6522)

The DNS server wrote version 2000120500 of zone movie.edu to file movie.edu.dns.
(ID 3150)
```

You'll also see that last message on the primary when you make a change to a zone through the DNS console and select **Action → Update Server Data Files**. After the server writes the updated file to disk, it logs that event.

If the primary is not authoritative for the zone—another error condition—you'll see this on the secondary:

```
Zone transfer request for secondary zone movie.edu refused by master server at 192.
249.249.3. Check the zone at the master server 192.249.249.3 to verify that zone
transfer is enabled to this server. To do so, use the DNS console, and select master
server 192.249.249.3 as the applicable server, then in secondary zone movie.edu
Properties, view the settings on the Zone Transfers tab. Based on the settings you
choose, make any configuration adjustments there (or possibly in the Name Servers
tab) so that a zone transfer can be made to this server.  (ID 6525)
```

Unfortunately, if the name server simply can't reach the primary (e.g., if it has gone down), the DNS server never logs an error.

On the other hand, a server that's a primary for a zone will notify you when a secondary does a zone transfer:

```
The DNS server successfully completed transfer of version 3 of zone movie.edu to DNS
server at 192.249.249.1.  (ID 6001)
```

If you're missing the cache file, *cache.dns*, or a zone datafile, the server will log a flurry of messages. A missing or empty cache file produces these events:

```
The DNS server could not open the file dns\cache.dns.  Check that the file exists in
the %SystemRoot%\System32\Dns directory and that it contains valid data. The event
data is the error code.  (ID 1000)

The DNS server could not find or open zone file dns\cache.dns.  in the %SystemRoot%\
System32\Dns directory.  Verify that the zone file is located in this directory and
that it contains valid data.  (ID 1004)

The DNS server is not root authoritative and no root hints were specified in the
cache.dns file.
Where the server is not a root server, this file must specify root hints in the form
of at least one name server (NS) resource record, indicating a root DNS server and a
corresponding host (A) resource record for that root DNS server.  Otherwise, the DNS
server will be unable to contact the root DNS server on startup and will be unable to
answer queries for names outside of its own authoritative zones.  To correct this
problem, use the DNS console to update the server root hints.  For more information,
see the online Help.  (ID 707)
```

```
The DNS server does not have a cache or other database entry for root name servers.
Either the root hints file, cache.dns, or Active Directory must have at least one
name server (NS) resource record, indicating a root DNS server and a corresponding
host (A) resource record for that root DNS server.  Otherwise, the DNS server will be
unable to contact the root DNS server on startup and will be unable to answer queries
for names outside of its own authoritative zones.  To correct this problem, use the
DNS console to update the server root hints.  For more information, see the online
Help.  (ID 706)
```

The somewhat cryptic message "The event data is the error code" makes more sense when viewing the message in Event Viewer. This message means there's a specific error code listed in the **Data** field at the bottom of the **Event Properties** window for this event.

A missing zone datafile, say *movie.edu.dns*, generates these events:

```
The DNS server could not open the file dns\movie.edu.dns.  Check that the file exists
in the %SystemRoot%\System32\Dns directory and that it contains valid data. The event
data is the error code.  (ID 1000)

The DNS server could not find or open zone file dns\movie.edu.dns.  in the
%SystemRoot%\System32\Dns directory.  Verify that the zone file is located in this
directory and that it contains valid data.  (ID 1004)
```

The server also logs a syntax error in a zone datafile. If you always make changes to your zones using the DNS console, you shouldn't see syntax errors. Editing by hand can get you into trouble, though. Here's what happens when the server encounters a syntax error (the exact error messages will vary based on the kind of syntax error):

```
The DNS server could not parse an unexpected token "terminator.movie.edu." in zone
file movie.edu.dns at line 24.  Although the DNS server continues to load, ignoring
this token, it is recommended that you either correct the token or remove the
resource record from the zone file, which is located in the %SystemRoot%\System32\Dns
directory.  (ID 1504)

The DNS server is ignoring an invalid resource record in zone file movie.edu.dns at
line 24.
See the previously logged event for a description of the error.
Although the DNS server continues to load, ignoring this RR, it is recommended that
you investigate the error associated with this record and either correct it or remove
it from the zone file.  (ID 1508)
```

For a list of most of the events logged by the Microsoft DNS Server, see article 259302 in the Microsoft Knowledge Base. This article lists events for the Windows 2000 version of the DNS Server since a Windows 2003 list was not available when this book went to press. However, in our experience, many of the events are identical between the Windows 2000 and Windows Server 2003 versions of the DNS Server.

Understanding Name Server Statistics

You should periodically look over the statistics on some of your name servers. Name server statistics are viewed with the System Monitor. To start it, select **Start** → **Administrative Tools** → **Performance**. Make sure **System Monitor** is selected in the left pane, right-click in the right pane, and select **Add Counters**. Select **DNS** in the **Performance object** pull-down list. You'll see a list of all the server parameters that you can monitor in real time. A brief explanation of each parameter is available in the Windows online help system document entitled "Monitoring DNS server performance." To view this document, choose **Start** → **Help** and type `Monitoring DNS Server Performance` in the search box and press **Enter**. Click the help topic button in the left pane and click on the document link when it appears.

Selecting all parameters is not useful—it produces too much information. To get an idea of the amount of memory being used by the server, choose **Caching Memory** and **Database Node Memory**. To see how busy the server is—that is, how many queries it is handling—look at **Total Query Received/sec** and **Total Response Sent/sec**. To select several parameters, hold down the **Ctrl** key while single-clicking. When you've selected all the ones you want, choose **Add**, then **Close**. Note that you have to save this list if you want to avoid selecting the list of parameters again. Select **File** → **Save As** to produce a *.msc* file that you can use for subsequent monitoring sessions.

Aging and Scavenging

Now let's shift gears a bit and discuss one other aspect of maintenance that may be applicable to some of your servers. If you have any zones with dynamic update enabled, they are prone to stale records. (See Chapter 11 for a description of dynamic update.) Stale records are A or PTR records that were dynamically added but were not properly removed when no longer necessary. Most DHCP clients—including Windows clients—don't release their addresses on shutdown, which means they don't send the corresponding dynamic update message to remove their A records (nor does the DHCP server send a dynamic update message to remove the PTR record). Imagine a transient host, such as a laptop, that receives but never releases an address, leaving A and PTR records in DNS. Microsoft refers to these records as *stale*, and the DNS server in Windows Server 2003 can track their age and remove, or *scavenge*, them when they are no longer necessary.

The DNS server knows a record is not stale when it receives a dynamic update request for it. A Windows 2000 or Windows XP host sends a dynamic update message for its A record (and PTR record, if configured with a static address) every 24 hours by default. These same Windows hosts also send dynamic updates on lease renewal. An update of an existing record is called a *refresh*. (Before sending the update to make any changes, clients actually probe for a record's existence by sending a dynamic update message with only a prerequisite section. The DNS server counts such a message as a refresh, too.) A refresh is the signal to the server that a particular client is still alive and using its records.

The idea behind aging and scavenging is to remove records that haven't been refreshed within a certain interval. The primary master server stores a timestamp for each resource record in zones with aging and scavenging enabled. Every time a record is created, modified, or refreshed, the server updates the timestamp with the current time. If the primary master is Active Directory–integrated, it replicates these timestamps to the other servers (since all primary masters may need to perform aging and scavenging). A large number of dynamic updates means a large number of refresh events and corresponding timestamp updates, which means a lot of replication traffic if the zone is Active Directory–integrated.

To reduce the replication burden of this algorithm, Microsoft introduced the concept of a "no-refresh" interval. After a record is refreshed and its timestamp is updated, the server will not process additional refresh events (nor update the record's timestamp) for the length of the no-refresh interval. Note that each record has its own refresh or no-refresh timer ticking away. The record can still be changed, though, which does cause its timestamp to be updated. Remember, a refresh is just a dynamic update that doesn't cause any changes* because the records specified in the update are already present in the zone. The no-refresh interval is like a cooling-off period that cuts down on replication: since refresh events aren't recorded during this interval, a record's timestamp isn't updated and therefore doesn't have to be replicated.

The DNS server's default refresh and no-refresh interval are both seven days. Aging and scavenging is enabled on a zone-by-zone basis. At a configurable interval, the server makes a scavenging pass to remove any stale records in zones enabled for aging and scavenging. Stale records have a timestamp older than the current time minus the no-refresh interval minus the refresh interval. Figure 7-5 shows the phases of a record from creation through refreshing to scavenging. Since this record was never refreshed, it's eligible for scavenging. Figure 7-6 corresponds to another record from a live client that is sending periodic dynamic updates to keep its A record refreshed. This record won't be scavenged.

Configuring Aging and Scavenging

Aging and scavenging is disabled by default since its improper use is dangerous. If you set the refresh and no-refresh intervals too low, records that aren't stale can be inadvertently removed. A global setting controls aging and scavenging for the entire DNS server. It's located on the **Advanced** tab of the server properties window, which

---

* Or the prerequisite check we described.

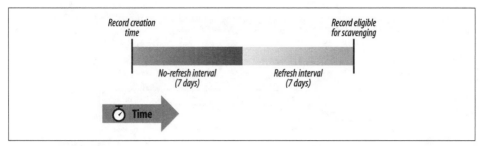

Figure 7-5. Nonrefreshed record

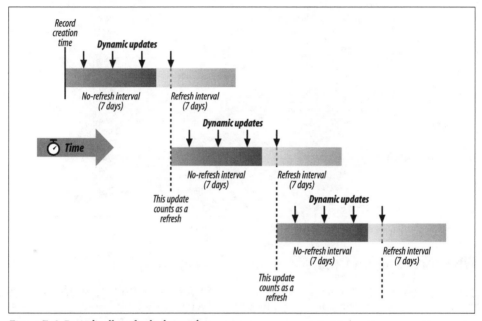

Figure 7-6. Periodically refreshed record

is shown in Figure 7-7. The **Scavenging period** setting controls how often the server makes a scavenging pass through all authoritative zones.

Once aging and scavenging has been enabled on a given server, you must still enable it for a particular zone. From the **General** tab of a zone's properties window, click the **Aging** button to produce a window like the one shown in Figure 7-8. Click **Scavenge stale resource records** to enable aging and scavenging for this zone. The refresh and no-refresh intervals are set on a per-zone basis.

In addition, a DNS server may be configured to apply the zone's values to all the existing and future zones.

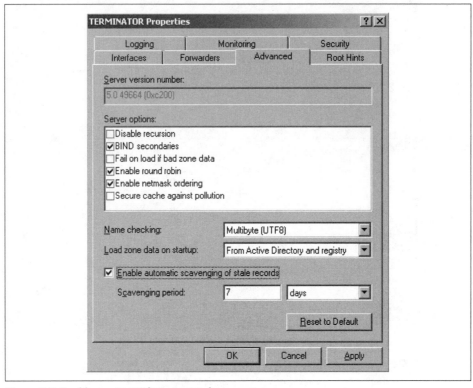

Figure 7-7. Enabling aging and scavenging for an entire server

When Scavenging Occurs

The server stores a parameter called StartScavenging for each primary zone, which is the time after which the zone is eligible for scavenging. A DNS server performs a zone-scavenging pass only if the current time is greater than StartScavenging. (In addition, scavenging must be enabled for the server and the zone, and dynamic update must be enabled for the zone.) The StartScavenging parameter is set to the current time plus the refresh interval of the zone when the following events happen:

- When scavenging is enabled for the zone
- When dynamic update is enabled for the zone
- When the zone is loaded
- When the zone is resumed

Other Notes on Aging and Scavenging

Static records (i.e., those added with the DNS console) are considered "permanent." They have a creation/refresh timestamp of zero and are ignored during a scavenging pass.

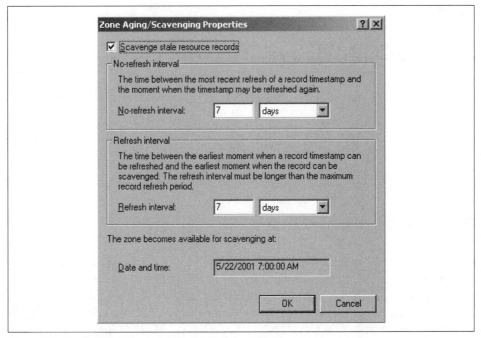

Figure 7-8. Enabling aging and scavenging for a particular zone

The DNS server needs to retain each record's creation/refresh timestamp across server restarts, which means writing this information to disk. For Active Directory–integrated zones, this information goes in—surprise!—Active Directory. For standard zones, the server has to store the information in the zone datafile. Thus, for standard zones with aging and scavenging enabled, the zone datafile format includes an extra field that is compatible only with name servers running on Windows 2000 or Windows Server 2003. An outbound zone transfer of a zone with aging and scavenging enabled is not affected, so you can still have other name servers as secondaries. But if aging and scavenging is enabled for a zone, you can't take the actual zone file from a Windows Server 2003 name server and load it on, say, a BIND name server.

CHAPTER 8

Integrating with Active Directory

*"The face is what one goes by, generally," Alice
remarked in a thoughtful tone.*

With the release of Windows 2000, Microsoft replaced the Windows NT Security
Account Manager (SAM) with Active Directory (AD), which serves as the repository
for information about users, groups, computers, and other network resources. In
contrast to the SAM, Active Directory is built on several well-known standards
including the Lightweight Directory Access Protocol (LDAP) for accessing and
manipulating data, Kerberos for authentication, and—you guessed it—DNS for
name resolution.

In fact, using DNS for name resolution is one of the major improvements of Active
Directory over Windows NT, which relied on the Windows Internet Naming Service
(WINS). Microsoft made the decision to develop WINS in the early days of Windows NT because, at the time, DNS did not support dynamic update capability,
which Microsoft needed for its clients. As a result, many companies had to implement both services: DNS for standard Internet-based name resolution and WINS for
the Windows NT environment. This often pitted the NT administrators against the
DNS administrators because of the need to maintain two separate namespaces. Over
time, dynamic update support was added to DNS, and WINS failed to garner industry support—in no small part because it was a proprietary Microsoft offering.

Even with the opportunity to get rid of WINS, migrating to Active Directory hasn't
always resulted in a harmonious union between AD and DNS administrators. While
Windows NT had virtually no DNS requirement, Active Directory is at the opposite
extreme. It is completely dependent on DNS. If DNS becomes unavailable, clients
may fail to authenticate or log in to Active Directory, and domain controllers will not
be able to replicate changes throughout the forest. This highly visible dependency on
DNS requires that the AD and DNS administrators work closely together (assuming
they are in separate groups) and agree on implementation details, which can sometimes be a challenge. It is not uncommon for DNS administrators to be reluctant to
delegate part of the namespace for Active Directory, and AD administrators are often

hesitant to entrust a critical component to another group and forgo the advantages of AD-integrated DNS.

This chapter explores many of the key DNS-related issues you need to be aware of when implementing and supporting Active Directory. We cover how Active Directory uses DNS for service advertisement and domain controller location; and, conversely, how Active Directory can be used to enhance DNS by providing robust replication and security for zone data. We do not—in fact, *cannot* in a single chapter—cover the numerous other Active Directory components. For more information on designing, implementing, and automating Active Directory, see *Active Directory, Second Edition* (O'Reilly) by our own Robbie Allen. For examples on how to perform common Active Directory administrative tasks, see *Active Directory Cookbook* (O'Reilly), also by Robbie.

Active Directory Domains

One of the first issues you have to consider when implementing an Active Directory infrastructure is how many domains you need and what to name them. Active Directory domain names are DNS domain names, but—and this is important—not every DNS domain name is an Active Directory domain name.* So while an organization's Active Directory namespace resembles its DNS namespace, the two don't have to be identical.

The number of domains you create in your forest is largely dependent on your administrative and replication requirements. A domain is mastered by one or more domain controllers, which are servers that have writeable copies of the data (about users, groups, computers, etc.) contained in the domain. Unfortunately, Active Directory is not like DNS, where a single name server can be authoritative for multiple zones. A domain controller can be authoritative only for a single Active Directory domain. To create a new Active Directory domain, you have to install a new domain controller—your existing domain controllers cannot be used. However, Active Directory uses a multimaster replication system, unlike DNS, and consequently any domain controller can process updates and replicate the changes to the other domain controllers in the domain.

Domains, Domain Trees, and Forests

Domain trees and forests are two important Active Directory concepts. A *domain tree* is simply a collection of one or more domains that share a common namespace. The *fx.movie.edu* and *movie.edu* domains would be considered part of the *movie.edu*

---

* And every square is a rectangle, but not all rectangles are squares. All registered mail is certified, but not all certified mail is registered. You get the idea.

domain tree; however, the *example.com* domain, if created after *movie.edu*, would be in a separate domain tree called *example.com*. If the domain you create does not contain the full name of the parent domain or forest root domain, it is considered part of a separate domain tree.

A *forest* is a collection of one or more domain trees. The domains in the *movie.edu* domain tree and the *example.com* domain tree could be part of the same forest. A domain tree is based on a common namespace, but a forest is not.

A forest is named after the first domain created in the forest. If *movie.edu* was the first domain we created, the forest is automatically named *movie.edu*. We can then create additional domains for *fx.movie.edu* and *example.com* all belonging to the *movie.edu* forest. Another option is to create the *example.com* domain in its own forest, which has certain implications for user access.

All domains within a forest, regardless of which domain tree they are part of, are trusted by each other from an authentication and authorization perspective. For this reason, the forest is considered the primary *security boundary* in Active Directory. By making the *example.com* domain part of the *movie.edu* forest, users in *example.com*, by default, have read access to much of the information in the *movie.edu* domains, and vice versa. Also, users in *example.com* can have control delegated to them over objects in the *movie.edu* domains and vice versa. If *example.com* is created in a separate forest, the users in that domain do not have access to the *movie.edu* forest, and they cannot have access delegated to it (unless a special cross-forest trust is created between the two forests).*

Domain Models

Two Active Directory domain models are commonly used. Your choice of domain model is important because it dictates DNS requirements, as we discuss later. One model consists of an empty root domain with geographic or organizational subdomains. We recommend that you do not create organizational-based subdomains if you can help it since they are very likely to change at some point.†

Some of the benefits of the multidomain model include the ability to delegate administration for management of portions of a forest, greater control over how data is replicated within the forest, and decreased exposure to problems that can impact a single domain. For example, if an application went out of control and mistakenly started creating tons of objects in a domain, at some point the hard disk on the

---

* Windows Server 2003 supports a new trust type called forest trust, which allows you to have a single transitive trust that spans two forests. If you want to understand more about how trusts work, get *Active Directory* (O'Reilly).

† Fortunately, a new feature of Windows Server 2003 allows you to rename domains, but the process is arduous. For more information on renaming domains, see *http://www.microsoft.com/windowsserver2003/downloads/domainrename.mspx*.

domain controllers in that domain would fill up. The domain would then enter an unstable and possibly unusable state. However, the domain controllers in other domains would continue to function without much impact. This example is admittedly contrived, but it shows you the benefits of autonomy in the multidomain model.

The downsides of this model include the increased support costs of setting up additional domain controllers—remember that each domain must have its own set of domain controllers—and additional domain configuration (configuring security, group policy objects, organizational units, etc.). Also, finding data in a multidomain forest is not always easy. Since data can be spread across several domains, you have to query the global catalog to perform forestwide searches. The global catalog contains a read-only copy of the objects in all domains in the forest. The drawback to the global catalog is that it contains only a subset of the attributes of objects. If the global catalog doesn't contain the attribute you want, you have to perform an additional query against the domain the object resides in after you've queried the global catalog.

The other common domain model is simply a single domain. Over time, many organizations have come to recognize the increased support costs associated with supporting additional domains and have found that their initial reasons for needing multiple domains may no longer be valid. With a single domain, you typically need fewer domain controllers, which results in decreased costs. Also, the global catalog does not play as big a role because you do not need to search across multiple domains.

The downside to the single domain model is decreased flexibility in replicating data. Since all of your objects are in a single domain, wherever you need to deploy a domain controller, you have to replicate all of the objects in the domain to it. This type of model does not lend itself well to branch office deployments where you have a lot of domain controllers, many of which may have slow WAN connections.

There are variations to these models, but this should give you the general idea. A good rule of thumb is the fewer domains the better. And if you can get by with a single domain, that's great.

Three Options for the Root Domain Name

Once you've decided on a domain model, you need to choose a name for your root domain, also known as the forest root domain. The root domain name is very important because it determines which name servers can be authoritative for the corresponding DNS namespace. You have three basic options for naming your root domain: use the same name as an existing DNS domain, create a new subdomain from an existing domain, or use a name that doesn't correspond to any of your DNS domains (i.e., a disjoint or private namespace). Each option has minor advantages and disadvantages based on your environment, but, as with most naming convention discussions, the decision is largely subjective.

Same name as an existing DNS domain

Consider Movie University. The apex (or top) of Movie U.'s DNS namespace is *movie.edu*, with subdomains named *fx.movie.edu*, *classics.movie.edu*, and *comedies. movie.edu*. This namespace is represented in Figure 8-1.

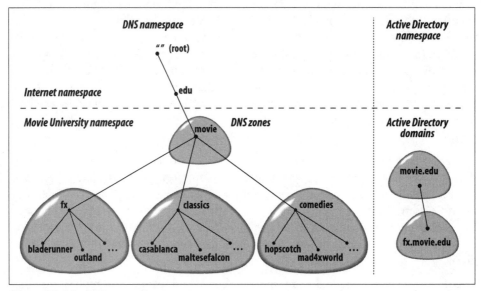

Figure 8-1. Movie University's namespace

We could root Active Directory's namespace at the root of Movie U's DNS namespace. That would result in *movie.edu* being the forest root domain. If we decide that the special effects lab needs a dedicated Active Directory domain, we can create the *fx.movie.edu* domain as a child domain in the *movie.edu* forest. Everyone else at Movie U. can be part of the *movie.edu* Active Directory domain, even though individual hosts may fall into different DNS domains. If we did nothing more, the resource records needed by Active Directory would be added to the *movie.edu* and *fx.movie.edu* zones.

If your authoritative name servers are not domain controllers and you want to use AD-integrated zones (more on this later), or you want some other name servers to be authoritative for the zone that contains the Active Directory resource records, you have to create delegations. All of the required Active Directory–specific resource records are stored in subdomains of the DNS domain whose name corresponds to the AD domain. These subdomains are named *_msdcs* (e.g., *_msdcs.movie.edu*), *_tcp*, *_udp*, *_sites*, and *DomainDNSZones*. The forest root domain will also have a

ForestDNSZones subdomain.* To delegate the Active Directory DNS responsibilities when the Active Directory domains are named after an existing DNS domain, you need to delegate those subdomains. In turn, those subdomains become zones on the delegated servers.

Subdomain of an existing DNS domain

Now let's say that Movie U. wanted to completely separate its AD namespace from its DNS namespace. Another common approach is to create a subdomain of an existing domain, such as the top-level domain for the organization. For example, we could name the forest root domain *ad.movie.edu* or *corp.movie.edu*. If we still needed to create a subdomain for the special effects lab, it could be named *fx.ad.movie.edu*.

This model is the easiest to implement if you want to delegate responsibility for the Active Directory–critical zones to name servers other than the main set of authoritative name servers for your organization. Instead of delegating subdomains as in the previous model, you need to delegate only the zone with the same name as the forest root domain (e.g., *ad.movie.edu*) from your main forward-mapping zone (e.g., *movie.edu*).

 Microsoft recommends this option for most deployments and uses it for its own corporate Active Directory deployment.

Disjoint or private name

The last major option for naming your forest root domain is not to base it on any of your top-level domain names and use a disjoint or private name. The most common suffix that is used in this scenario is *.local* (e.g., *movie.local*). This model is typically chosen by organizations that do not want their Active Directory DNS namespace to be public.

In nonproduction forests, we recommend following the guidelines in RFC 2606 and using *.test* or *.example* instead of *.local*, which are suffixes reserved for testing purposes. If you need to create a lab or test environment that your general community does not need to access, this is a good model to use. In fact, you can create a forest without requiring any delegations at all from your main forward-mapping zone, assuming you have control over the resolver configuration for the clients in the lab. To do this, you would need to create the *movie.test* forest, enable the DNS server on one or more domain controllers in the domain, and make the *movie.test* zone AD-integrated.

---

* The *DomainDNSZones* and *ForestDNSZones* domains are new in Windows Server 2003. They are used to support application partitions, described later in this chapter.

In order for clients to resolve DNS names outside of the forest, you would need to point the resolvers on the domain controllers to each other, and configure forwarders to forward unresolved requests to your organization's main authoritative name servers. At that point, all you need to do is point the resolvers of the clients that are going to use the *movie.test* forest to one of the domain controllers that are running the Microsoft DNS Server in *movie.test*. Now you have a fully functional Active Directory forest that didn't require any delegations from your main forward-mapping zone.

 Microsoft strongly discourages using a single-label domain name, such as *movie*, for your forest root domain name. If you do, it requires additional configuration on your servers. Microsoft's reasoning behind this is to limit the number of misconfigurations that result in hammering the top-level root name servers with unnecessary DNS requests.

Storing Zones in Active Directory

One of Microsoft's innovative uses of Active Directory is for storing (and replicating) DNS zone data. A traditional name server stores copies of the zones it supports in files on a local disk. In this model, you have a primary master name server that replicates the zone data to secondary name servers. A secondary can process updates to a zone from its master name server in two different ways. The original method supported by DNS is zone transfer, which allows secondary name servers to request a full copy of a zone. A newer method, which is an improvement on the zone transfer process, is incremental zone transfer. With incremental zone transfer, a secondary name server can request just the updates to the zone that occurred since its last transfer.

Active Directory provides another method for replicating zone content, albeit only for name servers running on domain controllers. You can make a zone *AD-integrated*, which means that instead of storing zone content in text files, it is stored in the Active Directory database. This makes a lot of sense because you take advantage of Active Directory's multimaster replication scheme, which means that any domain controller that is also a primary name server for the AD-integrated zone can update it directly, like a primary name server. With AD-integrated zones, replication is handled automatically, so you don't need to develop your own zone transfer replication topology.

One other note about Active Directory–integrated zones: strictly speaking, you don't have to make every domain controller into a name server for a zone that's AD-integrated within that domain. Since all authoritative servers can be configured to allow zone transfers, a server that loads a zone from Active Directory happily responds to allowed zone transfer requests. So you could conceivably make only a zone's primary master name server AD-integrated and have the secondaries continue to load from the primary, provided those secondaries are not domain controllers of the domain. However, this defeats one of the purposes of Active Directory integration—letting Active Directory handle zone replication. The other huge advantage of Active Directory integration is secure dynamic updates, which we'll cover in detail shortly.

The Impact on Replication

While AD-integrated zones have many advantages, the one potential drawback is how zone data gets replicated in Active Directory. Under Windows 2000, AD-integrated zones are stored in the System container in a domain. That means that every domain controller in that domain replicates that zone data regardless of whether the domain controller is a name server or not. For domain controllers that are not name servers, there is no benefit to replicating the data, which results in needless replication traffic. This can be a serious issue for those that have large zones with many domain controllers that are not name servers. Fortunately, a new feature in Windows Server 2003 called application partitions provides a better alternative.

Another issue with Windows 2000 AD-integrated zones is that domain controllers in subdomains could not replicate the forest root zone resource records through AD replication. You would have to configure the subdomain domain controller as a secondary and enable zone transfer. The requirement to replicate forest root records is common in branch office deployments where a certain amount of autonomy is needed due to potential network outages. Application partitions also help with this requirement.

Using Application Partitions

Active Directory segregates data into one of three partitions: schema, configuration, or domain. Partitions are used to organize and replicate data with a similar scope (i.e., forestwide or domainwide) among domain controllers. Conceptually, partitions are similar to zones. Zones are also used to segregate and replicate data (using zone transfer) among name servers.

In Windows Server 2003, Microsoft added a new type of partition called an *application partition*. Whereas the default partitions have a predefined replication scope, application partitions can be configured to replicate with any domain controller in a forest. Domain controllers that are configured to contain replicas of an application partition become the only servers that replicate the data contained within the partition. Application partitions are not limited by domain boundaries. You can configure domain controllers in completely different domains to replicate an application partition. For these reasons, application partitions make a lot of sense for storing AD-integrated zones. You no longer have to store zone data within the domain partition and replicate it to every domain controller in the domain, even if only a few are name servers. With application partitions, you can configure Active Directory to replicate DNS data only between the domain controllers running the DNS server in any domain of the forest. To help facilitate the transition from domain-based storage of zones to application partitions, Microsoft provides a couple of default DNS application partitions: one default DNS application partition for each domain in a forest and one for the forest itself. During the installation of a new Windows Server 2003 Active Directory forest, these partitions are created automatically and AD-integrated zones are stored there. If you upgrade from Windows 2000, the default DNS application partitions are still created automatically, but existing AD-integrated zones are not moved into them. You have to do that manually.

You are not required to use the default DNS application partitions. You can create your own or continue to use the System container in the domain partition, which is the only option under Windows 2000. The storage options are summarized in Table 8-1.

Table 8-1. Storage options for AD-integrated zones

Location	Replication scope
cn=System,DomainDN Example: cn=System,dc=movie,dc=edu	All domain controllers in the domain, regardless of whether they are a name server. This is the only storage method available under Windows 2000.
dc=DomainDnsZones,DomainDN Example: dc=DomainDnsZones,dc=fx, dc=movie,dc=edu	Domain controllers in the domain that are name servers.
dc=ForestDnsZones,ForestDN Example: dc=ForestDnsZones,dc=movie,dc=edu	Domain controllers in the forest that are name servers.
AppPartitionDN Example: dc=DnsData,dc=movie,dc=edu	Domain controllers that have been configured to replicate the custom application partition.

Application partitions are treated just like Active Directory domains by DNS. Each application partition has a corresponding DNS domain, which contains records that are used to locate domain controllers that replicate the partition. For the *movie.edu* forest root domain, the *ForestDnsZones* and *DomainDnsZones* default DNS application partitions would translate into *domaindnszones.movie.edu* and *forestdnszones.movie.edu* DNS domains. For the *fx.movie.edu* domain, there would be a *domaindnszones.fx.movie.edu* DNS domain.

Securing Dynamic Updates

Another huge advantage of storing zones in Active Directory is that you can enable secure dynamic updates. For zones that are not AD-integrated, you have two options for dynamic updates: allow anyone to make dynamic updates or don't allow dynamic updates at all. Allowing anyone has obvious drawbacks. A malicious client can easily hijack resource records in this mode.

However, when a zone is AD-integrated, you have the option to select **Secure only** for the **Dynamic Updates** configuration, found on the **General** tab for the zone properties in the DNS console. Figure 8-2 shows this window and the three dynamic update options.

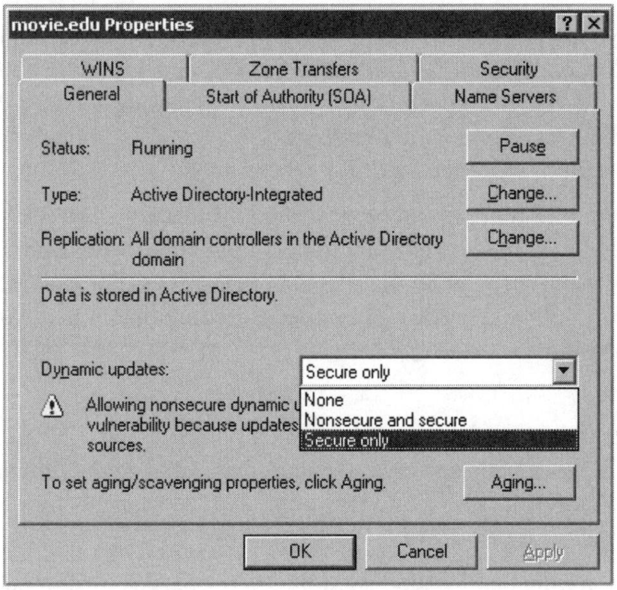

Figure 8-2. Dynamic update options

Microsoft uses access control lists (ACLs) on objects in Active Directory to secure zone data and provide secure dynamic update capability. A **Security** tab is available in the DNS console for AD-integrated zones, which allows you to configure whether a user, group, or computer can create and delete objects (i.e., resource records). By default, authenticated computers in a forest can create new records in a zone, and only the client that created a record is allowed to modify it.

DNS as a Service Location Broker

By now you probably want to hear more about how Active Directory makes use of DNS. At the beginning of the chapter, we dropped the little nugget that when DNS is not available, Active Directory clients may fail to log in. The reason for this is that Active Directory clients use DNS as a *service location broker*, that is, to find the closest server that is providing a certain Active Directory service. Prior to Active Directory,

Windows clients used NetBIOS and WINS to find domain controllers, but hosts running Windows 2000 and later use DNS.

Consider the case of a Windows XP Professional host at Movie U. that's been joined to the *movie.edu* Active Directory domain. When this system boots up, it sends a series of DNS SRV record queries to its configured name server to find the closest domain controller for the *movie.edu* domain.

The SRV Resource Record

Most of the DNS queries sent by Windows clients during the location process are for SRV (service location) records. The SRV record, introduced in RFC 2052 and updated in RFC 2782, is a general mechanism for locating services. Before we can talk in detail about exactly how a Windows client finds its domain controller using SRV records, we need to describe the SRV record itself.

Locating a service or a particular type of server within a zone is a difficult problem if you don't know which host it runs on. Some administrators have attempted to solve this problem by using service-specific aliases in their zones. For example, at Movie U. we created the alias *ftp.movie.edu* and pointed it to the domain name of the host that runs our FTP archive:

```
ftp.movie.edu.    IN    CNAME    plan9.fx.movie.edu.
```

This makes it easy for people to guess a domain name for our FTP archive and separates the domain name people use to access the archive from the domain name of the host on which it runs. If we were to move the archive to a different host, we could simply change the CNAME record.

Another option, for clients that understand it, is the SRV record. In addition to simply allowing a client to locate the host on which a particular service runs, SRV provides powerful features for load balancing and backup services, similar to what the MX record provides.

A unique aspect of the SRV record is the format of the domain name to which it's attached. Like the service-specific alias *ftp.movie.edu*, the domain name that a SRV record is attached to gives the name of the service sought along with the protocol it runs over, concatenated with a domain name. The labels representing the service name and the protocol begin with an underscore to distinguish them from labels in the domain name of a host. So, for example:

```
_ftp._tcp.movie.edu
```

represents the SRV records someone *ftp*ing to *movie.edu* should retrieve in order to find the *movie.edu* FTP servers, while:

```
_http._tcp.www.movie.edu
```

represents the SRV records someone accessing the URL *http://www.movie.edu* should look up in order to find the *www.movie.edu* web servers.

The names of the service and protocol must come from the latest Assigned Numbers RFC (the most recent as of this writing is RFC 1700) or be unique names used only locally. Don't use the port or protocol numbers, just the names. When entering SRV records through the DNS console, the service name is limited to eight common services.

The SRV record has four resource record-specific fields: *priority*, *weight*, *port*, and *target*. Priority, weight, and port are unsigned 16-bit numbers (between 0 and 65,535). Target is a domain name.

Priority works similarly to the preference in an MX record: the lower the number in the priority field, the more desirable the associated target. When searching for the hosts offering a given service, clients should try targets with the same priority value before trying those with a higher value in the priority field (lower priority values indicate higher priority—confusing, eh?).

Weight allows zone administrators to distribute load to multiple targets. Clients should query targets of the same priority in proportion to their weight. For example, if one target has a priority of zero and a weight of one and another target has a priority of zero but a weight of two, the second target should receive twice as much load (in queries, connections, etc.) as the first. It's up to the service's clients to direct that load: they typically use a system call to choose a random number. If the number is, say, in the top one-third of the range, they try the first target, and if the number is in the bottom two-thirds of the range, they try the second target.

Port specifies the port on which the service being sought is running. This allows zone administrators to run servers on nonstandard ports. For example, an administrator can use SRV records to point web browsers at a web server running on port 8000 instead of the standard HTTP port (80).

Finally, target specifies the hostname of a host on which the service is running (on the port specified in the port field). Target must be the canonical name of the host (not an alias), with address records attached to it.

So, for the *movie.edu* FTP server, we might add two SRV records to the *movie.edu* zone. Adding the first with the DNS console is shown in Figure 8-3.

After adding the second record, the *movie.edu* zone datafile (*movie.edu.dns*) contains these records:

```
_ftp._tcp.movie.edu.  IN  SRV  1  0  21  plan9.fx.movie.edu.
                      IN  SRV  2  0  21  thing.fx.movie.edu.
```

This instructs SRV-capable FTP clients to try the FTP server on *plan9.fx.movie.edu*'s port 21 first when accessing *movie.edu*'s FTP service and then to try the FTP server on *thing.fx.movie.edu*'s port 21 if *plan9.fx.movie.edu*'s FTP server isn't available.

The records:

```
_http._tcp.www.movie.edu.  IN  SRV  0  2  80    www.movie.edu.
                           IN  SRV  0  1  80    www2.movie.edu.
                           IN  SRV  1  1  8000  postmanrings2x.movie.edu.
```

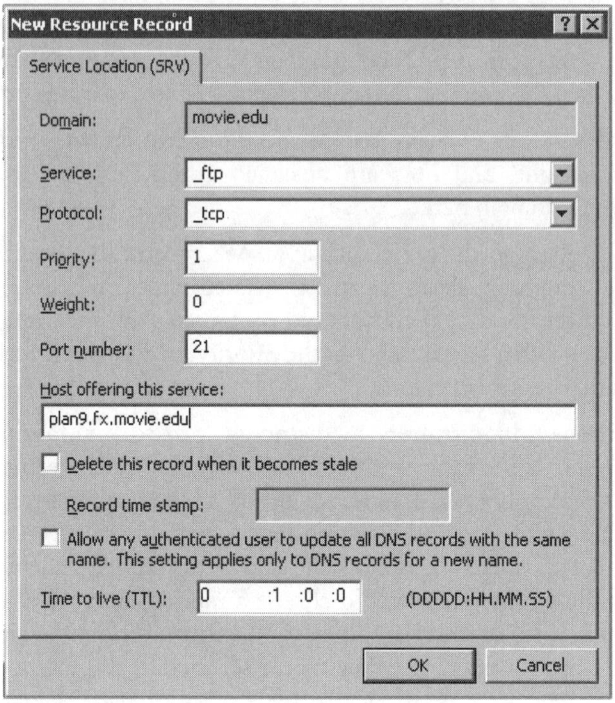

Figure 8-3. Adding an SRV record with the DNS console

direct web queries for *www.movie.edu* (the web site) to port 80 on *www.movie.edu* (the host) and *www2.movie.edu*, with *www.movie.edu* getting twice the queries *www2.movie.edu* does. If neither is available, queries go to *postmanrings2x.movie.edu* on port 8000.

But don't get excited and add SRV records for your FTP and web servers: currently few clients actually use SRV records to locate their servers. In fact, we're not aware of any FTP clients or web browsers that look up SRV records. On the other hand, when Microsoft was looking for a way to have Windows-based clients find their domain controllers, SRV records fit the bill perfectly.

DC Locator

One of the fundamental issues for clients in any networked environment is finding the optimal server to authenticate against. The process under Windows NT was not very efficient and could cause clients to authenticate to domain controllers in the least optimal location. With Active Directory, clients use DNS to locate domain controllers via the DC locator process. To illustrate at a high level how the DC locator process works, here's an example where a client has moved from one location to another and needs to find a domain controller (DC).

1. A client previously located in Site A logs in from Site B.

2. When the client boots up, it thinks it is still in Site A, so it proceeds to contact the DC it has cached locally in the registry.

3. The DC in Site A receives the request and realizes that the client should now be talking to a DC in Site B, since its IP address has changed. In its reply to the client, the DC in Site A refers the client to the DC in Site B.

4. The client then performs a DNS lookup to find a DC in Site B.

5. The client then contacts a DC in Site B. Three things can happen: the DC responds and authenticates the client; the DC fails to respond (it could be down), so the client attempts to use a different DC in Site B; or the DC fails to respond and the client fails to find another DC in Site B. In the last case, the client turns back to the DC in Site A and authenticates with the first server it contacted.

Two things are needed to support the DC locator process: the site topology must be properly defined in Active Directory, and DNS must contain the necessary Active Directory SRV records, which we describe in the next section. For a more detailed description of how the DC locator process works, including the specific resource records that are used during the process, check out Microsoft Knowledge Base articles 247811 and 314861.

Resource Records Used by Active Directory

When you promote a domain controller into a domain, the file *%SystemRoot%\System32\Config\netlogon.dns* is generated. This file contains the necessary resource records for the DC to function correctly within Active Directory. The NetLogon service keeps this file updated based on site membership, GC status, and site coverage.

The contents of the file looks like the following for a DC named *terminator.movie.edu* in the *movie.edu* domain with the IP address 10.1.1.1. We've reordered the file a bit to group records of similar purpose together. Note that some lines may wrap due to their length.

```
movie.edu. 600 IN A 10.1.1.1
ec4caf62-31b2-4773-bcce-7b1e31c04d25._msdcs.movie.edu. 600 IN CNAME↵
terminator.movie.edu.
gc._msdcs.movie.edu. 600 IN A 10.1.1.1
_gc._tcp.movie.edu. 600 IN SRV 0 100 3268 terminator.movie.edu.
_gc._tcp.Default-First-Site-Name._sites.movie.edu. 600 IN SRV 0 100 3268↵
terminator.movie.edu.
_ldap._tcp.gc._msdcs.movie.edu. 600 IN SRV 0 100 3268 terminator.movie.edu.
_ldap._tcp.Default-First-Site-Name._sites.gc._msdcs.movie.edu. 600 IN SRV 0 100 3268↵
terminator.movie.edu.
_kerberos._tcp.dc._msdcs.movie.edu. 600 IN SRV 0 100 88 terminator.movie.edu.
_kerberos._tcp.Default-First-Site-Name._sites.dc._msdcs.movie.edu. 600 IN SRV 0 100↵
88 terminator.movie.edu.
_kerberos._tcp.movie.edu. 600 IN SRV 0 100 88 terminator.movie.edu.
```

```
_kerberos._tcp.Default-First-Site-Name._sites.movie.edu. 600 IN SRV 0 100 88↵
terminator.movie.edu.
_kerberos._udp.movie.edu. 600 IN SRV 0 100 88 terminator.movie.edu.
_kpasswd._tcp.movie.edu. 600 IN SRV 0 100 464 terminator.movie.edu.
_kpasswd._udp.movie.edu. 600 IN SRV 0 100 464 terminator.movie.edu.
_ldap._tcp.movie.edu. 600 IN SRV 0 100 389 terminator.movie.edu.
_ldap._tcp.Default-First-Site-Name._sites.movie.edu. 600 IN SRV 0 100 389↵
terminator.movie.edu.
_ldap._tcp.pdc._msdcs.movie.edu. 600 IN SRV 0 100 389 terminator.movie.edu.
_ldap._tcp.97526bc9-adf7-4ec8-a096-0dbb34a17052.domains._msdcs.movie.edu. 600 IN SRV↵
0 100 389 terminator.movie.edu.
_ldap._tcp.dc._msdcs.movie.edu. 600 IN SRV 0 100 389 terminator.movie.edu.
_ldap._tcp.Default-First-Site-Name._sites.dc._msdcs.movie.edu. 600 IN SRV 0 100 389↵
terminator.movie.edu.
DomainDnsZones.movie.edu. 600 IN A 10.1.1.1
_ldap._tcp.DomainDnsZones.movie.edu. 600 IN SRV 0 100 389 terminator.movie.edu.
_ldap._tcp.Default-First-Site-Name._sites.DomainDnsZones.movie.edu. 600 IN SRV 0 100↵
389 terminator.movie.edu.
```

Let's go through what these records are actually used for, splitting them up into sections for ease of understanding. To start with, the first record is for the domain itself:

```
movie.edu. 600 IN A 10.1.1.1
```

This A record is for LDAP clients that don't understand SRV records. Since Windows clients use SRV records to locate the LDAP service on the domain controller, you don't need this A record (the one for *movie.edu*) unless you're running other LDAP clients. (And even then, you can just point those clients at the domain controller using its fully qualified name: *terminator.movie.edu*, in this case.) It's good that the A record isn't required because a lot of folks already have an A record at the apex of their DNS namespace. This record usually points to a web server, not to an Active Directory server. For example, Movie U.'s main web server is accessible via both *www.movie.edu* and *movie.edu*.

Next, we have the following record:

```
ec4caf62-31b2-4773-bcce-7b1e31c04d25._msdcs.movie.edu. 600 IN CNAME↵
terminator.movie.edu.
```

This CNAME record, found under the _msdcs subdomain, is used by domain controllers during replication. The left side of the record is the globally unique ID (GUID) for the server. DCs use this record if they know the server's GUID and want to determine its hostname. If this record isn't present for a DC, other DCs cannot replicate changes from it. The *DNSLint* command, available in the Windows Server 2003 Support Tools, can be used to make sure all DCs have this CNAME record present. Here is an example command line:

```
C:\> dnslint /ad 10.13.51.18 /s 10.13.52.15 /v
```

The required /ad switch is optionally followed by the IP address of a DC to perform LDAP queries against. If an IP address is not specified, the local host is assumed. The /s option, also required, must be followed by the IP address (or the text localhost) of a DNS server that is authoritative for the _msdcs subdomain of the DC's domain. See Chapter 15 for more on using *DNSLint* for troubleshooting.

Next, we have this A record:

```
gc._msdcs.movie.edu. 600 IN A 10.1.1.1
```

This record is registered only if the DC is a global catalog server. You can query *gc. _msdcs.movie.edu* to obtain a list of all the global catalog servers in the forest in much the same way you could query the AD domain's A record to get a list of all the domain controllers for a domain (if you allow registration of that record by domain controllers).

A few more global catalog–specific records are shown next:

```
_gc._tcp.movie.edu. 600 IN SRV 0 100 3268 terminator.movie.edu.
_gc._tcp.Default-First-Site-Name._sites.movie.edu. 600 IN SRV 0 100 3268↵
terminator.movie.edu.
_ldap._tcp.gc._msdcs.movie.edu. 600 IN SRV 0 100 3268 terminator.movie.edu.
_ldap._tcp.Default-First-Site-Name._sites.gc._msdcs.movie.edu. 600 IN SRV 0 100 3268↵
terminator.movie.edu.
```

Note that in the case of global catalog SRV records, the fourth record-specific data field—which is used for the port for the service—is 3268, the global catalog port. You may have also noticed the entries that contain **Default-First-Site-Name**. Each global catalog server registers site-specific records so clients can find the optimal global catalog server based on their site membership. If you renamed the default site and have other sites defined, you will see these site names used in the SRV records. See the "Site Coverage" sidebar for more information.

The next few SRV records are for Kerberos authentication (port 88) and the Kpasswd process (port 464), which allows users to change passwords:

```
_kerberos._tcp.dc._msdcs.movie.edu. 600 IN SRV 0 100 88 terminator.movie.edu.
_kerberos._tcp.Default-First-Site-Name._sites.dc._msdcs.movie.edu. 600 IN SRV 0 100↵
88 terminator.movie.edu.
_kerberos._tcp.movie.edu. 600 IN SRV 0 100 88 terminator.movie.edu.
_kerberos._tcp.Default-First-Site-Name._sites.movie.edu. 600 IN SRV 0 100 88↵
terminator.movie.edu.
_kerberos._udp.movie.edu. 600 IN SRV 0 100 88 terminator.movie.edu.
_kpasswd._tcp.movie.edu. 600 IN SRV 0 100 464 terminator.movie.edu.
_kpasswd._udp.movie.edu. 600 IN SRV 0 100 464 terminator.movie.edu.
```

Just as with the global catalog SRV records, there may be more of the site-specific Kerberos records for any additional sites the DC covers.

The rest of the SRV records are used to represent a domain controller for a particular domain, site, and application partition. One record to note is the *_ldap._tcp.pdc._msdcs. movie.edu.* entry, which is registered by the DC that is acting as the primary domain controller (PDC) emulator for the domain.

```
_ldap._tcp.movie.edu. 600 IN SRV 0 100 389 terminator.movie.edu.
_ldap._tcp.Default-First-Site-Name._sites.movie.edu. 600 IN SRV 0 100 389↵
terminator.movie.edu.
```

```
_ldap._tcp.pdc._msdcs.movie.edu. 600 IN SRV 0 100 389 terminator.movie.edu.
_ldap._tcp.97526bc9-adf7-4ec8-a096-0dbb34a17052.domains._msdcs.movie.edu. 600 IN SRV⏎
0 100 389 terminator.movie.edu.
_ldap._tcp.dc._msdcs.movie.edu. 600 IN SRV 0 100 389 terminator.movie.edu.
_ldap._tcp.Default-First-Site-Name._sites.dc._msdcs.movie.edu. 600 IN SRV 0 100 389⏎
terminator.movie.edu.
DomainDnsZones.movie.edu. 600 IN A 10.1.1.1
_ldap._tcp.DomainDnsZones.movie.edu. 600 IN SRV 0 100 389 terminator.movie.edu.
_ldap._tcp.Default-First-Site-Name._sites.DomainDnsZones.movie.edu. 600 IN SRV 0 100⏎
389 terminator.movie.edu.
```

Note the last three records—they are for the *DomainDnsZones* application partition. As we mentioned early, the DC locator process is used to find domain controllers for domains, but it is also used for application partitions as well. There will be records like those three for all the application partitions *terminator* replicates.

Based on all of these records, you can obtain a lot of information about an Active Directory environment by doing simple DNS queries. Some of the information you can retrieve includes:

- Global catalog servers in a forest or a particular site
- Kerberos servers in a domain or a particular site

- Domain controllers in a domain or a particular site
- PDC emulator for a domain

We could go on and on about Active Directory, but this is a book about DNS, so we won't. If you are interested in more information on Active Directory, see *Active Directory*, Second Edition and *Active Directory Cookbook*, both from O'Reilly. We return to a core DNS issue in the next chapter: growing your domain.

Growing Your Domain

"What size do you want to be?" it asked.
"Oh, I'm not particular as to size," Alice hastily
replied; "only one doesn't like changing so often, you
know...."
"Are you content now?" said the Caterpillar.
"Well, I should like to be a little larger, sir, if you
wouldn't mind...."

How Many Name Servers?

We set up two name servers in Chapter 4. Two servers are as few as you'll ever want to run and, depending on the size of your network, you may need to run many more. It is not uncommon to run four or more name servers, with one of them off-site. How many name servers are enough? You'll have to decide that based on your network. Here are some guidelines to help out:

- Run at least one name server on each network or subnet you have. This removes routers as a point of failure. Make the most of any multihomed hosts you may have since they are (by definition) attached to more than one network.

- If you have a file server and some diskless nodes, run a name server on the file server to serve this group of machines.

- Run name servers near, but not necessarily on, large multiuser computers. The users and their processes probably generate a lot of queries and, as administrators, you will work harder to keep a multiuser host up. But balance their needs against the risk of running a name server—a security-critical server—on a system to which lots of people have access.

- Run one name server off-site. This makes your data available when your network isn't. You might argue that it's useless to look up an address when you can't reach the host. Then again, the off-site name server may be available if your network is reachable but your other name servers are down. If you have a close relationship with an organization on the Internet—say another university or a business partner—they may be willing to run a secondary for you.

Figure 9-1 shows a sample topology to illustrate how this might work.

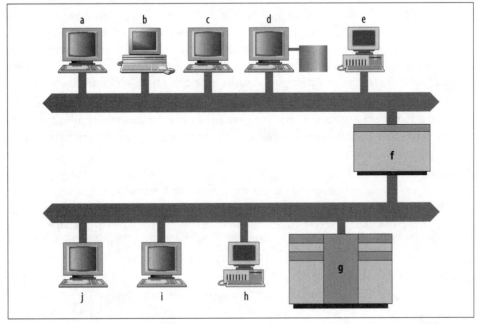

Figure 9-1. Sample network topology

Notice that, if you follow our guidelines, you still have a number of hosts on which you could choose to run a name server. Host *d*, the file server for hosts *a*, *b*, *c*, and *e*, could run a name server. Host *g*, a big, multiuser host, is another good candidate. But probably the best choice is host *f*, the smaller host with interfaces on both networks. You'll need to run only one name server, instead of two, and it will run on a closely watched host. If you want more than one name server on either network, you can also run one on *d* or *g*.

Where Do I Put My Name Servers?

In addition to giving you a rough idea of how many name servers you'll need, these criteria should help you decide *where* to run name servers (e.g., on file servers and multihomed hosts). But there are other important considerations when choosing the right host.

Other factors to keep in mind are the host's connectivity, the software it runs (for example, the Microsoft DNS Server or BIND), the security of your host, and maintaining the homogeneity of your name servers:

Connectivity

It's important that name servers be well connected. Running a name server on the fastest, most reliable host on your network won't do you any good if the host is mired in some backwater subnet of your network behind a slow, flaky serial line. Try to find a host close to your link to the Internet (if you have one) or find a well-connected Internet host to act as a secondary for your zone. On your own network, try to run name servers near the network's topological hubs.

It's doubly important that your primary master name server be well connected. For reliable zone transfers, the primary needs good connectivity to all the secondaries that update from it. And, like any name server, it will benefit from fast, reliable networking.

Software

Another factor to consider in choosing a host for a name server is the software the host runs. If you bought this book, we'll assume it's because you want to run the Microsoft DNS Server. Keep in mind that you'll be able to manage remote name servers with the DNS console only if they're running the Windows 2000 or Windows Server 2003 versions of the Microsoft DNS Server.

If managing servers with the DNS console isn't important to you (maybe you like the DNS console front-end for managing zone data, but you're comfortable editing BIND configuration files by hand), you might consider running some BIND name servers on your network. Newer BIND name servers are fast and robust and can interoperate with the Microsoft DNS Server. If you do decide to implement some BIND name servers, it would be a good idea to run the most recent version of BIND, BIND 9. BIND 9 servers can use a more efficient zone transfer protocol with Microsoft DNS Servers. (See Chapters 11 and 12 for more information on interoperability between the Microsoft DNS Server and BIND.)

Security

Since you would undoubtedly prefer that hackers not commandeer your name server to assist them in attacking your own hosts or other networks across the Internet, it's important to run your name server on a secure host. Don't run a name server on a big, multiuser system if you can't trust its users. Computers that are dedicated to hosting network services but don't permit general logins are good candidates for running name servers. If you have only one or a few really secure hosts, consider running the primary master name server on one of those, since its compromise would be more significant than the compromise of the secondaries.

Homogeneity

One last thing to take into account is the homogeneity of your name servers. Hopping between Windows and different versions of Unix can be frustrating and confusing. Avoid running name servers on lots of different platforms and even on different service packs if you can. You can waste a lot of time porting your scripts (or ours!) from one operating system to another or looking for the location of *nslookup* on three different operating systems.

Though these are really secondary considerations—it's more important to have a name server on a given subnet than to have it running on the perfect host—do keep these criteria in mind when deciding where to run your name servers.

Capacity Planning

If you have heavily populated< networks or users who do a lot of name server–intensive work, you may find you need more name servers than we've recommended to handle the load. Likewise, our recommendations may be fine for a little while, but as people add hosts to your networks or install new name server–intensive programs, you may find your name servers bogged down by queries.

Just which tasks are "name server–intensive"? Surfing the Web can be, as can sending electronic mail, especially to large mailing lists. Programs that make lots of remote procedure calls to different hosts can also be name server–intensive. Even running certain graphical user environments can tax your name server. The astute (and precocious) among you may be asking, "But how do I know when my name servers are overloaded? What do I look for?" An excellent question!

Memory utilization is probably the most important aspect of a name server's operation to monitor. *dns.exe*, the name server process, can get very large on a name server that is authoritative for many zones. If *dns.exe*'s size, plus the size of the other processes you run, exceeds the size of your host's real memory, your host may swap furiously ("thrash") and not get anything done. Another criterion you can use to measure the load on your name server is the load the name server process places on the host's CPU. Correctly configured name servers don't use much CPU time, so high CPU usage is often symptomatic of a configuration error. The Performance Monitor (*perfmon*) tool can help you characterize your name server's average CPU utilization. To see the name server's CPU utilization, start the Performance tool (**Start → Administrative Tools → Performance**) and select **System Monitor** in the left pane. Click on the add icon (shaped like a plus sign) in the right pane. In the resulting window, choose **Process** under **Performance object**, then choose **% Processor Time** in the left list and **dns** in the right list, as in Figure 9-2. Click on the **Add** button, then the **Close** button. A chart now shows the percentage of processor time the name server is using.

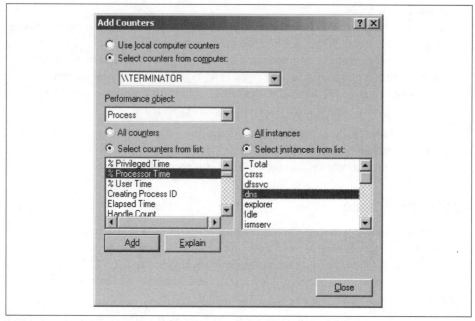

Figure 9-2. Adding counters to monitor DNS server CPU utilization

Unfortunately, there are no absolute rules when it comes to acceptable CPU utilization. We offer a rough rule of thumb, though: 5% average CPU utilization is probably acceptable; 10% is a bit high, unless the host is dedicated to providing name service.

Another statistic to look at is the number of queries the name server receives per minute (or second, if you have a busy name server). Again, there are no absolutes here: a multiprocessor server with oodles of RAM running Windows Server 2003 can handle thousands of queries per second without breaking into a sweat, while a less powerful PC might have problems with more than a few hundred queries per second.

To check the volume of queries your name server is receiving, use the Performance tool again. This time, select **DNS** under **Performance object**. You'll see there are several counters to choose from: you can monitor many different aspects of the name server's behavior. To see how busy your server is, pay particular attention to these counters: **Total Query Received, Total Query Received/sec, Total Response Sent**, and **Total Response Sent/sec**. More information about using the Performance tool to monitor name server performance can be found in "Understanding Name Server Statistics" in Chapter 7.

You should pay special attention to peak periods. For example, Monday morning is often busy because many people like to respond to mail they've received over the weekend first thing on Mondays.

You might also want to take a sample starting just after lunch, when people are returning to their desks and getting back to work—all at about the same time. Of course, if your organization is spread across several time zones, you'll have to use your judgment to determine a busy time.

Even if your host is fast enough to handle the volume of queries it receives, you should make sure the DNS traffic isn't placing undue load on your network. On most LANs, DNS traffic will be too small a proportion of the network's bandwidth to worry about. Over slow leased lines or dial-up connections, though, DNS traffic could consume enough bandwidth to merit concern.

To get a rough estimate of the volume of DNS traffic on your LAN, multiply the number of queries received plus the number of answers sent in an hour by 800 bits (100 bytes, a rough average size for a DNS message), and divide by 3,600 (seconds per hour) to find the bandwidth utilized. This should give you a feeling for how much of your network's bandwidth is being consumed by DNS traffic.

To give you an idea of what's normal, the last NSFNET traffic report (in April 1995) showed that DNS traffic constituted just over 5% of the total traffic volume (in bytes) on its backbone. The NSFNET's figures were based upon actual traffic sampling, not calculations like ours using the name server's statistics.* If you want to get a more accurate idea of the traffic your name server is receiving, you can always do your own traffic sampling with a LAN protocol analyzer.

If you find that your name servers are overworked, what then? First, it's a good idea to make sure that your name servers aren't being bombarded with queries by a misbehaving program. To do that, you'll need to find out the sources of all the queries.

Fortunately, Microsoft introduced some slick logging capabilities in Windows 2000 (the Windows NT version was woefully lacking in this area). Logging is configured through the **Debug Logging** tab of the server properties window (right-click on a name server in the DNS console and choose **Properties**, then click on the **Debug Logging** tab). Check the box labeled **Log packets for debugging** to enable logging. Be sure to check at least **Queries/Transfers** under **Packet contents**, which logs a record of every query to the file *%SystemRoot%\system32\dns\dns.log*. A sample logging properties window is shown in Figure 9-3.

When poring over the example, look for hosts sending repeated queries, especially for the same or similar information. That may indicate a misconfigured or buggy program running on the host or a foreign name server pelting your name server with queries.

---

* We're not sure how representative of the current state of the Internet these numbers are, because it's extremely difficult to wheedle equivalent numbers out of the commercial backbone providers that succeeded the NSFNET.

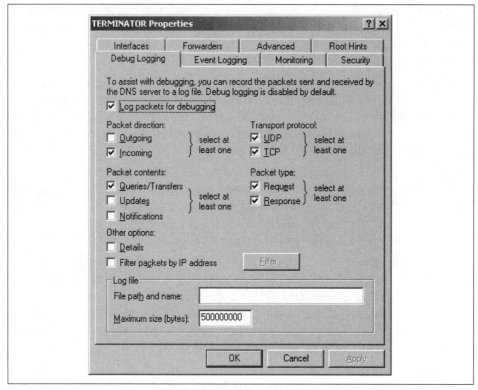

Figure 9-3. The Debug Logging tab of the properties window

If all the queries appear to be legitimate, add a new name server. Don't put the name server just anywhere, though; use the logging information to help you decide where it's best to run one. If DNS traffic is gobbling up your LAN, it won't help to choose a host at random and create a name server there. You need to consider which hosts are sending most of the queries, then figure out how to best provide them name service. Here are some hints to help you decide:

- Look for queries from resolvers on hosts that share the same file server. You could run a name server on that file server.

- Look for queries from resolvers on large, multiuser hosts. You could run a name server there.

- Look for queries from resolvers on another subnet. Those resolvers should be configured to query a name server on their local subnet. If there isn't one on that subnet, create one.

- Look for queries from resolvers on the same bridged segment (if you use bridging). If you run a name server on the bridged segment, the traffic won't need to be bridged to the rest of the network.

- Look for queries from hosts connected to each other via another, lightly loaded network. You could run a name server on the other network.

Adding More Name Servers

When you need to create new name servers for your domain, the simplest recourse is to add secondaries. You already know how—we went over it in Chapter 4—and once you've set up one secondary, cloning it is a piece of cake. But you can run into trouble if you add secondaries indiscriminately.

If you run a large number of secondary name servers for a zone, the primary master name server can take quite a beating just keeping up with the secondaries' polling to check that their zone data is current. There are a number of courses of action to take for this problem, as described in the sections that follow:

- Eliminate the secondary name servers altogether by using Active Directory integration.
- Increase the refresh interval so that the secondaries don't check so often.
- Direct some of the secondary name servers to load from other secondary name servers.
- Create caching-only name servers.
- Create partial-secondary name servers.

Active Directory Integration

We discuss Active Directory in Chapter 8. Briefly, this feature eliminates the load on the primary master from secondaries' polling by eliminating the secondaries! Remember that the main purpose of the primary master/secondary relationship is zone data replication: the DNS designers created the zone transfer mechanism as a way to spread zone data among multiple authoritative name servers. Windows stores all kinds of information about the network in Active Directory and replicates this information, too. With Windows Server 2003, you have the option of storing the definitive version of your zones' data in Active Directory rather than in zone datafiles on the primary master. All name servers running on domain controllers load the zone data stored in Active Directory, which also takes care of replicating changes to the data. See Chapter 8 for more details and instructions on setting up Active Directory.

Secondary Servers

You can have some of your secondaries load zone data from other secondary name servers instead of from a primary name server. The secondary name server can't tell if it's loading from a primary or another secondary. It's only important that the name server serving the zone transfer is authoritative for the zone. There's no trick to configuring this. Instead of specifying the IP address of the primary in the secondary's configuration, you simply specify the IP address of another secondary

When you go to this second level of distribution, though, be aware that it can take up to twice as long for the data to percolate from the primary name server to all the secondaries. Remember that the refresh interval is the period after which the secondary servers check to make sure that their zone data is still current. Therefore, it can take the first-level secondary servers the entire length of the refresh interval to get a new copy of the zone from the primary master server. Similarly, it can take the second-level secondary servers the entire refresh interval to get a new copy of the zone from the first-level secondary servers. The propagation time from the primary master server to all the secondary servers can therefore be twice the refresh interval.

Fortunately, using the DNS NOTIFY feature, which we'll describe in Chapter 11, avoids this delay. This feature is on by default and triggers zone transfers soon after the zone is updated on the primary master. Unfortunately, it doesn't work with any BIND Version 4 secondaries (they'll receive the NOTIFY messages, but will not understand them). Active Directory–integration, described in Chapter 8, also avoids zone synchronization delays.

If you decide to configure your network with two (or more) tiers of secondary servers, be careful to avoid updating loops. If we configured *wormhole* to update from *diehard* and then accidentally configured *diehard* to update from *wormhole*, neither would ever get data from the primary master. They would merely check their out-of-date serial numbers against each other and perpetually decide that they were both up-to-date.

Caching-Only Servers

Creating *caching-only name servers* is another alternative when you need more servers. Caching-only name servers are name servers not authoritative for any zones (except for the automatically created reverse-mapping zones). The name doesn't imply that primary master and secondary name servers don't cache—they do—but rather that the *only* function this server performs is looking up data and caching it. As with primary master and secondary name servers, a caching-only name server needs a *cache.dns* file and the automatically created zones, *0.in-addr.arpa*, *127.in-addr.arpa*, and *255.in-addr.arpa*. The configuration of a caching-only server looks like Figure 9-4.

A caching-only name server can look up domain names inside and outside your zone, as can primary master and secondary name servers. The difference is that when a caching-only name server initially looks up a name within your zone, it ends up asking one of your zone's primary master or secondary name servers for the answer. A primary or secondary would answer the same question out of its authoritative data. Which primary or secondary does the caching-only server ask? As with name servers outside of your domain, it finds out which name servers serve your zone from one of the name servers for your parent zone. Is there any way to prime a caching-only name server's cache so it knows which hosts run primary and secondary name

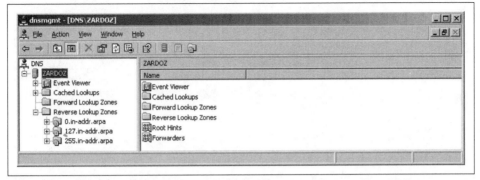

Figure 9-4. The DNS console showing a caching-only name server

servers for your zone? No, there isn't. You can't use *cache.dns*—the *cache.dns* file is only for root name server hints.

A caching-only name server's real value comes after it builds up its cache. Each time it queries an authoritative name server and receives an answer, it caches the records in the answer. Over time, the cache grows to include the information most often requested by the resolvers querying the caching-only name server. And you avoid the overhead of zone transfers—a caching-only name server doesn't need to do them.

Partial-Secondary Servers

In between a caching-only name server and a secondary name server is another varia-tion: a name server that is a secondary for only a few of the local zones. We call this a *partial-secondary name server* (although probably nobody else does). Suppose *movie. edu* had 20/24-sized (the old Class C) networks (and a corresponding 20 *in-addr.arpa* zones). Instead of creating a secondary server for all 21 zones (all the *in-addr.arpa* subdomains plus *movie.edu*), we could create a partial-secondary server for *movie. edu* and only those *in-addr.arpa* zones the host itself is in. If the host had two net-work interfaces, its name server would be a secondary for three zones: *movie.edu* and the two *in-addr.arpa* zones.

Let's say we scare up the hardware for another name server. We'll call the new host *zardoz.movie.edu*, with IP addresses 192.249.249.9 and 192.253.253.9. We'll create a partial-secondary name server on *zardoz*, with the configuration shown in Figure 9-5.

This server is a secondary for *movie.edu* and only 2 of the 20 *in-addr.arpa* zones. A "full" secondary would have 20 different zones (plus the three automatically cre-ated) under **Reverse Lookup Zones**.

What's so useful about a partial-secondary name server? They're not much work to administer because their configuration doesn't change much. On a server authorita-tive for all the *in-addr.arpa* zones, we'd need to add and delete *in-addr.arpa* zones as our network changed. That can be a surprising amount of work on a large network.

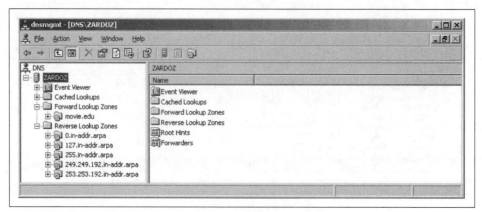

Figure 9-5. The DNS console showing a partial-secondary server

A partial secondary can still answer most of the queries it receives, though. Most of these queries are for data in *movie.edu* and the two *in-addr.arpa* zones. Why? Because most of the hosts querying the name server are on the two networks to which it's connected, 192.249.249/24 and 192.253.253/24. And those hosts probably communicate primarily with other hosts on their own network. This generates queries for data within the *in-addr.arpa* zone that corresponds to the local network.

Registering Name Servers

When you get around to setting up more and more name servers, a question may strike you—do I need to register *all* of my primary and secondary name servers with my parent zone? The answer is no. Only those servers you want to make available to name servers outside of your zone need to be registered with your parent. For example, if you run nine name servers for your zone, you may choose to tell the parent zone about only four of them. Within your network, you use all nine servers. Five of those nine servers, however, are queried only by resolvers on hosts that are configured to query them. Their parent name servers don't delegate to them, so they'll never be queried by remote name servers. Only the four servers registered with your parent zone are queried by other name servers, including caching-only and partial-secondary name servers on your network. This setup is shown in Figure 9-6.

Besides being able to pick and choose which of your name servers are hammered by outside queries, there's a technical motivation for registering only some of your zone's name servers: there is a limit to how many servers will fit in a UDP response packet. In practice, around 10 name server records should fit. Depending on the data (how many servers' names are in the same domain), you can get more or fewer.[*]

---

[*] The domain names of the Internet's root name servers were changed because of this. All the roots were moved into the same domain, *root-servers.net*, to take the most advantage of domain-name compression and to allow information about as many roots as possible to be stored in a single UDP packet.

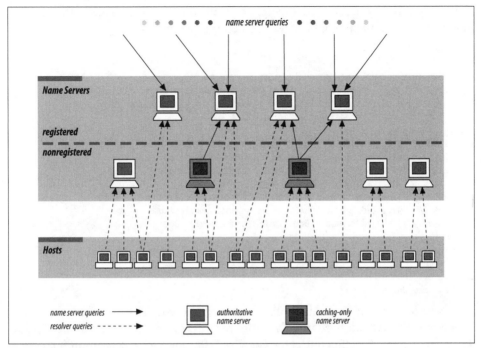

Figure 9-6. Registering only some of your name servers

There's not much point in registering more than 10 servers, anyway—if none of those 10 servers can be reached, it's unlikely the destination host can be reached.

If you've set up a new authoritative name server and you decide it should be registered, make a list of the parents of the zones for which it's authoritative. You'll need to contact the administrators for each of these parent zones. For example, let's say we want to register the name server we just set up on *zardoz*. To get this secondary registered in all the right zones, we'll need to contact the administrators of *edu* and *in-addr.arpa*. (For help determining who runs your parent zones, see Chapter 3.)

When you contact the administrators of a parent zone, be sure to follow the process they specify (if any) on their web site. If there's no standard modification process, you'll have to send them the domain name of the zone (or zones) for which the new name server is authoritative. If the new name server is in the new zone, you'll also need to give them the IP address(es) of the new name server. In fact, if there's no official format for submitting the information, it's often best just to send your parent the complete list of registered name servers for the zone, plus any addresses necessary, in zone datafile format. That avoids any potential confusion.

Since our networks were originally assigned by the InterNIC, we used the Network Modification form at *http://www.arin.net/library/templates/netmod.txt* to change our registration. If they hadn't had a template for us to use, our message to the administrator of *in-addr.arpa* might have read something like this:

```
Howdy!

I've just set up a new secondary name server on zardoz.movie.edu for the
249.249.192.in-addr.arpa and 253.253.192.in-addr.arpa zones. Would you
please add NS records for this name server to the in-addr.arpa zone?
That would make our delegation information look like:

253.253.192.in-addr.arpa. 86400 IN NS terminator.movie.edu.
253.253.192.in-addr.arpa. 86400 IN NS wormhole.movie.edu.
253.253.192.in-addr.arpa. 86400 IN NS zardoz.movie.edu.

249.249.192.in-addr.arpa. 86400 IN NS terminator.movie.edu.
249.249.192.in-addr.arpa. 86400 IN NS wormhole.movie.edu.
249.249.192.in-addr.arpa. 86400 IN NS zardoz.movie.edu.

Thanks!

Albert LeDomaine
al@robocop.movie.edu
```

Notice that we specified explicit TTLs on the NS records. That's because our parent name servers aren't authoritative for those records; *our* name servers are. By including them, we're indicating our choice of a TTL for our zone's delegation. Of course, our parent may have other ideas about what the TTL should be.

In this case, glue data—A records for each of the name servers—isn't necessary, since the domain names of the name servers aren't within the *in-addr.arpa* zones. They're within *movie.edu*, so a name server that was referred to *terminator.movie.edu* or *wormhole.movie.edu* could still find their addresses by following delegation to the *movie.edu* name servers.

Is a partial-secondary name server a good name server to register with your parent zone? Actually, it's not ideal because it's authoritative for only *some* of your *in-addr.arpa* zones. Administratively, it may be easier to register only servers backing up *all* the local zones; that way, you don't need to keep track of which name servers are authoritative for which zones. All of your parent zones can delegate to the same set of name servers: your primary master and your "full" secondaries.

If you don't have many name servers, though, or if you're good at remembering which name servers are authoritative for which zones, go ahead and register a partial-secondary.

Caching-only name servers, on the other hand, must *never* be registered. A caching-only name server rarely has complete information for any given zone; it just has the bits and pieces of the zone that it has looked up recently. If a parent name server were to mistakenly refer a foreign name server to a caching-only name server, the foreign name server would send the caching-only name server a nonrecursive query.

The caching-only name server might have the data cached, but then again, it might not. If it didn't have the data, it would refer the querier to the best name servers it knew (those closest to the domain name in the query)—which might include the caching-only name server itself! The poor foreign name server might never get an answer. This kind of misconfiguration—actually, delegating a zone to any name server not authoritative for that zone—is known as *lame delegation*.

Changing TTLs

An experienced zone administrator needs to know how to set the time to live on his zone's data to his best advantage. The TTL on a resource record, remember, is the time for which any server can cache that record. So if the TTL for a particular resource record is 3,600 seconds and a server outside your network caches that record, it will have to remove the entry from its cache after an hour. If it needs the same data after the hour is up, it'll have to query your name servers again.

When we introduced TTLs, we emphasized that your choice of a TTL would dictate how current you would keep copies of your data, at the cost of increased load on your name servers. A low TTL would mean that name servers outside your network would have to get data from your name servers often and that the data would therefore be kept current. On the other hand, your name servers would be peppered by the name servers' queries.

You don't *have* to choose a TTL once and for all, though. You can—and experienced administrators do—change TTLs periodically to suit your needs.

Suppose we know that one of our hosts is about to be moved to another network. This host houses the *movie.edu* film library, a large collection of files our site makes available to hosts on the Internet. During normal operation, outside name servers cache the address of our host according to the minimum (default) TTL in the SOA record. (We set the *movie.edu* TTL to be one day in our sample files.) A name server caching the old address record just before the change could have the wrong address for as long as a day. A loss of connectivity for a full day is unacceptable, though. What can we do to minimize the loss of connectivity? We can lower the TTL so that outside servers cache the address record for a shorter period. By reducing the TTL, we force the outside servers to update their data more frequently, which means that any changes we make when we actually move the system will be propagated to the outside world quickly. How short can we make the TTL? Unfortunately, we can't safely use a TTL of zero, which should mean "don't cache this record at all." (Some older BIND Version 4 name servers can't cope with a zero TTL.) Small TTLs, like 30 seconds, are okay, though. To add an explicit TTL on an individual resource record, you'll need the DNS console's advanced view so that you can actually see individual records' TTLs: choose **View** → **Advanced**.

Click on the domain name of the zone in the left panel, then double-click the record when it appears in the right panel. The **Properties** window is displayed, and you can type the TTL. Recall that the subfields in the TTL field are (from left to right) days, hours, minutes, and seconds.

Figure 9-7 provides an example of an explicit TTL from *movie.edu*.

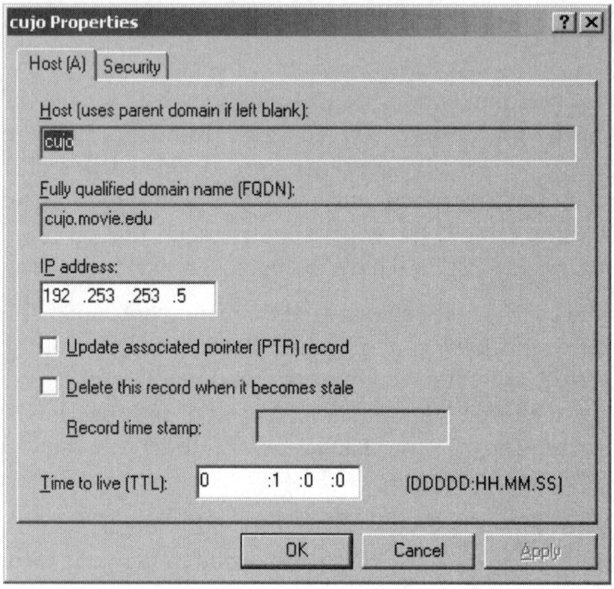

Figure 9-7. An explicit TTL on cujo.movie.edu

The record the DNS console adds to the *movie.edu* zone datafile looks like this:

```
cujo  3600  IN  A  192.253.253.5
```

Note the explicit TTL of 3,600 seconds (one hour) in the TTL field, overriding the TTL in the zone's SOA record.

You may have seen the last field of the SOA record called simply the "minimum" field (some versions of *nslookup* display it that way, for example). So why does it show up in the DNS console as "Minimum (default)"? (To see what we mean, take a look at the SOA record shown back in Chapter 4 in Figure 4-19.) If the Microsoft DNS Server followed the original DNS RFCs, the TTL field in the SOA record would really define the minimum TTL value for all resource records in the zone. Thus, you could specify only explicit TTLs larger than this minimum. Neither Microsoft nor BIND name servers work this way, though. In other words, in real life, "minimum" is not really minimum. Instead, the Microsoft DNS Server implements the minimum TTL field in the SOA record as a "default" TTL—hence the "Minimum (default)" wording. If there is no TTL on a record, the minimum applies. If there is a TTL on the resource record, the Microsoft DNS Server allows it even if it is smaller than the minimum. That one record is sent out in responses with the smaller TTL while all other records are sent out with the "Minimum (default)" TTL from the SOA record.

You should also know that when giving out answers, a secondary supplies the same TTL a primary master does—that is, if a primary gives out a TTL of one hour for a particular record, a secondary will, too. The secondary doesn't decrement the TTL according to how long it has been since it loaded the zone. So, if the TTL of a single resource record is set smaller than the SOA minimum, both the primary and secondary name servers give out the resource record with the same, smaller TTL. If the secondary name server has reached the expiration time for the zone, it expires the whole zone. It will never expire an individual resource record within a zone.

The Microsoft DNS Server does allow you to put a small TTL on an individual resource record if you know that the data is going to change shortly. Thus, any server caching that data caches it only for a brief time. Unfortunately, while the name server makes tagging records with a small TTL possible, most administrators don't take the time to do it. When a host changes addresses, you often lose connectivity to it for a while.

More often than not, the host having its address changed is not one of the main hubs on the site, so the outage affects few people. If one of the mail hubs or a major web server or *ftp* archive—like the film library—is moving, though, a day's loss of connectivity may be unacceptable. In cases like this, the administrator should plan ahead and reduce the TTL on the data to be changed.

Remember that the TTL on the affected data will need to be lowered *before* the change takes place. Reducing the TTL on a workstation's address record and changing the workstation's address simultaneously may do you little or no good; the address record may have been cached seconds before you made the change and may linger until the old TTL times out. You must also be sure to factor in the time it'll take your secondaries to load from your primary master. For example, if your minimum TTL is 12 hours and your refresh interval is 3 hours, be sure to lower the TTLs at least 15 hours ahead of time, so that by the time you move the host, all the old, longer TTL records will have timed out. Of course, if all of your secondaries are using NOTIFY, the secondaries shouldn't take the full refresh interval to sync up.

Changing Other SOA Values

We briefly mentioned increasing the refresh interval as a way of offloading your primary name server. Let's discuss refresh in a little more detail and go over the remaining SOA values, too.

The *refresh* value, you'll remember, controls how often a secondary checks whether its zone data is up-to-date. The *retry* value becomes the refresh time after the first failure to reach a master name server. The *expire* value determines how long zone data can be held before it's discarded when a master is unreachable. Finally, the *minimum TTL* sets how long zone information may be cached.

Suppose we've decided we want the secondaries to pick up new information every hour instead of every three hours. We change the refresh value to one hour in each of the zones. Since retry is related to refresh, we should probably reduce retry, too—to every 15 minutes or so. Typically, retry is less than refresh, but that's not required. Although lowering the refresh value will speed up the distribution of zone data, it will also increase the load on the server from which data is being loaded, since the secondaries will check more often. The added load isn't much, though; each secondary makes a single SOA query during each zone's refresh interval to check its master's copy of the zone. So with two secondary name servers, changing the refresh time from three hours to one hour will generate only four more queries (per zone) to the primary master in any three-hour span.

If all of your secondaries use NOTIFY, of course, refresh doesn't mean as much. But if you have even one BIND Version 4 slave, your zone data may take up to the full refresh interval to reach it.

Some older versions of BIND secondaries stopped answering queries during a zone load. As a result, BIND was modified to spread out the zone loads, reducing the periods of unavailability. So, even if you set a low refresh interval, your secondaries may not check exactly as often as you request. BIND Version 4 name servers attempt a certain number of zone loads and then wait 15 minutes before trying another batch. On the other hand, BIND Version 4.9 and later may also refresh *more often* than the refresh interval. These versions of BIND will wait a random number of seconds between one-half of the refresh interval and the full refresh interval to check serial numbers.

Expiration times on the order of a week—longer if you frequently have problems reaching your updating source—are common. The expiration time should always be much larger than the retry and refresh intervals; if the expire time is smaller than the refresh interval, your secondaries will expire their data before trying to load new data. If your zone's data doesn't change much, you might consider raising the minimum (default) TTL. The SOA's minimum (default) TTL value is typically one day (86,400 seconds), but you can make it longer. One week is about the longest value that makes sense for a TTL. If it's longer than that, you may find yourself unable to change bad, cached data in a reasonable amount of time.

Planning for Disasters

It's a fact of life on a network that things go wrong. Hardware fails, software has bugs, and people occasionally make mistakes. Sometimes this results in minor inconveniences, like having a few users lose connections. Sometimes the results are catastrophic and involve the loss of important data and valuable jobs.

Because the Domain Name System relies so heavily on the network, it is vulnerable to network outages. Thankfully, the design of DNS takes into account the imperfection of networks: it allows for multiple, redundant name servers, retransmission of queries, retrying zone transfers, and so on.

DNS doesn't protect itself from every conceivable calamity, though. DNS doesn't or can't protect against certain types of network failures—some of them quite common. But with a small investment of time and money, you can minimize the threat of these problems.

Outages

Power outages, for example, are relatively common in many parts of the world. In some parts of the U.S., thunderstorms or tornadoes may cause a site to lose power or have only intermittent power for an extended period. Elsewhere, typhoons, volcanoes, or construction work may interrupt electrical service. And you never know when those of you in California might lose power in a rolling blackout from a lack of electrical capacity.

If all your hosts are down, of course, you don't need name service. Quite often, however, sites have problems when power is *restored*. Following our recommendations, they run their name servers on file servers and big, multiuser machines. And when the power comes up, those machines are naturally the last to boot—because all those disks need to be checked and fixed first! Which means that all the on-site hosts that are quick to boot do so without the benefit of name service.

This can cause all sorts of wonderful problems, depending on what services your hosts access when they boot. For example, your PCs may mount your servers' drives (via *net use*) when they boot. If they do, they almost certainly specify the servers' domain names or NetBIOS names.

Using hostnames in commands is admirable because it allows administrators to change the servers' IP addresses without changing all the startup files on-site. However, if name service isn't available when your PCs boot, the *net use* command will fail, which may cause successive commands to fail, too. This will certainly not help your users' productivity.

Recommendations

Our recommendation is to add the names and IP addresses of critical hosts to your PCs' *HOSTS* files. Any host whose name is referenced during the boot process should appear in this file. You can synchronize the file by copying it from share to share. On Windows Server 2003, the default location for the file is *%SystemRoot%\System32\Drivers\Etc*, usually *C:\Windows\System32\Drivers\Etc*. The format of the file is just like the format of the Unix */etc/hosts* file: each line consists of an IP address (in dotted-octet notation), which starts in the first column, followed by whitespace and the canonical name of the host. Optionally, one or more aliases may follow the canonical name. For example:

```
192.249.249.1 wormhole.movie.edu wormhole
192.249.249.3 terminator.movie.edu terminator
```

Now, if a PC needs to look up *wormhole* or *wormhole.movie.edu* when it boots, it will be able to resolve the name.

However, using *HOSTS* files poses some danger: unless you take care to keep the files up-to-date, their information may become stale. And since the Windows Server 2003 resolver uses *HOSTS* before querying a name server, a stale entry can cause resolution failures that are hard to diagnose.

The best solution to this problem is to run a name server on a host with uninterruptible power. If you rarely experience extended power loss, battery backup might be enough. If your outages are longer and name service is critical to you, you should consider an uninterruptible power system (UPS) with a generator of some kind.

If you can't afford luxuries like these, you might just try to track down the fastest booting host around and run a name server on it. Hosts with small filesystems should boot quickly since they don't have many disks to check.

Once you've located the right host, you'll need to make sure the host's IP address appears in the resolver configurations of all of your hosts that need full-time name service. You'll probably want to list the backed-up host last since, during normal operation, hosts should use the name server closest to them. Then, after a power failure, your critical applications will still have name service, albeit at a small sacrifice in performance.

Coping with Disaster

When disaster strikes, it really helps to know what to do. Knowing to duck under a sturdy table or desk during an earthquake can save you from being pinned under a toppling monitor. Knowing how to turn off your gas can save your house from conflagration.

Likewise, knowing what to do in a network disaster (or even just a minor mishap) can help you keep your network running.

Long Outages (Days)

If you lose network connectivity for a long time, your name servers may have problems. If they lose connectivity to the root name servers for an extended period, they'll stop resolving queries outside their authoritative zone data. If the secondaries can't reach their master, sooner or later they'll expire the zone.

In case your name service really goes haywire because of the connectivity loss, it's a good idea to keep a sitewide or workgroup *HOSTS* file around, as we recommended earlier in this chapter. If your name servers all go down, your hosts will still be able to resolve the names of hosts in the *HOSTS* file.

As for secondaries, you can reconfigure a secondary that can't reach its master to run temporarily as a primary master. Just right-click on the zone's domain name in the DNS console, select **Properties**, make sure the **General** tab is selected, and click on **Change** to change the zone type from secondary to primary. If more than one secondary for the same zone is cut off, you can configure one as a primary master temporarily and reconfigure the other to load from the temporary primary.

Really Long Outages (Weeks)

If an extended outage cuts you off from the Internet—say for a week or more—you may need to restore connectivity to root name servers artificially to get things working again. Every name server needs to talk to a root name server occasionally. It's a bit like therapy: the name server needs to contact the root to regain its perspective on the world.

To provide root name service during a long outage, you can set up your own root name servers, *but only temporarily*. Once you're reconnected to the Internet, you *must* shut off your temporary root servers. The most obnoxious vermin on the Internet are name servers that believe they're root name servers but don't know anything about most top-level domains. A close second is the Internet name server configured to query—and report—a false set of root name servers.

That said, and our alibis in place, here's what you have to do to configure your own root name server. First, you need to create the root zone. The root zone will delegate to the highest level zones in your isolated network. For example, if *movie.edu* were to be isolated from the Internet, we might create a root zone datafile, *root.dns*, for *terminator*:

```
. IN SOA terminator.movie.edu. al.robocop.movie.edu. (
                1       ; Serial
                10800   ; Refresh after 3 hours
                3600    ; Retry after 1 hour
                604800  ; Expire after 1 week
                86400 ) ; Minimum TTL of 1 day

; Refresh, retry, and expire really don't matter since all
; roots are primaries.  Minimum TTL could be longer, since
; the data is likely to be stable.

   IN NS terminator.movie.edu. ; terminator is the temp. root

; Our root only knows about movie.edu and our two
; in-addr.arpa domains
```

```
movie.edu.  IN NS terminator.movie.edu.
            IN NS wormhole.movie.edu.

249.249.192.in-addr.arpa.  IN NS terminator.movie.edu.
                           IN NS wormhole.movie.edu.

253.253.192.in-addr.arpa.  IN NS terminator.movie.edu.
                           IN NS wormhole.movie.edu.

terminator.movie.edu.  IN A 192.249.249.3
wormhole.movie.edu.    IN A 192.249.249.1
                       IN A 192.253.253.1
```

Then we need to add the zone with the DNS console and update all of our name servers (except the new, temporary root) with a *cache.dns* file that includes just the temporary root name server (it's best to move the old cache file aside—we'll need it later, once connectivity is restored).

Here are the contents of the *cache.dns* file:

```
.  99999999  IN  NS  terminator.movie.edu.

terminator.movie.edu.  IN  A  192.249.249.3
```

This process will keep *movie.edu* name resolution going during the outage. Once Internet connectivity is restored, we can delete the root zone on *terminator* and restore the original cache files on all our other name servers.

## CHAPTER 10

Parenting

The way Dinah washed her children's faces was this: first she held the poor thing down by its ear with one paw, and then with the other paw she rubbed its face all over, the wrong way, beginning at the nose: and just now, as I said, she was hard at work on the white kitten, which was lying quite still and trying to purr— no doubt feeling that it was all meant for its good.

Once your domain reaches a certain size, or you decide you need to distribute the management of parts of your domain to various entities within your organization, you'll want to divide the domain into subdomains. These subdomains will be the children of your current domain on the domain tree; your domain will be the parent. If you delegate responsibility for your subdomains to another organization, each becomes its own zone, separate from its parent zone. We like to call the management of your subdomains—your children—*parenting.*

Good parenting starts with carving up your domain sensibly, choosing appropriate names for your subdomains, and then delegating the subdomains to create new zones. A responsible parent also works hard at maintaining the relationship between the name servers authoritative for her zone and its children; she ensures that delegation from parent to child is current and correct.

Good parenting is vital to the success of your network, especially as name service becomes critical to navigating between sites. Incorrect delegation to a child zone's name servers can render a site effectively unreachable while the loss of connectivity to the parent zone's name servers can leave a site unable to reach any hosts outside the local zone.

In this chapter we present our views on when to create subdomains, and we go over how to create and delegate them in some detail. We also discuss management of the parent-child relationship and, finally, how to manage the process of carving up a large domain into smaller subdomains with minimal disruption and inconvenience.

When to Become a Parent

Far be it from us to *tell* you when you should become a parent, but we will be so bold as to offer you some guidelines. You may find some compelling reason to implement subdomains that isn't on our list, but here are some of the most common reasons:

- A need to delegate or distribute management of the domain to a number of organizations
- The large size of your domain—dividing it would make it easier to manage and offload the name servers for the domain
- A need to distinguish hosts' organizational affiliations by including them in particular subdomains

Once you've decided to have children, the next question to ask yourself is, naturally, how many children to have.

How Many Children?

Of course, you won't simply say, "I want to create four subdomains." Deciding how many subdomains to implement is really choosing the organizational affiliations of those subdomains. For example, if your company has four branch offices, you might decide to create four subdomains, each of which corresponds to a branch office.

Should you create subdomains for each site, for each division, or even for each department? You have a lot of latitude in your choice because of DNS's scalability. You can create a few large subdomains or many small subdomains. You face trade-offs whichever you choose, though.

Delegating to a few large subdomains isn't much work for the parent because there's not much delegation to keep track of. However, you wind up with larger subdomains, which require more memory to load and faster name servers, and administration isn't as distributed. If you implement site-level subdomains, for example, you may force autonomous or unrelated groups at a site to share a single namespace and a single point of administration.

Delegating to many smaller subdomains can be a headache for the parent's administrator. Keeping delegation data current involves keeping track of which hosts run name servers and which zones they're authoritative for. The data changes each time a subdomain adds a new name server or the address of a name server for the subdomain changes. If the subdomains are all administered by different people, that means more administrators to train, more relationships for the parent's administrator to maintain, and more overhead for the organization overall. On the other hand, the subdomains are smaller and easier to manage, and the administration is more widely distributed, allowing closer management of zone data.

Given the advantages and disadvantages of either alternative, it may seem difficult to make a choice. Actually, there's probably a natural division in your organization. Some companies manage computers and networks at the site level; others have decentralized, relatively autonomous workgroups that manage everything themselves. Here are a few basic rules to help you find the right way to carve up your namespace:

- Don't shoehorn your organization into a weird or uncomfortable domain structure. Trying to fit 50 independent, unrelated U.S. divisions into four regional subdomains may save you work (as the administrator of the parent zone), but it won't help your reputation. Decentralized, autonomous operations demand different zones—that's the *raison d'être* of the Domain Name System.

- The structure of your domain should mirror the structure of your organization, especially your organization's support structure. If departments run networks, assign IP addresses, and manage hosts, they should also manage the subdomains.

- If you're not sure or can't agree about how the namespace should be organized, try to come up with guidelines for when a group within your organization can carve off its own subdomain (for example, how many hosts are needed to create a new subdomain and what level of support the group must provide) and grow the namespace organically, only as needed.

What to Name Your Children

Once you've decided how many subdomains you'd like to create and what they correspond to, you must choose names for them. Rather than unilaterally deciding on your subdomains' names, it's considered polite to involve your future subdomain administrators and their constituencies in the decision. In fact, you can leave the decision entirely to them if you like.

This can lead to problems, though. It's preferable to use a relatively consistent naming scheme across your subdomains. This practice makes it easier for users in one subdomain, or outside your domain entirely, to guess or remember your subdomain names and to figure out in which domain a particular host or user lives.

Leaving the decision to the locals can result in naming chaos. Some will want to use geographical names; others will insist on organizational names. Some will want to abbreviate; others will want to use full names.

Therefore, it's often best to establish a naming convention before choosing subdomain names. Here are some suggestions from our experience:

- In a dynamic company, the names of organizations can change frequently. Naming subdomains organizationally in a climate like this can be disastrous. One month the Relatively Advanced Technology group seems stable enough, the next month they've been merged into the Questionable Computer Systems organization, and the following quarter they're all sold to a German conglomerate. Meanwhile, you're stuck with well-known hosts in a subdomain whose name no longer has any meaning.

- Geographical names are more stable than organizational names but sometimes not as well known. You may know that your famous Software Evangelism Business Unit is in Poughkeepsie or Waukegan, but people outside your company may have no idea where it is (and might have trouble spelling either name).

- Don't sacrifice readability for convenience. Two-letter subdomain names may be easy to type, but impossible to recognize. Why abbreviate "Italy" to "it" and have it confused with your Information Technology organization when for a paltry three more letters you can use the full name and eliminate any ambiguity?

- Too many companies use cryptic, inconvenient domain names. The general rule seems to be the larger the company, the more indecipherable the domain names. Buck the trend: make the names of your subdomains obvious!

- Don't use existing or reserved top-level domain names as subdomain names. It might seem sensible to use two-letter country abbreviations for your international subdomains or to use organizational top-level domain names like *net* for your networking organization, but doing so can cause nasty problems. For example, naming your Communications department's subdomain *com* might impede your ability to communicate with hosts under the top-level *com* domain. Imagine the administrators of your *com* subdomain naming their new Sun workstation *sun* and their new HP 9000 *hp* (they aren't the most imaginative folks): users anywhere within your domain sending mail to friends at *sun.com* or *hp.com* could have their letters end up in your *com* subdomain, since the name of your parent zone may be in some of your hosts' search lists.

How to Become a Parent: Creating Subdomains

Once you've decided on names, creating the child domains is easy. But first, you've got to decide how much autonomy you're going to give your subdomains. Odd that you have to decide that before you actually create them....

Thus far, we've assumed that if you create a subdomain, you'll want to delegate it to another organization, thereby making it a separate zone from the parent. Is this always true, though? Not necessarily.

Think carefully about how the computers and networks within a subdomain are managed when choosing whether or not to delegate it. It doesn't make sense to delegate a subdomain to an entity that doesn't manage its own hosts or networks. For example, in a large corporation, the personnel department probably doesn't run its own computers: IT (Information Technology) department manages them. So while you may want to create a subdomain for personnel, delegating management for that subdomain to them is probably wasted effort.

Creating a Subdomain in the Parent's Zone

You can create a subdomain without delegating it, however. How? By creating resource records that refer to the subdomain within the parent's zone.

Say one day a group of students approaches us, asking for a DNS entry for a web server for student home pages. The name they'd like is *www.students.movie.edu*. You might think that we'd need to create a new zone, *students.movie.edu*, and delegate to it from the *movie.edu* zone. Well, that's one way to do it, but it's easier to create an A record for *www.students.movie.edu* in the *movie.edu* zone. We find that few people realize this is perfectly legal. You don't need a new zone for each new level in the namespace. A new zone would make sense if the students were going to run *students. movie.edu* by themselves and wanted to administer their own name servers. But they just want one A record, so creating a whole new zone is more work than necessary.

It's easy to add this record with the DNS console. First create a *students.movie.edu* subdomain in the *movie.edu* zone, then add the *www.students.movie.edu* A record. To create the subdomain, right-click on the zone in the left pane and select **New Domain**. You'll see a window like the one shown in Figure 10-1.

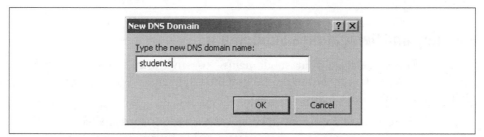

Figure 10-1. Creating a subdomain in a zone

Enter the name of the new subdomain. You don't need to append *movie.edu*—the DNS console knows what you mean. You'll then see a folder icon for the new domain in the DNS console, as shown in Figure 10-2.

To enter the *www.students.movie.edu* A record, just select the *students* folder and follow the procedures described previously to add a new host.

In fact, you can even skip the **Add Domain** step and use the **Add Host (A)** function to add the host's address record and implicitly create the *students.movie.edu* subdomain (if it hasn't already been created). Just specify *www.students* in the **Name** field and voila! You've created an address for *www.students.movie.edu*.

Now users can access *www.students.movie.edu* to get to the students' home pages. We could make this setup especially convenient for students by adding *students.movie.edu*

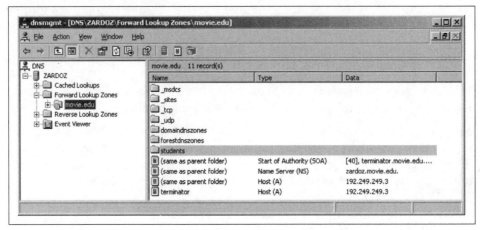

Figure 10-2. The students.movie.edu subdomain in the movie.edu zone

to their PCs' or workstations' search lists; they'd need to type only *www* as the URL to get to the right host.

Did you notice there's no SOA record for *students.movie.edu*? There's no need for one since the *movie.edu* SOA record indicates the start of authority for the entire *movie.edu* zone. Since there's no delegation to *students.movie.edu*, it's part of the *movie.edu* zone.

Creating and Delegating a Subdomain

If you decide to delegate your subdomains—to send your children out into the world, as it were—you'll need to do things a little differently. We're in the process of doing it now, so you can follow along with us.

We need to create a new subdomain of *movie.edu* for our special-effects lab. We've chosen the name *fx.movie.edu*—short, recognizable, unambiguous. Because we're delegating *fx.movie.edu* to administrators in the lab, it'll be a separate zone. The hosts *bladerunner* and *outland*, both within the special-effects lab, will serve as the zone's name servers (*bladerunner* will serve as the primary master). We've chosen to run two name servers for the zone for redundancy—a single *fx.movie.edu* name server would be a single point of failure that could effectively isolate the entire special-effects lab. Since there aren't many hosts in the lab, though, two name servers should be enough.

The special-effects lab is on *movie.edu*'s new 192.253.254/24 network. Here are the partial contents of *HOSTS*:

```
192.253.254.1 movie-gw.movie.edu movie-gw
# fx primary
192.253.254.2 bladerunner.fx.movie.edu bladerunner br
# fx secondary
```

```
192.253.254.3 outland.fx.movie.edu outland
192.253.254.4 starwars.fx.movie.edu starwars
192.253.254.5 empire.fx.movie.edu empire
192.253.254.6 jedi.fx.movie.edu jedi
```

First, we make sure the Microsoft DNS Server is installed on the new server, *bladerunner*. Then we create the new zone *fx.movie.edu* on *bladerunner* using the process described in the section "Creating a New Zone" in Chapter 4. We also create the corresponding *in-addr.arpa* zone, *254.253.192.in-addr.arpa*. Next, we populate the zone with all the hosts from our snippet of *HOSTS*, making sure the DNS console automatically adds the PTR records that correspond to our A records. We then add MX records for all of our hosts, pointing to *starwars.fx.movie.edu* and *wormhole.movie.edu*, at preferences 10 and 100, respectively.

The zone datafile we end up with, called *fx.movie.edu.dns*, looks like this:

```
;
;   Database file fx.movie.edu.dns for fx.movie.edu zone.
;       Zone version:   22
;

@                       IN  SOA bladerunner.fx.movie.edu.
administrator.fx.movie.edu. (
                        22          ; serial number
                        900         ; refresh
                        600         ; retry
                        86400       ; expire
                        3600        ) ; default TTL


;
;   Zone NS records
;

@                       NS          bladerunner.fx.movie.edu.
@                       NS          outland.fx.movie.edu.


;
;   Zone records
;

@                       MX          100     wormhole.movie.edu.
@                       MX          10      starwars.fx.movie.edu.

bladerunner             A 192.253.254.2
                        MX          100     wormhole.movie.edu.
                        MX          10      starwars.fx.movie.edu.

empire                  A 192.253.254.5
                        MX          100     wormhole.movie.edu.
                        MX          10      starwars.fx.movie.edu.

jedi                    A 192.253.254.6
                        MX          10      starwars.fx.movie.edu.
                        MX          100     wormhole.movie.edu.
```

```
outland                         A 192.253.254.3
                                MX        100      starwars.fx.movie.edu.
                                MX        10       starwars.fx.movie.edu.

starwars                        A 192.253.254.4
                                MX        100      wormhole.movie.edu.
                                MX        10       starwars.fx.movie.edu.
```

Note that we added an NS record for *outland.fx.movie.edu* even though we didn't strictly need to: the DNS console would have added it for us when we added *outland* as a secondary. But adding the NS record lets us restrict zone transfers to name servers listed in NS records and still set up the secondary on *outland*. We'll do this for the reverse-mapping zone, too.

The *254.253.192.in-addr.arpa.dns* file ends up looking like this:

```
;
;    Database file 254.253.192.in-addr.arpa.dns for 254.253.192.in-addr.arpa zone.
;        Zone version:  14
;

@                       IN  SOA bladerunner.fx.movie.edu.
administrator.fx.movie.edu. (
                        14              ; serial number
                        900             ; refresh
                        600             ; retry
                        86400           ; expire
                        3600            ) ; default TTL


;
;   Zone NS records
;

@                       NS        bladerunner.fx.movie.edu.
bladerunner.fx.movie.edu. A       192.253.254.2
@                       NS        outland.fx.movie.edu.
outland.fx.movie.edu.   A 192.253.254.3


;
;   Zone records
;

1                       PTR       movie-gw.movie.edu.
2                       PTR       bladerunner.fx.movie.edu.
3                       PTR       outland.fx.movie.edu.
4                       PTR       starwars.fx.movie.edu.
5                       PTR       empire.fx.movie.edu.
6                       PTR       jedi.fx.movie.edu.
```

Notice that the PTR record for *1.254.253.192.in-addr.arpa* points to *movie-gw. movie.edu*. That's intentional. The router connects to the other *movie.edu* networks, so it really doesn't belong in *fx.movie.edu*. There's no requirement that all the PTR records in *254.253.192.in-addr.arpa* map into a single zone, although they should correspond to the canonical names for those hosts.

Now we need to configure *bladerunner*'s resolver. Following the directions in Chapter 6, we configure *bladerunner* to send queries to its own IP address. Then we set *bladerunner*'s domain to *fx.movie.edu*.

Now we'll use *nslookup* to look up a few hosts in *fx.movie.edu* and in *254.253.192. in-addr.arpa*:

```
C:\> nslookup
Default Server:  bladerunner.fx.movie.edu
Address:  192.253.254.2

> jedi
Server:  bladerunner.fx.movie.edu
Address:  192.253.254.2

Name:    jedi.fx.movie.edu
Address:  192.253.254.6

> set type=mx
> empire
Server:  bladerunner.fx.movie.edu
Address:  192.253.254.2

empire.fx.movie.edu     MX preference = 10, mail exchanger = starwars.fx.movie.edu
empire.fx.movie.edu     MX preference = 100, mail exchanger = wormhole.movie.edu
starwars.fx.movie.edu internet address = 192.253.254.4

> ls fx.movie.edu
[bladerunner.fx.movie.edu]
 fx.movie.edu.            NS      server = bladerunner.fx.movie.edu
 fx.movie.edu.            NS      server = outland.fx.movie.edu
 bladerunner              A       192.253.254.2
 empire                   A       192.253.254.5
 jedi                     A       192.253.254.6
 outland                  A       192.253.254.3
 starwars                 A       192.253.254.4
> set type=ptr
> 192.253.254.3
Server:  bladerunner.fx.movie.edu
Address:  192.253.254.2

3.254.253.192.in-addr.arpa      name = outland.fx.movie.edu
> ls 254.253.192.in-addr.arpa
[bladerunner.fx.movie.edu]
 254.253.192.in-addr.arpa.    NS      server = bladerunner.fx.movie.edu
 254.253.192.in-addr.arpa.    NS      server = outland.fx.movie.edu
 1                            PTR     host = movie-gw.movie.edu
 2                            PTR     host = bladerunner.fx.movie.edu
 3                            PTR     host = outland.fx.movie.edu
 4                            PTR     host = starwars.fx.movie.edu
```

```
     5                              PTR     host = empire.fx.movie.edu
     6                              PTR     host = jedi.fx.movie.edu
  > exit
```

The output looks reasonable, so it's safe to set up a secondary name server for *fx.movie. edu* and then delegate *fx.movie.edu* from *movie.edu*.

An fx.movie.edu secondary

Setting up the secondary name server for *fx.movie.edu* is simple: use the DNS console to add *outland* as a new server, then add two secondary zones, according to the instructions in Chapter 4.

Like *bladerunner*, *outland*'s resolver will point to the local name server, and we'll configure the local domain to be *fx.movie.edu*.

On the movie.edu primary master name server

All that's left now is to delegate the *fx.movie.edu* subdomain to the new *fx.movie.edu* name servers on *bladerunner* and *outland*. Right-click on the parent domain, *movie.edu*, in the left pane and choose **New Delegation**, which starts the New Delegation Wizard. Click **Next** in the welcome screen to display a screen like the one shown in Figure 10-3. The first step is entering the name of the delegated subdomain, which we've done.

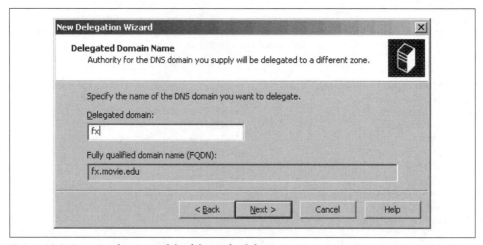

Figure 10-3. Entering the name of the delegated subdomain

Click **Next** and you'll be presented with a window to choose the name servers to host (i.e., be authoritative for) the delegated zone. Our two servers are *bladerunner. fx.movie.edu* and *outland.fx.movie.edu*, so we enter the appropriate information by clicking **Add** (we have to run through the add process twice, once for each name server), resulting in a window like Figure 10-4.

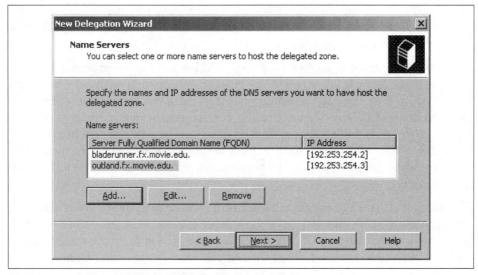

Figure 10-4. Choosing name servers for the delegated zone

The final window of the wizard is just for confirmation, so we won't bother to show it. Click **Finish** and you've delegated a zone. The DNS console adds a special gray icon for delegated zones; if you select this icon, you'll see the NS records added by the wizard. These records perform the actual delegation. A sample DNS console view showing the *fx.movie.edu* delegation appears in Figure 10-5.

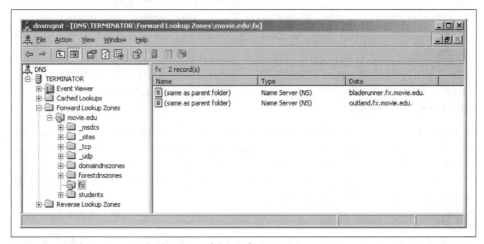

Figure 10-5. The DNS console showing a delegated zone

According to RFC 1034, the domain names in the resource record–specific portion (the "right side") of the *bladerunner.fx.movie.edu* and *outland.fx.movie.edu* NS records must be the canonical domain names for the name servers. A remote name server following delegation expects to find one or more address records attached to that domain name, not an alias (CNAME) record. Actually, the RFC extends this restriction to any type of resource record that includes a domain name as its value—all must specify the canonical domain name.

These two records alone aren't enough, though. Do you see the problem? How can a name server outside of *fx.movie.edu* look up information within *fx.movie.edu*? Well, a *movie.edu* name server would refer it to the name servers authoritative for *fx.movie.edu*, right? That's true, but the NS records in *movie.edu* give only the *names* of the *fx.movie.edu* name servers. The foreign name server needs the IP addresses of the *fx.movie.edu* name servers in order to send queries to them. Who can give it those addresses? Only the *fx.movie.edu* name servers. A real chicken-and-egg problem!

The solution is to include the addresses of the *fx.movie.edu* name servers in *movie.edu*. Although these aren't strictly part of the *movie.edu* zone, delegation to *fx.movie.edu* won't work without them. Of course, if the name servers for *fx.movie.edu* weren't within *fx.movie.edu*, these addresses—called *glue records*—wouldn't be necessary. A foreign name server would be able to find the address it needed by querying other name servers.

We don't have to worry about adding these records, though—the New Delegation Wizard takes care of it for us.

Also, remember to keep the glue up-to-date. If *bladerunner* gets a new network interface, and hence another IP address, you'll need to update the glue data. The DNS console doesn't let you edit the glue records directly, though. You have use the name server modification window. With the DNS console showing a view like Figure 10-5, double-click on an NS record in the right pane to produce a window like the one shown in Figure 10-6.

If *fx.movie.edu*'s delegation changes—i.e., a name server gets added or deleted or a name server's IP address changes—use the **Add**, **Edit**, or **Remove** buttons to make the appropriate changes.

We might also want to include aliases for any hosts moving into *fx.movie.edu* from *movie.edu*. For example, if we move *plan9.movie.edu*, a server with an important library of public-domain special-effects algorithms, into *fx.movie.edu*, we should create an alias under *movie.edu* pointing the old domain name to the new one. In the zone datafile, the record would look like this:

```
plan9    IN  CNAME  plan9.fx.movie.edu.
```

This will allow people outside of *movie.edu* to reach *plan9* even though they're using its old domain name, *plan9.movie.edu*.

Don't get confused about the zone in which this alias belongs. The *plan9* alias record is actually in the *movie.edu* zone, so it belongs in the file *movie.edu.dns*. An alias pointing

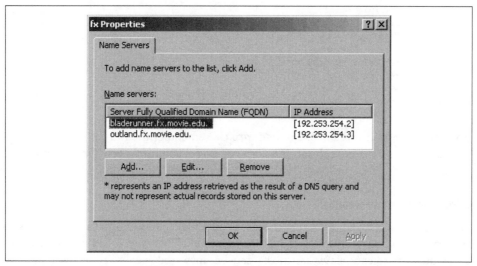

Figure 10-6. Name server modification window

p9.fx.movie.edu to *plan9.fx.movie.edu*, on the other hand, is in the *fx.movie.edu* zone and belongs in *fx.movie.edu.dns*.

Delegating an in-addr.arpa zone

We almost forgot to delegate the *254.253.192.in-addr.arpa* zone! This is a little trickier than delegating *fx.movie.edu* because we don't manage the parent zone.

First, we need to figure out what *254.253.192.in-addr.arpa*'s parent zone is and who runs it. Figuring this out may take some sleuthing; we covered how to do this in Chapter 3.

As it turns out, the *192.in-addr.arpa* zone is *254.253.192.in-addr.arpa*'s parent. And, if you think about it, that makes sense. There's no reason for the administrators of *192.in-addr.arpa* to delegate *253.192.in-addr.arpa* to a separate authority because, unless 192.253/16 is all one big CIDR block, networks like 192.253.253/24 and 192.253.254/24 don't have anything in common with each other. They may be managed by totally unrelated organizations.

To find out who runs *192.in-addr.arpa*, we can use *nslookup* or *whois*, as we demonstrated in Chapter 3. Here's how we'd use *nslookup* to find the administrator:

```
C:\> nslookup
Default Server:  bladerunner.fx.movie.edu
Address:  192.253.254.2

> set type=soa
> set norecurse
> 253.192.in-addr.arpa.
Server:  bladerunner.fx.movie.edu
Address:  192.253.254.2
```

```
192.in-addr.arpa
        primary name server = arrowroot.arin.net
        responsible  mail addr = bind.arin.net
        serial = 2003070219
        refresh = 1800 (30 mins)
        retry = 900 (15 mins)
        expire = 691200 (8 days)
        default TTL = 10800 (3 hours)
>
```

So ARIN is responsible for *192.in-addr.arpa*. (Remember them from Chapter 3?) All that's left is for us to submit the form at *http://www.arin.net/library/templates/ net-end-user.txt* to request registration of our reverse-mapping zone.

Adding a movie.edu secondary

If the special-effects lab gets big enough, it may make sense to put a *movie.edu* secondary somewhere on the 192.253.254/24 network. That way, a larger proportion of DNS queries from *fx.movie.edu* hosts can be answered locally. It seems logical to make one of the existing *fx.movie.edu* name servers into a *movie.edu* secondary, too—that way, we can make better use of an existing name server instead of setting up a brand-new name server.

We've decided to make *bladerunner* a secondary for *movie.edu*. This won't interfere with *bladerunner*'s primary mission as the primary master name server for *fx.movie. edu*. A single name server, given enough memory, can be authoritative for literally thousands of zones. One name server can load some zones as a primary master and others as a secondary.*

The configuration change is simple: we use the DNS console to add a secondary zone to *bladerunner* and tell *bladerunner* to get the *movie.edu* zone data from *terminator*'s IP address, per the instructions in Chapter 4.

Subdomains of in-addr.arpa Domains

Forward-mapping domains aren't the only domains you can divide into subdomains and delegate. If your *in-addr.arpa* namespace is large enough, you may need to divide it, too. Typically, you divide the domain that corresponds to your network number into subdomains that correspond to your subnets. How that works depends on the type of network you have and on your network's subnet mask.

---

* Clearly, though, a name server can't be both the primary master and a secondary for a single zone. The name server gets the data for a given zone either from a local zone datafile (and is a primary master for the zone) or from another name server (and is a secondary for the zone).

Subnetting on an Octet Boundary

Since Movie U. has just three /24 (Class C-sized) networks, one per segment, there's no particular need to subnet those networks. However, our sister university, Altered State, has a Class B-sized network, 172.20/16. Their network is subnetted between the third and fourth octet of the IP address; that is, their subnet mask is 255.255.255. 0. They've already created a number of subdomains of their domain: *altered.edu*, including *fx.altered.edu* (okay, we copied them); *makeup.altered.edu*; and *foley. altered.edu*. Since each of these departments also runs its own subnet (their Special Effects department runs subnet 172.20.2/24, Makeup runs 172.20.15/24, and Foley runs 172.20.25/24), they'd like to divvy up their *in-addr.arpa* namespace appropriately, too.

Delegating *in-addr.arpa* subdomains is no different from delegating subdomains of forward-mapping domains. First, they or their departments create three new zones, *2.20.172.in-addr.arpa*, *15.20.172.in-addr.arpa*, and *25.20.172.in-addr.arpa*. The *20.172.in-addr.arpa* administrators also need to add the NS records with the New Delegation Wizard, as we described in the *fx.movie.edu* example earlier in this chapter. Figure 10-7 shows how the second screen of the New Delegation Wizard would look when adding delegation to the *2.20.172.in-addr.arpa* zone:

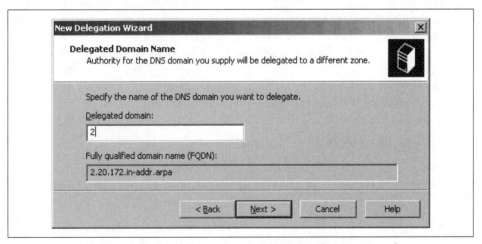

Figure 10-7. Adding reverse-mapping delegation using the New Delegation Wizard

After running the New Delegation Wizard, the NS records in *20.172.in-addr.arpa.dns* would look something like the following partial listing of the file's contents:

```
;
; Delegated sub-zone:  15.20.172.in-addr.arpa.
;
15                              NS      prettywoman.makeup.altered.edu.
prettywoman.makeup.altered.edu. A       172.20.15.2
15                              NS      priscilla.makeup.altered.edu.
```

```
priscilla.makeup.altered.edu.      A       172.20.15.3
; End delegation


;
; Delegated sub-zone:  2.20.172.in-addr.arpa.
;
2                                  NS      gump.fx.altered.edu.
gump.fx.altered.edu.               A       172.20.2.1
2                                  NS      toystory.fx.altered.edu.
toystory.fx.altered.edu.           A       172.20.2.5
; End delegation


;
; Delegated sub-zone:  25.20.172.in-addr.arpa.
;
25                                 NS      blowup.foley.altered.edu.
blowup.foley.altered.edu.          A       172.20.25.10
25                                 NS      muppetshow.foley.altered.edu.
muppetshow.foley.altered.edu.      A       172.20.25.2
; End delegation
```

The Altered State administrators needed to use the fully qualified domain names of the name servers in the NS records because the default origin in this file is *20.172.in-addr.arpa*. Strictly speaking, those glue address records aren't needed since the names of the name servers to which they delegated the zone weren't in the delegated zones. We were a little chagrined to discover that the DNS console forced us to enter IP addresses for these name servers and then put them in *20.172.in-addr.arpa.dns*. The name server even includes them in a zone transfer of the *20.172.in-addr.arpa* zone. Since the glue records are not required, all that is unnecessary.

Subnetting on a Nonoctet Boundary

What do you do about networks that aren't subnetted neatly on octet boundaries, like subnetted /24 (Class C-sized) networks? In these cases, you can't delegate along lines that match the subnets. This forces you into one of two situations: you have multiple subnets per *in-addr.arpa* zone or you have multiple *in-addr.arpa* zones per subnet. Neither is particularly pleasing.

Class A and B networks

Let's take the case of the /8 (Class A-sized) network 15/8, subnetted with the subnet mask 255.255.248.0 (a 13-bit subnet field and an 11-bit host field, or 8,192 subnets of 2,048 hosts). In this case, the subnet 15.1.200.0, for example, extends from 15.1.200.0 to 15.1.207.255. Therefore, the delegation for that single subdomain in *db.15*, the zone datafile for *15.in-addr.arpa*, might look like this:

```
200.1      NS      ns-1.cns.hp.com.
200.1      NS      ns-2.cns.hp.com.
```

```
201.1       NS      ns-1.cns.hp.com.
201.1       NS      ns-2.cns.hp.com.
202.1       NS      ns-1.cns.hp.com.
202.1       NS      ns-2.cns.hp.com.
203.1       NS      ns-1.cns.hp.com.
203.1       NS      ns-2.cns.hp.com.
204.1       NS      ns-1.cns.hp.com.
204.1       NS      ns-2.cns.hp.com.
205.1       NS      ns-1.cns.hp.com.
205.1       NS      ns-2.cns.hp.com.
206.1       NS      ns-1.cns.hp.com.
206.1       NS      ns-2.cns.hp.com.
207.1       NS      ns-1.cns.hp.com.
207.1       NS      ns-2.cns.hp.com.
```

That's a lot of delegation for one subnet!

You'd set this up with the DNS console by running the New Delegation Wizard (eight times!) and specifying two labels of the domain name of the delegated domain, as shown in Figure 10-8.

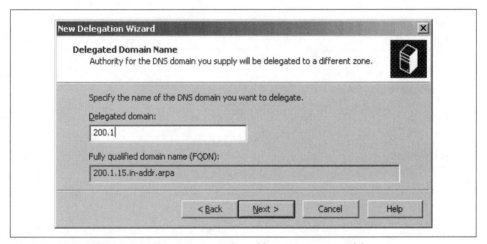

Figure 10-8. Using the New Delegation Wizard to add reverse-mapping delegation

/24 (Class C-sized) networks

In the case of a subnetted /24 (Class C-sized) network, say 192.253.254/24, subnetted with the mask 255.255.255.192, you have a single *in-addr.arpa* zone, *254.253.192.in-addr.arpa*, that corresponds to subnets 192.253.254.0/26, 192.253.254.64/26, 192.253.254.128/26, and 192.253.254.192/26. This can be a problem if you want to let different organizations manage the reverse-mapping information that corresponds to each subnet. You can solve this in one of three ways, none of which is pretty.

Solution 1. The first solution is to administer the *254.253.192.in-addr.arpa* zone as a single entity and not even try to delegate. This requires either cooperation between the administrators of the four subnets involved or the use of a tool like the DNS console to allow each of the four administrators to take care of her own data.

Solution 2. The second solution is to delegate at the *fourth* octet. That's even nastier than the /8 delegation we just showed. You'll need at least a couple of NS records per IP address. To set this up with the DNS console, you'd need to create the *254.253.192.in-addr.arpa* zone and run the New Delegation Wizard 254 times, one for each usable value in the fourth octet. Here's how the *254.253.192.in-addr.arpa.dns* file might end up looking (we've removed the unnecessary glue A records for clarity and brevity):

```
;
; Delegated sub-zone:  1.254.253.192.in-addr.arpa.
;
1                 NS           ns1.foo.com.
ns1.foo.com.      A      10.0.0.1
1                 NS           ns2.foo.com.
ns2.foo.com.      A      10.0.0.2
; End delegation


;
; Delegated sub-zone:  2.254.253.192.in-addr.arpa.
;
2                 NS           ns1.foo.com.
ns1.foo.com.      A      10.0.0.1
2                 NS           ns2.foo.com.
ns2.foo.com.      A      10.0.0.2
; End delegation


. . .


; Delegated sub-zone:  65.254.253.192.in-addr.arpa.
;
65                NS           gw.bar.com.
gw.bar.com.       A      10.0.1.1
65                NS           relay.bar.com.
relay.bar.com.    A      10.0.1.2
; End delegation

; Delegated sub-zone:  66.254.253.192.in-addr.arpa.
;
66                  NS         gw.bar.com.
gw.bar.com.     A      10.0.1.1
66                  NS         relay.bar.com.
relay.bar.com.  A      10.0.1.2
; End delegation


. . .
```

```
;
; Delegated sub-zone:  129.254.253.192.in-addr.arpa.
;
129                         NS            mail.baz.com.
mail.baz.com.      A     10.0.2.1
129                         NS            www.baz.com.
www.baz.com.       A     10.0.2.2
;  End delegation


;
; Delegated sub-zone:  193.254.253.192.in-addr.arpa.
;
193                         NS            mail.baz.com.
mail.baz.com.      A     10.0.2.1
192                         NS            www.baz.com.
www.baz.com.       A     10.0.2.2
;  End delegation
```

And so on, all the way down to *254.254.253.192.in-addr.arpa*. Of course, on *ns1.foo. com*, you'd also expect the name server to be authoritative for *1.254.253.192.in-addr. arpa*, and in the zone datafile for *1.254.253.192.in-addr.arpa*, you'd find just the one PTR record (plus an SOA and two NS records):

```
;
;  Database file 1.254.253.192.in-addr.arpa.dns for 1.254.253.192.in-addr.arpa zone.
;      Zone version:  4
;

@                          IN  SOA ns1.foo.com.  hostmaster.foo.com. (
                           4              ; serial number
                           900            ; refresh
                           600            ; retry
                           86400          ; expire
                           3600         ) ; default TTL


;
;  Zone NS records
;

@                          NS    ns1.foo.com.
ns1.foo.com.               A 10.0.0.1
@                          NS  ns2.foo.com.
ns2.foo.com.               A    10.0.0.2


;
;  Zone records
;

@                          PTR    thereitis.foo.com.
```

When you create the child zone with the DNS console, check the radio button labeled **Reverse lookup zone name** in the New Zone Wizard, since with **Network ID** checked, you can't enter all four octets of the IP address.

Note that the PTR record is attached to the zone's domain name, since the zone's domain name corresponds to just one IP address. Now, when a *254.253.192.in-addr.arpa* name server receives a query for the PTR record for *1.254.253.192.in-addr.arpa*, it will refer the querier to *ns1.foo.com* and *ns2.foo.com*, which will respond with the one PTR record in the zone.

Solution 3. Finally, there's a clever technique that obviates the need to maintain a separate zone datafile for each IP address.* The organization responsible for the over-all /24 network creates CNAME records for each of the domain names in the zone, pointing to domain names in new subdomains, which are then delegated to the proper servers. These new subdomains can be called just about anything, but names like *0-63*, *64-127*, *128-191*, and *192-255* clearly indicate the range of addresses each subdomain will reverse map. Each subdomain then contains only the PTR records in the range for which the subdomain is named.

Here is an excerpt from the *254.253.192.in-addr.arpa.dns* file:

```
;
;   Delegated sub-zone:  0-63.254.253.192.in-addr.arpa.
;

0-63                 NS        ns1.foo.com.
ns1.foo.com.         A 10.0.0.1
0-63                 NS        ns2.foo.com.
ns2.foo.com.         A 10.0.0.2
;   End delegation

1                    CNAME     1.0-63.254.253.192.in-addr.arpa.
...


;
;   Delegated sub-zone:  128-191.254.253.192.in-addr.arpa.
;

128-191              NS        mail.baz.com.
mail.baz.com.        A 10.0.2.1
128-191              NS        www.baz.com.
www.baz.com.         A 10.0.2.2
;   End delegation

129                  CNAME     129.128.191.254.253.192.in-addr.arpa.
130                  CNAME     130.128-191.254.253.192.in-addr.arpa.
2                    CNAME     2.0-63.254.253.192.in-addr.arpa.
...


;
```

---

* We first saw this explained by Glen Herrmansfeldt at CalTech in the newsgroup *comp.protocols.tcp-ip. domains*. It's now codified as RFC 2317.

```
;  Delegated sub-zone:  64-127.254.253.192.in-addr.arpa.
;

64-127                     NS        relay.bar.com.
relay.bar.com.            A 10.0.1.1
64-127                     NS        gw.bar.com.
gw.bar.com.               A 10.0.1.2
;  End delegation

65                         CNAME     65.64-127.254.253.192.in-addr.arpa.
66                         CNAME     66.64-127.254.253.192.in-addr.arpa.
...
```

The zone datafile for *0-63.254.253.192.in-addr.arpa, 0-63.254.253.192.in-addr. arpa.dns*, can contain just PTR records for IP addresses 192.253.254.1 through 192.253.254.63.

Here is part of the *0-63.254.253.192.in-addr.arpa.dns* file:

```
;
;  Database file 0-63.254.253.192.in-addr.arpa.dns for 0-63.254.253.192.in-addr.arpa
zone.
;      Zone version:  3
;

@                         IN  SOA ns1.foo.com.  hostmaster.foo.com. (
                          3               ; serial number
                          900             ; refresh
                          600             ; retry
                          86400           ; expire
                          3600          ) ; default TTL


;
;  Zone NS records
;

@                         NS      ns1.foo.com.
@                         NS   ns2.foo.com.


;
;  Zone records
;

1                         PTR     thereitis.foo.com.
2                         PTR     setter.foo.com.
...
```

The way this setup works is a little tricky, so let's go over it. A resolver requests the PTR record for *1.254.253.192.in-addr.arpa*, causing its local name server to go look up that record. The local name server ends up asking a *254.253.192.in-addr.arpa* name server, which will respond with the CNAME record indicating that *1.254.253. 192.in-addr.arpa* is actually an alias for *1.0-63.254.253.192.in-addr.arpa* and that the PTR record is attached to that name. The response will also include NS records telling the local name server that the authoritative name servers for *0-63.254.253.192.in-addr.arpa* are *ns1.foo.com* and *ns2.foo.com*. The local name server then queries either *ns1.foo.com* or *ns2.foo.com* for the PTR record for *1.0-63.254.253.192.in-addr.arpa* and receives the PTR record.

Good Parenting

Now that the delegation to the *fx.movie.edu* name servers is in place, we—responsible parents that we are—should check that delegation using *DNSLint*, available with the Windows Server 2003 Support Tools.

DNSLint makes it easy to check delegation. With *DNSLint,* you can look up the NS records for your zone on one of your zone's authoritative name servers and query each name server listed for the zone's SOA record. The query is nonrecursive, so the name server queried doesn't query other name servers to find the SOA record. If the name server replies, *DNSLint* checks the reply to see whether the *aa* (authoritative answer) bit in the reply packet is set. If it is, the name server checks to make sure that the packet contains an answer. If both these criteria are met, the name server is flagged as authoritative for the zone. Otherwise, the name server is not authoritative, and *DNSLint* reports an error.

Why all the fuss over bad delegation? Incorrect delegation can slow name resolution or cause the propagation of old and erroneous root name server information. When a name server is queried for data in a zone for which it is not authoritative, it does its best to provide useful information to the querier. This "useful information" comes in the form of NS records for the closest ancestor zone the name server knows. (We mentioned this briefly in Chapter 9, when we discussed why you shouldn't register a caching-only name server.)

For example, say one of the *fx.movie.edu* name servers mistakenly receives an iterative query for the address of *carrie.horror.movie.edu*. It knows nothing about the *horror.movie.edu* zone (except for what it might have cached), but it likely has NS records for *movie.edu* cached since those are its parent name servers. So it would return those records to the querier.

In that scenario, the NS records may help the querying name server get an answer. However, it's a fact of life on the Internet that not all administrators keep their root hints files up-to-date. If one of your name servers follows a bad delegation and queries a remote name server for records it doesn't have, look what can happen:

```
C:\> nslookup
Default Server:  terminator.movie.edu
Address:  192.249.249.3
> set type=ns
> .
Server:  terminator.movie.edu
Address:  192.249.249.3
```

```
Non-authoritative answer:
(root)   nameserver = D.ROOT-SERVERS.NET
(root)   nameserver = E.ROOT-SERVERS.NET
(root)   nameserver = I.ROOT-SERVERS.NET
(root)   nameserver = F.ROOT-SERVERS.NET
(root)   nameserver = G.ROOT-SERVERS.NET
(root)   nameserver = A.ROOT-SERVERS.NET
(root)   nameserver = H.ROOT-SERVERS.NETNIC.NORDU.NET
(root)   nameserver = B.ROOT-SERVERS.NET
(root)   nameserver = C.ROOT-SERVERS.NET
(root)   nameserver = A.ISI.EDU              These three name
(root)   nameserver = SRI-NIC.ARPA          servers are no longer
(root)   nameserver = GUNTER-ADAM.ARPA      roots.
```

A remote name server tried to "help out" our local name server by sending it the current list of roots. Unfortunately, the remote name server was corrupt and returned NS records that were incorrect. And our local name server, not knowing any better, cached that data.

Queries to misconfigured *in-addr.arpa* name servers often result in bad root NS records because the *in-addr.arpa* and *arpa* zones are the closest ancestors of most *in-addr.arpa* subdomains, and name servers very seldom cache either *in-addr.arpa*'s or *arpa*'s NS records. (The roots rarely give them out since they delegate directly to lower-level subdomains.) Once your name server has cached bad root NS records, your name resolution will almost certainly suffer: your name server won't be contacting the "official" root name servers, and who knows what information they will hand out?

Those root NS records may have your name server querying a root name server that is no longer at that IP address or a root name server that no longer exists at all. If you're having an especially bad day, the bad root NS records may point to a real, non-root name server that is close to your network. Even though it won't return authoritative root zone data, your name server will favor it because of its proximity to your network.

Using DNSLint

If our little lecture has convinced you of the importance of maintaining correct delegation, you'll be eager to learn how to use *DNSLint* to ensure that you don't join the ranks of the miscreants.

The first step is to use *nslookup* to look up your zone's NS records on a name server for your parent zone and make sure they're correct. Here's how we'd check the *fx.movie.edu* NS records on one of the *movie.edu* name servers:

```
C:\> nslookup -type=ns fx.movie.edu. terminator.movie.edu.
```

If everything's okay with the NS records, we'll simply see the NS records in the output:

```
fx.movie.edu      nameserver = bladerunner.fx.movie.edu
fx.movie.edu      nameserver = outland.fx.movie.edu
```

This tells us that all the NS records delegating *fx.movie.edu* from *terminator.movie.edu* are correct.

Next, we'll use *DNSLint*'s "lame delegation check" mode to query each of the name servers in the NS records for the *fx.movie.edu* zone's SOA record. This will also check whether the response was authoritative:

```
C:\> dnslint /d fx.movie.edu. -s 192.249.253.2
```

We have to use the */s* switch to tell *DNSLint* the IP address of one of the authoritative name servers for *fx.movie.edu*. Normally it would get this from *whois*, but *whois* doesn't contain information about zones as far down in the namespace as *fx.movie.edu*.

This command produces HTML output that tells us the status of the *fx.movie.edu* name servers. Here's the text equivalent of that output (which you get by using *DNSLint*'s */t* switch):

```
DNSLint Report

System Date: Sat Jul 05 18:58:05 2003

Command run:

dnslint /d fx.movie.edu /t /s 192.253.254.2


Domain name tested:

fx.movie.edu


DNS servers were identified as authoritative for the domain:


DNS server: bladerunner.fx.movie.edu
IP Address: 192.253.254.2
UDP port 53 responding to queries: YES
TCP port 53 responding to queries: Not tested
Answering authoritatively for domain: YES

SOA record data from server:
Authoritative name server: bladerunner.fx.movie.edu
Hostmaster: administrator.fx.movie.edu
Zone serial number: 10
Zone expires in: 1.00 day(s)
Refresh period: 900 seconds
Retry delay: 600 seconds
Default (minimum) TTL: 3600 seconds
```

```
Additional authoritative (NS) records from server:
outland.fx.movie.edu    192.253.254.3
bladerunner.fx.movie.edu    192.253.254.2


Mail Exchange (MX) records from server (preference/name/IP address):
100 wormhole.movie.edu 192.253.253.1
10 starwars.fx.movie.edu 192.253.254.4

DNS server: outland.fx.movie.edu
IP Address: 192.253.254.3
UDP port 53 responding to queries: YES
TCP port 53 responding to queries: Not tested
Answering authoritatively for domain: YES

SOA record data from server:
Authoritative name server: bladerunner.fx.movie.edu
Hostmaster: administrator.fx..movie.edu
Zone serial number: 10
Zone expires in: 1.00 day(s)
Refresh period: 900 seconds
Retry delay: 600 seconds
Default (minimum) TTL: 3600 seconds

Additional authoritative (NS) records from server:
outland.fx.movie.edu    192.253.254.3
bladerunner.fx.movie.edu    192.253.254.2


Mail Exchange (MX) records from server (preference/name/IP address):
10 starwars.fx.movie.edu 192.253.254.4
100 wormhole.movie.edu 192.253.253.1
---------------------------------------------
```

If one of the *fx.movie.edu* name servers—*outland*, for example—were misconfigured, we might see this:

```
DNS server: outland.fx.movie.edu
IP Address: 192.253.254.3
UDP port 53 responding to queries: YES
TCP port 53 responding to queries: Not tested
Answering authoritatively for domain: NO

SOA record data from server:
Authoritative name server: Unknown
Hostmaster: Unknown
Zone serial number: Unknown
Zone expires in: Unknown
Refresh period: Unknown
Retry delay: Unknown
Default (minimum) TTL: Unknown
```

This indicates that the name server on *outland* is running, but it's not authoritative for *fx.movie.edu*.

If one of the *fx.movie.edu* name servers weren't running at all, we'd see:

```
DNS server: outland.fx.movie.edu
IP Address: 192.253.254.3
UDP port 53 responding to queries: NO
TCP port 53 responding to queries: Not tested
Answering authoritatively for domain: Unknown

SOA record data from server:
Authoritative name server: Unknown
Hostmaster: Unknown
Zone serial number: Unknown
Zone expires in: Unknown
Refresh period: Unknown
Retry delay: Unknown
Default (minimum) TTL: Unknown
```

In this case, the UDP port 53 responding to queries: NO message indicates that *DNSLint* sent *outland* a query and didn't get a response back in an acceptable amount of time.

Although we could have checked the *fx.movie.edu* delegation using *nslookup*, *DNSLint* makes the task especially easy. We'll see more of *DNSLint* in Chapter 15.

Managing Delegation

If the special-effects lab gets bigger, we may find that we need additional name servers. We dealt with setting up new name servers in Chapter 9 and even went over what information to send to the parent zone's administrator. But we never explained what the parent needed to do.

It turns out that the parent's job is relatively easy, especially if the administrators of the subdomain send complete information. Imagine that the special-effects lab expands to a new network, 192.254.20/24. They have a passel of new, high-powered graphics workstations. One of them, *alien.fx.movie.edu*, will act as the new network's name server.

The administrators of *fx.movie.edu* (we delegated it to the folks in the lab) send their parent zone's administrators (that's us) a short note:

```
Hi!

We've just set up alien.fx.movie.edu (192.254.20.3) as a name server for
fx.movie.edu.
Would you please update your delegation information?  I've attached the NS
records you'll need to add.

Thanks,

Arty Segue
ajs@fx.movie.edu

----- cut here -----
```

```
fx.movie.edu.   86400   IN   NS   bladerunner.fx.movie.edu.
fx.movie.edu.   86400   IN   NS   outland.fx.movie.edu.
fx.movie.edu.   86400   IN   NS   alien.fx.movie.edu.

bladerunner.fx.movie.edu.   86400   IN   A   192.253.254.2
outland.fx.movie.edu.       86400   IN   A   192.253.254.3
alien.fx.movie.edu.         86400   IN   A   192.254.20.3
```

Our job as the *movie.edu* administrator is straightforward: add the NS and A records to *movie.edu*. Once again, it's the New Delegation Wizard to the rescue: select the gray *fx.movie.edu* folder in the DNS console's left pane and then double-click on any of the NS records in the right pane. You'll see a window like the one shown previously in Figure 10-6. Select **Add** to add the new NS record for *alien.fx.movie.edu*.

The final step for the *fx.movie.edu* administrator is to send a similar message to *hostmaster@arin.net* (administrator of the *192.in-addr.arpa* zone), requesting that the *20. 254.192.in-addr.arpa* subdomain be delegated to *alien.fx.movie.edu*, *bladerunner.fx. movie.edu*, and *outland.fx.movie.edu*.

Managing delegation with stubs

In the Windows Server 2003 version of the Microsoft DNS Server, Microsoft now supports *stub zones*, which offer an automatic way to track changes to delegation. A name server that's configured as a stub for a zone periodically sends discrete queries for the zone's SOA and NS records, as well as any necessary glue A records. The name server then uses the NS records to delegate the zone from its parent, and the SOA record governs how often the name server sends these queries. Now, when the administrators of a subdomain make changes to the subdomain's name servers, they simply update their NS records (and increment the serial number in the SOA record, of course). The parent zone's authoritative name servers, configured as stub for the child zone, pick up the updated records within the refresh interval.

To make the *movie.edu* name servers stubs for *fx.movie.edu*, we'd right-click on **Forward Lookup Zones** in the left pane of the DNS console and choose **New Zone**. In the second window of the New Zone Wizard, we'd choose **Stub zone**, as shown in Figure 10-9.

The next window would prompt us for the name of the stub zone, *fx.movie.edu*, and the following for the name of the zone datafile, where we'll accept the default. In the next-to-last window, we'll add the address of an authoritative name server for *fx.movie.edu*, which our stub name server can query for the full list of the zone's NS records. (We can list more than one authoritative name server for robustness, if we like.)

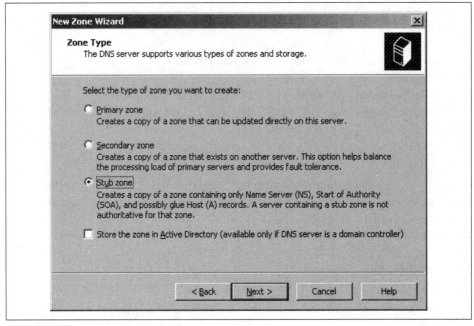

Figure 10-9. Adding a stub zone

Note that we must configure all *movie.edu* name servers—including secondaries—as stubs for *fx.movie.edu*. Since the *fx.movie.edu* NS records are part of the *fx.movie.edu* zone, they won't be included in *movie.edu* zone transfers.

Managing the Transition to Subdomains

We won't lie to you—the *fx.movie.edu* example we showed you was unrealistic for several reasons. The main one is the magical appearance of the special-effects lab's hosts. In the real world, the lab would have started out with a few hosts, probably in the *movie.edu* zone. After a generous endowment, an NSF grant, or a corporate gift, they might expand the lab a little and buy a few more computers. Sooner or later, the lab would have enough hosts to warrant the creation of a new subdomain. By that point, however, many of the original hosts would be well known by their names under *movie.edu*.

We briefly touched on using CNAME records in the parent zone (in our *plan9.movie. edu* example) to help people adjust to a host's change of domain. But what happens when you move a whole network or subnet into a new subdomain?

The strategy we recommend uses CNAME records in much the same way, but on a larger scale. Using the DNS console, you can create CNAMEs for hosts. This allows users to continue using the old domain names for any of the hosts that have moved.

When they *telnet* or *ftp* (or whatever) to those hosts, however, the command will report that they're connected to a host in *fx.movie.edu*:

```
C:\> telnet plan9

Trying...
Connected to plan9.fx.movie.edu.
Escape character is '^]'.

HP-UX plan9.fx.movie.edu A.09.05 C 9000/735 (ttyu1)

login:
```

Some users, of course, don't notice subtle changes like this, so you should also do some public relations work and notify folks of the change.

How do you create all these aliases? Well, you could do it manually using the DNS console, CNAME record by CNAME record. Or you could use a Perl script to create CNAME records for every host in *fx.movie.edu.dns:*

```
#
# Simple Perl script to create aliases
# Run with <script> <domain name of child zone>
#
die "Usage: $0 <child zone>\n" if $#ARGV!=0;

open(ZDF, "$ARGV[0].dns") || die "Couldn't open $ARGV[0]: $!\n";

($label, $parent) = split(/\./, $ARGV[0], 2);
$parent .= ".dns";

open(PZDF, ">>$parent") || die "Couldn't open $parent: $!\n";

while (<ZDF>) {
        if (/\s+IN\s+A\s+/) {
            ($host, $rest) = split(/[\s\.]/, $_, 2);
            printf PZDF "%s  IN  CNAME  %s.%s.\n", $host, $host, $ARGV[0];
        }
};
```

Removing Parent Aliases

Although parent-level aliases are useful for minimizing the impact of moving your hosts, they're also a crutch of sorts. Like a crutch, they'll restrict your freedom. They'll clutter up your parent namespace when one of your motivations for implementing a subdomain may have been making the parent zone smaller. And they'll prevent you from using the names of hosts in the subdomain as names for hosts in the parent zone.

After a grace period—which should be well advertised to users—you should remove all the aliases, with the possible exception of aliases for extremely well-known Internet hosts. During the grace period, users can adjust to the new domain names and modify scripts and the like. But don't get suckered into leaving all those aliases in the parent zone; they defeat part of the purpose of DNS because they prevent you and your subdomain administrator from naming hosts autonomously.

You might want to leave CNAME records for well-known Internet hosts or central network resources intact because of the potential impact of a loss of connectivity. On the other hand, rather than moving the well-known host or central resource into a subdomain at all, it might be better to leave it at the parent zone level.

The Life of a Parent

That's a lot of parental advice to digest in one sitting, so let's recap the highlights of what we've talked about. The life cycle of a typical parent goes something like this:

1. You have a single zone with all of your hosts in that zone.
2. You break your zone into a number of subdomains, some of them in the same zone as the parent, if necessary. You provide CNAME records in the parent zone for well-known hosts that have moved into subdomains.
3. After a grace period, you delete any remaining CNAME records.
4. You handle subdomain delegation updates, either manually or by using stubs, and periodically check delegation.

Okay, now that you know all there is to parenting, let's go on to talk about more advanced name server features. You may need some of these tools to keep those kids in line.

## CHAPTER 11

Advanced Features and Security

"What's the use of their having names," the Gnat
said, "if they won't answer to them?"

In this chapter, we'll cover some of the Microsoft DNS Server's more advanced features and suggest how they might come in handy in your DNS infrastructure. We cover some new ways to make changes to zone data, how DNS is linked with WINS and what to do about it, load balancing, using forwarders to set up a sitewide cache, and IPv6. We cover DNS security as well, though we save some of the hardcore firewall material for Chapter 16.

New Ways to Make Changes

In Chapter 4 we described the traditional method for making changes to zone data and how those changes are propagated: any changes to a zone are made on the zone's primary server, and secondary servers periodically poll the primary to check if the zone has changed. If the zone has new information, the secondaries perform a zone transfer to download the entire zone. This scheme is effective but inefficient and it's not suitable for every environment. The DNS console is great for making changes by hand, but what about automated changes (say you want to have a program change information in a zone)? It can also be frustrating to wait for all the secondaries to be updated with the new information. And for a large zone, it's a waste of time and bandwidth to transfer the entire zone if only a single record was added or deleted.

The next three sections describe relatively recent changes to the DNS protocol called dynamic update, NOTIFY, and incremental zone transfer that work together to address these issues. The Microsoft DNS Server implements all three.

Dynamic Update

Dynamic update was implemented in the Microsoft DNS Server starting with Windows 2000. Like many other protocols used by Windows, it's an Internet standard, defined in RFC 2136. Dynamic update allows a name server to be updated by sending it a message over the network. This is a big improvement over the traditional method, which requires a human to fire up the DNS console to make the change in person. Dynamic update allows nonhumans—i.e., programs—to easily update DNS information. Dynamic update is now used extensively in Windows: a modern Windows client uses it to add an A record to DNS for its IP address and recent Windows DHCP servers also use dynamic update to add PTR records as they assign leases.

No security is built into the dynamic update protocol. It's up to an individual name server to decide whether or not to accept an update message. About the only means of authentication a name server has is to look at the source IP address of the dynamic update message, and that's not a very strong means of authentication at all: it's easy to "spoof" or forge a packet's source IP address. And since a complete dynamic update message travels in a single UDP packet, all an attacker needs to know is an IP address that the name server accepting dynamic updates trusts. The Bad Guy just creates a dynamic update with a spoofed source IP address and sends it to the unsuspecting name server.

This deficiency begs for some stronger security based on cryptography, which fortunately has been developed. The DNS standards community developed a protocol extension to use *transaction signatures* to sign any kind of DNS message—including dynamic updates—sent between two parties: client to server, server to server, dynamic updater to server, etc.

The transaction signatures, or TSIGs for short, in DNS use a technique called HMAC—Keyed-Hashing for Message Authentication (see RFC 2104)—which employs a shared secret and a one-way cryptographic hash function to sign data. A shared secret is like a password known only to the two parties involved in exchanging data. A one-way cryptographic hash function computes a fixed-size checksum based on any amount of input. What differentiates a cryptographic hash function, such as MD5 or SHA1, from a run-of-the-mill checksum, such as a CRC (Cyclic Redundancy Check), is that it's computationally infeasible to find two different input streams that produce the same hash output. With a CRC checksum, on the other hand, the algorithm is easily reversible: given any checksum, it's trivial to calculate an input stream to generate that checksum. Another property of a good cryptographic hash function is that varying the input by even a small amount—such as changing just one bit—produces a major change in the hash output. In other words, the hash output is like a fingerprint of the original input.

A transaction signature is so-named because it's ephemeral: the signature applies only to a single transaction and is not reusable. Let's say a client wants to send a dynamic update signed with a TSIG to the appropriate name server. After generating the dynamic update message, it appends the secret it shares with the server to the message and runs everything through MD5. The output is the TSIG itself, which is placed into a TSIG resource record that goes in the dynamic update message. Since TSIGs are generated on the fly like this, you see a TSIG record only on a packet sniffer, never in the DNS console or a zone datafile. Note that TSIG doesn't encrypt the data being sent: it only authenticates it. HMAC is illustrated in Figure 11-1.

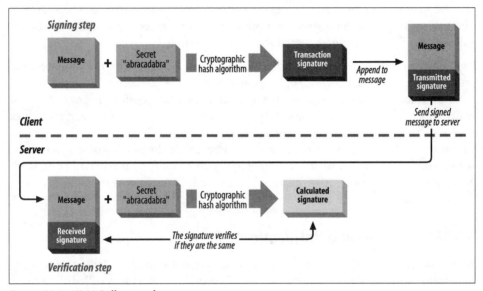

Figure 11-1. HMAC illustrated

One difficulty with TSIG is distributing the shared secrets. Imagine having hundreds of clients that need to send TSIG-signed dynamic updates to a name server: that would require generating hundreds of keys and distributing them securely to each client. Microsoft found itself in just such a predicament. As we discussed in Chapter 8, individual Windows clients do send dynamic updates to name servers. TSIG is a requirement for these transactions to happen securely, but it's not feasible to statically configure shared secrets on each Windows client. The solution: Kerberos to the rescue!

Windows Server 2003 (and Windows 2000 before it) uses Kerberos for authentication and authorization. Kerberos allows two parties who want to communicate securely to negotiate the necessary information to do so. Every Windows Server 2003 domain controller is a Kerberos Key Distribution Center, or KDC. Every modern Windows client and server is a Kerberos "principal." Every Kerberos principal shares a secret with the KDC. (This shared secret is generated when the host is joined to the domain.) The KDC acts as a trusted third party that allows two principals to communicate securely. For example, suppose a client named Alice wants to send an encrypted message to a client named Bob. Alice asks the KDC to help negotiate a session key* with Bob. Alice and Bob don't (yet) trust each other, but they do trust the KDC, which facilitates distributing the session key to each of them. This explanation is quite an oversimplification of how Kerberos actually works, but it does show the underlying concepts.

Microsoft extended TSIG in Windows to use Kerberos. A Windows client that wants to send a TSIG-signed dynamic update message to a name server doesn't have to be statically configured to share a secret with that server. The client uses Kerberos to obtain a session key, which serves as a one-time shared secret. This variant of TSIG is called GSS-TSIG and is documented in an Internet-Draft.†

The Microsoft DNS Server supports GSS-TSIG for securing dynamic updates, but only for zones that are AD-integrated (stored in Active Directory as opposed to a zone datafile). GSS-TSIG-secured dynamic updates allow quite fine-grained access control to a zone's contents. For example, the server can allow only the specific host that added an A record for itself to change or remove that record. This extra authorization can't be stored in a zone datafile—there aren't the necessary fields—so the server needs to store a zone in Active Directory to support secure dynamic updates. More information about AD-integrated zones and secure dynamic updates can be found in Chapter 8.

NOTIFY (Zone Change Notification)

As we described earlier, secondaries have traditionally used a polling scheme to determine when they need a zone transfer. The polling interval is called the *refresh time* and it's specified as a field in a zone's SOA record. Other parameters in the zone's SOA record govern other aspects of the polling mechanism.

But this scheme requires the secondaries to ask the primary, "Has the zone changed yet?", over and over. Wouldn't it be nice if the primary name server could tell its secondary servers when the information in a zone changed? After all, the primary name server knows the data has changed: every time a zone is changed with the DNS console or a dynamic update message is received, the server immediately changes the zone in its memory. The primary's notification can come soon after the actual modification instead of waiting for the refresh interval to expire.

RFC 1996 describes a mechanism that allows primary servers to notify their secondaries of changes to a zone's data. The Microsoft DNS Server implements this protocol, called NOTIFY for short.

---

* As the name implies, a session key is a short-lived key usually used for a single conversation.

† GSS stands for Generic Security Service. At the time of this writing, GSS-TSIG was not yet an Internet standard but was on track to become one. Internet-Drafts may be found at *http://www.ietf.org/1id-abstracts.html/*.

NOTIFY works like this: when a primary name server notices a change to data in a zone, it sends a special notification message to all secondary servers for that zone. It uses the list of NS records in the zone to build the list of servers to notify. The primary removes any NS record corresponding to the local host, which prevents it from sending a notification message to itself. You can also override using the list of NS records and specify your own list of secondary servers to notify.

The special NOTIFY request is identified by its opcode in the query header. The opcode for most queries is QUERY. NOTIFY messages have a special opcode, NOTIFY. Other than that, the request looks much like a query for the SOA record for the zone: it specifies the zone's domain name, class, and a type of SOA.

When a secondary receives a NOTIFY request for a zone from one of its configured master name servers, it sends a NOTIFY response. The response tells the master that the secondary received the NOTIFY request and to stop sending NOTIFY messages for the zone. Then the secondary proceeds just as if the zone's refresh timer had expired: it queries the master server for the SOA record for the zone the master claimed had changed. If the serial number is higher, the secondary performs the zone transfer, using an incremental zone transfer if possible (see the next section for details on this new kind of zone transfer).

Why doesn't the secondary simply take the master's word that the zone has changed? It's possible that a miscreant could forge NOTIFY requests to our secondaries, causing lots of unnecessary zone transfers that might amount to a denial-of-service attack against our master server.

If the secondary actually transfers the zone, RFC 1996 says that it should issue its own NOTIFY requests to the other authoritative name servers for the zone. The idea is that the primary may not be able to notify all the secondary servers for the zone itself, since it's possible that some secondaries can't communicate directly with the primary and so use another secondary as their master. The Microsoft DNS Server follows this behavior if NOTIFY is enabled for a secondary zone (it's disabled by default for secondary zones) and you don't list a specific set of name servers to NOTIFY.

Here's how this process works in practice: on our network, *terminator.movie.edu* is the primary for *movie.edu*, and *wormhole.movie.edu* and *zardoz.movie.edu* are secondaries (as shown in Figure 11-2).

When we update *movie.edu* on *terminator*, *terminator* sends NOTIFY messages to *wormhole* and *zardoz*. Both secondaries check to see whether *movie.edu*'s serial number has been incremented and, if they find it has, perform a zone transfer.

Let's also look at a more complicated zone transfer scheme. In Figure 11-3, *a* is the primary name server for the zone and *b*'s master server, but *b* is *c*'s master server. Moreover, *b* has two network interfaces.

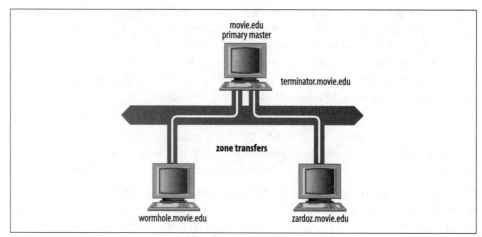

Figure 11-2. movie.edu zone transfer example

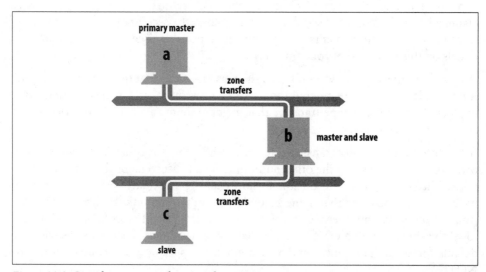

Figure 11-3. Complex zone transfer example

In this scenario, *a* notifies both *b* and *c* after the zone is updated. *b* checks to see whether the zone's serial number has been incremented and initiates a zone transfer. However, *c* ignores *a*'s NOTIFY message because *a* is not *c*'s configured master name server (*b* is). If *b* is explicitly configured to notify *c*, after *b*'s zone transfer completes it sends *c* a NOTIFY message, which prompts *c* to check the serial number *b* holds for the zone.

Older BIND secondary name servers, and other name servers that don't support NOTIFY, respond with a "Not Implemented" (NOTIMP) error, wait until their refresh timers expire, and then transfer the zone. The Microsoft DNS Server just ignores the NOTIMP error.

NOTIFY is controlled on a zone-by-zone basis and is enabled by default for primary zones (and disabled by default for secondary zones). The controls for NOTIFY are somewhat hidden: highlight a zone in DNS console's left pane, select **Action** → **Properties**, and choose the **Zone Transfers** tab of the zone properties window, which produces a window like the one shown in Figure 11-4.

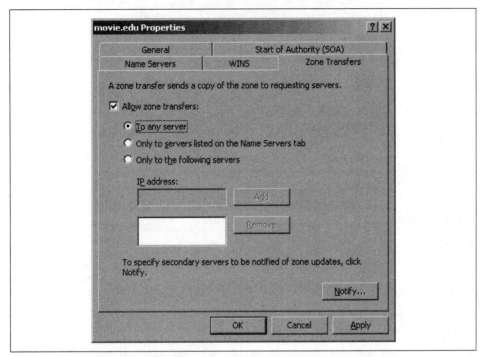

Figure 11-4. Zone transfer configuration for movie.edu

Select the **Notify** button to open the window shown in Figure 11-5, which illustrates the NOTIFY configuration for the *movie.edu* zone on the zone's primary, *terminator*. You have two choices for configuring which servers get NOTIFY messages for a zone. The first is to check the **Servers listed on the Name Servers** tab, which lets the server decide based on the name servers listed in the zone's NS records. (The **Name Servers** tab of the zone properties window simply shows the name servers listed in the zone's NS records.) The second choice is to specify exactly which secondary servers should receive NOTIFY messages. This option is required if you have secondary servers not listed in the zone's NS records: such secondaries are effectively hidden, and the only way the primary knows to send NOTIFY messages to them is if you tell it to.

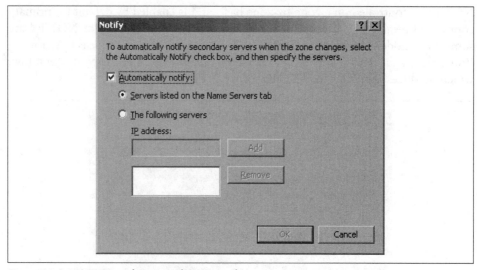

Figure 11-5. NOTIFY configuration for movie.edu

Incremental Zone Transfer

The Microsoft DNS Server in Windows 2003 supports a new kind of zone transfer. Incremental zone transfer, or IXFR for short, is specified in RFC 1995, and it does exactly what you'd expect based on its name. A traditional zone transfer always transfers the entire contents of a zone, even if only one record has changed. Incremental zone transfers allow a name server to send a list of just the records that have changed since the last zone transfer (whether it was a full or incremental one).

This new feature is critical for zones that change frequently. Imagine the scenario with dynamic update: every dynamic update is a change to the zone that requires a zone transfer. Doing a full zone transfer with every small change wastes bandwidth and CPU time. The situation is compounded when the zone being updated and transferred is large.

For IXFR to function, the master servers need to keep track of the differences between successive versions of the zone. A secondary requests an incremental zone transfer and presents its current serial number. The master server calculates and sends the changes needed on the secondary to make its version of the zone current. If the master server can't calculate the changes for whatever reason—perhaps the secondary has an old version of the zone and the primary hasn't kept a record of changes that far back—the primary is allowed to say "Sorry, but you've got to accept a full zone transfer."

A Microsoft DNS Server acting as a secondary requests an incremental zone transfer by default. If the master server doesn't support incremental zone transfer, the Microsoft DNS Server asks for a standard full zone transfer. A Microsoft DNS Server acting as a primary master stores a record of changes going back several versions. The number of versions the server keeps in memory depends on the zone's size: it keeps 25% of the total number of resource records of the zone, up to a total of 64,000. For example, given a zone of 100 resource records, the server would store changes corresponding to the last 25 versions of the zone. It responds with a full zone transfer instead of an incremental when it doesn't have the necessary information to produce the list of changes to the zone or when the list of changes would be larger than a full zone transfer.

AD-integrated zones introduce an extra wrinkle. Recall that every server for an AD-integrated zone stores the zone in Active Directory. Because of Active Directory's multimaster replication scheme, the notion of one server being a "primary" doesn't apply anymore. Instead, any of the zone's authoritative servers can accept a dynamic update for the zone. The change is stored locally and replicated to the other servers using Active Directory. This situation means that different servers can potentially apply changes to the zone in a different order. To maintain a consistent view of changes to a zone, a secondary must always use the same master server. If a particular master server becomes unavailable and a secondary is forced to use another, it automatically requests a full zone transfer for the first transfer from that server to avoid inconsistencies.

More Efficient Zone Transfers

As long as we're on the topic of zone transfers, we should mention another enhancement. A zone transfer comprises many DNS messages sent end-to-end over a TCP connection. Traditional zone transfers put only a single resource record in each DNS message. That's a waste of space: you need a full header on each DNS message, even though you're carrying only a single record. It's like being the only person in a Chevy Suburban. A DNS message can carry many more records.

The Microsoft DNS Server understands a newer zone-transfer format that puts as many records as possible into a single DNS message. The resulting "many answers" zone transfer takes less bandwidth because there's less overhead and less CPU time because less time is spent unmarshaling DNS messages.

The DNS server uses the "many answers" format by default, which is fine if all your secondaries can understand it. Older BIND name servers (prior to Version 4.9.4) can't cope with this format and require the traditional one. Fortunately, you can tell the Microsoft DNS Server to use the traditional method with a server properties setting. Right-click on a server in the left pane of the DNS console and choose **Properties**, then select the **Advanced** tab. Click the box next to **BIND secondaries**. When this box is checked, the server sends traditional zone transfers to satisfy older BIND servers. The box is checked by default, but that doesn't affect zone transfers between two Microsoft DNS Servers. They recognize each other, and the master uses the "many answers" format to the secondary.

You should change this setting only if you have no BIND secondaries or if all your BIND secondaries are running Version 4.9.4 or later.

WINS Linkage

Our next topic requires a short detour into the world of Microsoft networking. Networks based on NetBT (NetBIOS over TCP) need to perform name resolution, too: hosts need a way to map NetBIOS names* to IP addresses. The way this name resolution works has evolved over time. In the early days, hosts broadcasted a query on the LAN to resolve a NetBIOS name. This forced all hosts to listen to every broadcast. Since broadcasts don't leave the local LAN, this method didn't allow name resolution beyond the local network segment. The next evolutionary step was the *LMHOSTS* file, which is just a list of NetBIOS names and IP addresses. Every host needed an *LMHOSTS* file to resolve names beyond the local subnet. This model didn't scale very well, either: it was tough to keep the *LMHOSTS* files up to date and distribute them. And the introduction of the Dynamic Host Configuration Protocol (DHCP) essentially made basing a network's NetBIOS name resolution on *LMHOSTS* files impossible.

A detailed description of DHCP is beyond the scope of this book,† but suffice it to say that DHCP eliminates the requirement of configuring a static IP address on every one of your hosts. If those hosts support DHCP, they can contact a DHCP server when they boot to obtain an IP address and other configuration parameters, such as the IP addresses of the default router, name servers, and WINS servers.

WINS, which stands for Windows Internet Naming Service, is a Microsoft invention introduced in Windows NT 3.5. The server component of WINS is an implementation of a NetBIOS Name Server as described in RFCs 1001 and 1002. The idea is nothing new; the RFCs date from early 1987. The function of a NetBIOS Name Server is simple: it maps NetBIOS names to IP addresses.

The name and IP address information in a WINS server comes from the various hosts on the network. Once a host sets its IP address using the value sent by a DHCP server, the host registers its name with the WINS server the DHCP server told it about. Actually, any modern NetBT host registers its name with a WINS server (if it is configured to use a WINS server, of course), regardless of how it obtained its IP

---

* A host's NetBIOS name is simply the name by which it's known for NetBT networking purposes. NetBIOS names are limited to one label of up to 15 octets (that is, no multiple-label names like DNS domain names). On Windows Server 2003 systems, a host's NetBIOS name is derived automatically from the host's fully qualified DNS name, which is called the computer name and is set in the **System Properties** window's **Computer Name** tab (choose **Control Panel** → **System**). The NetBIOS name is forced to be the first label (i.e., everything to the left of the leftmost dot) of the host's DNS name. Windows 2000 allowed the NetBIOS name to be different from the DNS name, but that feature didn't carry over to Windows Server 2003.

† But see another book from O'Reilly: *TCP/IP Network Administration* by Craig Hunt.

address (e.g., dynamically from a DHCP server or statically from a user-input configuration). Modern NetBT hosts also know to contact a WINS server for NetBIOS name resolution, rather than relying solely on broadcasting or an LMHOSTS file.

So where does DNS fit in to all this? Before Windows 2000's support of dynamic update, it wasn't possible to make the new name-to-IP address mappings generated by the DHCP server visible to DNS. Microsoft realized there would be some value to enabling a DNS server to query a WINS server, which knows about names for dynamically assigned IP addresses. After all, a NetBIOS name in the WINS server is usually the same as a machine's hostname (the first label of its fully qualified domain name in DNS), which is what it would be in the DNS server if there were an easy way to get it there. (Remember, we're talking about the days before Windows 2000 with its improved integration with DNS.) So a Microsoft DNS Server can be configured to ask a WINS server when it receives a query for a domain name that's not in its zone data.

You may be thinking that a name server contacting a WINS server is kind of silly; isn't there a way for name servers to know what the DHCP servers are doing directly? There is. In a network with Windows 2000 or Windows Server 2003, DHCP servers can update name servers using dynamic update after every address assignment, as we discussed earlier in this chapter. The importance of WINS in recent versions of Windows (Windows 2000 and Windows Server 2003) is greatly reduced, too. Modern Windows hosts allow domain names (which are resolved with DNS) to be used in places where previously only NetBIOS names (typically resolved with WINS) were allowed. WINS is still required to support older, legacy clients. You can find more information about how modern Windows hosts use DNS for hostname lookups in Chapter 6.

Configuring WINS Lookup

WINS lookup, as it's called, is enabled on a zone-by-zone basis using the **WINS** tab of a forward zone's properties window. When the DNS server receives an address (A) record query for which it doesn't know the answer, if the zone where the record would exist has WINS lookup enabled, the DNS server queries a WINS server. The NetBIOS name sent to the WINS server is the first label of the domain name in the A record query. For example, if the domain name in the A record query is *terminator. movie.edu*, the NetBIOS name queried is *terminator*. If the WINS server responds with an IP address for *terminator*, the DNS server synthesizes an A record for *terminator.movie.edu* and returns it to the original querier.

The WINS lookup configuration for the *movie.edu* zone on the zone's primary, *terminator*, is shown in Figure 11-6.

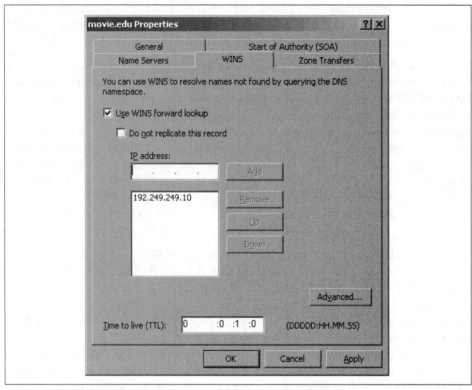

Figure 11-6. WINS lookup settings for movie.edu

WINS lookup is enabled by checking the **Use WINS forward lookup** box. You can specify the IP addresses of up to eight WINS servers, and the DNS server will try them in the order listed.

By default, the WINS lookup configuration you establish on the primary takes effect on the secondaries as well. The primary inserts a special WINS record that gets transferred with the rest of the zone to the secondaries. If the secondaries are Microsoft DNS Servers, they understand the WINS record and perform WINS lookups accordingly. If the secondaries are BIND name servers, they complain about the unknown WINS record. You can suppress sending this WINS record to the secondaries by checking **Do not replicate this record**.

The **Time to live (TTL)** field in the lower left corner specifies the TTL for the synthesized A records that result from WINS lookups.

Pressing the **Advanced** button yields a window like that in Figure 11-7. **Cache timeout** controls how long the DNS server will cache the synthesized A records. The default value is 15 minutes. That value may seem small, but it's a good choice: information in the WINS server is transient by nature, so you don't want the DNS server to hold onto it for a long time. If it needs a name again, the DNS server can just ask the WINS server for it. **Lookup time-out** controls how long the DNS server will wait after querying a WINS server. The default is 2 seconds.

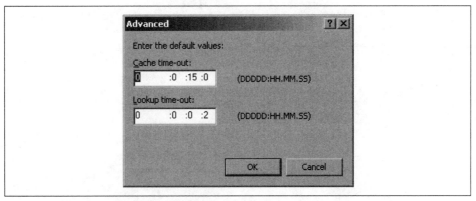

Figure 11-7. Advanced WINS lookup settings

You can enable WINS lookup on *in-addr.arpa* zones, too. It's called WINS reverse lookup, and it's implemented differently than plain WINS lookup. When the name server receives a PTR query it can't answer and WINS reverse lookup is enabled for the zone, it sends a NetBIOS Adapter Status request directly to the IP address referenced by the PTR record. In other words, the name server asks the host directly what its name is. The name server can't ask a WINS server because lookups based on IP address aren't supported: you can't give a WINS server an IP address and get the corresponding NetBIOS name back. WINS servers have obviously never heard of *Jeopardy!* ("The host with IP address 192.249.249.3.," "What is *terminator?*")

WINS reverse lookup is configured similarly to WINS lookup: select the **WINS-R** tab of the zone properties window of any *in-addr.arpa* zone. The WINS reverse lookup configuration for the *249.249.192.in-addr.arpa* zone on the zone's primary, *terminator*, is shown in Figure 11-8.

Use WINS-R lookup enables the NetBIOS Adapter Status requests for unknown PTR records in this zone. **Do not replicate this record** has the same effect as its WINS forward-lookup counterpart. If you look in an *in-addr.arpa* zone datafile, though, you'll see a WINS-R record instead of a WINS record. The **Domain to append to returned name** field takes a DNS domain name that will be appended to the NetBIOS name returned by the host to form a fully qualified domain name. The **Advanced** button controls cache and lookup timeouts, just like its WINS forward-lookup counterpart.

Using WINS Lookup and WINS Reverse Lookup

What's WINS lookup good for? In most networks, not a lot. For one thing, Windows Server 2003 integrates tightly with DNS so that in a properly configured network, all Windows hosts have forward- and reverse-mapping information in DNS.

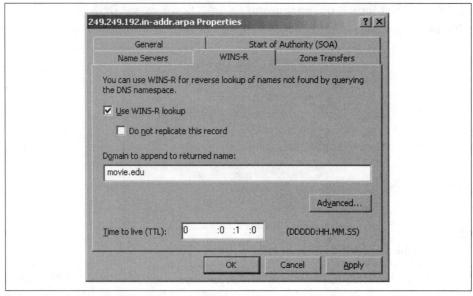

Figure 11-8. WINS reverse lookup settings for 249.249.192.in-addr.arpa

(More information about this new integration with DNS is found in Chapter 8.) But let's say you still have a lot of older Windows hosts on your network. Do you need WINS lookup? Well, we still can't get excited about it. Think about it this way: the names that get resolved the most are the servers, and they usually have fixed IP addresses and thus static DNS entries. They're resolved directly in DNS, not via the WINS lookup detour. Most networks don't have much peer-to-peer networking; your average desktop host usually doesn't offer network services, such as a web server, name server, and so on. It's the need to reach those kinds of network services that requires DNS name resolution to work for every host. (Sure, there's a lot of Net-BIOS-based file and print sharing among desktop hosts, but that process uses WINS natively.)

If you do need to support WINS lookup in your network, a big problem with it is that the standard BIND name server doesn't support it.* Many people find that they need WINS lookup after they have a DNS infrastructure in place using BIND name servers. One option is to replace all those name servers with the Microsoft DNS Server and enable WINS lookup. That's not realistic for most people. A better, but not perfect, option is to create a new subdomain for DHCP clients resolvable via WINS lookup and delegate the subdomain to a set of Microsoft DNS Servers.

---

* MetaInfo, a subsidiary of Check Point, has ported BIND to Windows and added WINS lookup and WINS reverse lookup. See *http://www.metainfo.com/*.

For example, let's say the folks running the domain *acme.com* suddenly find themselves with dozens of PCs doing peer-to-peer networking with DHCP-assigned IP addresses. Since they've already got a BIND infrastructure in place, they decide to create the domain *pcs.acme.com* for these PCs. (The domain name could be anything: *dhcp.acme.com*, *wins.acme.com*, whatever.) They configure a couple of Microsoft DNS Servers for this zone and enable WINS lookup. Finally, they delegate to the *pcs.acme.com* zone from the *acme.com* zone.

In practice, we find WINS reverse lookup is much more useful. It's really nice to have complete reverse-mapping information for your network in DNS. Network-management applications can report names rather than IP addresses. Web servers can log usage statistics by name and make named-based authorization decisions, such as giving access only to hosts in the *movie.edu* domain. Troubleshooting is easier as well. Without WINS reverse lookup, the name server can't reverse map dynamically assigned IP addresses in networks with older Windows hosts. Of course, for you to be able to use WINS reverse lookup in your network, all the name servers for your *in-addr.arpa* zones need to support it.

Building Up a Large, Sitewide Cache with Forwarders

Certain network connections discourage sending large volumes of traffic off-site, either because the network connection is pay-per-packet or because it is a slow link with a high delay, as with a remote office's satellite connection to the company's network. In other cases, a firewall might allow only certain name servers to send queries off the local network to the Internet. In these situations, you don't necessarily want your name server to follow the standard DNS resolution algorithm and start by sending a query to a root name server. A solution is called *forwarding*, which changes the way a name server resolves queries it can't answer itself.

If you designate one or more servers at your site as forwarders, all off-site queries are sent to the forwarders first. The idea is that the forwarders handle all off-site queries generated at the site, building up a rich cache of information. For any given query for a remote domain, there is a high probability that the forwarder can answer the query from its cache, avoiding the need for the other servers to send packets off-site. Nothing special is done to these servers to make them forwarders; you modify all the other servers at your site to direct their queries through the forwarders. It's worth pointing out that the terminology is a little funny: a name server configured to forward (or, if you prefer, with forwarding enabled) doesn't have an official name, but we use the term *forwarding name server*. A name server that receives queries forwarded from forwarding name servers is called a *forwarder*.

A primary or secondary name server's mode of operation changes slightly when it is directed to use a forwarder. If the requested information is already in its database of authoritative data and cache data, it answers with this information; this part of the operation hasn't changed. However, if the information is not in its database, the name server sends the query to its configured forwarders and waits a short period for an answer before resuming normal operation and contacting the remote servers itself. What the name server is doing that's different is sending a *recursive* query to the forwarder, expecting it to find the answer. At all other times, the name server sends out *nonrecursive* queries to other name servers and deals with responses that refer only to other name servers.

Microsoft has introduced a new feature called conditional forwarding that makes forwarding even more flexible under Windows Server 2003. In prior versions of the Microsoft DNS Server, all queries that couldn't be resolved locally were sent to the same set of forwarders. Using conditional forwarding, you can configure the DNS server to use a different set of forwarders depending on the domain name of the query. In our experience, this feature is most useful in large networks or networks with a restrictive security policy that limits Internet connectivity to certain hosts. For example, consider a large network where, as in most networks, the name servers need to know how to resolve both internal and external names. One set of forwarders—call them set A—might have complete knowledge of the organization's namespace, while a different bunch of forwarders—set B—might have access through the firewall to resolve Internet domain names. An individual name server is authoritative only for a small number of zones. This name server can resolve queries for names in its local authoritative zones, but how does it resolve other names? If a query is for an internal name, the name server needs to forward to the "A" forwarders, but any external names can only be resolved by the "B" forwarders. With conditional forwarding, such a configuration is a snap.

Forwarding is configured by selecting the **Forwarders** tab on the server properties window. Figure 11-9 shows how a *movie.edu* name server is configured to forward all queries to *wormhole* and *terminator*. And remember, forwarding is configured on every name server *except* the forwarders themselves—*wormhole* and *terminator* in this case.

To enable forwarding, you need to specify forwarders for a specific domain or the default of **All other DNS domains**. The default applies when no other configured domain matches. You can specify up to six forwarders for each domain. The name server forwards to them in the order in which they're listed, using a default timeout of five seconds per forwarder; that is, if the first forwarder doesn't respond within five seconds, try the next, wait five more seconds, try the next, and so on. The forwarding timeout can be changed with the **Number of seconds before forward queries time out** field.

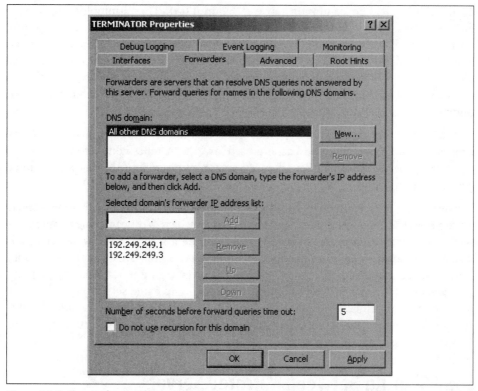

Figure 11-9. Forwarders configuration tab

When you use forwarders, try to keep your site configuration simple. Otherwise, you can end up with configurations that are really twisted. Follow these tips:

- Avoid having "midlevel" servers forward packets (that is, avoid configuring forwarding on your midlevel name servers). Midlevel servers mostly refer name servers to subdomain name servers. If they have been configured to forward packets, do they refer to subdomain name servers, or do they contact the subdomain name server to find out the answer? Whichever way it works, you're probably making your site configuration too hard for mere mortals (and subdomain administrators) to understand.

- Avoid chaining your forwarders. Don't configure server *a* to forward to server *b*, and configure server *b* to forward to server *c* (or worse yet, back to server *a*).

A More Restricted Forwarding Name Server

You may want to restrict your name servers even further—stopping them from even *trying* to contact an off-site server if their forwarder is down or doesn't respond. You can do this by telling the server not to fall back to using the recursive resolution process if no forwarders respond: check the **Do not use recursion for this domain** box on the **Forwarders** configuration tab (see Figure 11-9). The terminology is confusing: this checkbox has nothing to do with the kind of query being sent to the forwarders. As we said earlier, a name server that's forwarding always sends a recursive query to its forwarders. What this checkbox determines is what happens after that recursive query is sent, which we discuss next. The BIND name server configuration syntax calls this kind of forwarding name server a *forward-only* server, which we think is a good name.

A forward-only server is a variation on a server that forwards. It still answers queries from its authoritative data and cache data. However, it relies completely on its forwarders; it doesn't try to contact other servers for information if the forwarders don't give it an answer.

However, you must ask yourself if it ever makes sense to use a forward-only server. Such a server is completely dependent on the forwarders. You can achieve much the same configuration (and dependence) by not running a forward-only server at all; instead, configure your hosts' resolvers to point to the forwarders you were using. Thus, you are still relying on the forwarders, but now your applications are querying the forwarders directly instead of having a forward-only name server query them for the applications. You lose the local caching the forward-only server would do, but you reduce the overall complexity of your site configuration by running fewer "restricted" name servers.

Load Sharing Between Mirrored Servers

The Microsoft DNS Server has a feature called *round robin* (named after the equivalent feature in the BIND name server): the server rotates address records for the same domain name between responses. For example, if the domain name *foo.bar.baz* has three address records for IP addresses 192.1.1.1, 192.1.1.2, and 192.1.1.3, the round-robin feature causes the name server to give them out first in the order:

```
192.1.1.1 192.1.1.2 192.1.1.3
```

then in the order:

```
192.1.1.2 192.1.1.3 192.1.1.1
```

and then in the order:

```
192.1.1.3 192.1.1.1 192.1.1.2
```

before starting over again with the first order and repeating the rotation ad infinitum.

This functionality is enormously useful if you have a number of equivalent network resources, such as mirrored FTP servers, web servers, or terminal servers, and you'd like to spread the load among them. You establish one domain name that refers to the group of resources and configure clients to access that domain name, and the name server inverse-multiplexes the accesses between the IP addresses you list.

It's a good idea to reduce the records' TTLs, too. This ensures that, if the addresses are cached on an intermediate name server that doesn't support round robin, they'll time out of the cache quickly. If the intermediate name server looks up the name again, your authoritative name server can round-robin the addresses again.

Note that this is really load sharing, not load balancing: the name server gives out the addresses in a completely deterministic way, without regard to the actual load or capacity of the servers servicing the requests. In our example, the server at address 192.1.1.3 could be a 486 running Linux and the other two servers could be quad-processor Itanium2s, and the Linux box would still get a third of the load.

The ABCs of IPv6 Addressing

The Microsoft DNS Server supports the new AAAA record necessary for IPv6. We thought some information on the representation and structure of IPv6 addresses would be appropriate to help you understand the record.

IPv6 addresses are 128 bits long. The preferred representation of an IPv6 address is eight groups of as many as four hexadecimal digits, separated by colons. For example:

```
0123:4567:89ab:cdef:0123:4567:89ab:cdef
```

The first group of hex digits (0123, in this example) represents the most significant (or highest order) four bits of the address.

Groups of digits that begin with one or more zeros don't need to be padded to four places, so you can also write the previous address as:

```
123:4567:89ab:cdef:123:4567:89ab:cdef
```

Each group must contain at least one digit, though, unless you're using the :: notation. The :: notation allows you to compress sequential groups of zeros. This comes in handy when you're specifying just an IPv6 prefix. For example, this notation:

```
dead:beef::
```

specifies the first 32 bits of an IPv6 address as *dead:beef* and the remaining 96 as zeros.

You can also use :: at the beginning of an IPv6 address to specify a suffix. For example, the IPv6 loopback address is commonly written as:

```
::1
```

or 127 zeros followed by a single one. You can even use :: in the middle of an address as a shorthand for contiguous groups of zeros:

```
dead:beef::1
```

You can use the :: shorthand only once in an address since more than one could be ambiguous.

IPv6 prefixes are specified in a format similar to IPv4's CIDR notation. As many bits of the prefix as are significant are expressed in the standard IPv6 notation, followed by a slash and a decimal count of exactly how many significant bits there are. So the following three prefix specifications are equivalent (though obviously not equivalently terse):

```
dead:beef:0000:00f1:0000:0000:0000:0000/64
dead:beef::00f1:0:0:0:0/64
dead:beef:0:f1::/64
```

IPv6 Forward and Reverse Mapping

Clearly, the existing A record won't accommodate IPv6's 128-bit addresses. RFC 1886 defines the solution: an address record that's four times as long as an A record. That's the AAAA (pronounced "quad A") record. The AAAA record takes as its record-specific data the textual format of an IPv6 record as described earlier. So for example, you'd see AAAA records like this one:

```
ipv6-host    IN    AAAA    4321:0:1:2:3:4:567:89ab
```

RFC 3152 established *ip6.arpa*, a new reverse-mapping namespace for IPv6 addresses.* Each level of subdomain under *ip6.arpa* represents four bits of the 128-bit address, encoded as a hexadecimal digit just like in the record-specific data of the AAAA record. The least significant (lowest order) bits appear at the far left of the domain name. Unlike the format of addresses in AAAA records, omitting leading zeros is not allowed, so there are always 32 hexadecimal digits and 32 levels of subdomain below *ip6.arpa* in a domain name corresponding to a full IPv6 address. The domain name that corresponds to the address in the previous example is:

```
b.a.9.8.7.6.5.0.4.0.0.0.3.0.0.0.2.0.0.0.1.0.0.0.0.0.0.0.1.2.3.4.ip6.arpa.
```

These domain names have PTR records attached, just as the domain names under *in-addr.arpa* do:

```
b.a.9.8.7.6.5.0.4.0.0.0.3.0.0.0.2.0.0.0.1.0.0.0.0.0.0.0.1.2.3.4.ip6.arpa.    IN    PTR
mash.ip6.movie.edu.
```

Securing Your Name Server

Compared to a modern BIND name server, the Microsoft DNS Server is short on security features, but you do have some options. In this section, we discuss how to prevent unauthorized zone transfers from your servers and how to "lock down" a name server that receives queries from other name servers on the Internet.

---

* Several aspects of IPv6 addressing have been a moving target within the Internet standards community. We should point out that the original domain for IPv6 reverse mapping as defined in RFC 1886 was *ip6.int*. This domain was changed to *ip6.arpa* by RFC 3152 for both technical and political reasons.

Preventing Unauthorized Zone Transfers

It's important to ensure that only the intended name servers—usually this means the secondary name servers listed in the zone's NS records—can transfer zones from your primary name server. Users on remote hosts that can query your name server's zone data can look up data (for example, addresses) only for hosts whose domain names they already know, one at a time. Users who can start zone transfers from your server can list all the hosts in your zones. It's the difference between letting random folks call your company's switchboard and ask for John Q. Cubicle's phone number and sending them a copy of your corporate phone directory.

You control which name servers can perform a zone transfer with settings on the **Zone Transfers** tab of the zone properties window (see Figure 11-4). You can allow any host to perform zone transfers, or only those name servers listed in the zone's NS records, or only a specific set of name servers you list by IP address.

For a primary name server accessible from the Internet, you definitely want to limit zone transfers to just authorized secondary name servers. You probably don't need to restrict zone transfers on name servers inside your firewall, unless you're worried about your own employees listing your zone data.

Disabling Recursion on Delegated Name Servers

Some of your name servers answer nonrecursive queries from other name servers on the Internet because those name servers appear in NS records delegating your zones to them. We'll call these name servers *delegated* name servers. You can take special measures to secure your delegated name servers by disabling recursion.

Recall that by default, resolvers send recursive queries, and name servers do the work required to answer the queries. (If you don't remember how recursion works, refer to Chapter 2.) In the process of finding the answer to recursive queries, the name servers build up a cache of nonauthoritative information about other zones.

But for security reasons, you don't want delegated name servers to do the extra work required to answer a recursive query or to build up a cache of data. Answering recursive queries opens them up to a potential denial of service (DoS) attack: the Bad Guys can send these servers repeated recursive queries, making them do all kinds of unnecessary work. Answering recursive queries from just anyone is also a bad idea because of caching: the most common spoofing attacks involve inducing the target name server to query name servers under the Bad Guy's control by sending the target a recursive query for a domain name in a zone served by the Bad Guy's servers. The Bad Guys can force your name servers to cache known bad data in this way.

Disabling recursion on delegated servers eliminates these attack vectors. But to do so, you need to make sure these servers don't receive any legitimate recursive queries. Don't configure any resolvers to use these servers and don't list a nonrecursive name server as a forwarder. (When a name server is using another server as a forwarder, it sends the query to the forwarder as a recursive query instead of a nonrecursive query.)

You can induce the Microsoft DNS Server to run as a nonrecursive name server by checking the **Disable recursion (also disables forwarders)** box on the **Advanced** tab of the server properties window. By default, the name server supports recursion, and this box is unchecked. Disabling recursion doesn't break a delegated server because name servers send nonrecursive queries between themselves.

nslookup and dig

To be proficient at troubleshooting name server problems, you'll need a special tool to make DNS queries, one that gives you complete control. We'll cover *nslookup* in this chapter because it's distributed with Windows Server 2003 and with many other operating systems. We'll also cover another query tool, *dig*, that isn't part of Windows. It provides similar functionality and doesn't suffer from *nslookup*'s deficiencies.

Is nslookup a Good Tool?

Much of the time you'll use *nslookup* to make queries in the same way the resolver makes them. Sometimes, though, you'll use *nslookup* to query other name servers as a name server would. Which one you emulate will depend on the problem you're trying to debug. You might wonder, "How accurately does *nslookup* emulate a resolver or a name server? Does *nslookup* actually use the Windows resolver library routines?" No, *nslookup* uses its own routines for querying name servers, but those routines are based on the resolver routines. Consequently, *nslookup*'s behavior is very similar to the resolver's behavior, but it does differ slightly. We'll point out some of those differences. As for emulating name server behavior, *nslookup* allows you to query another server with the same query message that a name server would use, but the retransmission scheme is quite different. Like a name server, though, *nslookup* can perform a zone transfer to pull a copy of a zone's data. So *nslookup* does not exactly emulate either the resolver or the name server, but it does emulate them well enough to make a good troubleshooting tool. Let's delve into those differences we've alluded to.

Multiple Servers

nslookup talks to only one name server at a time. This is the major difference between *nslookup*'s behavior and the resolver's behavior. The resolver makes use of all the name servers listed in the Windows resolver configuration window. If two name servers are listed, the resolver tries the first name server, then the second, then the first, then the second, until it receives a response or gives up. The resolver does this for every query. On the other hand, *nslookup* tries only the first name server listed. But you *want* your troubleshooting tool to talk with only one name server so you can reduce the number of variables when analyzing a problem. If *nslookup* used more than one name server, you wouldn't have as much control over your troubleshooting session.

Timeouts

The *nslookup* timeouts are similar to the resolver timeouts when the resolver is querying only one name server. A name server's timeouts, however, are based on how quickly the remote server answered the last query, a dynamic measure. *nslookup* will never match name server timeouts, but that's not a problem either. When you're querying remote name servers with *nslookup*, you probably care only what the response was, not how long it took.

The Search List

nslookup implements the search list just as the resolver code does. Name servers don't implement search lists, so, to act like a name server, the *nslookup* search function must be turned off—more on that later.

Zone Transfers

nslookup will do zone transfers just like a name server. Unlike the name server, though, *nslookup* does not check SOA serial numbers before pulling the zone data; you'll have to do that manually, if you want to.

Using NetBIOS Names

This last point doesn't compare *nslookup* to the resolver or name server but rather to ways of looking up names in general. *nslookup*, as distributed by Microsoft, uses only DNS; you can't use it to look up NetBIOS names via broadcast, *LMHOSTS*, or

WINS. Before using *nslookup* to diagnose your problem, you need to determine if your problem is really with DNS. For example, if an application is using a different IP address than you expect, perhaps it's treating a value as a NetBIOS name and not a DNS name. To diagnose this kind of problem, you need to understand how the Windows resolver, which we discussed in Chapter 6, works. Just remember that *nslookup* talks only to name servers.

Interactive Versus Noninteractive

Let's start our tutorial on *nslookup* by looking at how to start and stop it. You can run *nslookup* either interactively or noninteractively. If you want to look up only one piece of data, you should use the noninteractive form. If you plan on doing something more extensive, such as changing servers or options, use an interactive session.

To start an interactive session, just type *nslookup*:

```
C:\> nslookup
Default Server:  terminator.movie.edu
Address:  192.249.249.3

> ^Z
```

If you need help, type *?* or *help*.

When you want to exit, type ^Z (Ctrl-Z) and press Enter. You can also exit from *nslookup* with ^C or *^Break* (Ctrl-Break). This behavior is different from *nslookup*'s operation on a Unix host, where if you send *nslookup* an interrupt, it catches it, stops whatever it is doing (like a zone transfer), and gives you the > prompt. There's no way to just interrupt Microsoft's *nslookup*: you just have to stop *nslookup* completely and restart it.

For a noninteractive lookup, include the name you are looking up on the command line:

```
C:\> nslookup carrie
Server:  terminator.movie.edu
Address:  192.249.249.3

Name:    carrie.movie.edu
Address:  192.253.253.4
```

Option Settings

nslookup has its own set of dials and knobs called *option settings*. All the option settings can be changed. We'll discuss here what each of the options means. We'll use the rest of the chapter to show you how to use them.

```
C:\> nslookup
Default Server:  terminator.movie.edu
Address:  192.249.249.3
```

```
> set all
Default Server:  terminator.movie.edu
Address:  192.249.249.3

Set options:
  nodebug
  defname
  search
  recurse
  nod2
  novc
  noignoretc
  port=53
  type=A
  class=IN
  timeout=2
  retry=1
  root=A.ROOT-SERVERS.NET.
  domain=movie.edu
  MSxfr
  IXFRversion=1
  srchlist=movie.edu

> ^Z
```

Before we get into the options, we need to cover the introductory lines. The default name server is *terminator.movie.edu*. This means that every query sent by *nslookup* will be sent to *terminator*.

The options come in two flavors: *Boolean* and *value*. The options that do not have an equals sign after them are Boolean options and they are either "on" or "off." The value options can take on different, well, values. How can we tell which Boolean options are on and which are off? The option is *off* when a "no" precedes the option's name. *nodebug* means that debugging is off. As you might guess, the option *search* is on.

How you change Boolean or value options depends on whether or not you are using *nslookup* interactively. In an interactive session, you change an option with the *set* command, as in *set debug* or *set domain=classics.movie.edu*. From the command line, you omit the word *set* and precede the option with a hyphen, as in *nslookup -debug* or *nslookup -domain=classics.movie.edu*. The options can be abbreviated to their shortest unique string—for example, *nodeb* for *nodebug*. In addition to its abbreviation, the *querytype* option can also be entered simply as *type*.

Let's go through each of the options:

[no]debug
> Debugging is turned off by default. If it is turned on, *nslookup* displays the complete contents of the response messages from the name server. See *[no]d2* for a discussion of debug level 2.

[no]defname

This option reflects *nslookup*'s BIND heritage. By default, *nslookup* adds the default domain name to names without a dot in them. Before search lists existed, the BIND resolver code would add the default domain only to names without any dots in them; this option reflects that behavior. *nslookup* can implement the pre-search list behavior (with *search* off and *defname* on), or it can implement the search list behavior (with *search* on).

[no]search

The *search* option "overshadows" the default domain name (*defname*) option. That is, *defname* applies only if *search* is turned off. By default, *nslookup* appends the domain names in the search list (*srchlist*) to names that don't end in a dot. *nslookup*'s search list is constructed from the **Append these DNS suffixes** field on the **DNS** tab of the **Advanced TCP/IP Settings** window.

[no]recurse

nslookup requests recursive service by default. This turns on the recursion-desired bit in query messages. The Windows resolver sends recursive queries in the same way. Name servers, however, send nonrecursive queries to other name servers.

[no]d2

Debugging at level 2 is turned off by default. If it is turned on, you see the query messages sent to the name server in addition to the regular debugging output. Turning on *d2* also turns on *debug*. Turning off *d2* turns off *d2* only; *debug* is left on. Turning off *debug* turns off both *debug* and *d2*.

[no]vc

By default, *nslookup* makes queries using UDP instead of over a TCP connection (virtual circuit). Most Windows resolver queries are made with UDP, so the default *nslookup* behavior matches the resolver.

[no]ignoretc

By default, *nslookup* doesn't ignore truncated messages. If a message is received that has the "truncated" bit set—indicating that the name server couldn't fit all the important information in the UDP response message—*nslookup* doesn't ignore it; it retries the query using a TCP connection instead of UDP.

port=53

The DNS service is on port 53. You can start a name server on another port—for debugging purposes, for example—and *nslookup* can be directed to use that port.

type=A

By default, *nslookup* looks up A (address) resource record types. In addition, if you type in an IP address (and the *nslookup* query type is address or pointer), *nslookup* inverts the address, appends *in-addr.arpa*, and looks up PTR (pointer) data instead.

class=IN

The only class that matters is Internet. Well, there's the Hesiod (HS) class, too, if you are an MITer or run Ultrix.

timeout=2

If the name server doesn't respond within two seconds, *nslookup* resends the query and waits another two seconds before giving up and printing a timeout message. The Windows resolver uses different timeouts when querying a single name server (see Chapter 6).

retry=1

The query is sent just once before giving up. Again, the Windows resolver behaves slightly differently as discussed in Chapter 6.

root=A.ROOT-SERVERS.NET

A convenience command called *root* switches your default server to the server named here. Executing the *root* command from *nslookup*'s prompt is equivalent to executing *server A.ROOT-SERVERS.NET*. You can change the default "root" server with *set root=server*.

domain=movie.edu

This is the default domain name appended if the *defname* option is on. If the *defname* option is not on, no default domain name is appended.

[no]MSxfr

The Microsoft DNS Server implements a feature that Microsoft calls "fast" zone transfers. Those of you familiar with the BIND name server know this as the "many answers" zone-transfer format, in which multiple records are packed into the answer section of a single DNS message during a zone transfer. (The method implemented by older BIND name servers uses one DNS message per record, which is somewhat wasteful of bandwidth.) This option indicates whether or not to request one of these "fast" zone transfers.

IXFRversion=1

The Microsoft DNS Server also supports a protocol called incremental zone transfer (IXFR). IXFR requests include a version number. The default value of 1 corresponds to the IXFR version supported by the Microsoft DNS Server. At this point, there's no reason to change this value.

srchlist=movie.edu

If *search* is on, these domain names are appended to names that do not end in a dot. The domain names are listed in the order in which they will be tried and are separated by slashes.

Avoiding the Search List

nslookup implements the search list, as the resolver does. When you are debugging, the search list can get in your way. You need to either turn the search list off completely (*set nosearch*) or add a trailing dot to the fully qualified domain name you are looking up. We prefer the latter, as you'll see in our examples.

Common Tasks

You'll come to use *nslookup* for little chores almost every day: for example, finding out the IP address or MX records for a given domain name or querying a particular name server for data. We'll cover these common tasks before moving on to the more occasional stuff.

Looking Up Different Data Types

By default, *nslookup* looks up the address for a name or the name for an address. You can look up any data type by changing the *querytype*, as we show in this example:

```
C:\> nslookup
Default Server:  terminator.movie.edu
Address:  192.249.249.3

> misery          Look up address.
Server:  terminator.movie.edu
Address:  192.249.249.3

Name:    misery.movie.edu
Address:  192.253.253.2

> 192.253.253.2    Look up name.
Server:  terminator.movie.edu
Address:  192.249.249.3

Name:    misery.movie.edu
Address:  192.253.253.2

> set type=mx      Look up MX data.
> wormhole
Server:  terminator.movie.edu
Address:  192.249.249.3
wormhole.movie.edu     MX preference = 10, mail exchanger = wormhole.movie.edu
wormhole.movie.edu     internet address = 192.249.249.1
wormhole.movie.edu     internet address = 192.253.253.1

> set q=any        Look up data of any type.
> diehard
Server:  terminator.movie.edu
Address:  192.249.249.3

diehard.movie.edu      internet address = 192.249.249.4
diehard.movie.edu      MX preference = 10, mail exchanger = diehard.movie.edu
diehard.movie.edu      internet address = 192.249.249.4
```

These are only a few of the valid DNS data types, of course. For a more complete list, see Appendix A.

Authoritative Versus Nonauthoritative Answers

If you've used *nslookup* before, you might have noticed that it sometimes precedes its answers with the phrase "Non-authoritative answer":

```
C:\>nslookup
Default Server:  terminator.movie.edu
Address:  192.249.249.3

> slate.mines.colorado.edu.
Server:  terminator.movie.edu
Address:  192.249.249.3

Non-authoritative answer:
Name:    slate.mines.colorado.edu
Address:  138.67.1.38
```

This phrase indicates that the name server is not authoritative for the data in the answer. (Recall that a name server is authoritative for data when it's a primary or secondary for the zone containing the data.) You'll see a nonauthoritative response for one of two reasons. The first is that the name server you queried didn't have the data you were looking for and had to query a remote name server to get it. The remote name server is authoritative for the data (that's the reason it was queried!) and returns it with the "authoritative answer" bit set in the DNS message header. The Microsoft DNS Server you queried puts this data in its cache and returns it to you marked nonauthoritative. If you ask for the same data again, this time the name server can answer from its cache and will mark the data nonauthoritative: that's the second reason you'll see a nonauthoritative answer.

Authoritative answers are not announced by *nslookup*: the absence of the nonauthoritative message means the answer is authoritative.

Notice that we ended the domain name with a trailing dot. The response would have been the same had we left it off. Sometimes it is critical that you use the trailing dot while debugging, but not always. Rather than stopping to decide if *this* name needs a trailing dot, we always add one if we know the name is fully qualified (except, of course, for the example where we turn off the search list).

Switching Servers

Sometimes you want to query another name server directly—for example, if you think it is misbehaving. You can switch servers with *nslookup* by using the *server* or *lserver* commands. The difference between *server* and *lserver* is that *lserver* queries your "local" server—the one you started out with—to get the address of the server you want to switch to; *server* uses the default server instead of the local server. This difference is important because the server that you just switched to may not be responding, as we'll show in this example:

```
C:\> nslookup
Default Server:  relay.hp.com
Address:  15.255.152.2
```

When we start up, our first server, *relay.hp.com*, becomes our *lserver* (this will matter later on in this session):

```
> server galt.cs.purdue.edu.
Default Server:  galt.cs.purdue.edu
Address:  128.10.2.39

> cs.purdue.edu.
Server:  galt.cs.purdue.edu
Address:  128.10.2.39

*** galt.cs.purdue.edu can't find cs.purdue.edu: No response from server
```

At this point we try to switch back to our original name server. But there is no name server running on *galt* to look up *relay*'s address:

```
> server relay.hp.com.
*** Can't find address for server relay.hp.com: No response from server
```

Instead of being stuck, though, we use the *lserver* command to have our local server look up *relay*'s address:

```
> lserver relay.hp.com.
Default Server:  relay.hp.com
Address:  15.255.152.2

>
```

Since the server on *galt* did not respond—it's not even running a name server—it wasn't possible to look up the address of *relay* to switch back to using *relay*'s name server. Here's where *lserver* comes to the rescue: the local name server, *relay*, was still responding, so we used it. Instead of using *lserver*, we could have recovered by using *relay*'s IP address directly—*server 15.255.152.2*.

You can even change servers on a per-query basis. To specify that you'd like *nslookup* to query a particular server for information about a given domain name, you can specify the server as the second argument on the line, after the domain name to look up—like so:

```
C:\> nslookup
Default Server:  relay.hp.com
Address:  15.255.152.2

> saturn.sun.com. ns.sun.com.
Server:  ns.sun.com
Address:  192.9.9.3
```

```
Name:    saturn.sun.com
Address: 192.9.25.2
```

And, of course, you can change servers from the command line. You can specify the server to query as the argument after the domain name to look up, like this:

```
C:\> nslookup -type=mx fisherking.movie.edu. terminator.movie.edu.
```

This instructs *nslookup* to query *terminator.movie.edu* for MX records for *fisherking.movie.edu*.

To specify an alternate default server and enter interactive mode, you can use a hyphen in place of the domain name to look up:

```
C:\> nslookup - terminator.movie.edu.
```

Less Common Tasks

The following sections describe tricks you'll probably have to use less often but are still handy to have in your repertoire. Most of these will be helpful when you're trying to troubleshoot a DNS problem; they'll enable you to grub around in the messages the resolver sees and mimic a name server querying another name server or transferring zone data.

Seeing the Query and Response Messages

If you need to, you can direct *nslookup* to show you the queries it sends out and the responses it receives. Turning on *debug* shows you the responses. Turning on *d2* shows you the queries as well. When you want to turn off debugging completely, you have to use *set nodebug*, since *set nod2* turns off only level 2 debugging. After the following trace, we'll explain some parts of the message output. If you want, you can pull out your copy of RFC 1035, turn to page 25, and read along with our explanation.

```
C:\> nslookup
Default Server:  terminator.movie.edu
Address:  192.249.249.3

> set debug
> set type=mx
> oreilly.com.
Server:  terminator.movie.edu
Address:  192.249.249.3

------------
Got answer:
    HEADER:
        opcode = QUERY, id = 11, rcode = NOERROR
        header flags:  response, want recursion, recursion avail.
        questions = 1,  answers = 1,  authority records = 0,  additional = 1
```

```
          QUESTIONS:
              oreilly.com, type = MX, class = IN
          ANSWERS:
          ->  oreilly.com
              MX preference = 20, mail exchanger = smtp2.oreilly.com
              ttl = 21598 (5 hours 59 mins 58 secs)
          ADDITIONAL RECORDS:
          ->  smtp2.oreilly.com
              internet address = 209.58.173.10
              ttl = 21598 (5 hours 59 mins 58 secs)


    ------------
    Non-authoritative answer:
    oreilly.com
              MX preference = 20, mail exchanger = smtp2.oreilly.com
              ttl = 21598 (5 hours 59 mins 58 secs)

    smtp2.oreilly.com
              internet address = 209.58.173.10
              ttl = 21598 (5 hours 59 mins 58 secs)
    >
    > set d2
    > oreilly.com.
    Server:  terminator.movie.edu
    Address:  192.249.249.3
```

This time the query is also shown:

```
    ------------
    SendRequest( ), len 29
        HEADER:
              opcode = QUERY, id = 12, rcode = NOERROR
              header flags:  query, want recursion
              questions = 1,  answers = 0,  authority records = 0,  additional = 0

        QUESTIONS:
              oreilly.com, type = MX, class = IN


    ------------
    ------------
    Got answer (67 bytes):
```

The answer is the same as in the previous example.

Between the dashes are the query and response messages. As promised, we will go through the message contents. DNS messages are composed of five sections:

Header section

> The Header section is present in every query and response. The operation code is always QUERY. (Other opcodes are used for other DNS operations, such as the Notify and Dynamic Update protocol extensions described in Chapter 11.) The ID is used to associate a response with a query and to detect duplicate queries or responses. You have to look in the header flags to see which messages are

queries and which are responses. The string "want recursion" indicates that the querier wants the name server to do all the work. The flag is parroted in the response. The string "auth. answer," when present, means that the response is authoritative—in other words, that the response comes from the name server's authoritative data, not from its cache data. (This response isn't authoritative, so that string is absent.) The response code, rcode, can be one of no error, server failure, name error (also known as "NXDOMAIN" or "nonexistent domain"), not implemented, or refused. The server failure, name error, not implemented, and refused response codes cause the nslookup "Server failed," "Nonexistent domain," "Not implemented," and "Query refused" errors, respectively. The last four entries in the Header section are counters—they indicate how many resource records there are in each of the next four sections.

Question section

A DNS message always contains one and only one question; it includes the name and the requested data type and class. There is never more than one question. Handling more than one question in a DNS message would require a redesign of its format. For one thing, the single authority bit would have to be changed, because the Answer section could contain a mix of authoritative answers and nonauthoritative answers. In the present design, setting the authoritative answer bit means that the name server is an authority for the domain name in the Question section.

Answer section

This section contains the resource records that answer the question. There can be more than one resource record in the response. For example, if the host is multihomed, there will be more than one address resource record.

Authority section

The Authority section is where name server records are returned. When a response refers the querier to some other name servers, those name servers are listed here.

Additional section

The Additional records section adds information that may complete information included in other sections. For instance, if a name server is listed in the Authority section, the name server's address is added to the Additional records section. After all, to contact the name server, you need to have its address.

Querying Like a Name Server

You can make *nslookup* send out the same query message a name server would. Name server query messages are not much different from resolver messages. The primary difference in the query messages is that resolvers request recursion and name servers seldom do. Recursion is the default with *nslookup*, so you have to explicitly turn it off. The difference in *operation* between a resolver and a name server is that the resolver implements the search list and the name server doesn't. By default, *nslookup* implements the search list, so that, too, has to be turned off. Of course, judicious use of the trailing dot will have the same effect.

In *nslookup* terms, this means that to query like a resolver, you use *nslookup*'s default settings. To query like a name server, use *set norecurse* and *set nosearch*. On the command line, that's *nslookup -norecurse -nosearch*.

When a name server gets a query, it looks for the answer in its cache. If it doesn't have the answer and it is authoritative for the zone, the name server responds that the name doesn't exist or that there is no data for that type. If the name server doesn't have the answer and it is *not* authoritative for the zone, it starts walking up the namespace looking for NS records. There will always be NS records somewhere higher in the domain tree. As a last resort, it will use the NS records at the root domain, the highest level.

If the name server received a nonrecursive query, it would respond to the querier by giving the NS records that it had found. On the other hand, if the original query was a recursive query, the name server would then query the remote name servers in the NS records that it found. When the name server receives a response from one of the remote name servers, it caches the response and repeats this process, if necessary. The remote server's response will contain either the answer to the question or a list of name servers lower in the namespace and closer to the answer.

Let's assume for our example that we are trying to satisfy a recursive query and that we didn't find any NS records until we checked the *com* domain. That is, in fact, the case when we ask the name server on *terminator.movie.edu* about *www.theonion.com*—it doesn't find any NS records in its cache until the *com* domain. From there we switch servers to a *com* name server and ask the same question. It directs us to the *theonion.com* servers. We then switch to a *theonion.com* name server and ask the same question:

```
C:\> nslookup
Default Server:  terminator.movie.edu
Address:  192.249.249.3

> set norec            Query like a name server: turn off recursion.
> set nosearch         Turn off the search list.
> www.theonion.com     We don't need to dot-terminate since we've turned search off.
Server:  terminator.movie.edu
Address:  192.249.249.3

Name:    www.theonion.com
Served by:
- a.gtld-servers.net
        192.5.6.30
        COM
- b.gtld-servers.net
        192.33.14.30
        COM
```

```
- c.gtld-servers.net
        192.26.92.30
        COM
- d.gtld-servers.net
        192.31.80.30
        COM
- e.gtld-servers.net
        192.12.94.30
        COM
- f.gtld-servers.net
        192.35.51.30
        COM
- g.gtld-servers.net
        192.42.93.30
        COM
- h.gtld-servers.net
        192.54.112.30
        COM
- i.gtld-servers.net
        192.43.172.30
        COM
- j.gtld-servers.net
        192.48.79.30
        COM
```

Switch to a *com* name server. You may have to turn recursion back on temporarily, if the name server doesn't have the address already cached:

```
> server a.gtld-servers.net.
Default Server:  a.gtld-servers.net
Address:  192.5.6.30
```

Ask the same question of the *com* name server. It will refer us to name servers closer to our desired answer:

```
> www.theonion.com.
Server:  a.gtld-servers.net
Address:  192.5.6.30

Name:    www.theonion.com
Served by:
- ns2.rackspace.com
        207.71.44.121
        theonion.com
- ns.rackspace.com
        207.235.16.2
        theonion.com
```

Switch to a *theonion.com* name server—either of them will do:

```
> server ns.rackspace.com.
Default Server:  ns.rackspace.com
Address:  207.235.16.2
```

```
> www.theonion.com.
Server:  ns.rackspace.com
Address:  207.235.16.2

Name:    theonion.com
Address:  66.216.104.235
Aliases:  www.theonion.com
```

We hope this example gives you a feeling for how name servers look up names. If you need to refresh your understanding of what this looks like graphically, see Figures 2-12 and 2-13.

Before we move on, notice that we asked each of the servers the very same question: "What's the address for *www.theonion.com?*" What do you think would happen if the *com* name server itself had already cached *www.theonion.com*'s address? The *com* name server would have answered the question out of its cache instead of referring us to the *theonion.com* name servers. Why is this significant? Suppose you messed up a particular host's address in your zone. Someone points it out to you, and you clean up the problem. Even though your name server now has the correct data, some remote sites find the old, messed-up data when they look up the name. One of the name servers higher up in the domain tree has cached the incorrect data; when it receives a query for that host's address, it returns the incorrect data instead of referring the querier to your name servers. What makes this problem hard to track down is that only one of the "higher up" name servers has cached the incorrect data, so only some of the remote lookups get the wrong answer—the ones that use this server. Fun, huh? Eventually, though, the "higher up" name server will time out the old record. If you're pressed for time, you can contact the administrators of the remote name server and ask them to kill and restart their name servers to flush the cache. Of course, if the remote name server is an important, much-used name server, they may tell you where to go with that suggestion.

Zone Transfers

You can use *nslookup* to transfer a whole zone with the *ls* command. This feature is useful for troubleshooting, for figuring out how to spell a remote host's name, or just for counting how many hosts are in some remote zone. Since the output can be substantial, *nslookup* allows you to redirect the output to a file.

Beware: a lot of hosts won't let you pull a copy of their zones, either for security reasons or to limit the load on their name server hosts.

nslookup filters zone transfer data: it shows you only some of the zone unless you tell it otherwise. By default, you see only address and name server data. You will see all of the zone data if you tell *nslookup* to display data of *any* type. The *nslookup* help (available from the Help and Support Center) or command summary (shown by typing *help* at the *nslookup* prompt) tells you all the parameters to the *ls* command. We are going to show only the *-t* parameter, since the others can be emulated with *-t*. The *-t* option takes one argument: the data type to filter. So, to pull a copy of a zone and see all the MX data, use *ls -t mx*. Let's do some zone transfers:

```
C:\> nslookup
Default Server:  terminator.movie.edu
Address:  192.249.249.3

> ls movie.edu.          List NS and A records for movie.edu.
[terminator.movie.edu]
 movie.edu.                  NS      server = terminator.movie.edu
 movie.edu.                  NS      server = wormhole.movie.edu
 carrie                      A       192.253.253.4
 diehard                     A       192.249.249.4
 misery                      A       192.253.253.2
 robocop                     A       192.249.249.2
 shining                     A       192.253.253.3
 terminator                  A       192.249.249.3
 wh249                       A       192.249.249.1
 wh253                       A       192.253.253.1
 wormhole                    A       192.253.253.1
 wormhole                    A       192.249.249.1
> ls -t any movie.edu > /temp/movie.edu.txt      List data into \temp\movie.edu.txt.

[terminator.movie.edu]
Received 25 records.
```

Those forward slashes in the *ls* command aren't a misprint—*nslookup* was originally written for Unix as part of the BIND distribution. Microsoft must have missed the slashes when porting *nslookup* to Windows.

Troubleshooting nslookup Problems

The last thing you want is to have problems with your troubleshooting tool. Unfortunately, some types of failures render the troubleshooting tool mostly useless. Other types of *nslookup* failures are, at best, confusing because they don't give you any direct information to work with. Although there may be a few problems with *nslookup* itself, most of the problems you encounter will be with name server configuration and operation. We'll cover a few odd problems here.

Looking Up the Right Data

This isn't really a problem, per se, but it can be awfully confusing. If you use *nslookup* to look up a type of data for a domain name and the domain name exists but no data of the type you're looking for exists, you'll get an error like this:

```
C:\> nslookup
Default Server:  terminator.movie.edu
Address:  192.249.249.3
```

```
> movie.edu.

Name:    movie.edu

>
```

Huh? It looks like we got an empty answer. In fact, that's exactly what happened: there are no A records for *movie.edu*, and the response from the name server has no records in the Answer section of the message. *nslookup* renders this empty response from the name server as an empty response to us. It's not very helpful or clear (previous versions of *nslookup* printed a better response).

So what types of records *do* exist? You can use *set type=any* to find out:

```
> set type=any
> movie.edu.
Server:  terminator.movie.edu
Address:  192.249.249.3

movie.edu        nameserver = terminator.movie.edu
movie.edu        nameserver = wormhole.movie.edu
movie.edu
        primary name server = terminator.movie.edu
        responsible mail addr = hostmaster.movie.edu
        serial  = 21
        refresh = 900 (15 mins)
        retry   = 600 (10 mins)
        expire  = 86400 (1 day)
        default TTL = 3600 (1 hour)
movie.edu        MX preference = 10, mail exchanger = wormhole.movie.edu
terminator.movie.edu    internet address = 192.249.249.3
wormhole.movie.edu      internet address = 192.249.249.1
wormhole.movie.edu      internet address = 192.253.253.1
wormhole.movie.edu      internet address = 192.253.253.1
wormhole.movie.edu      internet address = 192.249.249.1
```

Why are the IP addresses for *terminator* and *wormhole* returned? If you receive the NS records for *movie.edu* listing these two hosts as that zone's name servers, chances are the next thing you'll want are those hosts' IP addresses. The name server anticipates that and sends along address records in the Additional section. The same thing goes for the *movie.edu* MX record pointing to *wormhole*: if you get that record, you'll want *wormhole*'s IP address next. That explains why *wormhole*'s IP addresses show up twice, but this is arguably a bug in the Microsoft DNS Server.

No PTR Data for Name Server's Address

Here's a cryptic message:

```
C:\> nslookup
*** Can't find server name for address 192.249.249.3: Non-existent domain
```

```
Default Server:  UnKnown
Address:  192.249.249.3

>
```

The "Non-existent domain" message means that there's no PTR record for *3.249. 249.192.in-addr.arpa*. In other words, *nslookup* couldn't find the name for 192.249. 249.3, which is the first name server the resolver is configured to query. The only reason *nslookup* looks up this address is to print the "Default Server" startup message. Obviously, this name server's data is messed up, at least for the *249.249.192.in-addr.arpa* zone, so *nslookup* prints "UnKnown."

Timeouts

What if your resolver is pointing to a name server that isn't running or a host that can't be reached? Here's what happens:

```
C:\> nslookup
DNS request timed out.
    timeout was 2 seconds.
*** Can't find server name for address 192.249.249.4: Timed out
Default Server:  UnKnown
Address:  192.249.249.4

>
```

The resolver is configured to use the name server 192.249.249.4 (and only that name server). *nslookup* tries valiantly to contact it but times out, prints "UnKnown" for the default server, and gives you a prompt. You can't really do anything productive without changing servers at this point—after all, no server is running at that IP address—but at least you've got a prompt.

Occasionally you'll see timeouts during the course of an *nslookup* session. If you are looking up some remote information, the name server could fail to respond because it is still trying to look up the item and *nslookup* gave up waiting. How can you tell the difference between a name server that isn't running and a name server that is running but didn't respond? *nslookup*'s responses point out the difference. In this case, the response indicates no name server process is running:

```
C:\> nslookup
Default Server:  terminator.movie.edu
Address:  192.249.249.3

> movie.edu.
Server:  terminator.movie.edu
Address:  192.249.249.3

*** terminator.movie.edu can't find movie.edu.: No response from server
```

The "No response from server" message is quite misleading because *nslookup* actually did get a response from the server. What actually happened was this: *nslookup* sent a DNS query in a UDP packet addressed to port 53 on *terminator*. Since no name server was running on *terminator*, there was no process listening on UDP port 53 and the TCP/IP software on *terminator* responded with an ICMP destination port unreachable message. *nslookup* received this response and printed the misleading message shown previously.

If a name server is simply not responding, you'll see the following timeout message:

```
C:\> nslookup
Default Server:  terminator.movie.edu
Address:  192.249.249.3

> movie.edu.
Server:  terminator.movie.edu
Address:  192.249.249.3

DNS request timed out.
    timeout was 2 seconds.
*** Request to terminator.movie.edu timed-out
```

Query Refused

You generally see a "query refused" error message under two conditions. The first is when you attempt a zone transfer and the server refuses for security reasons (for example, based on the settings in the **Zone Transfers** tab of the zone properties window). This is what you'll see:

```
C:\> nslookup
Default Server:  terminator.movie.edu
Address:  192.249.249.3

> ls movie.edu    This attempts a zone transfer
[terminator.movie.edu]
*** Can't list domain movie.edu.: Query refused
The DNS server refused to transfer the zone movie.edu. to your computer. If this
is incorrect, check the zone transfer security settings for movie.edu. on the DNS
server at IP address 192.249.249.3.
>
```

You might also see a "query refused" error from a name server running a recent version of BIND, which has the ability to restrict queries to different zones based on the querier's source IP address.

Best of the Net

System administrators have a thankless job. They are asked certain questions, usually quite simple ones, over and over again. And sometimes, in a creative mood, they come up with a clever way to help their users. When the rest of us find out about their ingenuity, we can only sit back, smile admiringly, and wish we had thought of it ourselves.

Here is one such case, where a system administrator found a way to communicate the solution to the sometimes perplexing puzzle of how to end an *nslookup* session:

```
C:\> nslookup
Default Server: envy.ugcs.caltech.edu
Address: 131.215.134.135

> quit
Server: envy.ugcs.caltech.edu
Addresses: 131.215.134.135, 131.215.128.135

Name:   ugcs.caltech.edu
Addresses: 131.215.128.135, 131.215.134.135
Aliases: quit.ugcs.caltech.edu
         use.exit.to.leave.nslookup.-.-.-.ugcs.caltech.edu

> exit
```

Using dig

That's one way to< deal with what's arguably a shortcoming in *nslookup*. Another is just to chuck *nslookup* and use *dig*, the Domain Information Groper (a reverse-engineered acronym if we've ever heard one). *dig* is a powerful DNS query tool that comes with BIND. Unfortunately, it isn't shipped with Windows Server 2003, but you can get a version of *dig* that runs on Windows NT, Windows 2000, and Windows Server 2003 from *ftp://ftp.isc.org/isc/bind/contrib/ntbind-8.4.1/BIND8.4.1Tools. zip*. You may also need to download the other DLLs available at *ftp://ftp.isc.org/isc/ bind/contrib/ntbind-8.4.1*. Follow the installation instructions in the *readme1sttools. txt* file and note the *Known Problems* section of that file. It tells you, for example, that on Windows 2000 and Windows Server 2003, *dig* can't read the resolver configuration from the Registry, so it has no idea what name servers to query by default. You'll need to create the file *%SystemRoot%\system32\drivers\etc\resolv.conf* that contains at least one line specifying a name server to query:

```
nameserver 4.2.2.2
```

Now, all this might seem like a lot of trouble when *nslookup* is already installed. But for our DNS troubleshooting purposes, we left *nslookup* in the dust years ago. We hope you'll come to appreciate *dig* as much as we do.

With *dig*, you specify all aspects of the query you'd like to send on the command line; there's no interactive mode. You specify the domain name you want to look up as an argument, and the type of query you want to send (e.g., *a* for address records, *mx* for MX records) as another argument; the default is to look up address records. You specify the name server you'd like to query after an "@." You can use either a domain name or an IP address to designate a name server.

dig is smart about arguments, too. You can specify the arguments in any order you like, and *dig* will figure out that *mx* is probably the type of record, not the domain name, you want to look up.

One major difference between *nslookup* and *dig* is that *dig* doesn't apply the search list so always give *dig* fully qualified domain names as arguments. So:

```
C:\> dig plan9.fx.movie.edu
```

looks up address records for *plan9.fx.movie.edu* using the first name server in *resolv. conf*, while:

```
C:\> dig acmebw.com mx
```

looks up MX records for *acmebw.com* on the same name server, and:

```
C:\> dig @wormhole.movie.edu. movie.edu. soa
```

queries *wormhole.movie.edu* for the SOA record of *movie.edu*.

dig's Output Format

dig shows you the complete DNS response message in all its glory with the various sections (header, question, answer, authority, and additional) clearly called out, and with resource records in those sections printed in master file format. This can come in handy if you need to use some of your troubleshooting tool's output in a zone datafile or in your root hints file. For example, the output produced by:

```
C:\> dig @a.root-servers.net ns .
```

looks like this:

```
; <<>> DiG 8.4 <<>> @a.root-servers.net ns .
; (1 server found)
;; res options: init recurs defnam dnsrch
;; got answer:
;; ->>HEADER<<- opcode: QUERY, status: NOERROR, id: 13297
;; flags: qr aa rd; QUERY: 1, ANSWER: 13, AUTHORITY: 0, ADDITIONAL: 13
;; QUERY SECTION:
;;      ., type = NS, class = IN

;; ANSWER SECTION:
.                       6D IN NS        A.ROOT-SERVERS.NET.
.                       6D IN NS        H.ROOT-SERVERS.NET.
.                       6D IN NS        C.ROOT-SERVERS.NET.
.                       6D IN NS        G.ROOT-SERVERS.NET.
.                       6D IN NS        F.ROOT-SERVERS.NET.
.                       6D IN NS        B.ROOT-SERVERS.NET.
.                       6D IN NS        J.ROOT-SERVERS.NET.
.                       6D IN NS        K.ROOT-SERVERS.NET.
.                       6D IN NS        L.ROOT-SERVERS.NET.
.                       6D IN NS        M.ROOT-SERVERS.NET.
.                       6D IN NS        I.ROOT-SERVERS.NET.
.                       6D IN NS        E.ROOT-SERVERS.NET.
.                       6D IN NS        D.ROOT-SERVERS.NET.
```

```
;; ADDITIONAL SECTION:
A.ROOT-SERVERS.NET.    5w6d16h IN A    198.41.0.4
H.ROOT-SERVERS.NET.    5w6d16h IN A    128.63.2.53
C.ROOT-SERVERS.NET.    5w6d16h IN A    192.33.4.12
G.ROOT-SERVERS.NET.    5w6d16h IN A    192.112.36.4
F.ROOT-SERVERS.NET.    5w6d16h IN A    192.5.5.241
B.ROOT-SERVERS.NET.    5w6d16h IN A    128.9.0.107
J.ROOT-SERVERS.NET.    5w6d16h IN A    192.58.128.30
K.ROOT-SERVERS.NET.    5w6d16h IN A    193.0.14.129
L.ROOT-SERVERS.NET.    5w6d16h IN A    198.32.64.12
M.ROOT-SERVERS.NET.    5w6d16h IN A    202.12.27.33
I.ROOT-SERVERS.NET.    5w6d16h IN A    192.36.148.17
E.ROOT-SERVERS.NET.    5w6d16h IN A    192.203.230.10
D.ROOT-SERVERS.NET.    5w6d16h IN A    128.8.10.90

;; Total query time: 0 msec
;; FROM: typhoon to SERVER: 198.41.0.4
;; WHEN: Tue Aug 12 14:48:50 2003
;; MSG SIZE  sent: 17  rcvd: 436
```

Let's examine this output section by section.

The first line, beginning with the master file comment character (;) and *<<>> DiG 8.4 <<>>*, simply parrots the options we specified in the command line, namely, that we were interested in the NS records that *a.root-servers.net* had for the root zone.

The next line, (*1 server found*), tells us that when *dig* looked up the addresses associated with the domain name we specified after the "@," *a.root-servers.net*, it found one. (If *dig* finds more than three, the maximum number of name servers most resolvers can query, it'll report three.)

The line beginning with ->> *HEADER* <<- is the first part of the header of the reply message that *dig* received from the remote name server. The opcode in the header is always QUERY, just as it is with *nslookup*. The status is NOERROR; it can be any of the statuses mentioned earlier in this chapter. The ID is the message ID, a 16-bit number used to match responses to queries.

The flags tell us a bit more about the response. *qr* indicates that the message was a response, not a query. *dig* decodes responses, not queries, so *qr* will always be present. Not so with *aa* or *rd*, though. *aa* indicates that the response was authoritative, and *rd* indicates that the recursion desired bit was set in the query (since the responding name server just copies the bit from the query to the response). Most of the time *rd* is set in the query, you'll also see *ra* set in the response, indicating that recursion was available from the remote name server. However, *a.root-servers.net* is a root name server and has recursion disabled, so it handles recursive queries the same as it does iterative queries. So it ignores the *rd* bit and correctly indicates that recursion wasn't available by leaving *ra* unset.

The last fields in the header indicate that *dig* asked one question and received 13 records in the answer section, zero records in the authority section, and 13 records in the additional data section.

The line after the line that contains *QUERY SECTION* shows us the query *dig* sent: for the NS records in the IN class for the root zone. After *ANSWER SECTION*, we see the 13 NS records for the root name servers, and after *ADDITIONAL SECTION*, we have the 13 A records that correspond to those 13 root name servers. If the response had included an authority section, we'd have seen that, too, after *AUTHORITY SECTION*.

At the very end, *dig* includes summary information about the query and response. The first line shows you how long it took the remote name server to return the response after *dig* sent the query. The second line shows you from which host you sent the query and to which name server you sent it. The third line is a timestamp showing when the response was received. And the fourth line shows you the size of the query and the response, in bytes.

Zone Transfers with dig

As with *nslookup*, you can use *dig* to initiate zone transfers. Unlike *nslookup*, though, *dig* has no special command to request a zone transfer. Instead, you simply specify *axfr* (as the query type) and the domain name of the zone as arguments. Remember that you can only transfer a zone from a name server that's authoritative for the zone.

So to transfer the *movie.edu* zone from *wormhole.movie.edu*, you could use:

```
C:\> dig @wormhole.movie.edu movie.edu axfr

; <<>> DiG 8.4 <<>> @wormhole.movie.edu movie.edu axfr
; (1 server found)
$ORIGIN movie.edu.
@                       1D IN SOA       terminator al.robocop (
                                        2000091402      ; serial
                                        3H              ; refresh
                                        1H              ; retry
                                        1W              ; expiry
                                        1H )            ; minimum

                        1D IN NS        terminator
                        1D IN NS        wormhole
                        1D IN NS        outland.fx
outland.fx              1D IN A         192.253.254.3
wormhole                1D IN A         192.249.249.1
                        1D IN A         192.253.253.1
wh249                   1D IN A         192.249.249.1
robocop                 1D IN A         192.249.249.2
bigt                    1D IN CNAME     terminator
cujo                    1D IN TXT       "Location:" "machine" "room" "dog" "house"
wh253                   1D IN A         192.253.253.1
```

```
wh                  1D IN CNAME     wormhole
shining             1D IN A         192.253.253.3
terminator          1D IN A         192.249.249.3
localhost           1D IN A         127.0.0.1
fx                  1D IN NS        bladerunner.fx
bladerunner.fx      1D IN A         192.253.254.2
fx                  1D IN NS        outland.fx
outland.fx          1D IN A         192.253.254.3
dh                  1D IN CNAME     diehard
carrie              1D IN A         192.253.253.4
diehard             1D IN A         192.249.249.4
misery              1D IN A         192.253.253.2
@                   1D IN SOA       terminator al.robocop (
                                    2000091402      ; serial
                                    3H              ; refresh
                                    1H              ; retry
                                    1W              ; expiry
                                    1H )            ; minimum

;; Received 25 answers (25 records).
;; FROM: terminator.movie.edu to SERVER: wormhole.movie.edu
;; WHEN: Tue Aug 12 14:50:03 2003
```

Note that as with *nslookup*, the SOA record appears twice, at the beginning and the end of the zone.

dig Options

There are too many *dig* command-line options to show here, so look at *dig*'s manual page for an exhaustive list. Here's a list of the most important ones, though, and what they do:

-x address

> *nslookup* is smart enough to recognize an IP address and look up the appropriate domain name in *in-addr.arpa*, so why not *dig*? If you use the *-x* option, *dig* assumes that the domain name argument you've specified is really an IP address, so it inverts the octets and tacks on *in-addr.arpa*. Using *-x* also changes the default record type looked up to ANY, so you can reverse map an IP address with *dig -x 10.0.0.1*.

-p port

> Send queries to the specified port instead of port 53, the default.

+norec[urse]

> Turn off recursion (recursion is on by default).

+vc

> Send TCP-based queries (queries are UDP by default).

## CHAPTER 13

Managing DNS from the Command Line

*"I daresay you haven't had much practice," said the
Queen. "When I was your age, I always did it for half-
an-hour a day. Why, sometimes I've believed as many
as six impossible things before breakfast. There goes
the shawl again!"*

Knowledgeable administrators can perform tasks much faster using command-line tools than with graphical tools, such as the DNS console. Fortunately for us, Microsoft has steadily improved in this area, and the DNS command-line tools available with Windows Server 2003 are just as rich in features as the DNS console. In fact, many query and configuration tasks can be done *only* with a command-line tool.

Another benefit of understanding how to use command-line tools is that you can create batch scripts that automate repetitive processes. In this chapter, we will show you how easy it is to create a simple batch script that installs the Microsoft DNS Server, configures some name server settings, adds a zone, creates a resource record, and toasts some bread. All right, maybe it can't toast bread, but you get the idea. And don't worry if scripting isn't your cup of tea; Windows batch scripts, in their most basic form, contain nothing more than a list of commands to execute. Our script is a little more complicated than that, but not much.

Throughout this book we've shown you how to configure a Microsoft DNS Server using the DNS console. The command-line counterpart to the DNS console is *dnscmd*, which is available in the Windows Support Tools on the Windows Server 2003 CD. *dnscmd* includes the proverbial kitchen sink of options for managing a Microsoft DNS Server. We spend most of our time in this chapter reviewing *dnscmd*. We also cover other useful utilities such as *sysocmgr,* for installing the DNS server; and *sc*, which can be used to query, start, and stop the DNS server. At the end of the chapter, we provide a list of other DNS-related command-line tools that are useful for querying and troubleshooting DNS.

Installing the DNS Server

The Microsoft DNS Server is an optional Windows networking component that can be installed from the command line with the *sysocmgr* utility, which is installed with the operating system. It can be found in *%SystemRoot%\system32*.

To use *sysocmgr*, you first need to create an answer file. An answer file specifies one or more optional components that you want to install. In our case, we will just install the DNS server. Here is what our answer file looks like:

```
[netoptionalcomponents]
dns=1
```

When running *sysocmgr*, we need to specify two options. The first is /i, followed by a colon and the path to the *sysoc.inf* file, which is stored in the *%SystemRoot%\inf* directory by default. The second option is /u, followed by a colon and the path to the answer file. If the answer file is stored in the root of the *C:* drive and is called *dns_install.txt*, the full command line would look like this:

```
C:\> sysocmgr /i:%SystemRoot%\inf\sysoc.inf /u:c:\dns_install.txt
```

This starts installation of the service. You will see screens pop up as if you were installing the service through the GUI. You are prompted for the location of the Windows Server 2003 CD files, unless the *sysoc.inf* file points to a local drive or network share that contains the *\i386* directory that can be found on the CD.

Additional options available with *sysocmgr* can install the DNS server silently. If you want to suppress all screens during installation, you can use the /x and /q options. See Figure 13-1 for the complete list of options that are supported.

You can also use *sysocmgr* to uninstall the DNS server. To do that, change the contents of the *dns_install.txt* answer file to the following:

```
[netoptionalcomponents]
dns=0
```

Run *sysocmgr* with the same command-line options shown previously.

For more information about unattended installation options and the syntax of answer files, check out the *ref.chm* help file that can be extracted from the *\support\tools\deploy.cab* file on the Windows Server 2003 CD.

Stopping and Starting the DNS Server Service

There are a couple of options for stopping and starting the DNS server on Windows Server 2003. The *net stop* and *net start* commands have been around since the early days of Windows NT and are commonly used to stop and start services, if for no other reason than their availability and simplicity. You specify the name of the service

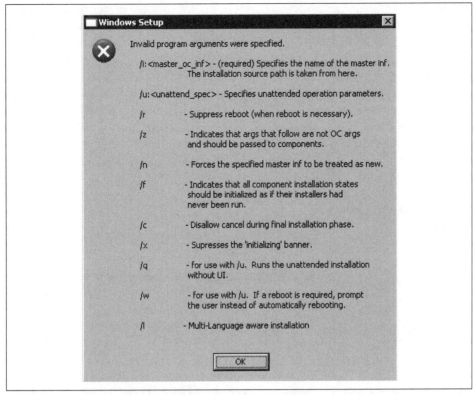

Invalid program arguments were specified.

/i: <master_oc_inf> - (required) Specifies the name of the master inf.
    The installation source path is taken from here.

/u: <unattend_spec> - Specifies unattended operation parameters.

/r   - Suppress reboot (when reboot is necessary).

/z   - Indicates that args that follow are not OC args
         and should be passed to components.

/n   - Forces the specified master inf to be treated as new.

/f   - Indicates that all component installation states
         should be initialized as if their installers had
         never been run.

/c   - Disallow cancel during final installation phase.

/x   - Supresses the 'initializing' banner.

/q   - for use with /u. Runs the unattended installation
         without UI.

/w   - for use with /u. If a reboot is required, prompt
         the user instead of automatically rebooting.

/l   - Multi-Language aware installation

[OK]

Figure 13-1. syscomgr command-line options

after the command to stop or start it. Here is an example of restarting the DNS server in two steps using these commands:

```
C:\> net stop dns
The DNS Server service is stopping.
The DNS Server service was stopped successfully.
```

```
C:\> net start dns
The DNS Server service is starting.
The DNS Server service was started successfully.
```

While these commands are certainly easy to use, they don't work on a remote server. If you need to stop, start, or restart the DNS server on a remote server, you'll need to use the *sc* utility.

In Windows 2000, the *sc* utility was available in the Resource Kit. In Windows Server 2003, it's installed with the operating system, like the *syscomgr* and *net* commands we described earlier.

Not only can *sc* be run against remote servers, but it provides options to perform just about any action you would need to do against a service. To restart the DNS server on a remote server named *matrix*, we would use the following commands:

```
C:\> sc \\matrix stop dns

SERVICE_NAME: dns
    TYPE               : 10  WIN32_OWN_PROCESS
    STATE              : 3  STOP_PENDING
                            (STOPPABLE, PAUSABLE, ACCEPTS_SHUTDOWN)
    WIN32_EXIT_CODE    : 0  (0x0)
    SERVICE_EXIT_CODE  : 0  (0x0)
    CHECKPOINT         : 0x1
    WAIT_HINT          : 0x7530
```

```
C:\> sc \\matrix start dns

SERVICE_NAME: dns
    TYPE               : 10  WIN32_OWN_PROCESS
    STATE              : 2  START_PENDING
                            (NOT_STOPPABLE, NOT_PAUSABLE, IGNORES_SHUTDOWN))

    WIN32_EXIT_CODE    : 0  (0x0)
    SERVICE_EXIT_CODE  : 0  (0x0)
    CHECKPOINT         : 0x0
    WAIT_HINT          : 0x7d0
    PID                : 504
    FLAGS              :
```

As you can see, the second command returned a START_PENDING state. To verify the service started successfully, we can use the *query* option:

```
C:\> sc \\matrix query dns

SERVICE_NAME: dns
    TYPE               : 10  WIN32_OWN_PROCESS
    STATE              : 4  RUNNING
                            (STOPPABLE, PAUSABLE, ACCEPTS_SHUTDOWN)
    WIN32_EXIT_CODE    : 0  (0x0)
    SERVICE_EXIT_CODE  : 0  (0x0)
    CHECKPOINT         : 0x0
    WAIT_HINT          : 0x0
```

We recommend using *sc* instead of the *net* command. In its most basic form, *sc* is just as simple but much more powerful. The following help entry lists all the options supported by *sc*:

```
DESCRIPTION:
        SC is a command line program used for communicating with the
        Service Control Manager and services.
USAGE:
        sc <server> [command] [service name] <option1> <option2>...
```

```
The option <server> has the form "\\ServerName"
Further help on commands can be obtained by typing: "sc [command]"
Commands:
query-----------Queries the status for a service, or
                enumerates the status for types of services.
queryex---------Queries the extended status for a service, or
                enumerates the status for types of services.
start-----------Starts a service.
pause-----------Sends a PAUSE control request to a service.
interrogate-----Sends an INTERROGATE control request to a service.
continue--------Sends a CONTINUE control request to a service.
stop------------Sends a STOP request to a service.
config----------Changes the configuration of a service (persistent).
description-----Changes the description of a service.
failure---------Changes the actions taken by a service upon failure.
qc--------------Queries the configuration information for a service.
qdescription----Queries the description for a service.
qfailure--------Queries the actions taken by a service upon failure.
delete----------Deletes a service (from the registry).
create----------Creates a service. (adds it to the registry).
control---------Sends a control to a service.
sdshow----------Displays a service's security descriptor.
sdset-----------Sets a service's security descriptor.
GetDisplayName--Gets the DisplayName for a service.
GetKeyName------Gets the ServiceKeyName for a service.
EnumDepend------Enumerates Service Dependencies.

The following commands don't require a service name:
sc <server> <command> <option>
boot------------(ok | bad) Indicates whether the last boot should
                be saved as the last-known-good boot configuration
Lock------------Locks the Service Database
QueryLock-------Queries the LockStatus for the SCManager Database
EXAMPLE:
sc start MyService
```

Managing the DNS Server Configuration

The DNS server is one of the few Microsoft services that you can configure completely from a command line. The *dnscmd* utility has been around since Windows NT. Microsoft has added new options with every major operating system release. With it, you can modify server settings and create, query, and manipulate zones and resource records. In the Windows Server 2003 version, there are even *dnscmd* commands for managing Active Directory application partitions.

Using *dnscmd* is straightforward. Here is the generic syntax:

```
dnscmd ServerName Command AdditionalOptions
```

The *ServerName* parameter is used to target a remote name server. It is optional and, if not included, runs the command against the local server (which must be a name server). You can also use a single dot (.) to target the local server.

The *Command* parameter is required and corresponds to an action you can perform against the server. The Windows Server 2003 version of *dnscmd* supports 37 different commands. Running *dnscmd* from a command line without passing any parameters displays the complete list of supported commands.

The *AdditionalOptions* parameter is optional for some commands, required for some, and not used for others. To see what additional parameters are needed for a command, run **dnscmd *Command* /?** from the command line.

The final point worth mentioning about *dnscmd* is that it does not communicate with a name server via dynamic updates, zone transfers, or any other standard DNS communication protocol. Instead, it uses RPC to talk directly to the DNS Server service on the target name server. This is why, if the DNS Server service is not running on a name server, you can't run *dnscmd* against it; start it with *sc* first.

We will now take a tour through the *dnscmd* command options (all 37 of them). Normally, we wouldn't go into so much detail about a utility's options but, unfortunately, much of the Microsoft documentation on *dnscmd* is inconsistent. We've tested each command and attempted to provide definitive information about its usage and syntax. A positive side effect of reading through each command is that you will become well-versed in the capabilities and limitations of the Microsoft DNS Server.

dnscmd Server Commands

You can view the settings for a name server by using the */Info* command. Likewise, you can use the */Config* command to change any of these settings. (Table 14-1 provides a complete list of supported settings.) Commands are also available to configure the addresses the server listens on (*/ResetListenAddresses*), configure forwarding (*/ResetForwarders*), initiate scavenging (*/StartScavenging*), clear the server cache (*/ClearCache*), and view DNS utilization statistics (*/Statistics*).

/Info [<PropertyName>]

    This command displays the DNS server settings. These settings are stored under the following registry key:

        `HKLM\SYSTEM\CurrentControlSet\Services\DNS\Parameters`

    If you run this command without other options, all settings and their values are displayed. Alternatively, you can display a single setting by specifying the name of the setting after the command.

    This example displays the *ForwardingTimeout* setting on *matrix*:

        `C:\> dnscmd matrix /info ForwardingTimeout`

/Config /<PropertyName> <PropertyValue>

    This command sets a server setting. The first parameter should be the name of the property you want to set, followed by the value.

This example shows how to change the *ForwardingTimeout* setting to 3 (seconds) on *matrix*:

```
C:\> dnscmd matrix /config /ForwardingTimeout 3
```

/ResetListenAddresses [<ServerIPAddresses>]

By default, the Microsoft name server listens for client requests on all networks to which it is directly connected. With this command, you can limit the networks that the server listens on by specifying a whitespace-separated list of one or more IP addresses. These IP addresses must be valid addresses configured on network adapters on the server or the command fails. To reset to the default, run this command without any IP addresses.

This example sets the listen addresses on *matrix* to 10.13.19.84 and 10.7.19.76:

```
C:\> dnscmd matrix /resetlistenaddresses 10.13.19.84 10.7.19.76
```

/ResetForwarders [<ForwarderIPAddresses>]

Use this command to enable forwarding on a name server. Specify a whitespace-separated list of the IP addresses of the name servers to which it should forward requests. If you run this command without any IP addresses, it disables forwarding.

This example enables forwarding on *matrix* and forwards unresolved queries to 10.13.19.84 and 10.7.19.76:

```
C:\> dnscmd matrix /resetforwarders 10.13.19.84 10.7.19.76
```

/StartScavenging

This command starts the scavenging process on all zones configured for scavenging on the name server. Even though it may return a success message, successful scavenging depends on the following:

1. Scavenging must have previously been enabled on the server. This command enables scavenging and sets it to run every 168 hours (7 days):

   ```
   C:\> dnscmd matrix /config /scavenginginterval 168
   ```

2. Scavenging must have previously been enabled on one or more zones. This command enables scavenging on the *fx.movie.edu* zone:

   ```
   C:\> dnscmd matrix /config fx.movie.edu /aging
   ```

3. Resource records must have previously had aging enabled. By default, resource records that are added via dynamic update have aging enabled. You can also configure a record to be aged when you create it using the /aging option with the /recordadd command. To enable aging on all resource records in a zone, see the /ageallrecords command.

   This example initiates scavenging on *matrix*:

   ```
   C:\> dnscmd matrix /startscavenging
   ```

This command causes scavenging to start, but it does not wait for scavenging to complete so it will pretty much always return success. To see the results of the scavenging, you'll want to view the DNS event log once scavenging has had enough time to run.

/ClearCache

The Microsoft DNS Server keeps a cache in memory of records that it has resolved locally or through recursive queries. These records are cached for the duration of the time to live (TTL) setting on each record. If a record was recently changed and you want to update the cache so the server returns the latest version, you can flush the cache using this command.

This example clears the server cache on *matrix*:

```
C:\> dnscmd matrix /clearcache
```

/Statistics [<StatNumber>]

The Microsoft DNS Server keeps track of performance statistics related to the number of requests, queries, updates, zone transfers, packets, and Active Directory reads and writes it processes. This is useful information for monitoring the utilization of your name server. Running this command without any parameters prints all statistics.

You can also view a subset of statistics. Several statistics categories group similar metrics together, such as query-related metrics. You can view a subset of metrics by summing the hexadecimal numbers associated with the categories you want to see. Here is a list of each category and its number.

Start number	Category
000001	Time
000002	Query
000004	Query2
000008	Recurse
000010	Master
000020	Secondary
000040	Wins
000100	Wire Update
000200	Security
000400	Ds
000800	Internal Update
010000	Memory
040000	Dbase
080000	Records
100000	PacketMem

This example displays the query-related statistics (2 + 4) for *matrix*:

```
C:\> dnscmd matrix /statistics 6
```

Keep in mind that these are numbers are in hex, so 4 + 8 would equal C, not 12.

dnscmd Zone Commands

Over half of the *dnscmd* command options relate to configuring or querying zones.

/AgeAllRecords <ZoneName> [<NodeName>] [/Tree] [/f]

In order for resource records to be scavenged after a period of time, a timestamp must be associated with the record. The */AgeAllRecords* command allows you to set the current time as the timestamp for all records in a zone, or for a specific node in a zone. The node name can be any node in the zone, @ to represent all records, or the name of a subdomain. If you specify a subdomain for the node, use the */tree* option to set a timestamp on all records in the subdomain.

By default, you are prompted for confirmation before records are aged. To disable this prompt, use the */f* option.

This example shows how to age all resource records in the *cgi* subdomain of the *fx.movie.edu* zone:

```
C:\> dnscmd /ageallrecords fx.movie.edu cgi /tree
```

/Config <ZoneName> /<PropertyName> [<PropertyValue>]

This command configures settings for both name servers and zones. To configure zone settings, specify the zone name followed by the property name and value (if necessary).

This example turns on aging for the *fx.movie.edu* zone:

```
C:\> dnscmd /config fx.movie.edu /aging
```

/EnumZones [<Filters>]

This command lists the zones stored on a server. Several filter options are available if you want to view a subset of zones. These include: */Primary, /Secondary, /Forwarder, /Stub, /Cache, /Auto-Created, /Forward, /Reverse, /Ds, /File, /DomainDirectoryPartition, /ForestDirectoryPartition, /CustomDirectoryPartition, /LegacyDirectoryPartition,* and */DirectoryPartition.*

This example enumerates all AD-integrated zones stored on the local server:

```
C:\> dnscmd /enumzones /ds
```

/WriteBackFiles [<ZoneName>]

This command allows you to write to persistent storage any updates to the zone that are stored only in memory. If you do not specify a zone name, changes to any zone stored on the server are written to persistent storage.

This example writes to disk any changes to the *fx.movie.edu* zone that are stored in memory:

```
C:\> dnscmd /writebackfiles fx.movie.edu
```

/ZoneAdd <ZoneName> <ZoneType> [<ZoneOptions>]

This command adds a zone to a server. The first parameter is the name of the zone, and the second is the zone type. Based on the zone type, there may be additional zone options that you can also specify. Here is the list of zone types and associated zone options:

- */DsPrimary [/dp <AppPartitionName> | /domain | /forest | /legacy]*
- */Primary /file <FileName>*
- */Secondary <MasterIPAddresses> [/file <FileName>]*
- */Stub <MasterIPAddresses> [/file <FileName>]*
- */DsStub <MasterIPAddresses> [/dp <AppPartitionName> | /domain | /forest | /legacy]*
- */Forwarder <MasterIPAddresses> [/Timeout <Time>] [/Slave]*
- */DsForwarder <MasterIPAddresses> [/Timeout <Time>] [/Slave] [/dp <AppPartitionName> | /domain | /forest | /legacy]*

This example creates an AD-integrated zone named *fx.movie.edu* and stores it in the forest DNS application partition:

```
C:\> dnscmd /zoneadd fx.movie.edu /dsprimary /forest
```

/ZoneDelete <ZoneName> [/DsDel] [/f]

This command deletes a zone from a server. When deleting an AD-integrated zone, you must specify the */DsDel* option or an error will be returned.

Before deleting the zone, you are prompted to confirm the deletion. The */f* option skips the confirmation step.

This example deletes the AD-integrated *fx.movie.edu* zone from the local server and from Active Directory:

```
C:\> dnscmd /zonedelete fx.movie.edu /DsDel
```

/ZoneExport <ZoneName> <ZoneFileName>

This command exports the contents of a zone into a standard zone file. This is useful when troubleshooting AD-integrated zones, which do not generate zone files.

The first parameter is the zone name, followed by the filename to which to export the zone. This file is created in *%systemroot%\System32\dns* on the target server.

This example shows how to export the contents of the *fx.movie.edu* zone to a file named *fx-export.dns*:

```
C:\> dnscmd /zoneexport fx.movie.edu fx-export.dns
```

/ZoneInfo <ZoneName> [<PropertyName>]

This command displays the settings for a zone. These settings are stored under the following registry key:

```
HKLM\SOFTWARE\Microsoft\Windows NT\CurrentVersion\DNS Server\Zones\ZoneName
```

By default, all settings for a zone are displayed, but you can optionally specify a property name to display the value for only that setting.

This example displays all settings for the *fx.movie.edu* zone:

```
C:\> dnscmd /zoneinfo fx.movie.edu
```

/ZonePause <ZoneName>

With this command, you can stop the name server from responding to queries for a zone and from processing updates. Use the */ZoneResume* command to restart the zone.

This example shows how to pause the *fx.movie.edu* zone:

```
C:\> dnscmd /zonepause fx.movie.edu
```

/ZonePrint <ZoneName>

This command prints the resource records for the specified zone. This is similar to the */ZoneExport* command, except that the contents of the zone are printed to the screen instead of to a file. You can obviously redirect the contents to a file if desired.

This example prints the resource records in the *fx.movie.edu* zone:

```
C:\> dnscmd /zoneprint fx.movie.edu
```

/ZoneRefresh <ZoneName>

This command is run against a secondary name server to force a zone transfer of a particular zone. The zone transfer occurs only if the serial number in the zone's SOA record on the master server is higher than the serial number on the secondary server the command is run against.

This example causes the local server to perform a zone transfer of the *fx.movie.edu* zone if the master server has a higher SOA serial number:

```
C:\> dnscmd /zonerefresh fx.movie.edu
```

/ZoneReload <ZoneName>

This command causes the specified zone to be reloaded from its zone file or from Active Directory for AD-integrated zones.

This example shows how to reload the *fx.movie.edu* zone:

```
C:\> dnscmd /zonereload fx.movie.edu
```

/ZoneResetMasters <ZoneName> [/local] [<MasterIPAddresses>]

This command sets the list of master IP addresses that the server uses to perform zone transfers for the specified zone. To remove the current master IP addresses, run this command without any parameters.

If you specify */local* against an AD-integrated stub zone, the new master list is "local" to the target server only. All other servers will use the master list stored in AD.

This example configures 10.7.52.25 as the master server for the *fx.movie.edu* zone:

```
C:\> dnscmd /zoneresetmasters fx.movie.edu 10.7.52.25
```

/ZoneResetScavengeServers <ZoneName> [<ServerIPAddresses>]

> For AD-integrated zones that have scavenging enabled, you can limit the servers that perform scavenging with this command. By default, all servers that have scavenging enabled remove out-of-date records in zones that also have scavenging enabled. If you omit the list of servers, it reverts to the default, which is all servers performing a periodic scavenge.
>
> This example shows how to restrict scavenging of the *fx.movie.edu* zone to the name servers 10.7.19.76 and 10.7.25.63:
>
> ```
> C:\> dnscmd /zoneresetscavengeservers fx.movie.edu 10.7.19.76 10.7.25.63
> ```

/ZoneResetSecondaries <ZoneName> [<ZoneTransferOptions>] [<NotifyOptions>]

> This command configures which secondary servers can perform zone transfers and receive NOTIFY messages for the specified zone. *ZoneTransferOptions* is optional and, if included, can be one of the following:

/NoXfr

> Zone transfers are not allowed to any server.

/NonSecure

> Zone transfers are allowed to any server.

/SecureNs

> Only servers listed in the NS records for the zone can perform zone transfers.

/SecureList <IPAddresses>

> Only servers specified by *IPAddresses* can perform zone transfers.

> *NotifyOptions* is also optional and can be one of the following:

/NoNotify

> Change notifications are not sent to any servers.

/Notify

> Change notifications are sent to all servers listed in the NS records for the zone.

/NotifyList <IPAddresses>

> Change notifications are only sent to the servers specified by *IPAddresses*.

> This example enables NOTIFY and allows only servers that have NS records in the zone to perform zone transfers for the *fx.movie.edu* zone:
>
> ```
> C:\> dnscmd /zoneresetsecondaries fx.movie.edu /securens /notify
> ```

/ZoneResetType <ZoneName> <ZoneType> [<ZoneOptions>] [/OverWrite_Mem | /OverWrite_Ds]

> This command changes the type of a zone. For example, you can change a secondary zone to become a primary zone. See the *ZoneType* options for the */ZoneAdd* command because they are nearly identical for this command. The only difference is that for AD-integrated zones, you need to use */DirectoryPartition* instead of */dp* to specify the application partition to store the zone in.
>
> The */OverWrite_Mem* and */OverWrite_Ds* options can be used when converting non-AD-integrated zones to AD-integrated zones. */OverWrite_Mem* causes the

contents of the zone in AD to overwrite what is stored locally. */OverWrite_Ds* causes the contents of the locally stored zone to overwrite what is in AD.

This example shows how to change the primary zone *fx.movie.edu* to be AD-integrated, and store it in the forest DNS application partition:

```
C:\> dnscmd /zoneresettype fx.movie.edu /dsprimary forestdnszones.movie.edu
```

/ZoneResume <ZoneName>

This command can be used to start a zone that has been stopped with the */ZonePause* command. When a zone is paused or stopped, the name server does not answer queries or process updates for the zone.

This example resumes the *fx.movie.edu* zone:

```
C:\> dnscmd /zoneresume fx.movie.edu
```

/ZoneUpdateFromDs <ZoneName>

Name servers that support AD-integrated zones periodically poll Active Directory for changes to those zones. By default, this happens every five minutes. You can use the */ZoneUpdateFromDs* command to force the name server to check Active Directory for changes. You can also change the polling frequency by running this command where *<Minutes>* is how often to poll Active Directory:

```
C:\> dnscmd /config /dspollinginterval Minutes
```

This example shows you how to force the local name server to check Active Directory for changes to the *fx.movie.edu* zone:

```
C:\> dnscmd /zoneupdatefromds fx.movie.edu
```

/ZoneWriteBack <ZoneName>

When a Microsoft DNS Server receives updates for a file-based zone, it does not immediately commit those changes to disk. Instead, it stores them in memory and periodically writes the changes to its permanent storage. The */ZoneWrite-Back* command allows you to manually initiate the write-back action for a zone.

For AD-integrated zones, all changes are written immediately to Active Directory as they are processed.

This example shows how to write to disk any changes stored in memory for the *fx.movie.edu* zone:

```
C:\> dnscmd /zonewriteback fx.movie.edu
```

dnscmd Application Partition Commands

In Windows Server 2003, AD-integrated zones can be stored in application partitions, which we described in Chapter 8. Not only can you use *dnscmd* to store a particular zone in an application partition, but you can query, create, delete, and control which domain controllers replicate an application partition. In short, *dnscmd* is not only your primary command-line interface for managing DNS, but for managing DNS application partitions as well.

/CreateBuiltinDirectoryPartitions /domain | /forest | /alldomains

If you install a new Windows Server 2003 Active Directory forest, the default DNS application partitions are installed automatically. If you delete these application partitions and need to recreate them, you can use this command. The type of built-in application partition to create is a required parameter. */domain* creates a domainwide application partition (e.g., *domaindnszones.movie.edu*) for the domain of the server this command is run against. */forest* creates a forestwide DNS application partition (e.g., *forestdnszones.movie.edu*). */alldomains* creates a domainwide application partition for all domains in the forest. (This does not include the forestwide application partition.)

This example shows how to create the built-in domainwide DNS application partitions in the forest that the target server is in:

```
C:\> dnscmd  /CreateBuiltinDirectoryPartitions /alldomains
```

/CreateDirectoryPartition <AppPartitionName>

This command creates an application partition, which can be used either for replicating AD-integrated zone data or for other application data.

This example shows how to create an application partition named *apps.fx. movie.edu*:

```
C:\> dnscmd /CreateDirectoryPartition apps.fx.movie.edu
```

/DeleteDirectoryPartition <AppPartitionName>

This command deletes an application partition. Deleting an application partition deletes all objects that are stored in it.

This example shows how to delete an application partition named *apps.fx. movie.edu*:

```
C:\> dnscmd /DeleteDirectoryPartition apps.fx.movie.edu
```

/DirectoryPartitionInfo <AppPartitionName> [/detail]

Use this command to display information about an application partition. The information includes the distinguished name in Active Directory, the corresponding *crossRef* object in the Partitions container, a list of replica servers, and the number of zones stored (if AD-integrated zones are stored in it). By default, very long domain names are truncated in the output. You can use the optional */detail* switch to make sure long names are not truncated.

This example displays the properties of the *forestdnszones.movie.edu* application partition:

```
C:\> dnscmd /DirectoryPartitionInfo forestdnszones.movie.edu
```

/EnlistDirectoryPartition <AppPartitionName>

With this command, you make the target name server a replica server for the specified application partition. This causes the server to replicate the contents of the application partition. Note that you cannot use this command to "enlist" servers that are not running the DNS Server service.

This example causes *matrix* to become a replica server for the *apps.movie.edu* application partition:

```
C:\> dnscmd matrix /EnlistDirectoryPartition apps.movie.edu
```

/EnumDirectoryPartitions [/custom]

This command prints a list of the application partitions in the forest that the target server is a member of. The output includes whether the server is enlisted with each application partition or not. */custom* is optional and can be used to display only the non-default application partitions. (These are the ones created by */CreateBuiltinDirectoryPartitions*.)

This example displays all of the custom application partitions in a forest:

```
C:\> dnscmd /EnumDirectoryPartitions /custom
```

/UnenlistDirectoryPartition <AppPartitionName>

Whereas the */EnlistDirectoryPartition* adds a server to an application partition, this command removes (or "unenlists") a server from an application partition.

This example removes *matrix* from the *apps.fx.movie.edu* application partition:

```
C:\> dnscmd matrix /UnenlistDirectoryPartition apps.fx.movie.edu
```

/ZoneChangeDirectoryPartition <ZoneName> [<AppPartitionName> | /domain | /forest | /legacy]

Use this command to move an AD-integrated zone between application partitions and the System container. The first two parameters must be the name of the zone to move followed by the application partition to move it to. This can take the form of a FQDN of an application partition, */domain* to move it to the default domain application partition for name servers, */forest* for the default forest application partition for name servers, or */legacy* to move it to the System container of a domain.

This example moves the *fx.movie.edu* zone to the default domain application partition for name servers:

```
C:\> dnscmd /ZoneChangeDirectoryPartition fx.movie.edu /domain
```

dnscmd Resource Record Commands

The *dnscmd* utility can query, create, and delete resource records using the */Enum-Records*, */RecordAdd*, */RecordDelete*, and */NodeDelete* commands. Each of these commands requires the same two parameters following the command option. The first is the name of the zone (*ZoneName*) you want to perform the task against. The second is the name of the node (*NodeName*) that corresponds to the owner of the target resource record (or records).

/EnumRecords <ZoneName> <NodeName> [/Type <RRType> <RRData>] [/Author-ity] [/Glue] [/Additional] [/Node | /Child | /StartChild <Child>] [/Continue | /Detail]

This command has several options that provide flexibility with enumerating resource records in a zone.* The only required parameters are *ZoneName* and *NodeName*. If you want to match all resource records, you can replace *Node-Name* with @ instead of a specific node name. Here are the other optional parameters used to control the types of records enumerated and the information that is displayed for each.

/Type <RRType>
Restrict the records that are returned to a specific resource record type (*RRType*).

/Authority
Display only authoritative data.

/Glue
Display any glue information for each record.

/Additional
Display any additional information for each record.

/Node
Display only the records for the specified node.

/Child
Display only the child records of the specified node.

/StartChild <ChildNodeName>
Display only the records starting at a particular child node (i.e., subdomain)

/Continue
Display all matching records regardless of the number. By default, after the buffer has been filled, it stops displaying records.

/Detail
Display detailed debugging information for each record.

This example displays all records associated with the node *matrix* in the *fx.movie.edu* zone:

```
C:\> dnscmd /enumrecords fx.movie.edu matrix
```

This example displays all A records in the *fx.movie.edu* zone:

```
C:\> dnscmd /enumrecords fx.movie.edu @ /Type A
```

---

* Besides providing different options for querying records, */EnumRecords* is different from the *nslookup* command because it uses RPC to communicate with the Microsoft DNS Server instead of the standard DNS protocol. This also means that the */EnumRecords* command does not work with non-Microsoft DNS Servers.

/NodeDelete <ZoneName> <NodeName> [/tree] [/f]
> This command deletes all resource records associated with a node. You can delete a subdomain of records by specifying the name of the subdomain for *<NodeName>* along with the /tree option.
>
> By default, you are prompted to confirm the deletion. To disable the confirmation request, use the /f switch.
>
> This example deletes the *cgi.fx.movie.edu* subdomain and all the resource records contained within it:
>
> ```
> C:\> dnscmd /nodedelete cgi.fx.movie.edu /tree
> ```

/RecordAdd <ZoneName> <NodeName> [/Aging] [/OpenAcl] [<TTL>] <RRType> <RRData>
> This command allows you to create any of the resource records supported by the Microsoft DNS Server. The first two required parameters are the zone name and node name. You can then specify any of these optional parameters:
>
> */Aging*
> > Enables aging for the record. If scavenging has been turned on for the server and zone, the record is deleted after the refresh and no-refresh intervals unless the record is updated.
>
> */OpenAcl*
> > For AD-integrated zones, the ACL on this record is configured so that anyone can modify it initially. After a client updates the record, only that client (by default) has permission to modify the record. An administrator who is pre-populating records for clients might use this option. The first time each client touches the record the record becomes locked down to only that client for future updates.
>
> *<TTL>*
> > Time-to-live value for the record.
>
> The next two parameters are required. They are the record type (*RRType*) and record data (*RRData*) fields.
>
> This example adds an A record for *matrix* in the *fx.movie.edu* zone:
>
> ```
> C:\> dnscmd /recordadd fx.movie.edu matrix A 10.7.19.76
> ```

/RecordDelete <ZoneName> <NodeName> <RRType> <RRData> [/f]
> While */NodeDelete* allows you to delete all of the resource records associated with a specific node, you can delete individual records with */RecordDelete*. After the *ZoneName* and *NodeName* parameters, you must specify the *RRType* and *RRData*.
>
> This command prompts for confirmation before proceeding with the deletion. You can disable the confirmation prompt using the */f* option.
>
> This example deletes the A record for *matrix* in the *fx.movie.edu* zone:
>
> ```
> C:\> dnscmd /recorddelete fx.movie.edu matrix A 10.7.19.76
> ```

An Installation and Configuration Batch Script

Now that we've covered the DNS installation and configuration commands, we'll show you a short batch script that automates the initial setup of a secondary name server. This script performs the following tasks:

1. Installs the DNS Server service using *sysocmgr*
2. Adds a zone called *fx.movie.edu* using *dnscmd*
3. Configures the server to use a forwarder using *dnscmd*
4. Adds an A record for the name of the new server in the *fx.movie.edu* zone on the primary master server using *dnscmd*
5. Performs a zone transfer from the primary master server to receive the latest updates using *dnscmd*

The only other utility used in the script is the *sleep* command, which is available in the Resource Kit. The sleep command is used to allow time for the changes initiated by each command to be committed.

Here is the script:

```
@echo off

:: IP address of primary master server
set PRIMARY_MASTER_IP=64.10.57.21
:: Forward-mapping zone to add to this server
set FWD_ZONE=fx.movie.edu
:: IP address of this server
set SERVER_IP=10.50.23.7

echo Installing the DNS Server service...
sysocmgr /i:%windir%\inf\sysoc.inf /u:c:\dns_install.txt
:: The sleep command is part of the Resource Kit
sleep 5

echo Adding a zone...
dnscmd /zoneadd %FWD_ZONE% /Secondary %PRIMARY_MASTER_IP%
sleep 5

echo Configuring this server to use a forwarder...
dnscmd /resetforwarders %PRIMARY_MASTER_IP%
sleep 5

echo Adding an A record for this server in %FWD_ZONE%
dnscmd %PRIMARY_IP% /recordadd %FWD_ZONE% %COMPUTERNAME% A %SERVER_IP%
sleep 5

echo Performing a zone transfer
dnscmd /zonerefresh %FWD_ZONE%

echo Done
```

As you can see, the script isn't terribly complex. The @echo off line turns off printing of each command as it is run. You may want to comment this out if you need to debug the script. Commented lines in batch scripts are designated by : : at the beginning of the line.

The rest of the code runs the commands to perform the steps we outlined earlier. We used the *set* command to initialize some variables that we use throughout the script. The *echo* command was used to print some status messages. The output from each command is also displayed.

This example script may not be applicable in your environment, but it should give you an idea of how easy it is to create simple batch scripts to automate the installation and configuration of your name servers. If you're interested in learning more about using scripts to manage DNS, see Chapter 14.

Other Command-Line Utilities

The command-line utilities we've seen so far cover the spectrum of installing and configuring the DNS Server service. There are, however, several other utilities that you are likely to run across as a DNS administrator. They are used for querying and troubleshooting DNS.

nslookup

The *nslookup* utility is one of the oldest and most widely used DNS tools. With it, you can perform all types of resource record queries and even zone transfers. This tool is so important that we spent most of Chapter 12 describing how to use it.

The *nslookup* utility is installed by default on Windows 2000, Windows XP, and Windows Server 2003.

ipconfig

The *ipconfig* utility is most commonly used for releasing and renewing DHCP addresses, but it is also a handy client-side DNS tool. The DNS-related *ipconfig* options include the following:

/displaydns
: This option displays the contents of the client resolver cache. For each cached resource record, it displays the Record Name, Record Type, Time To Live (TTL), Data Length, Section, and RR data. If a record resides in the cache and another query is made for the record, the client uses that record (until the TTL expires) instead of querying a name server again.

/flushdns

> This option erases the contents of the resolver cache. Subsequent lookups are sent to a name server and cached again by the client after receiving a response.

/registerdns

> This option causes the client to refresh its DHCP lease and its network registration (A and PTR records).

The *ipconfig* utility is installed by default on Windows 2000, Windows XP, and Windows Server 2003.

netdiag

The *netdiag* utility performs a variety of network connectivity tests, including a DNS test. The *netdiag /test:DNS* command iterates over each active network adapter and checks whether the hostname has an A record in the domain specified by the domain suffix for the adapter. If you receive an error message for the DNS test, you should run **netdiag /test:DNS /debug**, which will produce verbose output and help pinpoint the cause of the failure.

If you run **netdiag /test:DNS** on a domain controller and receive errors, you can run it again with the **/fix** option to force all the records in the *netlogon.dns* file to be refreshed in DNS. See Chapter 8 for more details on the *netlogon.dns* file.

The *netdiag* utility is available in the Windows 2000 and Windows Server 2003 Support Tools.

dcdiag

DNS can be hard to configure correctly when initially building an Active Directory infrastructure. The *dcdiag* utility provides two commands that help assess whether your DNS infrastructure is configured correctly to support Active Directory. The */test: DcPromo* option can be used to simulate creating a new forest, domain tree, domain, or replica domain controller. For this test, you have to include the */DnsDomain:* option and the name of the target domain. You also need to specify one additional option that indicates the type of test to run. These include: */NewForest, /NewTree, /ChildDomain,* and */ReplicaDC*. If you use the */NewTree* option, you must also include the */ForestRoot:* option followed by the name of the forest root domain. Here is an example command line to test creating a new child Active Directory domain called *matrix*:

```
C:\> dcdiag test:DcPromo /DnsDomain:matrix.movie.edu /ChildDomain
```

The other *dcdiag* test is *RegisterInDNS*. It verifies whether a domain controller can register an A record for its hostname as well as the various locator records required by Active Directory. The only additional option that is required for this command is */DnsDomain:* followed by the domain that the domain controller is in. Here is an example:

```
C:\> dcdiag test:RegisterInDNS /DnsDomain:movie.edu
```

You can specify the /s: option followed by the name of a target domain controller if you want to run *dcdiag* remotely.

The *dcdiag* utility is available in the Windows 2000 and Windows Server 2003 Support Tools, but the *DcPromo* and *RegisterInDNS* tests are available only in the latter.

DNSLint

The *DNSLint* utility is new in Windows Server 2003 and provides a way to quickly check for the existence of one or more resource records on several name servers. Additionally, it can check for lame delegations, and the resource records necessary for Active Directory replication to occur as well as performing connectivity tests for well known email protocols (i.e., SMTP, POP, and IMAP).

The *DNSLint* utility is part of the Windows Server 2003 Support Tools. For more information on *DNSLint*, see Chapter 15.

dnsdiag

The *dnsdiag* utility can be used to troubleshoot email delivery problems that stem from DNS misconfigurations. It works by simulating the DNS activity performed by an SMTP agent that is attempting to deliver email. In order for *dnsdiag* to work, either Exchange or SMTP service needs to be installed on the computer that *dnsdiag* is run from. If neither is installed, you will see a cryptic error stating that *ISATQ.dll* was not found.

dnsdiag can be found in the Windows Server 2003 Resource Kit.

CHAPTER 14

Managing DNS Programmatically

"It's MY opinion that you never think AT ALL," the
Rose said in a rather severe tone.

In the last chapter, we reviewed the *dnscmd* utility, which can be used to manage a Microsoft DNS Server from the command line. But what if you want more control over automating your DNS environment with scripts? Until recently, your only option would have been to run *dnscmd* from within batch files or from VBScript or Perl scripts. In fact, the lack of a good DNS API has always been a big shortcoming of Microsoft's DNS solution. Starting with Windows 2000, Microsoft answered the call by providing a Windows Management Instrumentation (WMI) DNS Provider. WMI is Microsoft's API of choice for managing and monitoring Windows-based systems and services. With the WMI DNS Provider, you have complete programmatic control over the Microsoft DNS environment, much like you do with *dnscmd* from a command line.

In this chapter, we cover the WMI DNS Provider by providing real-world scripts that should serve as good examples to get your automation efforts jumpstarted. If you need a more detailed introduction to WMI, check out Alain Lissior's books from Digital Press: *Understanding Windows Management Instrumentation (WMI) Scripting* and *Leveraging Windows Management Instrumentation (WMI) Scripting*.

WMI and the DNS Provider

The WMI API was developed by Microsoft in 1998 in response to developers' and system administrators' ever-growing need for a common, scriptable API to manage the components of the Windows operating systems. Before WMI, if you wanted to manage some component of the operating system, you had to resort to using one of the component-specific Win32 APIs, such as the Registry API or Event Log API. Each API typically had its own implementation quirks and required way too much work to do simple tasks. The other big problem with the Win32 APIs was that scripting languages, such as VBScript, could not access them. This limited how much an inexperienced programmer or system administrator could manage systems programmatically. WMI changes all this by providing a single API that can be used to query and manage the Event Log, the Registry, system processes, the file system, or almost any other operating system component.

WMI is the Microsoft implementation of the Common Information Model (CIM) developed by the Distributed Management Task Force (DMTF). The DMTF is an association of various hardware and software companies (e.g., Novell, Microsoft, Cisco, and HP) developing standards in enterprise management. As large enterprises have many computers with many software environments, managing these diverse environments can be a real challenge. In order to unify the management techniques for the sake of simplicity, DMTF defined CIM to represent real-world manageable entities in a unified way. The CIM object model provides a generic set of definitions for hardware and software components. Vendors use this generic object model as a basis for extending CIM to support their own products. WMI is based on the CIM object model and includes extensions that represent the various Windows components.

The WMI DNS Provider was first released as part of the Windows 2000 Resource Kit Supplement 1, but unfortunately, it wasn't ready for prime time. That version was buggy, didn't include all the documented features, and, in several cases, behaved differently from what the documentation described. Also, since the DNS Provider was included as part of a Resource Kit, it was not fully supported by Microsoft, which meant that if you encountered problems, you were largely on your own. That said, much of the functionality you probably need is present in the Windows 2000 version so it may be suitable. You can download the Windows 2000 DNS Provider separately from the Resource Kit via anonymous FTP from the following location: *ftp:// ftp.microsoft.com/reskit/win2000/dnsprov.zip.*

With Windows Server 2003, the DNS Provider is fully functional and supported, although some discrepancies still exist between the Microsoft documentation and the implementation. It is installed automatically whenever you install the DNS Server service.

 All of our sample code has been tested using the Windows Server 2003 DNS Provider.

Quick Overview

The three main areas of interest when it comes to managing DNS include server configuration, zone management, and the creation and deletion of resource records. The

DNS Provider has several classes to manipulate each of these components, all stored under the *root\MicrosoftDNS* namespace. With the MicrosoftDNS_Server class, you can manipulate server configuration settings, start and stop the DNS Server service, and initiate scavenging. The MicrosoftDNS_Zone class allows you to create, delete, and modify zone configurations. The MicrosoftDNS_ResourceRecord class and child classes provide methods for manipulating the various resource record types. Each of these is explained in more detail in the next few sections.

Several additional classes supported by the DNS Provider manage other aspects of DNS including the root hints (MicrosoftDNS_RootHints), DNS server cache (MicrosoftDNS_Cache), and server statistics (MicrosoftDNS_Statistics) classes. For more information on these classes, including sample scripts in VBScript and Perl, search for "DNS WMI Provider" in the Microsoft Developer Network Library (*http://msdn.microsoft.com/library/*).

WMI Scripting with VBScript and Perl

The learning curve to develop WMI scripts is relatively short if you have any experience with a scripting language. In fact, once you understand how to reference, enumerate, and query objects of a particular class with WMI, it is straightforward to adapt the code to work with any managed component, including DNS. And fortunately, by understanding just a few guidelines, you can convert VBScript code to Perl and vice versa.

Referencing an Object

To reference objects in WMI, you use a UNC-style path name. Here is an example of how to reference the *C:* drive on the host *terminator*:

```
\\terminator\root\CIMv2:Win32_LogicalDisk.DeviceID="C:"
```

The first part of the path (\\terminator\) is a reference to the computer on which the object resides. To reference the computer on which the script is running, you can use a dot (.) for the computer name. The second part (root\CIMv2) is the namespace the object resides in. Each WMI provider uses a namespace to store its associated objects. The third part (Win32_LogicalDisk) is the class of the object to reference. The fourth part is the key/value pairs representing an object of that class. Generically, the path can be described as follows:

```
\\ComputerName\NameSpace:ClassName.KeyName="KeyValue"[,KeyName2="KeyValue2"...]
```

Now that we know how to reference WMI objects, let's instantiate an object using VBScript's GetObject function. In order for GetObject to understand we are referencing WMI objects, we have to include one additional piece of information: the moniker. If you've done any Active Directory scripting before, you're probably familiar with the LDAP: and WinNT: monikers used in ADSI. For WMI, we need to use the winmgmts: moniker:

```
set objDisk = GetObject("winmgmts:\\terminator" & _
                        "\root\CIMv2:" & _
                        "Win32_LogicalDisk.DeviceID='C:'")
```

To accomplish the same thing in Perl, we need to use the Win32::OLE module. (The sidebar details differences between VBScript and Perl.) Here is the same code written in Perl:

```
use Win32::OLE;
$objDisk = Win32::OLE->GetObject("winmgmts:\\\\terminator" .
                        "\\root\\CIMv2:" .
                        "Win32_LogicalDisk.DeviceID='C:'");
```

Differences Between VBScript and Perl

Here are some of the main differences between VBScript and Perl:

- With Perl, you have to use the Win32::OLE module to access the WMI Scripting interface. With VBScript, you simply need to call the GetObject function.
- Perl uses the arrow operator (->) to invoke a method on an object whereas VBScript uses a dot (.).
- In Perl, the backslash (\) character is the escape character, so we need to use two backslashes when using it within double quotes.
- Perl uses the dollar sign ($) to indicate a variable whereas VBScript doesn't use a character to distinguish variables.
- VBScript requires an underscore to continue a statement to the next line whereas Perl does not.
- Perl uses the dot (.) for concatenation whereas VBScript uses the ampersand (&).
- Perl requires that each statement end with a semicolon (;) whereas VBScript assumes the end of the line is the end of the statement (unless the underscore continuation character is used).
- Perl uses pound (#) for comments whereas VBScript uses a single quote (').

If you can keep these differences in mind, along with being able to convert basic language constructs (for loops, if then else conditionals, etc.), you should have no problems converting VBScript to Perl.

Enumerating Objects of a Particular Class

Now let's enumerate all logical disks on a machine. To do so, we need to use the InstancesOf method on a WMI object pointing to the namespace of the provider that contains the class. An example should make this clear:

```
strComputer = "."
set objWMI = GetObject("winmgmts:\\" & strComputer & "\root\cimv2")
set objDisks = objWMI.InstancesOf("Win32_LogicalDisk")
for each objDisk in objDisks
    Wscript.Echo "DeviceID: " &  objDisk.DeviceID
    Wscript.Echo "FileSystem: " &  objDisk.FileSystem
    Wscript.Echo "FreeSpace: " & objDisk.FreeSpace
    Wscript.Echo "Name: " & objDisk.Name
    Wscript.Echo "Size: " & objDisk.Size
    WScript.Echo ""
next
```

Here we get a WMI object pointing to the *root\CIMv2* namespace, after which we call the InstancesOf method and pass the Win32_LogicalDisk class. That method returns a collection of Win32_LogicalDisk objects, which we then iterate over with a for loop.

Since we used a for loop in the last example, we'll show the equivalent code in Perl:

```
use Win32::OLE 'in';
my $strComputer = ".";
my $objWMI = Win32::OLE->GetObject("winmgmts:\\\\$strComputer\\root\\cimv2");
my $objDisks = $objWMI->InstancesOf("Win32_LogicalDisk");
for my $objDisk (in $objDisks) {
    print "DeviceID: ", $objDisk->DeviceID,"\n";
    print "FileSystem: ", $objDisk->FileSystem,"\n";
    print "FreeSpace: ", $objDisk->FreeSpace,"\n";
    print "Name: ", $objDisk->Name,"\n";
    print "Size: ", $objDisk->Size,"\n";
    print "\n";
}
```

As you can see, the Perl code is very similar to the VBScript code. One thing to note is that we had to import the in function on the first line, which was later used in the for loop to iterate over the $objDisks collection. VBScript provides this function natively within the language whereas Perl does not.

Having the capability to easily obtain the instances of a certain type of class is very powerful. As you can imagine, you could adapt the code to retrieve a list of all CPUs, services, processes, etc., on a computer. The only issue with the last example is that we needed to know which property methods of the Win32_LogicalDisk class we wanted to print. We can instead retrieve all properties of the `Win32_LogicalDisk` class using the `Properties_` method on each object as shown here:

```
strComputer = "."
strWMIClass = "Win32_LogicalDisk"

set objWMI = GetObject("winmgmts:\\" & strComputer & "\root\cimv2")
set objDisks = objWMI.InstancesOf(strWMIClass)
for each objDisk in objDisks
    for each objProp in objDisk.Properties_
        ' Print out NULL if the property is blank
        if IsNull(objProp.Value) then
            Wscript.Echo " " & objProp.Name & " : NULL"
        else
        ' If the value is an array, we need to iterate through each element
        ' of the array
            if objProp.IsArray = TRUE then
                For I = LBound(objProp.Value) to UBound(objProp.Value)
                    wscript.echo " " & objProp.Name & " : " & objProp.Value(I)
                next
            else
            ' If the property was  not NULL or an array, we print it
                wscript.echo " " & objProp.Name & " : " & objProp.Value
            end if
        end if
    next
    WScript.Echo ""
next
```

Searching with WQL

So far we've shown how to instantiate specific objects, such as a logical drive, and also how to enumerate all the objects of a particular class using the `InstancesOf` method. Knowing how to do both of these functions will take us a long way with WMI, but we are missing one other important capability: the ability to find objects that meet certain criteria.

The creators of WMI found an elegant way to handle this problem. They implemented a subset of the Structured Query Language (SQL) known as the WMI Query Language (WQL). WQL greatly increases the power of WMI by giving the programmer complete control over locating objects.

With WQL, we can even perform the same function as the `InstancesOf` method we used earlier. The following query retrieves all the `Win32_LogicalDisk` objects on the system:

```
select * from Win32_LogicalDisk
```

We can use any property available on Win32_LogicalDisk objects as criteria in our search. As an example, let's say we wanted to find all NTFS logical disks that have less than 100 MB of available space. The query would look like the following:

```
select * from Win32_LogicalDisk
where FreeSpace < 104857600
and    filesystem = 'NTFS'
```

Pretty easy, huh? Now let's put WQL to use. First, we need to get a WMI object to the namespace we want to query. After we've done that, we can call the ExecQuery method on that object and pass the WQL query to use. The next example uses the "less than 100 MB" query we just described to print out all logical disks on the local computer that match that criterion:

```
strComputer = "."
set objWMI = GetObject("winmgmts:\\" & strComputer & "\root\cimv2")
set objDisks = objWMI.ExecQuery _
             ("select * from Win32_LogicalDisk " & _
              "where FreeSpace < 104857600 " & _
              "and filesystem = 'NTFS' ")
for each objDisk in objDisks
    Wscript.Echo "DeviceID: " & objDisk.DeviceID
    Wscript.Echo "Description: " & objDisk.Description
    Wscript.Echo "FileSystem: " & objDisk.FileSystem
    Wscript.Echo "FreeSpace: " & objDisk.FreeSpace
next
```

Authentication with WMI

So far, the examples we've shown assume that the caller of the script has the necessary rights to access the WMI information on the target machine. In most cases in which you are trying to automate a task that may not be the case. Luckily, using alternate credentials in WMI is very straightforward.

Previously, to connect to a WMI namespace, we would have used the following:

```
strComputer = "terminator.movie.edu"
set objWMI = GetObject("winmgmts:\\" & strComputer & "\root\cimv2")
```

But let's say that the person calling the script does not have any privileges on *terminator*. We must now use the following:

```
strComputer = "terminator.movie.edu"
strUserName = "administrator"
strPassword = "password"

set objLocator = CreateObject("WbemScripting.SWbemLocator")
set objWMI = objLocator.ConnectServer(strComputer, "root\cimv2", _
                                      strUserName, strPassword)
```

We've replaced the single call to GetObject with a call to CreateObject to instantiate a WbemScripting.SWbemLocator object. The SWbemLocator object has a method called ConnectServer, which allows us to specify the target machine, username, and password.* We can then use the object returned from ConnectServer to get the instances of a class, perform a WQL search, or any other function.

This was a quick introduction into WMI scripting. We'll cover additional tasks, such as invoking an action or modifying properties of an object, as we walk through specific DNS examples later in the chapter. Now, back to the good stuff…

Server Classes

Nearly 50 different settings can be configured on a Microsoft DNS Server. They range from scavenging and logging settings to settings that customize the name server's behavior, such as how zone transfers are sent to secondaries and whether to round-robin responses that include multiple A records. A name server is represented by an instance of the MicrosoftDNS_Server class. Table 14-1† contains all the property methods defined in the MicrosoftDNS_Server class.

Table 14-1. MicrosoftDNS_Server class properties

Property name	Property description
AddressAnswerLimit	Maximum number of records to return for address requests (i.e., A records). This value can be a number between 5 and 28. The default value is 0, which does not limit the number of records that can be returned.
AllowUpdate	Determines whether dynamic updates are allowed. The value of this property can be any sum of the following values:
	0 No restrictions.
	1 Dynamic updates to SOA records are not allowed.
	2 Dynamic updates to NS records at the apex of the zone are not allowed.
	4 Dynamic updates to NS records of delegated zones are not allowed.
	The default value is 0.

---

* Obviously it is less than ideal to include passwords in plain text scripts. An alternative would be to require the user to use the *runas* command to authenticate as the privileged user. If you plan on running the script via Scheduled Tasks, you can provide credentials when you configure the task.

† For the latest list of supported properties and methods for any of the DNS Provider classes, check out the MSDN documentation: *http://msdn.microsoft.com/library/en-us/dns/dns/microsoftdns_server.asp*. If that link becomes out of date, you should be able to find the documentation by going to *http://msdn.microsoft.com/* and searching on *MicrosoftDNS_Server*.

Table 14-1. MicrosoftDNS_Server class properties (continued)

Property name	Property description
AutoCacheUpdate	Boolean that indicates whether the name server dynamically attempts to update its root hints (also known as cache) file. The default value is TRUE, which means the server auto-updates its root hints.
AutoConfigFileZones	Indicates whether the name server attempts to automatically update any zone it knows about that has an A, NS, or SOA record when the name of the server changes. The value for this property can be one of the following: 0 None 1 Only zones that have name servers that allow dynamic updates 2 Only zones that have name servers that do not allow dynamic updates 4 All zones The default value is 1.
BindSecondaries	Boolean that if TRUE causes the name server to send zone transfers in a less efficient (but more interoperable) format to non-Microsoft DNS Servers. The default value is TRUE.
BootMethod	Determines where the server reads its zone information. The value for this property can be one of the following: 1 Boot from the zone file. 2 Boot from the Registry. 3 Boot from Active Directory and the Registry. The default value is 3.
DefaultAgingState	Boolean that indicates whether aging is enabled for AD-integrated zones. The default value is FALSE (not enabled).
DefaultNoRefreshInterval	For AD-integrated zones, the default no-refresh interval in hours. The default value is 168 (one week).
DefaultRefreshInterval	For AD-integrated zones, the default refresh interval in hours. The default value is 168 (one week).
DisableAutoReverseZones	Boolean that determines whether the name server automatically creates reverse zones for *0.in-addr.arpa*, *127.in-addr.arpa*, and *255.in-addr.arpa*. The default value is FALSE (the reverse zones are created).
DisjointNets	Boolean that indicates whether the default port binding for a socket used to send queries to remote name servers can be overridden.
DsAvailable	Boolean that indicates whether Active Directory is available on the server.
DsPollingInterval	For AD-integrated zones, the interval in minutes to poll Active Directory for updates. The default value is 5 minutes.
DsTombstoneInterval	For AD-integrated zones, the length of time in seconds for which tomb-stoned (i.e., deleted) records should remain in Active Directory. In 99.99% of deployments the default of 604800 (one week) should not need changing.
EdnsCacheTimeout	Length of time, in seconds, that the Extension Mechanisms for DNS (EDNS0) version information about a remote name server is cached. (You can find more information on EDNS0 in RFC 2671.) Valid values range from 3600 (one hour) to 15724800 (182 days). The default value is 604800 (one week).

Table 14-1. MicrosoftDNS_Server class properties (continued)

Property name	Property description
EnableDirectoryPartitionSupport	Boolean that indicates whether application partition support has been enabled. Valid only for domain controllers in a forest at the Windows Server 2003 functional level.
EnableDnsSec	Flag indicating whether DNSSEC resource records are returned if queried. The value of this property can be one of the following: 0 DNSSEC records are returned only if the query specifically queried for it. 1 Return DNSSEC records according to RFC 2535 *only* if the client query includes an OPT record 2 DNSSEC records are always returned, basically according to RFC 2535 regardless of whether the client is using EDNS0. The default is 1.
EnableEDnsProbes	When TRUE, the name server probes other DNS servers to determine if they support EDNS0. The default is 1 (TRUE).
EventLogLevel	Determines the type of events (i.e., errors or warnings) that are logged to the DNS Event Log. The value of this property can be one of the following: 0 Log nothing. 1 Log errors. 2 Log errors and warnings. 4 Log all events. The default value is 4.
ForwardDelegations	Determines whether queries for data in delegated subzones are sent to forwarders or follow the delegation. The value of this property can be one of the following: 0 Automatically send queries referring to delegated subzones to the appropriate subzone. 1 Forward queries referring to the delegated subzone to the existing forwarders. The default value is 0.
Forwarders	Array of IP addresses the server forwards queries to.
ForwardingTimeout	Time in seconds to wait for a response from a forwarded query. The default value is 5 seconds.
IsSlave	Boolean that indicates how the name server responds when forwarded queries do not receive a response. If FALSE, the server attempts to resolve the query and if TRUE the server returns a failure. The default value is FALSE.
ListenAddresses	Array of addresses the name server can receive queries on.
LocalNetPriority	If TRUE, the name server orders records that have a similar IP address to it at the top of the response. If FALSE, then no priority is given based on IP address. This is called "netmask ordering" in the DNS console. The default value is TRUE.
LogFileMaxSize	Maximum size in bytes of the DNS debug log. The default value is 500000000.
LogFilePath	Filename and path to the DNS debug log. The default is *%SystemRoot%\ system32\dns\dns.log*.

Table 14-1. MicrosoftDNS_Server class properties (continued)

Property name	Property description
LogIPFilterList	Array of IP addresses used to filter entries written to the DNS debug log

LogLevel	Determines which events should be written to the debug log. The value of this property can be the sum of any of the following values:
	
	1 Query
	
	16 Notify
	
	32 Update
	
	254
	    Nonquery transactions
	
	256
	    Questions
	
	512
	    Answers
	
	4096
	    Send
	
	8192
	    Receive
	
	16384
	    UDP
	
	32768
	    TCP
	
	65535
	    All packets
	
	65536
	    AD write transaction
	
	131072
	    AD update transaction
	
	16777216
	    Full packets
	
	2147483648
	    Write through

LooseWildcarding	Boolean that indicates whether the server supports wildcards. The default value is FALSE (do not use loose wildcarding).
MaxCacheTTL	Maximum time-to-live value, in seconds, to accept for records from a remote name server. The default value is 86400 (one day).
MaxNegativeCacheTTL	Maximum time-to-live value, in seconds, to accept from a remote name server for a negative response (e.g., one that indicates that a particular domain name doesn't exist). The default value is 86400 (one day).
Name	Domain name or IP address of server

Table 14-1. MicrosoftDNS_Server class properties (continued)

Property name	Property description
NameCheckFlag	Indicates the set of eligible characters to be used in domain names. The value for this property can be one of the following: 0 Strict RFC ANSI 1 Non-RFC ANSI 2 Multibyte UTF8 3 All characters The default value is 2.
NoRecursion	Boolean indicating whether the name server processes recursive queries. The default value is FALSE, which means the name server performs recursive resolution.
RecursionRetry	Time in seconds before retrying a recursive look up. The default value is 3 seconds.
RecursionTimeout	Time in seconds before the name server gives up on processing a recursive query. The default value is 15 seconds.
RoundRobin	Boolean that indicates whether the name server round-robins addresses in responses that return multiple A records. The default value is TRUE.
RpcProtocol	Protocol to run administrative RPC over. The value of this property can be any sum of the following: 0 None 1 TCP 2 Named Pipes 3 LPC The default value is all protocols.
ScavengingInterval	Interval in hours between scavenging runs. The default value is 168 hours (one week).
SecureResponses	Boolean that indicates whether the name server exclusively caches records of names in the same subtree as the server that provided them. If FALSE, all records are cached, but if TRUE, records are cached only if the name server that responded to the forwarded query is in the same subtree as the returned record. The default value is TRUE. This setting is called "Secure cache against pollution" in the DNS console.
SendPort	Port number from which the name server sends UDP queries to other name servers. The default value is 0, which means a port number is randomly selected.
ServerAddresses	Array of IP addresses for the server.
StrictFileParsing	Boolean that indicates whether the name server parses zone files strictly, which means that if bad data is encountered, the zone fails to load. The default value is FALSE, which means the server continues to load the zone.

Table 14-1. MicrosoftDNS_Server class properties (continued)

Property name	Property description
UpdateOptions	Flag that restricts the type of records that can be updated via DDNS. Used in conjunction with AllowUpdate. The value of this property can be any sum of the following values:
	0 No restrictions.
	1 Exclude SOA records.
	2 Exclude NS records.
	4 Exclude delegation NS records.
	8 Exclude server host records.
	256 Exclude SOA records for secure dynamic updates.
	512 Exclude root NS records for secure dynamic updates.
	783 On standard dynamic updates, exclude NS, SOA, and server host records for dynamic updates, and for secure dynamic updates, exclude root NS and SOA records. Allows delegations and server host updates.
	1024 On secure dynamic updates, exclude delegation NS records.
	2048 Exclude server host records for secure dynamic updates.
	16777216 Exclude DS records.
	2147483648 Disable dynamic update.
	The default value is 0.
Version	Name server version.
WriteAuthorityNS	Boolean that indicates whether the server includes NS and SOA records in the authority section of all successful authoritative responses. The default is FALSE, which means it writes NS records in the Authority section for referrals only, per RFC 2181.
XfrConnectTimeout	Number of seconds the name server waits for a successful TCP connection to a remote name server when attempting a zone transfer. The default value is 30 seconds.

The MicrosoftDNS_Server class also provides a few methods to initiate certain actions on the name server. Two of the most useful are StartService and StopService, which allow you to start and stop the DNS Server service. Table 14-2 lists MicrosoftDNS_Server methods.

Table 14-2. MicrosoftDNS_Server class methods

Method name	Method description
GetDistinguishedName	For AD-integrated zones, gets the DN of the zone.
StartScavenging	Start the scavenging process for zones that have scavenging enabled.

Table 14-2. MicrosoftDNS_Server class methods (continued)

Method name	Method description
StartService	Start the DNS service.
StopService	Stop the DNS service.

Listing a Name Server's Properties

The first step to programmatically managing your name server's configuration is to see what settings you currently have in place and determine whether any need to be modified. With WMI, it's really easy to list all properties for a name server. The following example shows how to do it:

```
strServer = "terminator.movie.edu"

' Instantiate a WMI object for the target server
set objDNS = GetObject("winmgmts:\\" & strServer & "\root\MicrosoftDNS")
' Get an instance of the MicrosoftDNS_Server  class
set objDNSServer = objDNS.Get("MicrosoftDNS_Server.Name="".""")

' Iterate over each property using Properties_
Wscript.Echo objDNSServer.Properties_.Item("Name") & ":"
for each objProp in objDNSServer.Properties_
    if IsNull(objProp.Value) then
        Wscript.Echo " " & objProp.Name & " : NULL"
    else
        if objProp.IsArray = TRUE then
            For I = LBound(objProp.Value) to UBound(objProp.Value)
                wscript.echo " " & objProp.Name & " : " & objProp.Value(I)
            next
        else
            wscript.echo " " & objProp.Name & " : " & objProp.Value
        end if
    end if
next
```

After getting a WMI object for the DNS Provider (*root\MicrosoftDNS*), we get a MicrosoftDNS_Server object by looking for the "." instance. Since there can be only one instance of MicrosoftDNS_Server running on any given computer, we do not need to worry about multiple objects. After getting a MicrosoftDNS_Server object, we iterate through all the properties of the object and print each one out. Note that we have added special checks for values that contain arrays in order to print each element of the array. In that case, we use Lbound and Ubound to iterate over all the values for the array.

Configuring a Name Server

Now that we can see what values have been set on our name server, we can change some of them. We simply need to set the property method (e.g., EventLogLevel) to the correct value. This example shows how to do it:

```
strServer = "terminator.movie.edu"

on error resume next

set objDNS = GetObject("winMgmts:\\" & strServer & "\root\MicrosoftDNS")
set objDNSServer = objDNS.Get("MicrosoftDNS_Server.Name=""."""")

Wscript.Echo objDNSServer.Name & ":"
' See Table 14-1 for an explanation of each of these settings
objDNSServer.EventLogLevel = 4
objDNSServer.LooseWildcarding = TRUE
objDNSServer.MaxCacheTTL = 900
objDNSServer.MaxNegativeCacheTTL = 60
objDNSServer.AllowUpdate = 3
objDNSServer.Put_

if Err then
    Wscript.Echo " Error occurred: " & Err.Description
else
    WScript.Echo " Change successful"
end if
```

Note that we had to call Put_ at the end. If we hadn't, none of the changes would have been committed. This is similar to ADSI's SetInfo method, which must be called after modifying an object's property cache to make the change actually take effect.

Restarting the DNS Server Service

Some changes you make to a DNS Server require the service to be restarted for the changes to take effect. We can utilize the StopService and StartService methods as shown in the following example to do this:

```
strServer = "terminator.movie.edu"

on error resume next

set objDNS = GetObject("winMgmts:\\" & strServer & "\root\MicrosoftDNS")
set objDNSServer = objDNS.Get("MicrosoftDNS_Server.Name=""."""")

objDNSServer.StopService
if Err Then
  WScript.Echo "StopService failed: " & Err.Description
  Wscript.Quit
end if
```

```
objDNSServer.StartService
if Err Then
  WScript.Echo "StartService failed: " & Err.Description
  Wscript.Quit
end if

WScript.Echo "Restart successful"
```

Putting It Together: Configuration Check Script

Building on the examples we've used so far in this chapter, we can now write a robust script to check name server configurations. Such a script can be very important, especially in large environments with many name servers. Unless you have a script that routinely checks the configuration on all of your name servers, it's very likely that those servers will not have an identical configuration. If they don't have identical configurations, then when problems pop up, you may end up spending a lot of time troubleshooting because of the discrepancies between the name servers.

To perform the configuration checking, we store each setting in a VBScript Dictionary object. For those accustomed to other languages such as Perl, a Dictionary object is the VBScript analog to a hash or associative array. Another option would be to store the settings in a text file and read them into a Dictionary object when the script starts up. The following example shows the configuration check code:

```
option explicit
on error resume next

Dim arrServers
Dim strUsername, strPassword
Dim dicDNSConfig

' Array of DNS servers to check
arrServers = Array("terminator.movie.edu","fx.movie.edu")

' User and password that can modify the config on the DNS servers
strUsername = "dnsadmin"
strPassword = "dnspwd"

' This dictionary object will contain the key value pairs for all the settings
' that you want to check and configure on the DNS servers
Set dicDNSConfig = CreateObject("Scripting.Dictionary")
dicDNSConfig.Add "AllowUpdate",            1
dicDNSConfig.Add "LooseWildCarding",       TRUE
dicDNSConfig.Add "MaxCacheTTL",            900
dicDNSConfig.Add "MaxNegativeCacheTTL",    60
dicDNSConfig.Add "EventLogLevel",          0
dicDNSConfig.Add "StrictFileParsing",      TRUE
dicDNSConfig.Add "DisableAutoReverseZones", TRUE

Dim arrDNSConfigKeys
arrDNSConfigKeys = dicDNSConfig.keys
```

```
Dim objLocator
Set objLocator = CreateObject("WbemScripting.SWbemLocator")

Dim x, y, boolRestart
For x = LBound(arrServers) to UBound(arrServers)
   boolRestart = False

   WScript.echo arrServers(x)

   Dim objDNS, objDNSServer
   Set objDNS = objLocator.ConnectServer(arrServers(x), "root\MicrosoftDNS", _
                                          strUserName, strPassword)
   set objDNSServer = objDNS.Get("MicrosoftDNS_Server.Name=""."""")

   for y = 0 To dicDNSConfig.Count - 1
      Dim strKey
      strKey = arrDNSConfigKeys(y)

      WScript.Echo "  Checking " & strKey
      if dicDNSConfig.Item(strKey) <> objDNSServer.Properties_.Item(strKey) then
         objDNSServer.Properties_.Item(strKey).value = dicDNSConfig(strKey)
         objDNSServer.Put_
         boolRestart = TRUE
         if Err Then
            WScript.Echo "     Error setting " & strKey & " : " & Err.Description
            Wscript.Quit
         else
            WScript.Echo "     " & strKey & " updated"
         end if
      end if
   Next

   if boolRestart then
      objDNSServer.StopService
      if Err Then
         WScript.Echo "StopService failed: " & Err.Description
         Wscript.Quit
      end if

      objDNSServer.StartService
      if Err Then
         WScript.Echo "StartService failed: " & Err.Description
         Wscript.Quit
      end if
      WScript.Echo "Restarted"
   end if

   WScript.Echo ""
next
```

Besides the use of the Dictionary object, most of the script is a combination of the
other three examples shown so far in this chapter. We added a server array so that

you can check multiple servers at once. For each server, the script simply checks each key in the Dictionary object to see if its value matches the key on the name server. If not, it modifies the server and commits the change via Put_. After it's done looping through all the settings, it restarts the DNS Server service if a change has been made to its configuration. It then proceeds to the next server.

One enhancement that would make the process even more automated would be to dynamically query the list of name servers instead of hard-coding them in an array. You would need to look up the NS records for one or more zones that your name servers are authoritative for. As long as an NS record is added for each new name server, the script would automatically discover new name servers on subsequent runs. Later in the chapter, we show how to query name servers with the DNS Provider.

Monitoring Server Performance

If you've ever wanted a programmatic way to access the output of the *dnscmd /statistics* command, now you have one. The MicrosoftDNS_Statistic class provides complete access to all the performance metrics you can get using *dnscmd* or Performance Monitor. And it's easy too! Check out this script, which prints out all of the statistics:

```
strServer = "terminator.movie.edu "

set objDNS = GetObject("winMgmts:\\" & strServer & "\root\MicrosoftDNS")
set objDNSServer = objDNS.Get("MicrosoftDNS_Server.Name=""."""")
set objStats = objDNS.ExecQuery("Select * from MicrosoftDNS_Statistic ")
for each objStat in objStats
    WScript.Echo " " & objStat.Name & " : " & objStat.Value
next
```

And if you want to access only a subset of the metrics (for example, all of the entries that start with "Records") you only need to modify the WQL query slightly:

```
set objStats = objDNS.ExecQuery("Select * from MicrosoftDNS_Statistic " & _
                           where Name like 'Records%' ")
```

Zone Classes

The MicrosoftDNS_Zone class offers a plethora of properties and methods to aid in managing your zones. Even if you are using AD-integrated zones, which help reduce the amount of work required to maintain DNS, inevitably you need to configure a zone's settings or create additional zones. In Tables 14-3 and 14-4, available properties and methods for the MicrosoftDNS_Zone class are listed.

Table 14-3. MicrosoftDNS_Zone class properties

Property name	Property description
Aging	Boolean that indicates whether scavenging is enabled for the zone. The default value is FALSE, which means it is disabled.
AllowUpdate	Flag indicating whether dynamic updates are allowed. The value for this property can be one of the following: 0 No updates allowed. 1 Zone accepts both secure and nonsecure updates. 2 Zone accepts secure updates only. The default for new zones is 0.
AutoCreated	Boolean that indicates whether the zone was auto-created , as is the case with the standard reverse zones (e.g., *255.in-addr.arpa*) that are automatically created by default.
AvailForScavengeTime	Time period when scavenging can be run (if configured for the zone).
DataFile	Name of the zone datafile.
DisableWINSRecordReplication	Boolean that if TRUE indicates that WINS record replication is disabled. The default value is FALSE (WINS record replication does occur).
DsIntegrated	Boolean that indicates whether the zone is AD-integrated.
ForwarderSlave	Boolean that indicates whether the name server relies entirely on its forwarders when resolving domain names in this zone. This can override the server *IsSlave* setting.
ForwarderTimeout	Number of seconds the name server waits after forwarding a query for domain names in this zone before trying to resolve the query itself. This overrides the server setting.
LastSuccessfulSoaCheck	Number of seconds from January 1, 1970, GMT since the zone's serial number was checked.
LastSuccessfulXfr	Number of seconds from January 1, 1970, GMT since the last successful zone transfer from a master.
LocalMasterServers	If zone is a secondary, this contains the list of master name servers to request zone transfers from. This overrides the *MasterServers* setting, which can be stored in AD.
MasterServers	If zone is a secondary, this contains the list of master name servers to request zone transfers from.
NoRefreshInterval	For AD-integrated zones, the no-refresh interval in hours. If not specified, the default server no-refresh interval is used.
Notify	If set to 1, the name server notifies secondaries of zone changes.
NotifyServers	Name servers that are notified when there are changes to the zone.
Paused	Flag indicating whether the zone is paused and therefore not responding to requests.
RefreshInterval	For AD-integrated zones, the refresh interval in hours. If not specified, the default server refresh interval is used.
Reverse	If TRUE, the zone is a reverse-mapping (*in-addr.arpa*) zone. If FALSE, zone is a forward-mapping zone.

Table 14-3. MicrosoftDNS_Zone class properties (continued)

Property name	Property description
ScavengeServers	Array of IP addresses of servers that are allowed to perform scavenging for the zone. If this is not set, any authoritative server in the zone can perform scavenging.
SecondaryServers	IP addresses of name servers allowed to receive zone transfers.
SecureSecondaries	Flag indicating whether zone transfers are allowed only to name servers speci- fied in SecondariesIPAddressesArray. The value for this property can be one of the following: 0 Send zone transfers to all secondary servers that request them. 1 Send zone transfers only to name servers that are authoritative for the zone. 2 Send zone transfers only to servers specified in SecondaryServers. 3 Do not send zone transfers. The default is 0 for standard primary zones and 3 for AD-integrated zones.
Shutdown	Boolean that if TRUE means the zone has expired (or shut down).
UseWins	Boolean that indicates whether the zone uses WINS lookups. The default is FALSE, which disables WINS lookups.
ZoneType	Type of zone: DS Integrated,[a] Primary, or Secondary.

[a] Most people refer to zones stored in Active Directory as AD-integrated. The WMI DNS Provider consistently uses DS Integrated instead.

Table 14-4. MicrosoftDNS_Zone class methods

Method name	Method description
AgeAllRecords	Age part or all of a zone.
ChangeZoneType	Convert zone to a different type and make it AD-integrated.
CreateZone	Create a new zone.
ForceRefresh	Force secondary to update its zone from master.
GetDistinguishedName	Get distinguished name of the zone.
PauseZone	Cause the name server not to respond to queries for the zone.
ReloadZone	Reload the contents of the zone. This may be necessary after making changes to a zone that you want to take effect immediately.
ResetSecondaries	Specify list of secondaries.
ResumeZone	Cause the name server to start responding to queries for the zone after pausing the zone.
UpdateFromDS	Reload the zone data from Active Directory; valid only for AD-integrated zones.
WriteBackZone	Save zone data to a file.

Creating a Zone

Creating a zone with the DNS Provider is a straightforward operation. You need to get a WMI object for the DNS namespace, instantiate an object from the `MicrosoftDNS_Zone` class, and call `CreateZone` on that object. The next example shows how to do this:

```
strNewZone = "movie.edu."
strServer = "terminator.movie.edu"

on error resume next

set objDNS = GetObject("winMgmts:\\" & strServer & "\root\MicrosoftDNS")
set objDNSZone = objDNS.Get("MicrosoftDNS_Zone")
strNull = objDNSZone.CreateZone(strNewZone,0,TRUE)

if Err then
   WScript.Echo "Error occurred creating zone: " & Err.Description
else
   WScript.Echo "Zone created..."
end if
```

The three parameters we passed into `CreateZone` include the zone name, the zone type flag, and the AD-integrated flag. A zone type of 0 creates a primary zone. When the AD-integrated flag is set to true, the primary zone is AD-integrated; if it is false, it is a standard primary. At the time of this writing, Microsoft had conflicting documentation about these parameters and their valid values. Refer to the MSDN Library for more information; hopefully, they'll get it straight eventually.

Configuring a Zone

Configuring a zone is not too different from configuring a name server. The primary difference is in how you instantiate a `MicrosoftDNS_Zone` object. In order to use the Get method on a WMI object, you have to specify the keys for the class you want to instantiate. For the `MicrosoftDNS_Zone` class, the keys include `ContainerName`, `DnsServerName`, and `Name`. In this case, `ContainerName` and `Name` are both the name of the zone. We retrieve `DnsServerName` by getting a `MicrosoftDNS_Server` object as we've done earlier in the chapter.

The following example lists all of the properties of the *movie.edu* zone before it modifies the `AllowUpdate` property and commits the change:

```
strZone = "movie.edu."
strServer = "terminator.movie.edu"

on error resume next

set objDNS = GetObject("winMgmts:\\" & strServer & "\root\MicrosoftDNS")
set objDNSServer = objDNS.Get("MicrosoftDNS_Server.Name=""."""")
set objDNSZone = objDNS.Get("MicrosoftDNS_Zone.ContainerName=""" & strZone & _
                    """,DnsServerName=""" & objDNSServer.Name & _
                    """,Name=""" & strZone & """")
```

```
' List all of the properties of the zone
Wscript.Echo objDNSZone.Name
for each objProp in objDNSZone.Properties_
    if IsNull(objProp.Value) then
        Wscript.Echo " " & objProp.Name & " : NULL"
    else
        if objProp.IsArray = TRUE then
            For I = LBound(objProp.Value) to UBound(objProp.Value)
                wscript.echo " " & objProp.Name & " : " & objProp.Value(I)
            next
        else
            wscript.echo " " & objProp.Name & " : " & objProp.Value
        end if
    end if
next

' Modify the zone
objDNSZone.AllowUpdate = 1
objDNSZone.Put_

WScript.Echo ""
if Err then
    Wscript.Echo "Error occurred: " & Err.Description
else
    WScript.Echo "Change successful"
end if
```

Listing the Zones on a Server

The last zone example we'll show lists the configured zones on a specific name
server. To make the following example a little more robust, we've added logic to
make the script configurable so it can be run against any name server using the specified credentials. That is accomplished by using the ConnectServer method on the
SWbemLocator object.

```
strServer   = "terminator.movie.edu"
strUsername = "dnsadmin"
strPassword = "dnspwd"

Set objLocator = CreateObject("WbemScripting.SWbemLocator")
Set objDNS = objLocator.ConnectServer(strServer, "root\MicrosoftDNS", _
                                      strUsername, strPassword)
set objDNSServer = objDNS.Get("MicrosoftDNS_Server.Name="".""")
set objZones = objDNS.ExecQuery("Select * from MicrosoftDNS_Zone " & _
                                "Where DnsServerName = '" & _
                                objDNSServer.Name & "'")
WScript.Echo objDNSServer.Name
for each objZone in objZones
    WScript.Echo " " & objZOne.Name
next
```

To retrieve the list of zones, we used a WQL query with ExecQuery to find all MicrosoftDNS_Zone objects that had a DnsServerName equal to the name of the server we are connecting to.

Resource Record Classes

Resource records are the basic unit of information in DNS. A name server's primary job is to respond to queries for resource records. Most people don't realize they are generating queries for resource records with nearly every network-based operation they do, including accessing a web site, pinging a host, or logging into Active Directory.

The WMI DNS Provider fully supports querying and manipulating resource records. Tables 14-5 and 14-6 list the supported properties and methods for the MicrosoftDNS_ResourceRecord class, which implements a generic interface for resource records.

Table 14-5. MicrosoftDNS_ResourceRecord class properties

Property name	Property description
ContainerName	Name of the WMI container that holds the resource record (RR). This is usually the same as the name of the zone.
DnsServerName	Domain name of the name server that contains the RR.
DomainName	Domain name of the node that is associated with the RR.
OwnerName	Owner of the RR.
RecordClass	Class of the RR. 1 represents IN.
RecordData	Resource record data.
TextRepresentation	Textual representation of the RR. For example: www.movie.edu. 1800 IN CNAME www1.movie.edu.
Timestamp	Time RR was last refreshed.
TTL	Time-to-live or maximum time a name server may cache the RR.

Table 14-6. MicrosoftDNS_ResourceRecord class methods

Method name	Method description
CreateInstanceFromTextRepresentation	Creates a new instance of a MicrosoftDNS_ResourceRecord subclass based on 1) the textual representation of the resource record, 2) server name, and 3) the container or zone name. A reference to the new object is returned as an out parameter.
GetObjectByTextRepresentation	Gets an instance of the appropriate MicrosoftDNS_ResourceRecord subclass as specified by 1) the textual representation of the resource record, 2) server name, and 3) the container or zone name.

The MicrosoftDNS_ResourceRecord class by itself is not enough. There are over two dozen types of resource records, and many have additional fields that don't have corresponding methods in the generic interface. To solve this problem, subclasses of MicrosoftDNS_ResourceRecord were created for each supported record type. Each subclass provides specific methods to access any field supported by the resource record type. Each supported resource record has a subclass with a name in the format of MicrosoftDNS_*RRType*Type where *RRType* is the name of the record type, such as SRV, A, or PTR.

Finding Resource Records in a Zone

With the marriage of DNS and WMI, sending DNS queries has never been so easy. By using WQL, you can write complex query routines that would not have been possible previously. To list all of the resource records on a server, you simply need to execute the WQL query select * from MicrosoftDNS_ResourceRecord against the target server. The following example shows how to run the query against the local name server:

```
set objDNS = GetObject("winMgmts:root\MicrosoftDNS")
set objRR = objDNS.ExecQuery("Select * from MicrosoftDNS_ResourceRecord")
for Each objInst in objRR
    WScript.Echo objInst.TextRepresentation
next
```

The TextRepresentation method is available to all resource record types since it's defined in MicrosoftDNS_ResourceRecord. It returns a text string representing the resource record, such as the following:

```
www.movie.edu.  IN  A  192.10.4.5
```

If you want to limit the query to only a specific zone, change the WQL query to include criteria for ContainerName, such as the following:

```
Select * from MicrosoftDNS_ResourceRecord
Where ContainerName = 'ZoneName'
```

Since Active Directory stores all of the global catalog servers for a forest and domain controllers for a domain in DNS, you can write scripts to access this information and integrate it into your applications. The following example does exactly this by selecting all SRV records with a particular OwnerName. To find all global catalog servers in a forest, you can look up _ldap._tcp.gc._msdcs.*ForestRootDNSName;* to find all domain controllers in a domain, look up _ldap._tcp.dc._msdcs.*DomainDNSName.*

```
option explicit

Dim strDomain
strDomain = "movie.edu"

Dim objDNS, objRRs, objRR
set objDNS = GetObject("winMgmts:root\MicrosoftDNS")
set objRRs = objDNS.ExecQuery("Select * from MicrosoftDNS_SRVType " & _
                        " Where OwnerName = '_ldap._tcp.gc._msdcs." & _
                        strDomain & "'")
```

```
WScript.Echo "Global Catalogs for " & strDomain
for Each objRR in objRRs
    Wscript.Echo " " & objRR.DomainName
next

Wscript.Echo

set objRRs = objDNS.ExecQuery("Select * from MicrosoftDNS_SRVType " & _
                              " Where OwnerName = '_ldap._tcp.dc._msdcs." & _
                              strDomain & "'")
WScript.Echo "Domain Controllers for " & strDomain
for Each objRR in objRRs
    Wscript.Echo " " & objRR.DomainName
next
```

Creating Resource Records

With the DNS Provider, creating resource records can be done in a couple of steps.
The CreateInstanceFromTextRepresentation method takes the following parameters:
the domain name of the name server to create the record on, the domain name of the
zone to add the record to, and the textual representation of the resource record. It
also provides an out parameter that is a MicrosoftDNS_ResourceRecord object representing the newly created record.

The following example goes through the process of creating both an A and a PTR
record. Both records are typically necessary when adding a new host to DNS:

```
option explicit

Dim strRR, strReverseRR, strDomain, strReverseDomain

' A record to add
strRR = "matrix.movie.edu. IN A 192.168.64.13"
strDomain = "movie.edu"

' PTR record to add
strReverseRR = "13.64.168.192.in-addr.arpa IN PTR matrix.movie.edu"
strReverseDomain = "168.192.in-addr.arpa."

Dim objDNS, objRR, objDNSServer, objRR2, objOutParam
set objDNS = GetObject("winMgmts:root\MicrosoftDNS")
set objRR = objDNS.Get("MicrosoftDNS_ResourceRecord")
set objDNSServer = objDNS.Get("MicrosoftDNS_Server.Name="".""")

' Create the A record
Dim strNull
strNull = objRR.CreateInstanceFromTextRepresentation( _
            objDNSServer.Name, _
            strDomain, _
            strRR, _
            objOutParam)
```

```
set objRR2 = objDNS.Get(objOutParam)
WScript.Echo "Created Record: " & objRR2.TextRepresentation
set objOutParam = Nothing

' Create the PTR record
strNull = objRR.CreateInstanceFromTextRepresentation( _
                objDNSServer.Name, _
                strReverseDomain, _
                strReverseRR, _
                objOutParam)

set objRR2 = objDNS.Get(objOutParam)
WScript.Echo "Created Record: " & objRR2.TextRepresentation
```

The WMI DNS Provider fills a much-needed gap for programmatic management of a Microsoft DNS environment. In this chapter, we gave an overview of WMI and covered the classes used for managing name server and zone configuration along with the available properties and methods. We described how to query, add, and delete resource records with the DNS Provider and showed how you can get a list of Active Directory domain controllers using a simple WQL query.

## CHAPTER 15

Troubleshooting DNS

*"Of course not," said the Mock Turtle. "Why, if a fish
came to me, and told me he was going on a journey, I
should say, 'With what porpoise?' "*

"Don't you mean 'purpose'?" said Alice.

*"I mean what I say," the Mock Turtle replied, in an
offended tone. And the Gryphon added, "Come, let's
hear some of your adventures."*

In Chapter 12, we demonstrated how to use *nslookup* to make queries. In this chapter, we'll show you how to use *nslookup*—plus traditional TCP/IP networking tools like trusty ol' *ping*—to troubleshoot real-life problems with DNS.

Troubleshooting, by its nature, is a tough subject to teach. You start with any of a world of symptoms and try to work your way back to the cause. We can't cover the whole gamut of problems you may encounter on the Internet, but we do our best to show you how to diagnose the most common of them. And along the way, we hope to teach you troubleshooting techniques that will be valuable in tracking down more obscure problems that we don't document.

Is DNS Really Your Problem?

Before we launch into a discussion of how to troubleshoot a DNS problem, we should make sure you know how to tell whether a problem is caused by DNS, not by another naming service. On Windows hosts, figuring out whether the culprit is actually DNS can be difficult. Windows supports a whole panoply of naming services: DNS, WINS, *HOSTS*, *LMHOSTS*, and more. The stock Windows Server 2003 version of *nslookup*, however, doesn't pay any attention to these other naming services. You can run *nslookup* on a Windows Server 2003 box and query the name server til the cows come home while the service with the problem is using a different naming service.

How do you know where to put the blame? First, you need to consider what kind of program is having the problem. If it's a TCP/IP client, such as *telnet* or *ftp*, the possible culprits are DNS and the *HOSTS* file. If it's a utility that supports NetBIOS naming, such as *net* (as in *net use*), the likely suspects also include WINS and the *LMHOSTS* file. Other clients, such as *ping*, that also take either a DNS name or a NetBIOS name as an argument can use any of these naming services.

Next, consider the order in which Windows uses the naming services. You should look through the various services in that order when troubleshooting the problem.

These hints should help you identify the guilty party or at least exonerate one suspect. If you narrow down the suspects and DNS is still implicated, you'll just have to read this chapter.

Checking the Cache

As we've said earlier, you can check the contents of your name server's cache with the DNS console. This can come in handy if you suspect that your name server has cached bad or out-of-date data from another server. To inspect a server's cache, click the plus sign to the left of the name of the server in the DNS console's left pane. You'll see a folder named **Cached Lookups**. Either click on the plus sign to the left of it or double-click the folder icon or the label to expand the next level, then do the same on the label **. (root)**. This shows you the top-level domains for which your name server has cached data. Expand your way to the domain name to which the cached data you're looking for is attached. In Figure 15-1, we've clicked our way down to *acmebw.com* to look for cached data.

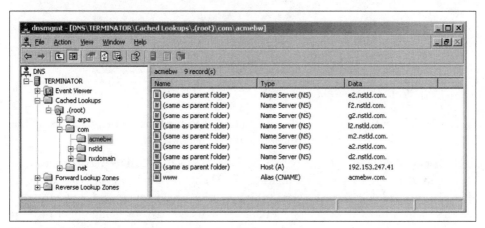

Figure 15-1. NS and A records for acmebw.com in the cache

As you can see in the right pane, our name server has cached seven NS records and one A record for *acmebw.com*. If we double-clicked **net** and then **acmebw**, we could find the cached addresses of these name servers, too.

If you'd like to see the TTL on the cached data, double-click on a record in the right pane. Provided the DNS console is in advanced view mode (select **View →** **Advanced**), the resulting window shows the record's TTL. For example, in Figure 15-2, we've double-clicked the **acmebw.com** A record.

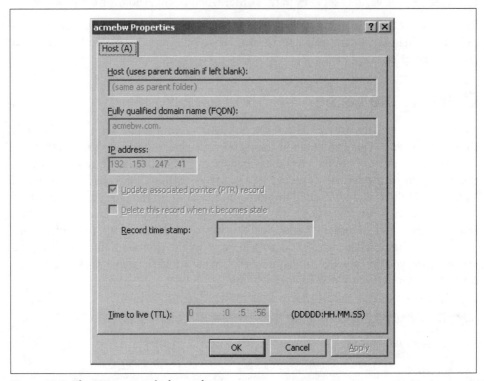

Figure 15-2. The TTL on a cached record

Be sure to refresh the DNS console with **Action → Refresh** or **F5** before checking the TTL, or the TTL you see may be bigger than the current TTL.

If you right-clicked the record, you may have noticed a **Delete Record** selection. Now there's something you can't do in BIND. Using the DNS console, you can actually delete cached data record by record! If you know that some records in your name server's cache are out of date, you can delete them and let your name server pick up updated records from an authoritative name server.

Using DNSLint

DNSLint, which we introduced back in Chapter 8, can also come in handy when you're troubleshooting. In Chapter 8, we mostly used it to verify the registration of records by Domain Controllers. But *DNSLint* can also come in handy in detecting delegation problems, as we showed in Chapter 9.

To use *DNSLint* to check delegation, use the */d* command-line option. Specify the domain name of the zone whose delegation you'd like to check as the argument. For example:

```
C:\> dnslint /d movie.edu
```

This produces a report on *movie.edu*'s delegation, displayed in a browser window. If you're checking a zone that's not registered on the InterNIC's *whois* servers (i.e., a subdomain of *com* or *net*), you'll also need to specify the */s* option and, as an argument, the IP address of a name server authoritative for the zone.

By default, *DNSLint* checks DNS over UDP. You can instruct it to test DNS over TCP, too, using the */test_tcp* option.

Finally, you can use the */c* option to tell *DNSLint* to check connectivity to the mail ports (SMTP, POP, and IMAP, by default) on the mail servers it finds for the zone. If you don't want it to check all three, you can enumerate the protocols to check after the option; for example:

```
C:\> dnslint /d movie.edu /c smtp,imap
```

Here's some sample *DNSLint* output (in text format, generated using */t*):

```
DNSLint Report

System Date: Sat Jul 05 18:58:05 2003

Command run:

dnslint /d fx.movie.edu /t /s 192.253.254.2 /c smtp


Domain name tested:

fx.movie.edu


DNS servers were identified as authoritative for the domain:


DNS server: bladerunner.fx.movie.edu
IP Address: 192.253.254.2
UDP port 53 responding to queries: YES
TCP port 53 responding to queries: Not tested
Answering authoritatively for domain: YES
```

```
SOA record data from server:
Authoritative name server: bladerunner.fx.movie.edu
Hostmaster: administrator.fx.movie.edu
Zone serial number: 10
Zone expires in: 1.00 day(s)
Refresh period: 900 seconds
Retry delay: 600 seconds
Default (minimum) TTL: 3600 seconds

Additional authoritative (NS) records from server:
outland.fx.movie.edu    192.253.254.3
bladerunner.fx.movie.edu    192.253.254.2


Mail Exchange (MX) records from server (preference/name/IP address):
100 wormhole.movie.edu 192.253.253.1
10 starwars.fx.movie.edu 192.253.254.4

DNS server: outland.fx.movie.edu
IP Address: 192.253.254.3
UDP port 53 responding to queries: YES
TCP port 53 responding to queries: Not tested
Answering authoritatively for domain: YES

SOA record data from server:
Authoritative name server: bladerunner.fx.movie.edu
Hostmaster: administrator.fx..movie.edu
Zone serial number: 10
Zone expires in: 1.00 day(s)
Refresh period: 900 seconds
Retry delay: 600 seconds
Default (minimum) TTL: 3600 seconds

Additional authoritative (NS) records from server:
outland.fx.movie.edu    192.253.254.3
bladerunner.fx.movie.edu    192.253.254.2


Mail Exchange (MX) records from server (preference/name/IP address):
10 starwars.fx.movie.edu 192.253.254.4
100 wormhole.movie.edu 192.253.253.1

Network Connectivity Tests

E-mail server: starwars.fx.movie.edu
IP address: 192.253.254.4

SMTP response: 220 starwars.fx.movie.edu ESMTP Postfix

POP response: Not Tested
IMAP response: Not Tested

E-mail server: wormhole.movie.edu
IP address: 192.253.253.1
```

```
SMTP response: 220 wormhole.movie.edu ESMTP Postfix

POP response: Not Tested
IMAP response: Not Tested

=================================================
```

Potential Problem List

Let's go through some common real-world DNS problems. Many of these problems are easy to recognize and correct. We cover these problems as a matter of course—they're some of the most common problems because they're caused by some of the most common mistakes. Here are the contestants, in no particular order.

1. Forget to Increment Serial Number

This particular problem occurs only if you make changes to your zone datafile by hand, without using the DNS console. The DNS console remembers to increment the serial number in the SOA record each time it changes zone data, so you don't have to worry about it. However, this also means that you probably won't be in the habit of updating the serial number, so you may forget when making that one-off manual modification.

The main symptom of this problem is that secondary name servers don't pick up any changes you make to the zone on the primary server. The secondaries think the zone data hasn't changed since the serial number is still the same.

How do you check if you remembered to increment the serial number? Unfortunately, that's not so easy. If you don't remember what the old serial number was and your serial number gives you no indication of when it was updated, there's no direct way to tell whether it has changed.* When you start the primary, it loads the updated zone datafile regardless of whether you've changed the serial number. About the best you can do is to use *nslookup* to compare the data returned by the primary and by a secondary. If they return different data, you probably forgot to increment the serial number. If you can remember a recent change you made, you can look for that data. If you can't remember a recent change, you can try transferring the zone from a primary and from a secondary, sorting the results, and using a file-comparison tool to compare them.

The good news is that, although determining whether the zone was transferred is tricky, making sure the zone is transferred is simple. Just increment the serial number

---

* On the other hand, if you encode the date into the serial number, as many people do (for example, 2004010500 is the first rev of data on January 5, 2004), you may be able to tell at a glance whether you updated the serial number when you made the change. However, the DNS console makes this almost impossible since it just increments by one for each change.

on the primary's copy of the zone by double-clicking the SOA record in the DNS console and clicking the **Increment** button on the **Start of Authority (SOA)** tab. The secondaries should pick up the new data within their refresh interval, or sooner if they use NOTIFY.

2. Forget to Restart Primary Master Server

Like the last problem, you'll see this problem only if you make changes to your zone datafiles by hand. The DNS console adds and deletes data on the fly, so there's no need to restart your primary master name server.

If you're not using the DNS console, though, you may forget to restart your primary master name server after editing a zone datafile. The name server won't know to load the new data—it doesn't automatically check the file to see if it has changed. Consequently, any changes you've made won't be reflected in the name server's data: new zones won't be loaded, and new records won't percolate out to the secondaries.

To check when you last restarted the name server, use the Event Viewer to scan the DNS Server event log for Event ID 2, which contains the following text:

```
The DNS server has started.
```

The date and time on these events tell you the last time you restarted the name server.

If the time of the restart doesn't correlate with the time you made the last change, use the DNS console to stop and restart the name server and reload its data. Check that you incremented the serial numbers on the zone datafiles you changed, too.

3. Name Server Loses Manual Changes

One final but important note about making manual changes: remember that the Microsoft DNS Server periodically updates its zone datafiles. Each time you make changes to a zone's data using the DNS console, a write is pending: before the name server exits, it must rewrite the zone's datafile or it will lose the changes you made. Think of this as a dirty page in memory: the operating system must write it to disk before exiting.

If you make a manual change to a zone datafile while a write is pending, you'll mysteriously lose the change when the name server exits. Say you add delegation to a new subdomain of *movie.edu* while the server is running and a write is pending. After you've made the change, you have to stop the server and start it again to get it to read the zone data again. But as the server exits, it rewrites the *movie.edu* zone datafile, and your delegation disappears. If you're watching the DNS Server event log carefully (like you should be), you'll see a message like this before the server stops:

```
The DNS server wrote version 37 of zone movie.edu to file movie.edu.dns.
```

Once you force the server to rewrite its zone datafiles with **Action** → **Update Server Data Files**, the server is in sync with the zone datafiles and doesn't have to rewrite them on exit. So, if you're going to make manual changes to the zone datafiles, you should either stop the server first (although that means your server won't answer queries while you make the change), or use the DNS console to sync the server with the zone datafiles and then make the change.

4. Secondary Server Can't Load Zone Data

If a secondary name server can't get the current serial number for a zone from its master server, you won't be warned about it initially. However, if the problem persists and the secondary can't determine within the expire interval whether or not its data is up to date, it expires the zone. On a Microsoft DNS Server, you'll see a message like this in the DNS Server event log:

```
Zone movie.edu expired before it could obtain a successful zone transfer or update
from a master server acting as its source for the zone.
The zone has been shut down.
```

Once the zone has expired and the name server has shut it down, you'll start getting **Query refused** errors when you query the name server for data in the zone:

```
C:\> nslookup robocop wormhole.movie.edu.
Server:  wormhole.movie.edu
Addresses:  192.249.249.1, 192.253.253.1

*** wormhole.movie.edu can't find robocop.movie.edu: Query refused
```

Three leading causes of this problem are a loss in connectivity to the master server due to network failure, an incorrect IP address configured for the master server, and a syntax error in the zone datafile on the master server.

First, use the DNS console to check the address of the master server(s) from which the secondary is attempting to load data. Right-click the domain name of the zone in the left pane, choose **Properties**, and look at the **General** tab, shown in Figure 15-3.

Make sure that's really the IP address of the master name server. If it is, check connectivity to that IP address:

```
C:\> ping 192.249.249.3
Pinging 192.249.249.3 with 32 bytes of data:

Request timed out.
Request timed out.
Request timed out.
Request timed out.
```

If the master server isn't reachable, make sure that the server's host is really running (for example, is powered on) or look for a network problem.

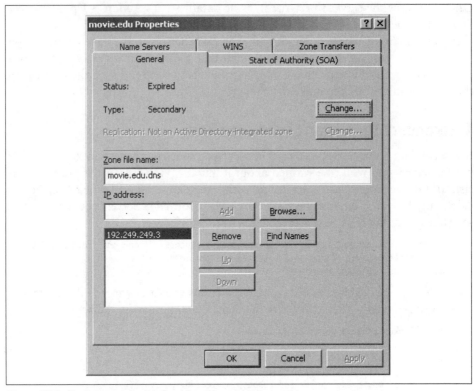

Figure 15-3. Zone properties window showing master server(s)

You may also want to check that the master server is returning authoritative responses to queries for data in the zone. If the master server is responding as not authoritative for the zone, the secondary won't transfer the zone from it. Here's how you could use *nslookup* to check for an authoritative response for the zone's SOA record from the master server:

```
C:\> nslookup -norec -type=SOA movie.edu. 192.249.249.3
```

This command sends a nonrecursive query for the SOA record for *movie.edu* to the name server at 192.249.249.3. We need to send a nonrecursive query so that the name server at 192.249.249.3 doesn't try to forward the query to another server.

If this master server is correctly configured, the answer to this query should be authoritative. (Remember that unless *nslookup* reports "Non-authoritative answer," the answer is authoritative.) A nonauthoritative reply may indicate that the master server had a problem loading the zone, usually because of a syntax error in the zone datafile. We've never seen a Microsoft DNS Server go nonauthoritative for a zone based on a syntax error in a zone datafile, but older BIND name servers exhibit this behavior. So if your name server is a secondary to a zone whose primary master is a BIND name server that's not claiming authority for the zone, a syntax error could be your problem. Contact the administrator of the master server and have him check his name server's *syslog* output for indications of a syntax error.

If the answer to the query is authoritative but the secondary server still can't transfer the zone successfully, you can use the *nslookup*'s *ls* command to try to transfer the zone manually (*ls*, as we said in Chapter 12, performs a zone transfer). If you see an error like this, it's a good bet that the master server restricts zone transfers:

```
C:\> nslookup - 192.249.249.3
Default Server:  terminator.movie.edu
Address:  192.249.249.3
> ls movie.edu
[terminator.movie.edu]
*** Can't list domain movie.edu: Query refused
>
```

Contact the administrator of the master server and ask whether he is restricting zone transfers. Ask him to check the options on the **Zone Transfers** tab of the **Properties** window for the zone you're trying to transfer (if he's running the Microsoft DNS Server). If the remote server is running BIND, ask if he's using the *xfrnets* or *allow-transfer* features to restrict zone transfers.

Once the problem has been cleared up and your server successfully transfers the zone, you'll see messages like these in the DNS Server event log:

```
A more recent version, version 212 of zone movie.edu was found at DNS server at 192.
249.249.3. Zone transfer is in progress.

The DNS server wrote version 212 of zone movie.edu to file movie.edu.dns.
```

5. Add Address to Zone, but Forget to Add Corresponding PTR Record

Because the mappings from hostnames to IP addresses are disjointed from the mappings from IP addresses to hostnames in DNS, it's easy to forget to add a PTR record for a new host. Adding the A record is intuitive, but many people who are used to host tables assume that adding an address record takes care of the reverse mapping, too. That's not true—you need to add a PTR record for the host to the appropriate *in-addr.arpa* zone. Thankfully, the DNS console makes that easy by providing a checkbox to **Create associated pointer (PTR) record** when you choose **New Host**.

Neglecting to add the PTR record for a host usually causes that host to fail authentication checks. For example, users on the host won't be able to *ssh* or *scp* to other hosts. The servers these programs talk to need to be able to map the connection's IP address to a domain name to check authorization files.

In addition, some large FTP archives, including *ftp.uu.net*, used to refuse anonymous *ftp* access to hosts whose IP addresses don't map back to domain names. *ftp.uu.net*'s FTP server emitted a message that read, in part:

```
530- Sorry, we're unable to map your IP address 140.186.66.1 to a hostname
530- in the DNS. This is probably because your nameserver does not have a
530- PTR record for your address in its tables, or because your reverse
530- nameservers are not registered. We refuse service to hosts whose
530- names we cannot resolve.
```

That made the reason you couldn't use anonymous *ftp* pretty evident. Other FTP sites, however, didn't bother printing informative messages; they simply denied service.

nslookup is handy for checking whether or not you've forgotten the PTR record:

```
C:\> nslookup
Default Server:  terminator.movie.edu
Address:  192.249.249.3

> beetlejuice        Check for a hostname-to-address mapping.
Server:  terminator.movie.edu
Address:  192.249.249.3

Name:     beetlejuice.movie.edu
Address:  192.249.249.23

> 192.249.249.23     Now check for a corresponding address-to-hostname mapping.
Server:  terminator.movie.edu
Address:  192.249.249.3

*** terminator.movie.edu can't find 192.249.249.23: Non-existent domain
```

On the primary master for *249.249.192.in-addr.arpa*, a quick check of the DNS console or the *249.249.192.in-addr.arpa.dns* file tell you whether the PTR record has been added to the zone yet.

6. Wrong Domain Name in RDATA of Record

When you add CNAME, MX, and NS records with the DNS console, remember to specify the fully qualified domain name of the host for the resource record-specific data. The DNS console assumes that the name you type as the RDATA field is fully qualified. So if you try to create a CNAME record as shown in Figure 15-4, the CNAME record looks like this in the zone datafile:

```
bigt   IN NS terminator.
```

This is probably not what you intended, since there's no top-level *terminator* domain. You probably assumed the DNS console would append the name of the zone to the name if you left off the dot. Nope.

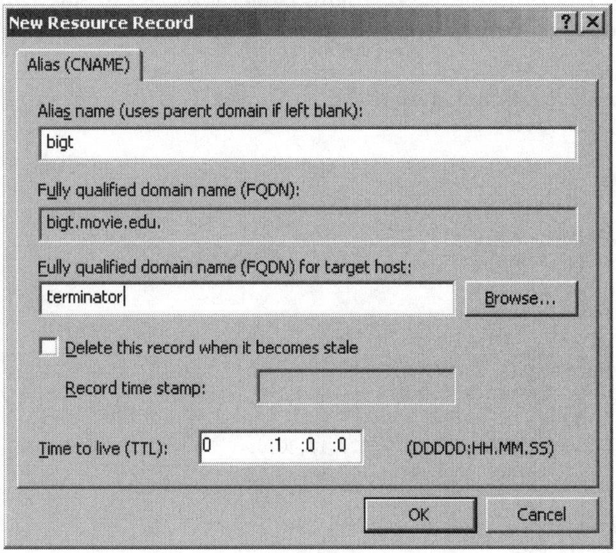

Figure 15-4. Creating a CNAME record (the wrong way)

These mistakes are easy to discover if you simply examine the zone datafile (after **Action → Update Server Data Files**) or use *nslookup*:

```
C:\> nslookup -type=cname bigt.movie.edu.
Server:  terminator.movie.edu
Address:  192.249.249.3

bigt.movie.edu  canonical name = terminator
```

7. Loss of Network Connectivity

Though the Internet is more reliable today than it was back in the wild and woolly days of the ARPANET, network outages are still relatively common. These failures usually look like poor performance:

```
C:\> nslookup nisc.sri.com.
Server:  terminator.movie.edu
Address:  192.249.249.3

DNS request timed out.
    timeout was 2 seconds.
DNS request timed out.
    timeout was 4 seconds.
DNS request timed out.
    timeout was 8 seconds.
*** Request to terminator.movie.edu timed-out
```

Using *nslookup*, you can look up the names and addresses of the name servers your
name server needs to talk to in order to resolve the name:

```
C:\> nslookup
Default Server: terminator.movie.edu
Address: 192.249.249.3

> set type=ns
> sri.com.
Server: terminator.movie.edu
Address: 192.249.249.3

Non-authoritative answer:
sri.com nameserver = ns.sri.com
sri.com nameserver = nsf.algx.net
sri.com nameserver = ns1.sri.com

ns.sri.com      internet address = 128.18.30.66
ns1.sri.com     internet address = 128.18.30.65
> com.
Server: terminator.movie.edu
Address: 192.249.249.3

Non-authoritative answer:
com     nameserver = j.gtld-servers.net
com     nameserver = k.gtld-servers.net
com     nameserver = l.gtld-servers.net
com     nameserver = m.gtld-servers.net
com     nameserver = a.gtld-servers.net
com     nameserver = b.gtld-servers.net
com     nameserver = c.gtld-servers.net
com     nameserver = d.gtld-servers.net
com     nameserver = e.gtld-servers.net
com     nameserver = f.gtld-servers.net
com     nameserver = g.gtld-servers.net
com     nameserver = h.gtld-servers.net
com     nameserver = i.gtld-servers.net
```

Then you can check your host's connectivity to those servers. Odds are, *ping* won't
have much better luck than your name server did. If it does, you should check that
the remote name servers are really running:

```
C:\> ping 128.18.30.66          Ping first sri.com name server.
Pinging 128.18.30.66 with 32 bytes of data:

Request timed out.
Request timed out.
Request timed out.
Request timed out.
C:\> ping 128.18.30.65          Ping second sri.com name server.
Pinging 128.18.30.65 with 32 bytes of data:

Request timed out.
Request timed out.
```

```
Request timed out.
Request timed out.
```

Now all that's left to do is to locate the break in the network. Utilities like *tracert* and *pathping* can help you determine whether the problem is on your network, on the destination network, or somewhere in the middle.

You should also use common sense when tracking down the break. If, for example, your *ping* testing showed that you couldn't reach any of the Internet's root name servers, it's not likely that each root's local network went down or that the Internet's commercial backbone networks collapsed entirely. Occam's razor says that the simplest condition that could cause this behavior—namely, the loss of *your* network's link to the Internet—is the most likely cause.

8. Missing Subdomain Delegation

Even though registrars do their best to process requests as quickly as possible, it may take some time for your subdomain's delegation to appear in the parent zone's name servers. If your parent zone isn't one of the generic top-level domains, your mileage may vary. Some parents are quick and responsive; others are slow and inconsistent. Just like in real life, though, you're stuck with them.

Until your delegation data appears in your parent zone's name servers, your name servers can look up data in the Internet domain namespace, but no one else on the Internet (outside of your domain) will know how to look up data in *your* namespace.

That means that even though you can send mail outside of your domain, the recipients won't be able to reply to it. Furthermore, no one can *telnet* to, *ftp* to, or even *ping* your hosts by name.

Remember that this applies equally to any *in-addr.arpa* subdomains you may run. Until the parent delegates those subdomains to your servers, name servers on the Internet won't be able to reverse-map addresses on your networks.

To determine whether or not your zone's delegation has made it into your parent zone's name servers, query a parent name server for the NS records for your zone. If the parent name server has the data, any name server on the Internet can find it:

```
C:\> nslookup
Default Server:  terminator.movie.edu
Address:  192.249.249.3

> server arrowroot.arin.net.        Query a 192.in-addr.arpa name server.
Default Server:  arrowroot.arin.net
Address:  198.133.199.110

> set norecurse                     Instruct the server to answer out of
> set type=ns                       its own data and to look for NS records
> 249.249.192.in-addr.arpa.         for 249.249.192.in-addr.arpa.
```

```
Server:  arrowroot.arin.net
Address:  198.133.199.110

*** arrowroot.arin.net can't find 249.249.192.in-addr.arpa.: Non-existent domain
```

Here, the delegation clearly hasn't been added yet. You can either wait patiently, or if an unreasonable amount of time has passed since you requested delegation from your parent zone, you can contact your parent zone's administrator and ask what's up.

9. Incorrect Subdomain Delegation

Incorrect subdomain delegation is another familiar problem on the Internet. Keeping delegation up-to-date requires human intervention—informing your parent zone's administrator of changes to your set of authoritative name servers. Consequently, delegation information often becomes inaccurate as administrators make changes without letting their parents know. Far too many administrators believe that setting up delegation is a one-shot deal: they let their parents know which name servers are authoritative once, when they set up their zones, and then they never talk to them again. They don't even call on Mother's Day.

An administrator may add a new name server, decommission another, and change the IP address of a third, all without telling the parent zone's administrator. Gradually, the number of name servers correctly delegated to by the parent zone dwindles. In the best case this leads to long resolution times, as querying name servers struggle to find an authoritative name server for the zone. If the delegation information becomes badly out of date and the last authoritative name server host is brought down for maintenance, the information within the zone becomes inaccessible.

If you suspect bad delegation, whether from your parent to your zone, from your zone to one of your children, or from a remote zone to one of its children, you can check with *nslookup*:

```
C:\> nslookup
Default Server:  terminator.movie.edu
Address:  192.249.249.3

> server a.gtld-servers.net.          Set server to the parent name server you suspect has bad
                                       delegation.
Default Server:  a.gtld-servers.net
Address:  198.41.0.4

> set type=ns          Look for NS records
> hp.com.              for the zone in question.
Server:  a.gtld-servers.net
Address:  198.41.0.4

Non-authoritative answer:
hp.com          nameserver = RELAY.HP.COM
hp.com          nameserver = HPLABS.HPL.HP.COM
```

```
hp.com            nameserver = NNSC.NSF.NET
hp.com            nameserver = HPSDLO.SDD.HP.COM

Authoritative answers can be found from:
hp.com            nameserver = RELAY.HP.COM
hp.com            nameserver = HPLABS.HPL.HP.COM
hp.com            nameserver = NNSC.NSF.NET
hp.com            nameserver = HPSDLO.SDD.HP.COM
RELAY.HP.COM       internet address = 15.255.152.2
HPLABS.HPL.HP.COM      internet address = 15.255.176.47
NNSC.NSF.NET          internet address = 128.89.1.178
HPSDLO.SDD.HP.COM      internet address = 15.255.160.64
HPSDLO.SDD.HP.COM      internet address = 15.26.112.11
```

Let's say you suspect that the delegation to *hpsdlo.sdd.hp.com* is incorrect. Query *hpsdlo* for data in the *hp.com* zone, and check the answer:

```
> server hpsdlo.sdd.hp.com.
Default Server:  hpsdlo.sdd.hp.com
Addresses:  15.255.160.64, 15.26.112.11

> set norecurse
> set type=soa
> hp.com.
Server:  hpsdlo.sdd.hp.com
Addresses:  15.255.160.64, 15.26.112.11

Non-authoritative answer:
hp.com
        origin = relay.hp.com
        mail addr = hostmaster.hp.com
        serial = 1001462
        refresh = 21600 (6 hours)
        retry   = 3600 (1 hour)
        expire  = 604800 (7 days)
        minimum ttl = 86400 (1 day)

Authoritative answers can be found from:
hp.com            nameserver = RELAY.HP.COM
hp.com            nameserver = HPLABS.HPL.HP.COM
hp.com            nameserver = NNSC.NSF.NET
RELAY.HP.COM       internet address = 15.255.152.2
HPLABS.HPL.HP.COM      internet address = 15.255.176.47
NNSC.NSF.NET       internet address = 128.89.1.178
```

If *hpsdlo* really were authoritative, it would have responded with an authoritative answer. The administrator of the *hp.com* zone can tell you whether *hpsdlo* should be an authoritative name server for *hp.com*, so that's who you should contact.

Checking delegation is even easier with *DNSLint*, which we introduced in Chapter 8. To check *hp.com*'s delegation, we could have run just:

```
C:\> dnslint /d hp.com
```

Interoperability Problems

The Microsoft DNS Server has a few interoperability issues with BIND name servers. Most of these involve zone transfers.

The WINS and WINS-R Records

Zone transfers sometimes fail because of Microsoft's proprietary WINS and WINS-R records. When a Microsoft DNS Server is configured to consult a WINS server for names it can't find in a given zone, it inserts a special record into the zone datafile. The record looks like this:

```
@   IN    WINS    <IP address of WINS server>
```

When configured to use WINS-R for reverse-mapping queries, the Microsoft DNS Server adds a similar WINS-R record to reverse-mapping zones.

Unfortunately, neither WINS nor WINS-R is a standard record type in the IN class. Consequently, any BIND secondaries that transfer this zone will choke on these records and refuse to load the zone. Here's the message the administrator of the BIND server might see in his *syslog* output:

```
May 23 15:58:43 terminator named-xfer[386]: "fx.movie.edu IN 65281" - unknown type
(65281)
```

The workaround for this problem is to configure the Microsoft DNS Server to filter out the proprietary record before transferring the zone. You do this by selecting the zone in the left pane of the DNS console, right-clicking it, and selecting **Properties**. For a forward-mapping zone, click on the **WINS** tab in the resulting properties window, which is shown in Figure 15-5.

Checking **Do not replicate this record** filters out the WINS record for that zone.

For a reverse-mapping zone, click on the **WINS-R** tab, shown in Figure 15-6. Check **Do not replicate this record** to prevent the name server from including the record in zone transfers.

BIND Secondaries for Active Directory–Integrated Zones

Another problem related to zone transfers can crop up when running a BIND or other non-Microsoft name server as a secondary to an AD-integrated zone. The serial number in an AD-integrated zone can vary on otherwise synchronized Microsoft DNS Servers. If a BIND secondary is configured to use multiple master name servers and the first of these isn't available, the second master may respond with a lower serial number, despite the fact that it has the same version of the zone as the previous master.

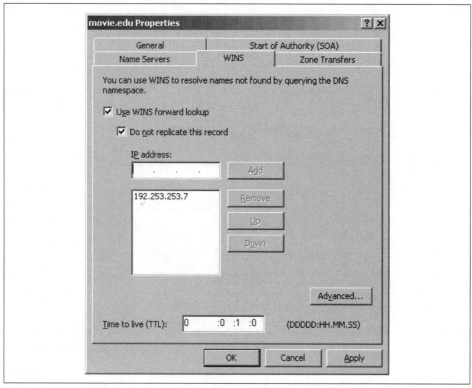

Figure 15-5. "Do not replicate this record" checkbox

Problem Symptoms

Some problems, unfortunately, aren't as easy to identify as the ones we've listed. You'll probably experience some misbehavior that you won't be able to attribute directly to its cause, often because any of a number of problems may cause the symptoms you see. For cases like this, we'll suggest some of the common causes of these symptoms and ways to isolate them.

Can't Look Up Local Name

The first thing to do when a program like *telnet* or *ftp* can't look up a local name is to use *nslookup* to try to look up the same name. When we say "the same name," we mean *literally* the same name—don't add a domain name and a trailing dot if the user didn't type either one. Don't query a different name server than the user did.

As often as not, the user mistyped the name or misunderstood how the search list works and just needs direction. Occasionally, you'll turn up real host configuration

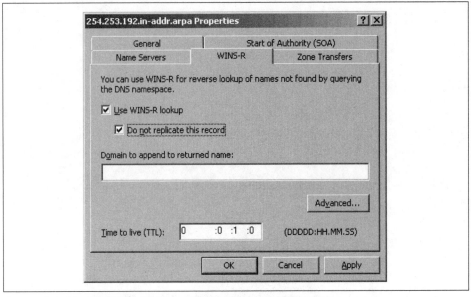

Figure 15-6. "Do not replicate this record" (for WINS-R) checkbox

errors, such as a mistake in the resolver configuration (e.g., the wrong IP address for a name server). You can check for errors like this using *nslookup*'s *set all* command.

If *nslookup* points to a problem with the name server, rather than with the host's configuration, check for the problems associated with the type of name server. If the name server is the primary master for the zone but it doesn't respond with data you think it should:

- Check that the zone or zone datafile contains the data in question.
- Ensure that the domain names in the records are correct (problem 6).

If the name server is a secondary server, you should first check whether or not its master has the correct data. If it does, and the secondary doesn't:

- Make sure you've incremented the serial number on the primary (problem 1).
- Look for a problem on the secondary in updating the zone (problem 4).

If the primary *doesn't* have the correct data, of course, diagnose the problem on the primary.

If the problem server isn't authoritative for the zone that contains the data, check that your parent zone's delegation to your zone exists and is correct (problems 8 and 9). Remember that to that name server, your zone looks just like any other remote zone. Even though the host it runs on may be inside your zone, the name server must be able to locate an authoritative server for your zone from your parent zone's servers.

Can't Look Up Remote Names

If your local lookups succeed but you can't look up names outside your local zones, there is a different set of problems to check:

- Can you *ping* the remote zone's name servers? Maybe you can't reach the remote zone's servers because of connectivity loss (see problem 7).

- Is the remote zone new? Maybe its delegation hasn't yet appeared (see problem 8). Alternatively, the delegation information for the remote zone may be wrong or out of date, due to neglect (see problem 9).

- Does the domain name actually exist on the remote zone's servers? Does it exist on all of them (see problems 1, 2, and 4)?

Wrong or Inconsistent Answer

If you get the wrong answer when looking up a local name or you get an inconsistent answer, depending on which name server you ask or when you ask, first check the synchronization between your name servers:

- Are they all holding the same serial number for the zone? Did you forget to increment the serial number on the primary after you made a manual change (see problem 1)? If you did, the name servers may all have the same serial number, but they will answer differently out of their authoritative data.

- Did you forget to restart the primary after making a manual change (see problem 2)? Then the primary returns (via *nslookup*, for example) a different serial number than the serial number in the zone datafile.

- Are the secondaries having trouble updating from the primary (see problem 4)?

- Is the name server's round-robin feature rotating the addresses of the domain name you're looking up?

If you get these results when looking up a name in a remote zone, you should check whether the remote zone's name servers have lost synchronization. You can use tools like *nslookup* to determine whether the remote zone's administrator has forgotten to increment the serial number, for example. If the name servers answer differently from their authoritative data but show the same serial number, the serial number probably wasn't incremented. If the primary's serial number is much lower than the secondary's, the primary's serial number was probably accidentally reset. We usually assume a zone's primary name server is running on the host listed as the origin in the SOA record.

You probably can't determine conclusively that the primary hasn't been restarted, though. It's also difficult to pin down updating problems between remote name servers. In cases like this, if you've determined that the remote name servers are giving out incorrect data, contact the zone administrator and (gently) relay what you've found. This helps the administrator track down the problem on the remote end.

Lookups Take a Long Time

Long name resolution periods are usually due to one of two problems:

- Connectivity loss (see problem 7), which you can diagnose with tools like *ping* and *tracert*
- Incorrect delegation information (see problem 9), which points to the wrong name servers or the wrong IP addresses

Usually, sending a few *ping*s points to one or the other of these causes. Either you can't reach the name servers at all, or you can reach the hosts but the name servers aren't responding.

Sometimes, though, the results are inconclusive. For example, the parent name servers may delegate to a set of name servers that don't respond to *ping*s or queries, but connectivity to the remote network seems all right (a *tracert*, for example, gets you to the remote network's "doorstep"—the last router between you and the host). Is the delegation information so badly out of date that the name servers have long since moved to other addresses? Are the hosts simply down? Or is there really a remote network problem? Usually, finding out requires a call or a message to the administrator of the remote zone. (And remember, *whois* gives you phone numbers!)

That's about all we can think of to cover. It's certainly a less than comprehensive list, but we hope it'll help you solve the more common problems you encounter with DNS and give you ideas about how to approach the rest. Boy, if we'd only had a troubleshooting guide when *we* started!

## CHAPTER 16

Miscellaneous

*"The time has come," the Walrus said, "To talk of
many things: Of shoes—and ships—and sealing-
wax—Of cabbages—and kings—And why the sea is
boiling hot—And whether pigs have wings."*

It's time we tied up loose ends. We've already covered the mainstream of DNS, but
we haven't explored a handful of interesting niches. Some of these, like instructions
on how to set up DNS on a network without Internet connectivity, may actually be
useful; others may just be interesting. But we can't in good conscience send you out
into the world without completing your education!

Using CNAME Records

We talked about CNAME resource records in Chapter 4. We didn't tell you *everything* about CNAME records, though; we saved that for this chapter. When you set
up your first name servers, you didn't care about the subtle nuances of the magical
CNAME record. Maybe you didn't realize there was more to it than we explained;
maybe you didn't care. Some of this trivia is interesting; some is arcane. We'll let you
decide which is which.

CNAMEs Attached to Interior Nodes

If you've ever renamed your zone because of a company reorganization, you may
have considered creating a single CNAME record that pointed from the zone's old
domain name to the new domain name. For instance, if the *fx.movie.edu* zone were
renamed to *magic.movie.edu*, we'd be tempted to create a single CNAME record to
map all the old names to the new names:

```
fx.movie.edu.   IN CNAME  magic.movie.edu.
```

With this record in place, you'd expect a lookup of *empire.fx.movie.edu* to result in a
lookup of *empire.magic.movie.edu*. Unfortunately, this doesn't work—you *can't* have

a CNAME record attached to an interior node like *fx.movie.edu* if it owns other records. Remember that *fx.movie.edu* has an SOA record and NS records, so attaching a CNAME record to it violates the rule that a domain name be either an alias or a canonical name, not both. So, instead of using a single CNAME record to rename a complete zone, we'll have to do it the old-fashioned way—a CNAME record for each individual host within the zone:

```
empire.fx.movie.edu.       IN  CNAME  empire.magic.movie.edu.
bladerunner.fx.movie.edu.  IN  CNAME  bladerunner.magic.movie.edu.
```

If the subdomain isn't delegated and consequently doesn't have an SOA record and NS records attached to it, you can create an alias for *fx.movie.edu*, but it will apply only to the domain name *fx.movie.edu* and not to domain names under *fx.movie.edu*.

CNAMEs Pointing to CNAMEs

You may have wondered whether it was possible to have an alias (CNAME record) pointing to another alias. This might be useful in situations where an alias points from a domain name outside of your zone to a domain name inside your zone. You may not have any control over the alias outside of your zone. What if you want to change the domain name to which it points? Can you simply add another CNAME record?

The answer is yes: you can chain together CNAME records. The Microsoft DNS Server supports it, and the RFCs don't expressly forbid it. But, while you *can* chain CNAME records, is it a wise thing to do? The RFCs recommend against it because of the possibility of creating a CNAME loop and because it slows resolution. You may be able to do it in a pinch, but you probably won't find much sympathy if something breaks.

CNAMEs in the Resource Record Data

For any other record besides a CNAME record, you must have the canonical domain name in the resource record data. Applications and name servers won't operate correctly otherwise. As we mentioned back in Chapter 5, for example, many mailers recognize only the canonical name of the local host on the right side of an MX record. If a mailer doesn't recognize the local host, it won't strip out the right MX records when paring down the MX list and may deliver mail to itself or to less-preferred mail exchangers, causing mail to loop.

Looking Up CNAMEs

At times you may want to look up a CNAME record itself, not data for the canonical name. With *nslookup*, this is easy to do. You can set the query type either to *cname* or to *any* and then look up the name:

```
C:\> nslookup
Default Server:  wormhole.movie.edu
Address:  192.249.249.1

> set query=cname
> bigt
Server:  wormhole.movie.edu
Address:  192.249.249.1

bigt.movie.edu  canonical name = terminator.movie.edu
> set query=any
> bigt
Server:  wormhole.movie.edu
Address:  192.249.249.1

bigt.movie.edu  canonical name = terminator.movie.edu
```

Finding Out a Host's Aliases

One thing you can't easily do with *nslookup*—or any query tool, for that matter—is find out a host's aliases. With the host table, it's easy to find both the canonical name of a host and any aliases. No matter which you look up, they're all there together on the same line, as shown in the following excerpt from *HOSTS*:

```
192.249.249.3  terminator.movie.edu terminator bigt
```

With DNS, however, if you look up the canonical name, all you get is the canonical name. There's no easy way for the name server or the application to know whether aliases exist for that canonical name:

```
C:\> nslookup
Default Server:  wormhole.movie.edu
Address:  192.249.249.1

> terminator
Server:  wormhole.movie.edu
Address:  192.249.249.1

Name:     terminator.movie.edu
Address:  192.249.249.3
```

If you use *nslookup* to look up an alias, you'll see that alias and the canonical name. *nslookup* reports both the alias and the canonical name in the packet. But you won't see any other aliases that might point to that canonical name:

```
C:\> nslookup
Default Server:  wormhole.movie.edu
Address:  192.249.249.1

> bigt
Server:  wormhole.movie.edu
Address:  192.249.249.1

Name:     terminator.movie.edu
Address:  192.249.249.3
```

```
   Aliases:  bigt.movie.edu
```

You can find out all the CNAMEs for a host *in a particular zone* by transferring the whole zone and picking out the CNAME records in which that host is the canonical name. You can have *nslookup* filter on CNAME records:

```
C:\> nslookup
Default Server:  wormhole.movie.edu
Address:  192.249.249.1

> ls -t cname movie.edu
[wormhole.movie.edu]
 bigt                           terminator.movie.edu
 wh                             wormhole.movie.edu
 dh                             diehard.movie.edu
```

You can also do this with *dnscmd*:

```
C:\> dnscmd /enumrecords movie.edu @ /type A
```

This method won't show you aliases in other zones that point to the canonical name, though.

Wildcards

Something else we haven't covered yet is DNS *wildcards*. At times you want a single resource record to cover any possible name, rather than creating zillions of resource records that are all the same except for the domain name to which they apply. DNS reserves a special character, the asterisk (*), to be used in a DNS datafile as a wildcard name. It will match any number of labels in a name, as long as that name isn't an exact match with a name already in the DNS database.

Most often, you'd use wildcards to forward mail to non-Internet-connected networks. Suppose our site weren't connected to the Internet, but we had a host that would relay mail between the Internet and our network. We could add a wildcard MX record to the *movie.edu* zone for Internet consumption that points all our mail to the relay. Here is an example:

```
*.movie.edu.  IN  MX  10 movie-relay.nea.gov.
```

Since the wildcard matches one or more labels, this resource record would apply to names like *terminator.movie.edu*, *empire.fx.movie.edu*, or *casablanca.bogart.classics. movie.edu*. The danger with wildcards is that they clash with search lists. This wildcard also matches *cujo.movie.edu.movie.edu*, making wildcards dangerous to use in your internal zone data. Remember that some mailers apply the search list when looking up MX records:

```
C:\>nslookup
Default Server:  wormhole.movie.edu
Address:  192.249.249.1
```

```
> set type=mx          Look up MX records
> cujo.movie.edu       for cujo.movie.edu.
Server:  wormhole.movie.edu
Address:  192.249.249.1

cujo.movie.edu.movie.edu        This isn't a real host's name!
        preference = 10, mail exchanger = movie-relay.nea.gov
```

What are the limitations of wildcards? Wildcards do not match names for which there is already data. Suppose you *did* use wildcards within your zone data:

```
*.movie.edu.    IN  MX  10 mail-hub.movie.edu.
et.movie.edu.   IN  MX  10 et.movie.edu.
jaws.movie.edu IN  A   192.253.253.113
```

Mail to *terminator.movie.edu* will be sent to *mail-hub*, but mail to *et.movie.edu* will be sent directly to *et*. An MX lookup of *jaws.movie.edu* would result in a response that says there is no MX data for that name. The wildcard doesn't apply because an A record exists. Can you use wildcards safely within your zone data? Yes. We'll cover that case a little later in this chapter.

A Limitation of MX Records

While we are on the topic of MX records, let's talk about how they can result in mail taking a longer path than necessary. The MX records are a list of data returned when a name is looked up. The list isn't ordered according to which mail exchanger is closest to the sender. Here is an example of this problem: Your non-Internet-connected network has two hosts capable of relaying Internet mail to your network. One host is in the U.S., and one host is in France. Your network is in Greece. Most of your mail comes from the U.S., so you have someone maintain your zone and install two wildcard MX records—giving the highest preference to the U.S. relay and a lower preference to the France relay. Since the U.S. relay is at a higher preference, *all* mail will go through that relay (as long as it is reachable). If someone in France sends you a letter, it will travel across the Atlantic to the U.S. mail relay and back across the Atlantic from the U.S. mail relay to your network in Greece because there is nothing in the MX list to indicate that the French relay is closer to that sender.

DNS and Internet Firewalls

The Domain Name System wasn't designed to work with Internet firewalls. It's a testimony to the flexibility of DNS that you can configure DNS to work with, or even through, an Internet firewall.

That said, configuring the Microsoft DNS Server to work in a firewalled environment, although not difficult, takes a good, complete understanding of DNS. Describing it also requires a large portion of this chapter, so here's a roadmap.

We start by describing the two major families of Internet firewall software: packet filters and application gateways. The capabilities of each family have a bearing on how you'll need to configure your DNS servers to work through the firewall. The next section details the two most common DNS architectures used with firewalls, forwarders, and internal roots, and describes the advantages and disadvantages of each. Finally, we discuss split namespaces and the configuration of the bastion host, the host at the core of your firewall system.

Types of Firewall Software

Before you start configuring your DNS servers to work with your firewall, it's important that you understand what your firewall is capable of. Your firewall's capabilities will influence your choice of DNS architecture and will determine how you implement it. If you don't know the answers to the questions in this section, track down someone in your organization who does know and ask. Better yet, work with your firewall's administrator when designing your DNS architecture to ensure it will coexist with the firewall.

Note that this is far from a complete explanation of Internet firewalls. These few paragraphs describe only the two most common types of Internet firewalls and only in enough detail to show how the differences in their capabilities affect name servers. For a comprehensive treatment of Internet firewalls, see Elizabeth Zwicky, Simon Cooper, and D. Brent Chapman's *Building Internet Firewalls* (O'Reilly).

Packet filters

The first type of firewall we'll cover is the packet-filtering firewall. Packet-filtering firewalls operate largely at the transport and network levels of the TCP/IP stack (layers three and four of the OSI reference model, if you dig that). They decide whether to route a packet based upon packet-level criteria, such as the transport protocol (e.g., whether it's TCP or UDP), the source and destination IP addresses, and the source and destination ports (see Figure 16-1).

What's most important to us about packet-filtering firewalls is that you can typically configure them to selectively allow DNS traffic between hosts on the Internet and your internal hosts. That is, you can let an arbitrary set of internal hosts communicate with Internet name servers. Some packet-filtering firewalls can even permit your name servers to query name servers on the Internet, but not vice versa. All router-based Internet firewalls are packet-filtering firewalls. Check Point's FireWall-1, Cisco's PIX, and NetScreen's products are popular commercial packet-filtering firewalls.

Application gateways

Application gateways operate at the application protocol level, several layers higher in the OSI reference model than most packet filters (see Figure 16-2). In a sense, they

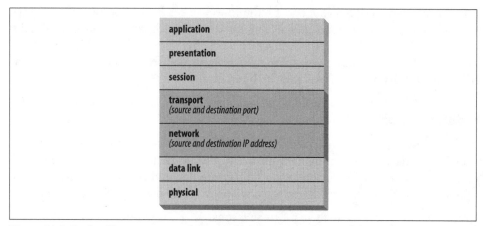

Figure 16-1. Packet filters operate at the network and transport layers of the stack

"understand" the application protocol in the same way a server for that particular application would. An FTP application gateway, for example, can make the decision to allow or deny a particular FTP operation, like a *RETR* (a *get*) or a *STOR* (a *put*).

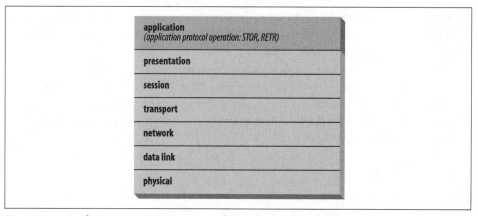

Figure 16-2. Application gateways operate at the application layer of the stack

The bad news, and what's important for our purposes, is that most application gateway-based firewalls handle only TCP-based application protocols. DNS, of course, is largely UDP-based, and we know of no application gateways for DNS. This implies that if you run an application gateway-based firewall, your internal hosts will likely not be able to communicate directly with name servers on the Internet.

The Firewall Toolkit from Trusted Information Systems (TIS, now part of Network Associates), a suite of application gateways for common Internet protocols, such as Telnet, FTP, and http, was used to build some of the first Internet firewalls. Many other firewall products include application gateways for various protocols. Note that these two categories of firewalls are really just generalizations. The state of the art in firewalls changes very quickly, and by the time you read this, you may have a fire-wall that includes an application gateway for DNS. Which family your firewall falls into is important only because it *suggests* what that firewall is capable of; what's more important is whether your particular firewall will let you permit DNS traffic between arbitrary internal hosts and the Internet.

A Bad Example

The simplest configuration is to allow DNS traffic to pass freely through your fire-wall (assuming you can configure your firewall to do that). That way, any internal name server can query any name server on the Internet, and any Internet name server can query any of your internal name servers. You don't need any special configuration.

Unfortunately, this is a bad idea, for two reasons:

Version control
> The developers of the Microsoft DNS Server are constantly finding and fixing security-related bugs in the code. Consequently, it's important to run a recent version of the server, especially for name servers that are directly exposed to the Internet. If one or just a few of your name servers communicate directly with name servers on the Internet, upgrading them to a new version is easy. If all of the name servers on your network do, upgrading all of them is more difficult.

Possible vector for attack
> Even if you're not running a name server on a particular host, a hacker might be able to take advantage of the fact that you allow DNS traffic through your fire-wall to attack that host. For example, a coconspirator working on the inside could set up a Telnet daemon listening on the host's DNS port, allowing the hacker to *telnet* right in.

For the rest of this chapter, we'll try to set a good example.

Internet Forwarders

Given the dangers of allowing bidirectional DNS traffic through the firewall unre-stricted, most organizations elect to limit the internal hosts that can "talk DNS" to the Internet. With an application gateway firewall, or any firewall without the ability to pass DNS traffic, the only host that can communicate with Internet name servers is the bastion host (see Figure 16-3).

With a packet-filtering firewall, the firewall's administrator can configure the fire-wall to let any set of internal name servers communicate with Internet name servers. Often, a small set of hosts runs name servers under the direct control of the network administrator (see Figure 16-4).

Internal name servers that can query name servers on the Internet directly don't require any special configuration. Their root hints files contain the Internet's root

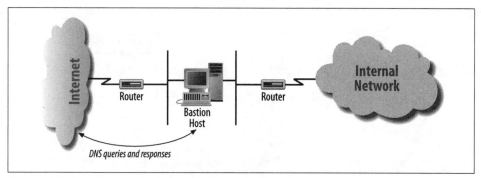

Figure 16-3. A small network, showing the bastion host

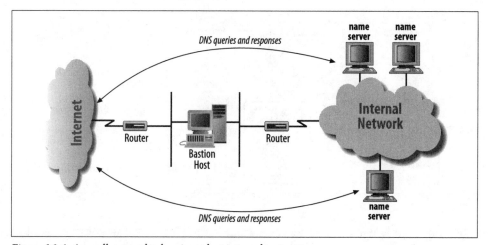

Figure 16-4. A small network, showing select internal name servers

name servers, which enables them to resolve Internet domain names. Internal name servers that *can't* query name servers on the Internet, however, need to know to forward queries they can't resolve to one of the name servers that can. This is done with the **Forwarders** tab on the server's **Properties** window, described in Chapter 11.

Figure 16-5 illustrates a common forwarding setup, with internal name servers forwarding queries to a name server running on a bastion host.

At Movie U., we put in a firewall to protect ourselves from the Big Bad Internet several years ago. Ours is a packet-filtering firewall, and we negotiated with our firewall administrator to allow DNS traffic between Internet name servers and two of our name servers, *terminator.movie.edu* and *wormhole.movie.edu*. (These negotiations involved the exchange of Krispy Kreme doughnuts.) Figure 16-6 shows how we configured the other internal name servers at the university.

When configuring different internal name servers, we vary the order in which the forwarders appear to help spread the load among them.

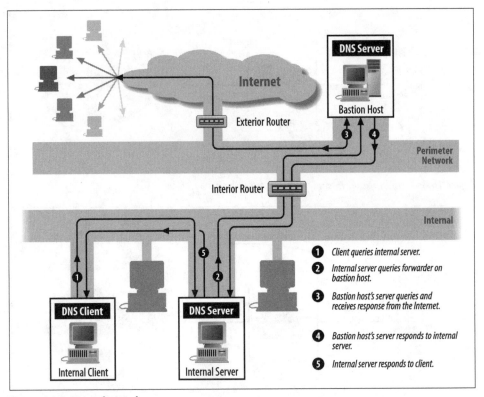

Figure 16-5. Using forwarders

When an internal name server receives a query for a name it can't resolve locally, such as an Internet domain name, it forwards that query to one of our forwarders, which can resolve the name using name servers on the Internet. Simple!

The trouble with forwarding

Unfortunately, it's a little too simple. Forwarding starts to get in the way once you delegate subdomains or build an extensive network. To explain what we mean, consider an internal caching-only name server, *darkcity.movie.edu. darkcity.movie.edu* is configured to use our two forwarders to resolve domain names. What happens when *darkcity.movie.edu* receives a query for a name in *fx.movie.edu*? Naturally, it'll forward the query to one of the forwarders. The response it gets may include NS records for *fx.movie.edu*, but *darkcity.movie.edu* will never use those NS records (unless they're looked up explicitly). It'll keep sending *fx.movie.edu* queries to the forwarders, even though it's perfectly capable of querying the *fx.movie.edu* name servers directly.

Now imagine the scale of the network is much larger: a corporate network that spans continents, with tens of thousands of hosts and hundreds or thousands of name serv-

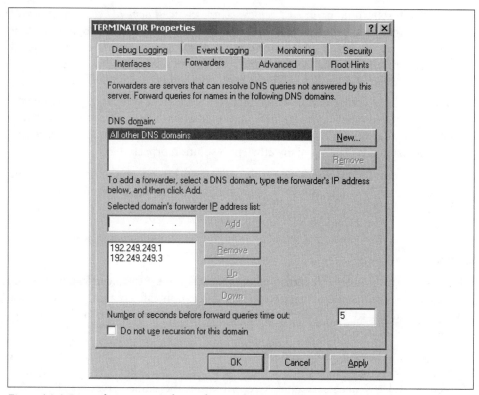

Figure 16-6. Internal name server forwarding configuration

ers. All of the internal name servers that don't have direct Internet connectivity—the vast majority of them—use a small set of forwarders. There are several things wrong with this picture:

Single point of failure

If the forwarders fail, your name servers lose the ability to resolve both Internet domain names and internal domain names that they don't have cached or authoritative data.

Concentration of load

The forwarders will have an enormous query load placed on them. This is both because of the large number of internal name servers that use them and because the queries are recursive and may require a good deal of work to answer.

Inefficient resolution

Imagine two internal name servers authoritative for *west.acmebw.com* and *east. acmebw.com*, respectively, both on the same network segment in Boulder, Colorado. Both are configured to use the company's forwarder in Bethesda, Maryland. To resolve a name in *east.acmebw.com*, the *west.acmebw.com* name server sends a query to the forwarder in Bethesda. The forwarder in Bethesda then sends a query back to Boulder to the *east.acmebw.com* name server, the original querier's neighbor. The *east.acmebw.com* name server replies by sending a response back to Bethesda, which the forwarder sends back to Boulder.

In a traditional configuration using iterative queries, the *west.acmebw.com* name server would quickly have learned that an *east.acmebw.com* name server was next door and would favor it (because of its low roundtrip time). Using forwarders "short-circuits" the normally efficient resolution process.

The upshot is that forwarding is fine for small networks and simple namespaces but usually inadequate for large networks and complex namespaces. We found this out the hard way at Movie U. as our network grew and we were forced to find an alternative.

Using stub zones

We can solve this problem by using stub zones, which we introduced in Chapter 10. In that chapter, we used stub zones to track delegation information. However, we can also use them to load certain NS records into our name server's cache and thereby disable forwarding for a domain.

We add *movie.edu* as a stub zone on our caching-only name server, as shown in Figure 16-7. With the stub zone configured, *darkcity.movie.edu* retrieves *movie.edu*'s NS records and any necessary glue A records from the name server we designate. More importantly, when it has queries in the *movie.edu* domain, it sends them directly to the name servers designated in those NS records rather than forwarding the queries.

We also need to set this up for any internal reverse-mapping zones to avoid having those sent to the forwarders.

If we set this up on all internal name servers that aren't authoritative for *movie.edu* and all of our reverse-mapping zones (they don't need it), we end up with a fairly robust resolution architecture that minimizes our exposure to the Internet: it uses efficient, resilient iterative name resolution to resolve internal domain names, and forwarders only when necessary to resolve Internet domain names. If our forwarders fail or we lose our connection to the Internet, we lose only our ability to resolve Internet domain names.

Internal Roots

If you want to avoid the scalability problems of forwarding and don't want to deal with stub zones, you can set up your own root name servers. These internal roots serve only the name servers in your organization. They'll know about only the portions of the namespace relevant to your organization.

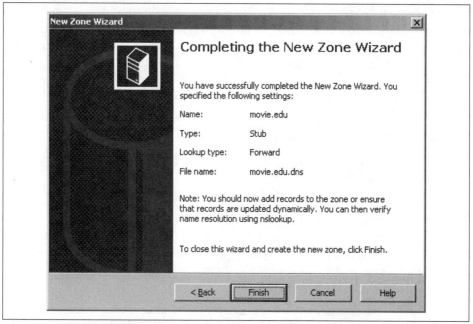

Figure 16-7. Adding movie.edu as a stub zone

What good are they? By using an architecture based on root name servers, you gain the scalability of the Internet namespace (which should be good enough for most companies), plus redundancy, distributed load, and efficient resolution. You can have as many internal roots as the Internet has roots—13 or so—whereas having that many forwarders may be an undue security exposure and a configuration burden. Most of all, the internal roots don't get used frivolously. Name servers need to consult an internal root only when they time out the NS records for your top-level zones. Using forwarders, name servers may have to query a forwarder once *per resolution*.

The moral of our story is that if you have, or intend to have, a large namespace and lots of internal name servers, internal root name servers scale better than any other solution.

Where to put internal root name servers

Since name servers "lock on" to the closest root name server by favoring the one with the lowest roundtrip time, it pays to pepper your network with internal root name servers. If your organization's network spans the U.S., Europe, and the Pacific Rim, consider locating at least one internal root name server on each continent. If you have three major sites in Europe, give each of them an internal root.

Forward-mapping delegation

Here's how an internal root name server is configured. An internal root delegates directly to any zones you administer. For example, on the *movie.edu* network, the root zone's datafile would contain:

```
;
;  Delegated sub-zone: movie.edu.
;
movie.edu               NS  terminator.movie.edu.
terminator.movie.edu    A   192.249.249.3
movie.edu               NS  wormhole.movie.edu.
wormhole.movie.edu      A   192.249.249.1
wormhole.movie.edu      A   192.253.253.1
movie.edu               NS  zardoz.movie.edu.
zardoz.movie.edu        A   192.249.249.9
zardoz.movie.edu        A   192.253.253.9
;  End delegation
```

On the Internet, this information would appear in the *edu* name servers' zone datafiles. On the *movie.edu* network, of course, there aren't any *edu* name servers, so you delegate directly to *movie.edu* from the root.

Notice that this example doesn't contain delegation to *fx.movie.edu* or any other subdomain of *movie.edu*. The *movie.edu* name servers know which name servers are authoritative for all *movie.edu* subdomains, and all queries for information in those subdomains pass through the *movie.edu* name servers, so there's no need to delegate them here.

in-addr.arpa delegation

We also need to delegate from the internal roots to the *in-addr.arpa* zones that correspond to the networks at the university:

```
;
;  Delegated sub-zone: 249.249.192.in-addr.arpa.
;
249.249.192.in-addr.arpa  NS  terminator.movie.edu.
terminator.movie.edu      A   192.249.249.3
249.249.192.in-addr.arpa  NS  wormhole.movie.edu.
wormhole.movie.edu        A   192.249.249.1
wormhole.movie.edu        A   192.253.253.1
249.249.192.in-addr.arpa  NS  zardoz.movie.edu.
zardoz.movie.edu          A   192.249.249.9
zardoz.movie.edu          A   192.253.253.9
;  End delegation


;
;  Delegated sub-zone: 253.253.192.in-addr.arpa.
;
253.253.192.in-addr.arpa  NS  terminator.movie.edu.
```

```
terminator.movie.edu        A   192.249.249.3
253.253.192.in-addr.arpa    NS  wormhole.movie.edu.
wormhole.movie.edu          A   192.249.249.1
wormhole.movie.edu          A   192.253.253.1
253.253.192.in-addr.arpa    NS  zardoz.movie.edu.
zardoz.movie.edu            A   192.249.249.9
zardoz.movie.edu            A   192.253.253.9
; End delegation


;
; Delegated sub-zone: 254.253.192.in-addr.arpa.
;
254.253.192.in-addr.arpa    NS  bladerunner.fx.movie.edu.
bladerunner.fx.movie.edu    A   192.253.254.2
254.253.192.in-addr.arpa    NS  outland.fx.movie.edu.
outland.fx.movie.edu        A   192.253.254.3
254.253.192.in-addr.arpa    NS  alien.fx.movie.edu.
alien.fx.movie.edu          A   192.253.254.86
; End delegation


;
; Delegated sub-zone: 20.254.192.in-addr.arpa.
;
20.254.192.in-addr.arpa     NS  bladerunner.fx.movie.edu.
bladerunner.fx.movie.edu    A   192.253.254.2
20.254.192.in-addr.arpa     NS  outland.fx.movie.edu.
outland.fx.movie.edu        A   192.253.254.3
20.254.192.in-addr.arpa     NS  alien.fx.movie.edu.
alien.fx.movie.edu          A   192.253.254.86
; End delegation
```

Notice that we *did* include delegation for the *254.253.192.in-addr.arpa* and *20.254. 192.in-addr.arpa* zones, even though they both correspond to the *fx.movie.edu* zone. We didn't need to delegate to *fx.movie.edu* because we'd already delegated to its parent, *movie.edu*. The *movie.edu* name servers delegate to *fx.movie.edu*, so by transitivity the roots delegate to *fx.movie.edu*. Since neither of the other *in-addr.arpa* zones is a parent of *254.253.192.in-addr.arpa* or *20.254.192.in-addr.arpa*, we needed to delegate both zones from the root.

As we've explained earlier, we don't *need* to add address records for the three Special Effects name servers, *bladerunner.fx.movie.edu*, *outland.fx.movie.edu*, and *alien.fx.movie.edu*, because a remote name server can already find their addresses by following delegation from *movie.edu*. However, the New Delegation Wizard adds their addresses anyway. Oh, well.

The root.dns file

All that's left is to add a root zone with an SOA record and NS records for this internal root name server and any others:

```
;
; Database file root.dns for . zone.
```

```
;      Zone version:  1
;
@              IN  SOA  rainman.movie.edu.  hostmaster.movie.edu.  (
               1               ; serial number
               900             ; refresh
               600             ; retry
               86400           ; expire
               3600  ) ; default TTL


;
; Zone NS records
;

@                    NS  rainman.movie.edu.
rainman.movie.edu A  192.249.249.254
@                    NS  awakenings.movie.edu
awakenings.movie.edu       A  192.253.253.254
```

rainman.movie.edu and *awakenings.movie.edu* are the hosts running internal root
name servers. We shouldn't run an internal root on a bastion host because if a name
server on the Internet accidentally queries it for data it's not authoritative for, the
internal root will respond with its list of roots—all internal!

So the whole *root.dns* file (by convention, we call the root zone's datafile *root.dns*)
looks like this:

```
;
; Database file root.dns for . zone.
;      Zone version:  4
;

@              IN  SOA  rainman.movie.edu.  hostmaster.movie.edu.  (
               1               ; serial number
               900             ; refresh
               600             ; retry
               86400           ; expire
               3600  )   ; default TTL


;
; Zone NS records
;
@                    NS  rainman.movie.edu.
rainman.movie.edu  A  192.249.249.254
@                    NS  awakenings.movie.edu.awakenings.movie.edu
                     A  192.253.253.254


;
; Zone records
;


;
; Delegated sub-zone:  movie.edu.
;
movie.edu                    NS  terminator.movie.edu.
terminator.movie.edu         A   192.249.249.3
```

```
movie.edu                 NS  wormhole.movie.edu.
wormhole.movie.edu        A   192.249.249.1
wormhole.movie.edu        A   192.253.253.1
movie.edu                 NS  zardoz.movie.edu.
zardoz.movie.edu          A   192.249.249.9
zardoz.movie.edu          A   192.253.253.9
; End delegation


;
; Delegated sub-zone:  249.249.192.in-addr.arpa.
;
249.249.192.in-addr.arpa  NS  terminator.movie.edu.
terminator.movie.edu      A   192.249.249.3
249.249.192.in-addr.arpa  NS  wormhole.movie.edu.
wormhole.movie.edu        A   192.249.249.1
wormhole.movie.edu        A   192.253.253.1
249.249.192.in-addr.arpa  NS  zardoz.movie.edu.
zardoz.movie.edu          A   192.249.249.9
zardoz.movie.edu          A   192.253.253.9
; End delegation


;
; Delegated sub-zone:  253.253.192.in-addr.arpa.
;
253.253.192.in-addr.arpa  NS  terminator.movie.edu.
terminator.movie.edu      A   192.249.249.3
253.253.192.in-addr.arpa  NS  wormhole.movie.edu.
wormhole.movie.edu        A   192.249.249.1
wormhole.movie.edu        A   192.253.253.1
253.253.192.in-addr.arpa  NS  zardoz.movie.edu.
zardoz.movie.edu          A   192.249.249.9
zardoz.movie.edu          A   192.253.253.9
; End delegation


;
; Delegated sub-zone:  254.253.192.in-addr.arpa.
;
254.253.192.in-addr.arpa  NS  bladerunner.fx.movie.edu.
bladerunner.fx.movie.edu  A   192.253.254.2
254.253.192.in-addr.arpa  NS  outland.fx.movie.edu.
outland.fx.movie.edu      A   192.253.254.3
254.253.192.in-addr.arpa  NS  alien.fx.movie.edu.
alien.fx.movie.edu        A   192.253.254.86
; End delegation


;
; Delegated sub-zone:  20.254.192.in-addr.arpa.
;
20.254.192.in-addr.arpa   NS  bladerunner.fx.movie.edu.
bladerunner.fx.movie.edu  A   192.253.254.2
20.254.192.in-addr.arpa   NS  outland.fx.movie.edu.
outland.fx.movie.edu      A   192.253.254.3
20.254.192.in-addr.arpa   NS  alien.fx.movie.edu.
alien.fx.movie.edu        A   192.253.254.86
```

```
;   End delegation
```

Creating the root zone with the DNS console on both of the internal root name servers, *rainman* and *awakenings*, is just like creating any primary zone: right-click on the server's name in the left pane, then choose **New Zone**. For the zone's domain name, choose "." (a single dot). The DNS console helpfully uses *root.dns* as the default filename for this zone.

If you don't have a lot of idle hosts sitting around that you can turn into internal roots, don't despair! Any internal name server (i.e., one that's not running on a bastion host or outside your firewall) can serve double duty as an internal root *and* as an authoritative name server for whatever other zones you need it to load. Remember, a single name server can be authoritative for many, many zones, including the root zone.

Configuring other internal name servers

Once you've set up internal root name servers, configure all the name servers on hosts anywhere on your internal network to use them. Any name server running on a host without direct Internet connectivity (i.e., behind the firewall) should list the internal roots in its root hints file:

```
;
;   Root Name Server Hints File:
;
;       These entries enable the DNS server to locate the root name servers
;       (the DNS servers authoritative for the root zone).
;       For historical reasons this is often referred to as the
;       "Cache File"
;

@                       NS  rainman.movie.edu.
@                       NS  awakenings.movie.edu
rainman.movie.edu       A   192.249.249.254
awakenings.movie.edu    A   192.253.253.254
```

To edit the root hints, you can open a name server's properties window and choose the **Root Hints** tab, shown in Figure 16-8. From here, you can delete the old root name servers and add the two new ones.

Once you've got one name server running with the new root hints, you can use the **Copy from Server** button to tell other name servers to import its list of root name servers.

Name servers running on hosts using this root hints file can resolve domain names in *movie.edu* and in Movie U.'s *in-addr.arpa* domains but not names outside of those domains.

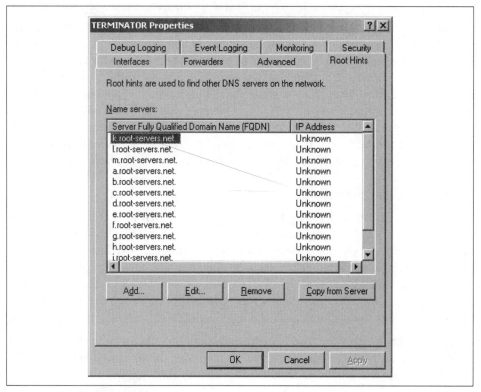

Figure 16-8. Editing the root hints

How internal name servers use internal roots

To tie together how this whole scheme works, let's go through an example of name resolution on an internal caching-only name server using these internal root name servers. First, the internal name server receives a query for a domain name in *movie.edu*, say the address of *gump.fx.movie.edu*. If the internal name server doesn't have any "better" information cached, it starts by querying an internal root name server. If it has communicated with the internal roots before, it has a roundtrip time associated with each, which tells it which of the internal roots is responding to it most quickly. It sends a nonrecursive query to that internal root for *gump.fx.movie.edu*'s address. The internal root answers with a referral to the *movie.edu* name servers on *terminator.movie.edu*, *wormhole.movie.edu*, and *zardoz.movie.edu*. The caching-only name server follows up by sending another nonrecursive query to one of the *movie.edu* name servers for *gump.fx.movie.edu*'s address. The *movie.edu* name server responds with a referral to the *fx.movie.edu* name servers. The caching-only name server sends the same nonrecursive query for *gump.fx.movie.edu*'s address to one of the *fx.movie.edu* name servers and finally receives a response.

Contrast this with the way a forwarding setup would have worked. Let's imagine that instead of using internal root name servers, our caching-only name server were configured to forward queries first to *terminator.movie.edu* and then to *wormhole.movie.edu*. In that case, the caching-only name server would have checked its cache for the address of *gump.fx.movie.edu* and, not finding it, would have forwarded the query to *terminator.movie.edu*. *terminator.movie.edu* would have queried an *fx.movie.edu* name server on the caching-only name server's behalf and returned the answer. Should the caching-only name server need to look up another name in *fx.movie.edu*, it would still ask the forwarder, even though the forwarder's response to the query for *gump.fx.movie.edu*'s address probably contained the names and addresses of the *fx.movie.edu* name servers.

The trouble with internal roots

Unfortunately, just as forwarding has its problems, internal root architectures have their limitations. Chief among these is the fact that your internal hosts can't see the Internet namespace. On some networks this isn't an issue, because most internal hosts don't have direct Internet connectivity. The few that do can have their resolvers configured to use a name server on the bastion host. Some of these hosts probably need to run proxy servers to allow other internal hosts access to services on the Internet.

On other networks, however, the Internet firewall or other software may require that all internal hosts have the ability to resolve names in the Internet namespace. For these networks, an internal root architecture won't work.

A Split Namespace

Many organizations would like to advertise different zone data to the Internet than they do internally. In most cases, much of the internal zone data is irrelevant to the Internet because of the organization's Internet firewall. The firewall may not allow direct access to most internal hosts and may also translate internal, unregistered IP addresses into a range of IP addresses registered to the organization. Therefore, the organization may need to trim out irrelevant information from the external view of the zone or change internal addresses to their external equivalents.

Unfortunately, the Microsoft DNS Server doesn't support automatic filtering and translation of zone data. Consequently, many organizations manually create what have become known as "split namespaces." In a split namespace, the real namespace is available only internally, while a pared-down, translated version of it, called the *shadow namespace*, is visible to the Internet.

The shadow *namespace* contains the name-to-address and address-to-name mappings of only those hosts that are accessible from the Internet through the firewall. The addresses advertised may be the translated equivalents of internal addresses. The shadow *namespace* may also contain one or more MX records to direct mail from the Internet through the firewall to a mail server.

Since Movie U. has an Internet firewall that greatly limits access from the Internet to the internal network, we elected to create a shadow namespace. For the *movie.edu* zone, we need to give out information about only the domain name *movie.edu* (an SOA record and a few NS records), the bastion host (*postmanrings2x.movie.edu*), and our new external name server, *ns.movie.edu*, which also functions as an external web server, *www.movie.edu*. The address of the external interface on the bastion host is 200. 1.4.2, while the address of the name/web server is 200.1.4.3. The shadow *movie.edu* zone datafile looks like this:

```
;
; Database file movie.edu.dns for movie.edu zone.
;      Zone version 1
;
@                 IN    SOA   ns.movie.edu.    hostmaster.movie.edu. (
                              1       ; serial number
                              900     ; refresh
                              600     ; retry
                              86400   ; expire
                              3600  ) ; default TTL


;
; Zone NS records
;
@                 NS    ns.movie.edu.
ns                A     200.1.4.3
@                 NS    ns1.isp.net
ns1.isp.net.      A     200.1.0.2


;
; Zone records
;
@                 A     200.1.4.3
@                 MX    10 postmanrings2x.movie.edu.
@                 MX    100 mail.isp.net.
*                 MX    10 postmanrings2x.movie.edu.
                  MX    100 mail.isp.net.
ns                A     200.1.4.3
                  MX    10 postmanrings2x.movie.edu.
                  MX    100 mail.isp.net.
postmanrings2x    A     200.1.4.2
                  MX    10 postmanrings2x.movie.edu.
                  MX    100 mail.isp.net.
www               CNAME movie.edu.
```

Note that there's no mention of any of the subdomains of *movie.edu*, including any delegation to the name servers for those subdomains. That information isn't necessary, since there's nothing in any of the subdomains you can get to from the Internet and inbound mail addressed to hosts in the subdomains is caught by the wildcard.

The *4.1.200.in-addr.arpa.dns* file, which we need to reverse map the two Movie U. IP addresses that hosts on the Internet might see, looks like this:

```
;
; Database file 4.1.200.in-addr.arpa.dns for 4.1.200.in-addr.arpa zone
;
@               SOA     ns.movie.edu.   hostmaster.movie.edu. (
                        1           ; serial number
                        900         ; refresh
                        600         ; retry
                        86400       ; expire
                        3600    ) ; default TTL


;
; Zone NS records
;
@               NS      ns.movie.edu.
ns.movie.edu.   A       200.1.4.3
@               NS      ns1.isp.net.
ns1.isp.net.    A       200.1.0.2


;
; Zone records
;
2               PTR     postmanrings2x.movie.edu.
3               PTR     ns.movie.edu.
```

As a precaution, we need to make sure that the resolver on our bastion host isn't configured to use the server on *ns.movie.edu*. Since that server can't see the real, internal *movie.edu*, using it would render *postmanrings2x.movie.edu* unable to map internal names to addresses or internal addresses to names.

Configuring the bastion host

The bastion host is a special case in a split-namespace configuration. The bastion host has a foot in each environment: one network interface connects it to the Internet and another connects it to the internal network. Now that we have split our namespace in two, how can our bastion host see both the Internet namespace and our internal namespace? If we configure it with the Internet's root name servers in its root hints file, it will follow delegation from the Internet's *edu* name servers to an external *movie.edu* name server with shadow zone data. It would be blind to our internal namespace, which it needs to see to log connections, deliver inbound mail, and more. On the other hand, if we configure it with our internal roots it won't see the Internet namespace, which it clearly needs to do in order to function as a bastion host. What to do?

If we have internal name servers that can resolve both internal and Internet domain names—using the forwarding configuration earlier in this chapter, for example—we can simply configure the bastion host's resolver to query those name servers. But if we use forwarding internally, depending on the type of firewall we're running, we may also need to run a forwarder on the bastion host itself. If the firewall won't pass DNS traffic, we'll need to run at least a caching-only name server, configured with the Internet roots, on the bastion host so that our internal name servers will have somewhere to forward their unresolved queries.

If our internal name servers don't support per-zone forwarding, the name server on our bastion host must be configured as a secondary for *movie.edu* and any *in-addr.arpa* zones in which it needs to resolve addresses. This way, if it receives a query for a domain name in *movie.edu*, it'll use its local authoritative data to resolve the name. (If our internal name servers support conditional forwarding and are configured correctly, the name server on our bastion host will never receive queries for names in *movie.edu*.) If the domain name is in a subdomain of *movie.edu*, it'll follow NS records in the zone data to query an internal name server for the name. Therefore, it doesn't need to be configured as a secondary for any *movie.edu* subdomains, such as *fx.movie.edu*, just the "topmost" zone (see Figure 16-9).

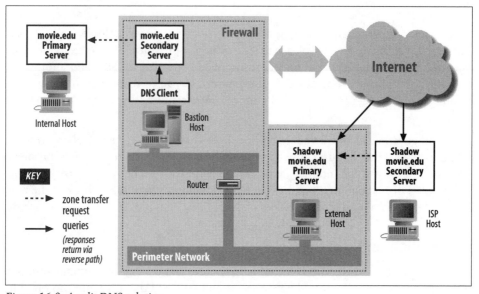

Figure 16-9. A split DNS solution

Dial-up Connections

Another relatively recent development in networking that presents a challenge to DNS is the dial-up Internet connection. When the Internet was young and DNS was born, there was no such thing as a dial-up connection. With the enormous explosion in the Internet's popularity and the propagation of Internet service providers who offer dial-up Internet connectivity to the masses, a whole new breed of problems with name service has been introduced.

We'll separate dial-up connections into two categories: simple dial-up, by which we mean a single computer that connects to the Internet occasionally, when a user manually initiates a connection; and dial-on-demand, which means one or more computers that connect to the Internet automatically whenever they generate traffic bound for the Internet. Often, the device that makes this dial-on-demand connectivity possible is a small dial-up router with an analog modem or ISDN interface.

Simple Dial-up

The easiest way to deal with simple dial-up is to use a name server provided by your ISP. Most ISPs run name servers for their subscribers' use. And in most cases, the addresses of your ISP's name servers are assigned to your resolver when you dial in. Occasionally, however, you'll need to configure them yourself. If you're not sure whether your ISP provides name servers for your use or if you don't know what their IP addresses are, check their web site, send them email, or—as a last resort—give them a call.

Some operating systems, including all modern versions of Windows, will let you define a set of name servers for a particular dial-up provider. So, for example, you can configure one set of name servers to use when you dial up SBC and another to use when you dial up your office. Unfortunately, if you're still using Windows 95, defining name servers for your LAN connection overrides all your precious dial-up settings.

This configuration is usually adequate for most casual dial-up users. Name resolution fails unless the dial-up connection is up, but that's not likely to be a problem since there's no use for Internet name service without Internet connectivity. If you have special needs that aren't addressed by this configuration, take a look at the recommendations in the next section.

Dial-on-Demand

A more sophisticated dial-up solution is dial-on-demand. Dial-on-demand Internet connections often use dedicated hardware, such as a small dial-up router, to provide connectivity whenever it's needed. If you initiate a connection to the Internet from the "remote" end of a dial-on-demand router, it dials up another router on the Internet and routes your packets across. If the connection is idle for more than a specified amount of time, the router drops the connection.

The challenge with DNS is to keep a local name server from continuously bringing the dial-on-demand connection up and down like a yo-yo. This could be costly, because you sometimes pay a premium for connection setup with technologies such as ISDN.

The most important strategy for minimizing this off-net traffic is to configure your resolvers to use a minimal search list (or DNS suffix list, as it's called in Windows). The default Windows search list (which you get when you don't specify an explicit list of DNS suffixes to search) searches the ancestors of your local domain, which can cause unnecessary remote traffic. For instance, say your local domain is *tinyoffice.majorcorp.com*, and you have a dial-on-demand connection to Major-corp's enterprise network. On hosts without an explicit DNS suffix list, your default search list includes:

```
tinyoffice.majorcorp.com
majorcorp.com
```

A user typing *telnet foo.tinyoffice.majorcorp.com* to log into the workstation next to him might inadvertently cause lookups of both of these addresses:

```
foo.tinyoffice.majorcorp.com.tinyoffice.majorcorp.com
foo.tinyoffice.majorcorp.com.majorcorp.com
```

before the correct domain name, *foo.tinyoffice.majorcorp.com*, is looked up.[*] Since your local name server is probably authoritative for *tinyoffice.majorcorp.com,* it can tell that the first domain name, *foo.tinyoffice.majorcorp.com.tinyoffice.majorcorp.com*, is bogus. (It ends in *com.tinyoffice.majorcorp.com*, so it would require the existence of a *com* subdomain of your local domain, and there isn't one.) But it can't tell about the second domain name without talking to a *majorcorp.com* name server first. If there isn't one locally, it'll have to bring up that dial-on-demand connection.

The easiest way to prevent these unnecessary queries is to trim the parent domain out of your search list explicitly by setting a DNS suffix list in the resolver configuration. In this example, a DNS suffix list *tinyoffice.majorcorp.com* (just one entry) would probably cause fewer failed off-site lookups.

If many of the names your users look up are in your parent zone, you might also consider configuring your local name server as a secondary for your parent zone. At least that way you'll bring up the link at most only once per refresh interval to resolve names in your parent zone. The same logic could be applied to nearly any zone your local name server queries often.

---

[*] The exact behavior depends on which version of Windows the user is running. Older versions of Windows exhibit this behavior, but newer versions of Windows try to resolve any domain names containing at least one dot by themselves before appending the search list. You'll find more details about resolver behavior in Chapter 6.

DNS Message Format and Resource Records

This appendix outlines the format of DNS messages and enumerates the most common resource record types. The resource records are shown in their textual format, as you would specify them in a zone datafile, and in their binary format, as they appear in DNS messages.

We've included the portions of RFC 1035, written by Paul Mockapetris, that deal with the textual format of master files (what we called *zone datafiles*) or with the DNS message format (for those of you who need to parse DNS packets).

Master File Format

(From RFC 1035, pages 33–35)

The format of these files is a sequence of entries. Entries are predominantly line-oriented, though parentheses can be used to continue a list of items across a line boundary, and text literals can contain CRLF within the text. Any combination of tabs and spaces acts as a delimiter between the separate items that make up an entry. The end of any line in the master file can end with a comment. The comment starts with a semicolon (;).

The following entries are defined:

```
blank[comment]

$ORIGIN domain-name [comment]

$INCLUDE file-name [domain-name] [comment]

domain-namerr [comment]

blankrr [comment]
```

Blank lines, with or without comments, are allowed anywhere in the file.

Two control entries are defined: $ORIGIN and $INCLUDE. $ORIGIN is followed by a domain name and resets the current origin for relative domain names to the stated name. $INCLUDE inserts the named file into the current file and may optionally specify a domain name that sets the relative domain name origin for the included file. $INCLUDE may also have a comment. Note that an $INCLUDE entry never changes the relative origin of the parent file, regardless of changes to the relative origin made within the included file.

The last two forms represent RRs. If an entry for an RR begins with a blank, then the RR is assumed to be owned by the last stated owner. If an RR entry begins with a *domain-name*, then the owner name is reset.

rr contents take one of the following forms:

```
[
TTL] [
class]
type RDATA
[
class] [
TTL]
type RDATA
```

The RR begins with optional TTL and class fields, followed by a type and RDATA field appropriate to the type and class. Class and type use the standard mnemonics; TTL is a decimal integer. Omitted class and TTL values default to the last explicitly stated values. Since type and class mnemonics are disjoint, the parse is unique.

*domain-name*s make up a large share of the data in the master file. The labels in the domain name are expressed as character strings and separated by dots. Quoting conventions allow arbitrary characters to be stored in domain names. Domain names that end in a dot are called absolute and are taken as complete. Domain names that do not end in a dot are called relative; the actual domain name is the concatenation of the relative part with an origin specified in an $ORIGIN, $INCLUDE, or argument to the master file-loading routine. A relative name is an error when no origin is available.

character-string is expressed in one of two ways: as a contiguous set of characters without interior spaces, or as a string beginning with " and ending with ". Inside a "-delimited string any character can occur, except for " itself, which must be quoted using a backslash (\).

Because these files are text files, several special encodings are necessary to allow arbitrary data to be loaded. In particular:

.   Of the root.

@   A free-standing @ is used to denote the current origin.

\X X is any character other than a digit (0–9), and \ is used to quote that character so that its special meaning does not apply. For example, \. can be used to place a dot character in a label (not implemented by BIND 4.8.3).

\DDD
Each D is a digit in the octet corresponding to the decimal number described by DDD. The resulting octet is assumed to be text and is not checked for special meaning (not implemented by BIND 4.8.3).

( ) Parentheses are used to group data that crosses a line boundary. In effect, line terminations are not recognized within parentheses. (BIND 4.8.3 allows parentheses only on SOA and WKS resource records.)

;   A semicolon is used to start a comment; the remainder of the line is ignored.

Time to Live

(From RFC 2308, pages 7–8)

The Master File format [RFC 1035 Section 5] is extended to include the following directive:

```
$TTL <TTL> [comment]
```

All resource records appearing after the directive, and which do not explicitly include a TTL value, have their TTL set to the TTL given in the $TTL directive.

The remaining of the current meanings, of being the TTL to be used for negative responses, is the new defined meaning of the SOA minimum field.

Character Case

(From RFC 1035, page 9)

For all parts of the DNS that are part of the official protocol, all comparisons between character strings (e.g., labels, domain names, etc.) are done in a case-insensitive manner. At present, this rule is in force throughout the domain system without exception. However, future additions beyond current usage may need to use the full binary octet capabilities in names, so attempts to store domain names in 7-bit ASCII or use of special bytes to terminate labels, etc., should be avoided.

Types

Following is a list of common resource record types. The textual representation is used in master files. The binary representation is used in DNS queries and responses. These resource records are described on pages 13–21 of RFC 1035.

A (address)

(From RFC 1035, page 20)

Textual representation

```
owner ttl class A address
```

Example

```
localhost.movie.edu.   IN A 127.0.0.1
```

Binary representation

```
Address type code: 1
    +--+--+--+--+--+--+--+--+--+--+--+--+--+--+--+--+
    |                    ADDRESS                    |
    +--+--+--+--+--+--+--+--+--+--+--+--+--+--+--+--+
```

where:

ADDRESS
Is a 32-bit Internet address.

CNAME (canonical name)

(From RFC 1035, page 14)

Textual representation

```
owner ttl class CNAME canonical-dname
```

Example

```
wh.movie.edu.  IN  CNAME  wormhole.movie.edu.
```

Binary representation

```
CNAME type code: 5
    +--+--+--+--+--+--+--+--+--+--+--+--+--+--+--+--+
    /                     CNAME                     /
    /                                               /
    +--+--+--+--+--+--+--+--+--+--+--+--+--+--+--+--+
```

where:

CNAME
Is a *domain-name* that specifies the canonical or primary name for the owner. The owner name is an alias.

MX (mail exchanger)

(From RFC 1035, page 17)

Textual representation

```
owner ttl class MX preference exchange-dname
```

Example

```
ora.com.  IN  MX  0  ora.ora.com.
          IN  MX  10 ruby.ora.com.
          IN  MX  10 opal.ora.com.
```

Binary representation

```
MX type code: 15
     +--+--+--+--+--+--+--+--+--+--+--+--+--+--+--+--+
     |                  PREFERENCE                   |
     +--+--+--+--+--+--+--+--+--+--+--+--+--+--+--+--+
     /                   EXCHANGE                    /
     /                                               /
     +--+--+--+--+--+--+--+--+--+--+--+--+--+--+--+--+
```

where:

PREFERENCE
Is a 16-bit integer that specifies the preference given to this RR among others at the same owner. Lower values are preferred.

EXCHANGE
Is a *domain-name* that specifies a host willing to act as a mail exchange for the owner name.

NS (name server)

(From RFC 1035, page 18)

Textual representation

```
owner ttl class NS name-server-dname
```

Example

```
movie.edu.  IN   NS  terminator.movie.edu
```

Binary representation

```
NS type code: 2
     +--+--+--+--+--+--+--+--+--+--+--+--+--+--+--+--+
     /                    NSDNAME                    /
     /                                               /
     +--+--+--+--+--+--+--+--+--+--+--+--+--+--+--+--+
```

where:

NSDNAME

Is a *domain-name* that specifies a host which should be authoritative for the specified class and domain.

PTR (pointer)

(From RFC 1035, page 18)

Textual representation

```
owner ttl class PTR dname
```

Example

```
1.249.249.192.in-addr.arpa.  IN PTR wormhole.movie.edu.
```

Binary representation

```
PTR type code: 12
    +--+--+--+--+--+--+--+--+--+--+--+--+--+--+--+--+
    /                    PTRDNAME                   /
    +--+--+--+--+--+--+--+--+--+--+--+--+--+--+--+--+
```

where:

PTRDNAME

Is a *domain-name* that points to some location in the domain name space.

SOA (start of authority)

(From RFC 1035, pages 19–20)

Textual representation

```
owner ttl class SOA source-dname mbox (serial refresh retry expire minimum)
```

Example

```
movie.edu. IN SOA terminator.movie.edu. al.robocop.movie.edu. (
                        1        ; Serial
                        10800    ; Refresh after 3 hours
                        3600     ; Retry after 1 hour
                        604800   ; Expire after 1 week
                        86400 )  ; Minimum TTL of 1 day
```

Binary representation

```
SOA type code: 6
    +--+--+--+--+--+--+--+--+--+--+--+--+--+--+--+--+
    /                     MNAME                     /
    /                                               /
```

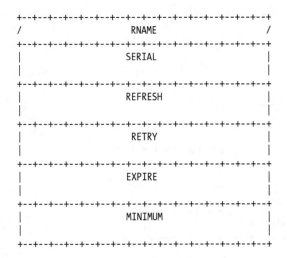

```
+--+--+--+--+--+--+--+--+--+--+--+--+--+--+--+--+
/                     RNAME                      /
+--+--+--+--+--+--+--+--+--+--+--+--+--+--+--+--+
|                     SERIAL                     |
|                                                |
+--+--+--+--+--+--+--+--+--+--+--+--+--+--+--+--+
|                     REFRESH                    |
|                                                |
+--+--+--+--+--+--+--+--+--+--+--+--+--+--+--+--+
|                     RETRY                      |
|                                                |
+--+--+--+--+--+--+--+--+--+--+--+--+--+--+--+--+
|                     EXPIRE                     |
|                                                |
+--+--+--+--+--+--+--+--+--+--+--+--+--+--+--+--+
|                    MINIMUM                     |
|                                                |
+--+--+--+--+--+--+--+--+--+--+--+--+--+--+--+--+
```

where:

MNAME

Is the *domain-name* of the name server that was the original or primary source of data for this zone.

RNAME

Is a *domain-name* that specifies the mailbox of the person responsible for this zone.

SERIAL

Is the unsigned 32-bit version number of the original copy of the zone. Zone transfers preserve this value. This value wraps and should be compared using sequence space arithmetic.

REFRESH

Is a 32-bit time interval before the zone should be refreshed.

RETRY

Is a 32-bit time interval that should elapse before a failed refresh should be retried.

EXPIRE

Is a 32-bit time value that specifies the upper limit on the time interval that can elapse before the zone is no longer authoritative.

MINIMUM

Is the unsigned 32-bit minimum TTL field that should be exported with any RR from this zone.

TXT (text)

(From RFC 1035, page 20)

Textual representation

```
owner ttl class TXT txt-strings
```

Example

```
cujo.movie.edu.  IN  TXT  "Location: machine room dog house"
```

Binary representation

```
TXT type code: 16
    +--+--+--+--+--+--+--+--+--+--+--+--+--+--+--+--+
    /                  TXT-DATA                    /
    +--+--+--+--+--+--+--+--+--+--+--+--+--+--+--+--+
```

where:

TXT-DATA
   Is one or more *character-strings*.

New Types from RFC 1183

RP (Responsible Person—experimental)

Textual representation

```
owner ttl class RP mbox-dname txt-dname
```

Example

```
; The current origin is fx.movie.edu
@            IN  RP   ajs.fx.movie.edu.    ajs.fx.movie.edu.
bladerunner  IN  RP   root.fx.movie.edu.   hotline.fx.movie.edu.
             IN  RP   richard.fx.movie.edu.  rb.fx.movie.edu.
ajs          IN  TXT  "Arty Segue, (415) 555-3610"
hotline      IN  TXT  "Movie U. Network Hotline, (415) 555-4111"
rb           IN  TXT  "Richard Boisclair, (415) 555-9612"
```

Binary representation

```
RP type code: 17
    +--+--+--+--+--+--+--+--+--+--+--+--+--+--+--+--+
    /                  MAILBOX                      /
    /                                               /
    +--+--+--+--+--+--+--+--+--+--+--+--+--+--+--+--+
    /                  TXTDNAME                     /
    /                                               /
    +--+--+--+--+--+--+--+--+--+--+--+--+--+--+--+--+
```

where:

MAILBOX
> Is a *domain-name* that specifies the mailbox for the responsible person.

TXTDNAME
> Is a *domain-name* for which TXT RRs exist. A subsequent query can be per-
> formed to retrieve the associated TXT resource records at *txt-dname*.

New Types from RFC 1886

AAAA (IPv6 Address)

Textual representation

```
owner ttl class AAAA ipv6-address
```

Example

```
bridgetjones.movie.edu.   IN AAAA 4321:0:1:2:3:4:567:89ab
```

Binary representation

```
Address type code: 28
    +--+--+--+--+--+--+--+--+--+--+--+--+--+--+--+--+
    |                    ADDRESS                     |
    |                                                |
    |                                                |
    |                                                |
    +--+--+--+--+--+--+--+--+--+--+--+--+--+--+--+--+
```

where:

ADDRESS
> Is a 128-bit Internet Protocol Version 6 address.

New Types from RFC 2052

SRV (service location)

Textual representation

```
owner ttl class SRV priority weight port target
```

Example

```
_http._tcp.movie.edu.  IN  SRV 1 2 80 www.fx.movie.edu.
                       IN  SRV 1 1 8080 www1.fx.movie.edu.
```

Binary representation

SRV type code: 33

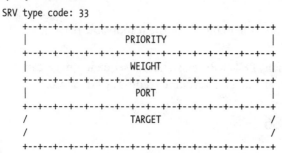

where:

PRIORITY

Is, as for MX, the priority of this target host. A client MUST attempt to contact the target host with the lowest-numbered priority it can reach; target hosts with the same priority SHOULD be tried in pseudorandom order. The range is 0–65535.

WEIGHT

Is a load-balancing mechanism. When selecting a target host among those that have the same priority, the chance of trying this one first SHOULD be proportional to its weight. The range of this number is 1–65535. Domain administrators are urged to use Weight 0 when there isn't any load balancing to do, to make the RR easier to read for humans (less noisy).

PORT

Is the port on this target host of this service. The range is 0–65535. This is often as specified in Assigned Numbers but need not be.

TARGET

Is, as for MX, the domain name of the target host. There MUST be one or more A records for this name. Implementors are urged, but not required, to return the A record(s) in the Additional Data section. Name compression is to be used for this field. A Target of "." means that the service is decidedly not available at this domain.

Classes

(From RFC 1035, page 13)

CLASS fields appear in resource records. The following CLASS mnemonics and values are defined:

IN 1: the Internet

CS 2: the CSNET class (obsolete—used only for examples in some obsolete RFCs)

CH 3: the CHAOS class

HS 4: the Hesiod class

DNS Messages

To write programs that parse DNS messages, you need to understand the message format. DNS queries and responses are most often contained within UDP datagrams. Each message is fully contained within a UDP datagram. If the query and response are sent over TCP, they are prefixed with a 2-byte value indicating the length of the query or response, excluding the 2-byte length. The format and content of the DNS messages are as follows.

Message Format

(From RFC 1035, page 25)

All communications inside of the domain protocol are carried in a single format called a message. The top-level format of the message is divided into five sections (some of which are empty in certain cases), which are shown here:

```
+---------------------+
|        Header       |
+---------------------+
|       Question      | the question for the name server
+---------------------+
|        Answer       | RRs answering the question
+---------------------+
|      Authority      | RRs pointing toward an authority
+---------------------+
|      Additional     | RRs holding additional information
+---------------------+
```

The Header section is always present. The header includes fields that specify which of the remaining sections are present, and also specify whether the message is a query or a response, a standard query or some other opcode, etc.

The names of the sections after the header are derived from their use in standard queries. The Question section contains fields that describe a question to a name server. These fields are a query type (QTYPE), a query class (QCLASS), and a query domain name (QNAME). The last three sections have the same format: a possibly empty list of concatenated resource records (RRs). The Answer section contains RRs that answer the question; the Authority section contains RRs that point toward an authoritative name server; and the Additional records section contains RRs which relate to the query, but are not strictly answers for the question.

Header Section Format

(From RFC 1035, pages 26-28)

The header contains the following fields:

```
                                    1 1 1 1 1 1
    0 1 2 3 4 5 6 7 8 9 0 1 2 3 4 5
```

```
+--+--+--+--+--+--+--+--+--+--+--+--+--+--+--+--+
|                      ID                       |
+--+--+--+--+--+--+--+--+--+--+--+--+--+--+--+--+
|QR|   Opcode  |AA|TC|RD|RA|   Z   |   RCODE    |
+--+--+--+--+--+--+--+--+--+--+--+--+--+--+--+--+
|                    QDCOUNT                     |
+--+--+--+--+--+--+--+--+--+--+--+--+--+--+--+--+
|                    ANCOUNT                     |
+--+--+--+--+--+--+--+--+--+--+--+--+--+--+--+--+
|                    NSCOUNT                     |
+--+--+--+--+--+--+--+--+--+--+--+--+--+--+--+--+
|                    ARCOUNT                     |
+--+--+--+--+--+--+--+--+--+--+--+--+--+--+--+--+
```

where:

ID

Is a 16-bit identifier assigned by the program that generates any kind of query. This identifier is copied into the corresponding reply and can be used by the requester to match up replies to outstanding queries.

QR

Is a 1-bit field that specifies whether this message is a query (0), or a response (1).

OPCODE

Is a 4-bit field that specifies the kind of query in this message. This value is set by the originator of a query and copied into the response. The values are:

0   A standard query (QUERY)

1   An inverse query (IQUERY)

2   A server status request (STATUS)

3–15

   Reserved for future use

AA (Authoritative Answer)

Is valid in responses and specifies that the responding name server is an authority for the domain name in the Question section. Note that the contents of the Answer section may have multiple owner names because of aliases. The AA-bit corresponds to the name which matches the query name, or the first owner name in the Answer section.

TC (TrunCation)

Specifies that this message was truncated due to length greater than that permitted on the transmission channel.

RD (Recursion Desired)

May be set in a query and is copied into the response. If RD is set, it directs the name server to pursue the query recursively. Recursive query support is optional.

RA (Recursion Available)

Is set or cleared in a response, and denotes whether recursive query support is available in the name server.

Z   Is reserved for future use. Must be 0 in all queries and responses.

RCODE (Response Code)

Is a 4-bit field set as part of responses. The values have the following interpretation:

0   No error condition.

1   Format Error. The name server was unable to interpret the query.

2   Server Failure. The name server was unable to process this query due to a problem with the name server.

3   Name Error. Meaningful only for responses from an authoritative name server, this code signifies that the domain name referenced in the query does not exist.

4   Not Implemented. The name server does not support the requested kind of query.

5   Refused. The name server refuses to perform the specified operation for policy reasons. For example, a name server may not wish to provide the information to the particular requester, or a name server may not wish to perform a particular operation (e.g., zone transfer) for particular data.

6–15

Reserved for future use.

QDCOUNT

Is an unsigned 16-bit integer specifying the number of entries in the Question section.

ANCOUNT

Is an unsigned 16-bit integer specifying the number of resource records in the Answer section.

NSCOUNT

Is an unsigned 16-bit integer specifying the number of name server resource records in the Authority records section.

ARCOUNT

Is an unsigned 16-bit integer specifying the number of resource records in the Additional records section.

Question Section Format

(From RFC 1035, pages 28–29)

The Question section is used to carry the "question" in most queries, i.e., the parameters that define what is being asked. The section contains QDCOUNT (usually 1) entries, each of the following format:

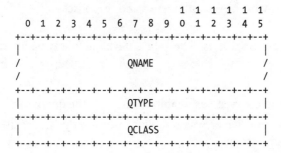

where:

QNAME

Is a domain name represented as a sequence of labels, in which each label consists of a length octet followed by that number of octets. The domain name terminates with the zero length octet for the null label of the root. Note that this field may be an odd number of octets; no padding is used.

QTYPE

Is a 2-octet code that specifies the type of the query. The values for this field include all codes valid for a TYPE field, together with some more general codes which can match more than one type of RR.

QCLASS

Is a 2-octet code that specifies the class of the query. For example, the QCLASS field is IN for the Internet.

QCLASS values

(From RFC 1035, page 13)

QCLASS fields appear in the Question section of a query. QCLASS values are a superset of CLASS values; every CLASS is a valid QCLASS. In addition to CLASS values, the following QCLASS is defined:

* 255 Any class

QTYPE values

(From RFC 1035, pages 12–13)

QTYPE fields appear in the Question part of a query. QTYPES are a superset of TYPEs, hence all TYPEs are valid QTYPEs. Also, the following QTYPEs are defined:

AXFR
> 252 A request for a transfer of an entire zone

MAILB
> 253 A request for mailbox-related records (MB, MG, or MR)

MAILA
> 254 A request for mail agent RRs (obsolete; see MX)

* 255 A request for all records

Answer, Authority, and Additional Section Format

(From RFC 1035, pages 29–30)

The Answer, Authority, and Additional sections all share the same format: a variable number of resource records, where the number of records is specified in the corresponding count field in the header. Each resource record has the following format:

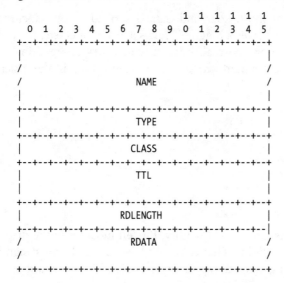

where:

NAME
> Is a domain name to which this resource record pertains.

TYPE
> Is two octets containing one of the RR type codes. This field specifies the meaning of the data in the RDATA field.

CLASS
> Is two octets that specify the class of the data in the RDATA field.

TTL

Is a 32-bit unsigned integer that specifies the time interval (in seconds) that the resource record may be cached before it should be discarded. Values of 0 are interpreted to mean that the RR can only be used for the transaction in progress, and should not be cached.

RDLENGTH

Is an unsigned 16-bit integer that specifies the length in octets of the RDATA field.

RDATA

Is a variable-length string of octets that describes the resource. The format of this information varies according to the TYPE and CLASS of the resource record. For example, if the TYPE is A and the CLASS is IN, the RDATA field is a 4-octet ARPA Internet address.

Data Transmission Order

(From RFC 1035, pages 8–9)

The order of transmission of the header and data described in this document is resolved to the octet level. Whenever a diagram shows a group of octets, the order of transmission of those octets is the normal order in which they are read in English. For example, in the following diagram, the octets are transmitted in the order they are numbered:

```
   0                   1
   0 1 2 3 4 5 6 7 8 9 0 1 2 3 4 5
  +-+-+-+-+-+-+-+-+-+-+-+-+-+-+-+-+
  |       1       |       2       |
  +-+-+-+-+-+-+-+-+-+-+-+-+-+-+-+-+
  |       3       |       4       |
  +-+-+-+-+-+-+-+-+-+-+-+-+-+-+-+-+
  |       5       |       6       |
  +-+-+-+-+-+-+-+-+-+-+-+-+-+-+-+-+
```

Whenever an octet represents a numeric quantity, the left most bit in the diagram is the high order or most significant bit. That is, the bit labeled 0 is the most significant bit. For example, the following diagram represents the value 170 (decimal).

```
   0 1 2 3 4 5 6 7
  +-+-+-+-+-+-+-+-+
  |1 0 1 0 1 0 1 0|
  +-+-+-+-+-+-+-+-+
```

Similarly, whenever a multi-octet field represents a numeric quantity, the left most bit of the whole field is the most significant bit. When a multi-octet quantity is transmitted the most significant octet is transmitted first.

Resource Record Data

Data Format

In addition to 2- and 4-octet integer values, resource record data can contain *domain-name*s or *character-string*s.

Domain name

(From RFC 1035, page 10)

Domain names in messages are expressed in terms of a sequence of labels. Each label is represented as a one octet length field followed by that number of octets. Since every domain name ends with the null label of the root, a domain name is terminated by a length byte of zero. The high order two bits of every length octet must be zero, and the remaining six bits of the length field limit the label to 63 octets or less.

Message compression

(From RFC 1035, page 30)

In order to reduce the size of messages, the domain system utilizes a compression scheme which eliminates the repetition of domain names in a message. In this scheme, an entire domain name or a list of labels at the end of a domain name is replaced with a pointer to a prior occurrence of the same name.

The pointer takes the form of a two octet sequence:

```
+--+--+--+--+--+--+--+--+--+--+--+--+--+--+--+--+
| 1  1|                OFFSET                   |
+--+--+--+--+--+--+--+--+--+--+--+--+--+--+--+--+
```

The first two bits are ones. This allows a pointer to be distinguished from a label, since the label must begin with two zero bits because labels are restricted to 63 octets or less. (The 10 and 01 combinations are reserved for future use.) The OFFSET field specifies an offset from the start of the message (i.e., the first octet of the ID field in the domain header). A zero offset specifies the first byte of the ID field, etc.

Character string

(From RFC 1035, page 13)

character-string is a single length octet followed by that number of characters. *character-string* is treated as binary information, and can be up to 256 characters in length (including the length octet).

Converting from BIND to the Microsoft DNS Server

This appendix covers the steps necessary to convert a BIND Version 4 name server to a Microsoft DNS Server. This process is straightforward, since the Microsoft DNS Server can read a BIND Version 4-style configuration file to obtain its configuration. If you're running BIND Version 8 or 9, you're no doubt aware that the configuration file format is drastically different. Unfortunately, the Microsoft DNS Server can't read this version of the BIND configuration file. You should still read through this appendix to see what's involved in the conversion, but you'll need to manually "downgrade" your BIND configuration file to a format readable by the Microsoft DNS Server.

Step 1: Change the DNS Server Startup Method to File

The first step is directing the DNS server to obtain its configuration from a file rather than the Registry or an Active Directory server (or a combination of both). Start the DNS console, right-click on the server name in the left pane, and choose **Properties**. In the server properties window, click on the **Advanced** tab, which produces a window like the one shown in Figure B-1.

Change the **Load zone data on startup** parameter to **From file** and click **OK**.

Step 2: Stop the Microsoft DNS Server

The next step is stopping the DNS server: right-click on the server name in the DNS console's left pane and choose **All Tasks → Stop**.

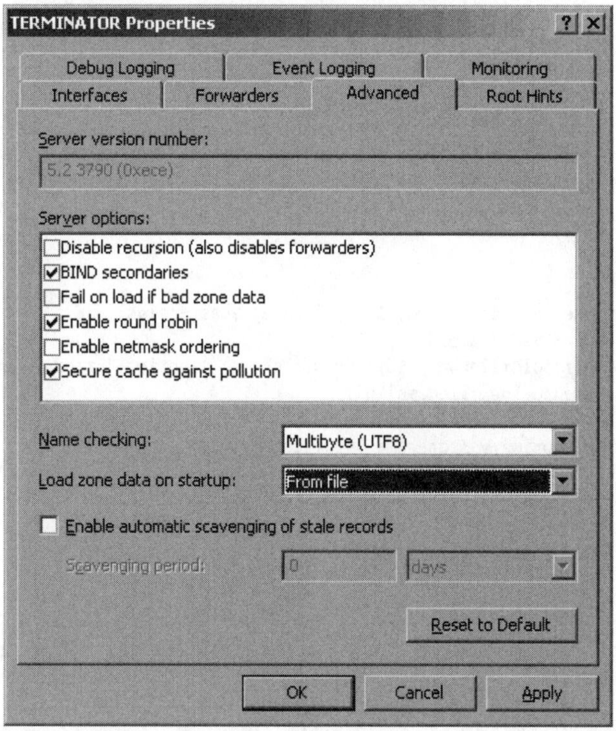

Figure B-1. Changing the DNS server startup method

Step 3: Change the Zone Datafile Naming Convention

This step is optional. Chances are, your BIND zone datafiles don't follow the same naming convention used by the Microsoft DNS Server. Recall from Chapter 4 that the Microsoft convention is the name of the zone followed by the *.dns* extension—for example, *movie.edu.dns*. You can continue to use your current naming convention, but if you add new zones with the DNS console, they'll have the *.dns* extensions unless you go out of your way to make the names conform to your scheme. If you're not particularly attached to your naming scheme and don't want to fight the DNS console every time you create a new zone, this Perl script will rename your zone datafiles in the *.dns* style and modify your *named.boot* file accordingly:

```
# name-convert.pl—Convert zone datafile naming convention in a BIND
#                  named.boot file to Microsoft *.dns format
#

die "usage: name-convert.pl path-to-named.boot\n" unless $ARGV[0];
```

```
open (BOOTIN, $ARGV[0]) || die "Can't open boot file for reading: $!\n";
open (BOOTOUT, ">boot") || die "Can't open boot file for writing: $!\n";

while (<BOOTIN>) {
    $dir="$1/" if /^directory\s+(.+).*$/;
    &changeit (1, $1, $2) if /^primary\s+(.+)\s+(.+)$/;
    &changeit (2, $1, $5, $2) if /^secondary\s+([\w\.]+)\s+(((\d{1,3}\.){3}\
    d{1,3}\s+)+)(.+)$/;
    &changeit (3, "cache", $1) if /^cache\s+\.\s+(.+)$/;
}

sub changeit {
    local ($zonetype, $zonename, $oldfilename, $mastersips) = @_;
    $newfilename="$zonename.dns";
    rename ($dir.$oldfilename, $dir.$newfilename) || print "Error renaming
    $oldfilename to $newfilename!\n";
    if ($zonetype == 1) {
    print BOOTOUT "primary $zonename $newfilename\n";
    } elsif ($zonetype == 2) {
    print BOOTOUT "secondary $zonename $mastersips $newfilename\n";
    } else {
    print BOOTOUT "cache . $newfilename\n";
    }
}
```

The script takes one argument, the name of the name server boot file. For example:

```
name-convert.pl /etc/named.boot
```

It outputs a file called *boot* in the current directory, which is a Microsoft DNS Server boot file with the zone datafile names changed. It's probably easiest to run the script on the BIND name server (which is probably running on Unix and therefore has Perl installed), then copy over *boot* and the newly renamed *.dns* zone datafiles.

Step 4: Copy the Files

The next step is copying the necessary files from the BIND name server's machine to the Windows Server 2003 machine. You'll need to copy the name server configuration file, called the *boot* file (which is usually */etc/named.boot*) and all the zone datafiles for which the BIND server is a primary master. The zone datafiles will be in the directory specified by the *directory* directive in the boot file. The files should be copied to the *%SystemRoot%\system32\dns* directory on the Windows server. The *named.boot* file goes in that directory, too, but you need to rename it to just *boot*. One final note: only the *primary*, *secondary*, and *cache* directives are supported. Any other directives are ignored.

Step 5: Get a New Root Name Server Cache File

Now is a good time to make sure you've got the latest and greatest root name server cache file. Follow the instructions in Chapter 4 to retrieve the file from *ftp.rs.internic.net*. Be sure the name matches the one in the boot file's *cache* directive. If you went through the name conversion process (step two), the file should be called *cache.dns*.

Step 6: Restart the DNS Server

Restart the DNS server. The server will now read the BIND boot file for its configuration information and—here's the nice part—update its configuration information in the Registry to match what it read from the boot file.

If you want to the server to use the boot file permanently, you're finished now. You can even add or delete zones using the DNS console; the server will update the boot file. That's a nice improvement over Windows NT, which silently converted back to loading startup data from the Registry if you made any changes with its DNS Manager administration tool.

Step 7: Change the DNS Server Startup Method to Registry

Finally, you can configure the DNS server to load its configuration information from the Registry or Active Directory (or both). Using the instructions from step one above, change the boot method back to **From registry** or **From Active Directory and registry**.

Top-Level Domains

The following table lists all the two-letter country codes and all the top-level domains that aren't countries. Not all of the countries are registered in the Internet namespace at the time of this writing, but there aren't many missing.

Domain	Country or organization
AC	Ascension Island
AD	Andorra
AE	United Arab Emirates
AERO	Aviation Community
AF	Afghanistan
AG	Antigua and Barbuda
AI	Anguilla
AL	Albania
AM	Armenia
AN	Netherlands Antilles
AO	Angola
AQ	Antarctica
AR	Argentina
ARPA	ARPA Internet
AS	American Samoa
AT	Austria
AU	Australia
AW	Aruba
AZ	Azerbaijan
BA	Bosnia and Herzegovina
BB	Barbados
BD	Bangladesh

Domain	Country or organization
BE	Belgium
BF	Burkina Faso
BG	Bulgaria
BH	Bahrain
BI	Burundi
BIZ	Commercial
BJ	Benin
BM	Bermuda
BN	Brunei Darussalam
BO	Bolivia
BR	Brazil
BS	Bahamas
BT	Bhutan
BV	Bouvet Island
BW	Botswana
BY	Belarus
BZ	Belize
CA	Canada
CC	Cocos (Keeling) Islands
CD	Congo, Democratic Republic of the
CF	Central African Republic
CG	Congo
CH	Switzerland
CI	Côte d'Ivoire
CK	Cook Islands
CL	Chile
CM	Cameroon
CN	China
CO	Colombia
COM	Generic (formerly Commercial)
COOP	Cooperatives
CR	Costa Rica
CU	Cuba
CV	Cape Verde
CX	Christmas Island
CY	Cyprus
CZ	Czech Republic

Domain	Country or organization
DE	Germany
DJ	Djibouti
DK	Denmark
DM	Dominica
DO	Dominican Republic
DZ	Algeria
EC	Ecuador
EDU	Education
EE	Estonia
EG	Egypt
EH	Western Sahara
ER	Eritrea
ES	Spain
ET	Ethiopia
FI	Finland
FJ	Fiji
FK	Falkland Islands (Malvinas)
FM	Micronesia, Federated States of
FO	Faroe Islands
FR	France
GA	Gabon
GB	United Kingdom (in practice, the United Kingdom uses "UK" for its top-level domain)
GD	Grenada
GE	Georgia
GF	French Guiana
GG	Guernsey, Alderney, and Sark (British Channel Islands)
GH	Ghana
GI	Gibraltar
GL	Greenland
GM	Gambia
GN	Guinea
GOV	U.S. Federal Government
GP	Guadeloupe
GQ	Equatorial Guinea
GR	Greece
GS	South Georgia and the South Sandwich Islands

Domain	Country or organization
GT	Guatemala
GU	Guam
GW	Guinea-Bissau
GY	Guyana
HK	Hong Kong
HM	Heard Island and McDonald Islands
HN	Honduras
HR	Croatia
HT	Haiti
HU	Hungary
ID	Indonesia
IE	Ireland
IL	Israel
IM	Isle of Man
IN	India
INFO	Generic
INT	International entities
IO	British Indian Ocean Territory
IQ	Iraq
IR	Iran, Islamic Republic of
IS	Iceland
IT	Italy
JE	Jersey (British Channel Island)
JM	Jamaica
JO	Jordan
JP	Japan
KE	Kenya
KG	Kyrgyzstan
KH	Cambodia
KI	Kiribati
KM	Comoros
KN	Saint Kitts and Nevis
KP	Korea, Democratic People's Republic of
KR	Korea, Republic of
KW	Kuwait
KY	Cayman Islands
KZ	Kazakhstan

Domain	Country or organization
LA	Lao People's Democratic Republic
LB	Lebanon
LC	Saint Lucia
LI	Liechtenstein
LK	Sri Lanka
LR	Liberia
LS	Lesotho
LT	Lithuania
LU	Luxembourg
LV	Latvia
LY	Libyan Arab Jamahiriya
MA	Morocco
MC	Monaco
MD	Moldova, Republic of
MG	Madagascar
MH	Marshall Islands
MIL	U.S. Military
MK	Macedonia, the Former Yugoslav Republic of
ML	Mali
MM	Myanmar
MN	Mongolia
MO	Macao
MP	Northern Mariana Islands
MQ	Martinique
MR	Mauritania
MS	Montserrat
MT	Malta
MU	Mauritius
MUSEUM	Museums
MV	Maldives
MW	Malawi
MX	Mexico
MY	Malaysia
MZ	Mozambique
NA	Namibia
NAME	Individuals
NC	New Caledonia

Domain	Country or organization
NE	Niger
NET	Generic (formerly Networking Organizations)
NF	Norfolk Island
NG	Nigeria
NI	Nicaragua
NL	Netherlands
NO	Norway
NP	Nepal
NR	Nauru
NU	Niue
NZ	New Zealand
OM	Oman
ORG	Generic (formerly Organizations)
PA	Panama
PE	Peru
PF	French Polynesia
PG	Papua New Guinea
PH	Philippines
PK	Pakistan
PL	Poland
PM	St. Pierre and Miquelon
PN	Pitcairn
PR	Puerto Rico
PRO	Professionals
PS	Palestinian Territory, Occupied
PT	Portugal
PW	Palau
PY	Paraguay
QA	Qatar
RE	Réunion
RO	Romania
RU	Russian Federation
RW	Rwanda
SA	Saudi Arabia
SB	Solomon Islands
SC	Seychelles
SD	Sudan

Domain	Country or organization
SE	Sweden
SG	Singapore
SH	St. Helena
SI	Slovenia
SJ	Svalbard and Jan Mayen
SK	Slovakia
SL	Sierra Leone
SM	San Marino
SN	Senegal
SO	Somalia
SR	Suriname
ST	Sao Tome and Principe
SU	Union of Soviet Socialist Republics
SV	El Salvador
SY	Syrian Arab Republic
SZ	Swaziland
TC	Turks and Caicos Islands
TD	Chad
TF	French Southern Territories
TG	Togo
TH	Thailand
TJ	Tajikistan
TK	Tokelau
TL	Timor-Leste (still uses TP)
TM	Turkmenistan
TN	Tunisia
TO	Tonga
TP	See TL
TR	Turkey
TT	Trinidad and Tobago
TV	Tuvalu
TW	Taiwan, Province of China
TZ	Tanzania, United Republic of
UA	Ukraine
UG	Uganda
UK	United Kingdom
UM	United States Minor Outlying Islands

Domain	Country or organization
US	United States
UY	Uruguay
UZ	Uzbekistan
VA	Holy See (Vatican City State)
VC	Saint Vincent and The Grenadines
VE	Venezuela
VG	Virgin Islands (British)
VI	Virgin Islands (U.S.)
VN	Viet Nam
VU	Vanuatu
WF	Wallis and Futuna
WS	Samoa
YE	Yemen
YT	Mayotte
YU	Yugoslavia
ZA	South Africa
ZM	Zambia
ZW	Zimbabwe

Index

Symbol

* (asterisk) wildcard, 332
@ (at sign), 76
. (dot)
    in domain names, 12
    root domain, 78
    trailing, 76

A

A records, 66, 71
    stale, 141
aa (authoritative answer) bit, 206
AAAA ipv6-address records, 363
absolute pathnames, 5
access to name servers, 26
Active Directory, xi
    application partitions, 153
        dnscmd commands, 273
    domains, 147–152
    integration, 142, 171
    resource records, 159
    service location broker, 155
    sites, 162
    zones, 152–155, 161–163
adding
    aliases, 69
    caching-only name servers, 172
    CNAME records, 70
    domains, 92
    MX records, 99
    name servers, 174
    NS records, 89
    primary master name servers, 59
    resource records, 68–71, 130–132
    secondary name servers, 87, 171, 198
    servers, 59–60
    subdomains, 188–198
    zones, 60, 87, 92

Additional section (DNS messages), 248
AdditionalOptions parameter, 266
addresses
    address type, 17
    forward/reverse mapping, 234
    in MX records, 103
    incorrect, 315
    IP, 38
    local, 85, 325
    loopback, 77
    mapping, 31–33, 67, 78
    network numbers, registering, 46
    records, 141
    round robin, 234
    types, 17
address-to-name mapping, 234
AD-integrated zones
    application partitions, 153
    BIND, 324
    classes, 299–304
    dnscmd commands, 273
administration, xiii
    administrators, contacting, 175
    capacity planning, 167
    delegation, 210, 322
    disasters, preventing and handling, 180
    mail exchangers, 102
    servers, 265–277
    subdomains, 212–214
    WMI, 282–284
        scripting, 284–289
aging, 141–145
algorithms, MX records, 103
aliases, 6
    to other aliases, 330
    creating, 69
    deleting, 213
    determining, 331
    in MX records, 103
allwhois.com web site, 42

We'd like to hear your suggestions for improving our indexes. Send email to *index@oreilly.com*.

Answer section (DNS messages), 248
APNIC registry, 46
appending
    origin in zone datafiles, 76
    parent suffixes, 113
applications, x
    gateways, 334
    name servers, 36–39
    nslookup, 38
arguments, search lists, 113
ARIN registry, 46
arpa domain, 18, 197
ARPAnet, 1
at sign (@), 76
attacks, 235
authentication
    Kerberos, 161
    WMI, 288
authority
    aa bit, 206
    delegating, 5
    nslookup and, 244
    root domains, 149
    SOA records, 41
    unauthorized zone transfers, 235
    zones, 22–31
Authority section (DNS messages), 248
automating secondary name servers, 278

B

backups, battery power, 182
bastion hosts, configuring, 350
batch scripts, 278
benefits of use, DNS, 9, 10
BIND, 8
    AD-integrated zones, 324
    interoperability with Microsoft DNS
        Server, 324
    name servers, 372–375
    obtaining, 37
    ports of, xi, 37
    versions of, xi
    WINS records and, 324
Boolean options, nslookup, 240
boundaries
    nonoctets, 200
    octets, 199

C

cache.dns file, 78, 135
caching, 33–35, 78, 118–119
    caching-only name servers, 172, 176
    checking, 309–310
    forwarding servers, 229–232
    negative caching, 33
    root name servers, 375
canonical domain names, 6
capacity planning, 167
case sensitivity, 75
chaining, 28

Chaosnet class, 16
characters, 357
Check Point, 228, 334
children, 185
    domains, 5
    naming, 187–188
    selecting number of, 186
CIDR (Classless Inter-Domain Routing), 47
CIM (Common Information Model), 283
Class A networks, subnetting, 200
Class B networks, subnetting, 200
Class C networks, subnetting, 201
CLASS mnemonics, 364
classes
    class option, nslookup, 242
    objects, 286
    resource records, 304–307, 364
    servers, 289–299
    zones, 299–304
Classless Inter-Domain Routing (CIDR), 47
clients
    domain controllers, 158
    name servers, 116–118
    resolvers, 106
        caching, 118
        configuring, 107–118, 124–126
        subnet prioritization, 119
        Windows 2000, 106–120
        Windows 95, 120
        Windows 98, 122
        Windows NT 4.0, 122
        Windows XP, 106–120
    service location broker, 155
closest known name servers, 29
CNAME records, 329–332, 358
    adding/creating, 70
    name servers and, 69
    transition to subdomains, 212
collisions, 3
com domain, 17
Command parameter, 266
command-line tools, 279–281
Common Information Model (CIM), 283
computer names, modifying, 109
conditional formatting, forwarding name
        servers, 230
configuration
    Active Directory
        names, 147–152
        sites, 162
    aging, 141–145
    application partition, 153
    batch script, example, 278
    check script, example, 297
    dial-up connections, 351
    DNS console
        adding resource records, 68–71
        adding servers, 59
        adding zones, 92
        creating zones, 60–67
        formatting loopback addresses, 77

formatting zone datafiles, 75–77
mapping zones, 67–68
searching root hints, 78–81
starting primary master name
servers, 82–86
starting secondary name servers, 86–92
storing resource records, 71
viewing zone datafiles, 72–74
firewalls, 333
internal name servers, 346
large sitewide caches, 229–232
managing, 265–277
master file formats, 355–364
name servers, 296
resolvers, 107–118, 124–126, 193
caching, 118
subnet prioritization, 119
Windows 2000, 106–120
Windows 95, 120
Windows 98, 122
Windows NT 4.0, 122
Windows Server 2003, 106–120
Windows XP, 106–120
resource records, 130–132, 306
scavenging, 141–145
searching, 114
security, 333–336, 348
servers, 295
subdomains, 186
delegating, 206–212
in-addr.arpa domains, 198–206
life cycles, 214
naming children, 187
parent, 188–198
transitions, 212–214
TTL, 118, 177–180
TXT records, 134
WINS lookup, 225
WINS reverse lookup, 227
zones, 10, 302
Configure Your Server Wizard, 53
connections, 101
ARPAnet, 1
dial-up, 351–353
extranets, 2
Internet, 10
internets, 2
master name servers, 315
multiple name servers, 166
troubleshooting, 319
consistency, 3
in domain names, 23
controls, zone datafiles, 136–145
converting BIND to Microsoft DNS
servers, 372–375
copying files, 374
cost of registering domains, 49
creating subdomains, 188

D

d2 option (nslookup), 241, 246
data types, nslookup and, 243
databases
indexes, 6
structure of, 4–8
whois, 48
datafiles
controls, 136–145
zones, 26, 72–74, 75–77
dcdiag, 280
DC-less sites, creating, 162
Debug Logging tab, 129
debug option (nslookup), 240, 246
debugging
nslookup and, 240, 241
writing, 128
(see also troubleshooting)
default domain, with nslookup, 242
default search lists, 113
(see also searching)
defname option (nslookup), 241
delegation, 21, 25
checking, 206, 321
disabling, 235
DNSLint, 311–313
forward-mapping, 342
in-addr.arpa domain, 49, 197, 342
lame, 177
managing, 210
nonoctet boundaries and, 200
number of, 186
octet boundaries and, 199
of authority, 5
parents, 206–212
registration and, 40
subdomains, 190, 321
creating without, 189
troubleshooting, 321, 322
deleting
aliases, 213
hosts, 317
objects, 129
records, 141
resource records, 130–132
stale, 141
DHCP (Dynamic Host Configuration
Protocol), 224, 229
diagnostics, 325
inconsistent answers, 327
names, 325
remote hostnames, 327
response time, 328
(see also troubleshooting)
dial-on-demand connections, 352
dial-up connections, 351–353
Dictionary object, 299
dig (Domain Information Groper), 256–260
directories, 4
namespaces, 13

disabling recursion, 235
disadvantages of use, DNS, 9
disaster planning, 180–184
disjoint domain names, 151
Distributed Management Task Force (DMTF), 283
dividing in-addr.arpa domains, 198–206
DMTF (Distributed Management Task Force), 283
DNS console, 55
   addresses, checking, 315
   aliases, 69
   CNAME records, 70
   configuring, 225
      adding resource records, 68–71
      adding servers, 59
      adding zones, 92
      creating zones, 60–67
      formatting loopback addresses, 77
      formatting zone datafiles, 75–77
      mapping zones, 67
      starting primary master name
         servers, 82–86
      starting secondary name servers, 86–92
      storing resource records, 71
      using root hints, 78–81
      viewing zone datafiles, 72–74
   error messages, 83
   MX records, 99
   name servers, 59, 60
   NS records, 89, 318
   Properties selection in, 92
   reverse lookup, 227
   reverse-mapping, 67
   secondary name servers, 87
   subdomains, 189
   TTL on resource records, 177
   WINS lookup, 227
   WINS reverse lookup, 227
   zones, 60, 87
DNS (Domain Name System), ix
   benefits of use, 9
   clients, 116–118
   disadvantages of use, 9
   disasters, preventing and handling, 180
   dynamic update protocol, 216
   message format, 247
   resources for, 38
   structure of, 4–8
   suffixes, 112–115
   troubleshooting, 308
DNS NOTIFY, 218
DNS Provider
   resource records, 307
   zones, 302
DNS Server
   logging, 129
   signals, 127–129
dnscmd commands, 265
   application partitions, 273
   resource records, 275
   zones, 269
dnsdiag, 281

DNSEXT, 38
DNSLint, 281
   testing delegation, 206–212
   troubleshooting, 311–313
documentation, x
   BIND, 37
   firewalls, 334
   network numbers, 48
domain controllers
   application partitions, 153
   promoting, 159
   searching, 158
Domain Information Groper (see dig)
Domain Name System (see DNS)
domain names, 5, 11, 12
   choosing, 39
   CIDR and, 47
   consistency of, 23
   FQDNs, 12
   mapping, 31
   MX records, 102
   reading, 20
   resolving, 26
   resource records and, 75
   servers for, 25
   subdomains, 16
   visibility of, 350
domains, 4, 13
   Active Directory, 147–152
   adding, 92
   appending, 76
   CNAME records, 329–332
   controllers (see domain controllers)
   default, 242
   delegating, 21, 25, 190, 321
   forests, 147
   generic top-level, 44
   hosts, 15
   in-addr.arpa, 49, 198–206
   international, 43
   levels of, 16
   life cycles, 214
   managing transition to subdomains, 212
   models, 148
   names (see domain names)
   parenting, 185
   registering, 46
   root, 11
   searching for, 238
   shadow namespaces, 348
   state- and city-level, 19
   subdomains, 151
   testing setup, 84
   top-level, 17, 376–??
   trees, 147
   troubleshooting, 318
   whois service, 42
   zones versus, 22
dot (.)
   root domain, 78
   trailing, 76

dotted-octet representation, 32
dumping servers, 128
Dunlap, Kevin, 9
Dynamic Host Configuration Protocol (see DHCP)
dynamic updates, 154, 216–224

E

edu domain, 17
EDUCAUSE, 40
email, 96
  administrator address, 65
  mail exchangers, 97, 102
  MX records, 97–99
  routing loops, 102
encryption, 216
enumeration of objects, 286
errors
  messages, 83
  nonexistent domain (nslookup), 254
  rcodes for, 247
  SERVFAIL, 315
  (see also troubleshooting)
Event Log, 83
Event Viewer, 138
  DNS console, 83
example programs, obtaining, xiv, xv
existing domains, 149
expire value, 91
expiring cached data
  changing TTL, 177–180
extensions, 373
extranets, 2

F

files
  cache.dns, 78
    updating, 135
  copying, 374
  HOSTS.TXT, 3
  root name server hints, 78
  root.dns, 343
  troubleshooting, 128
  zone data, 26, 61, 72
filesystems, 4
  remote management, 7
Filter option, View menu (DNS console), 57
filtering packets (firewalls), 334
finding
  IP addresses, 38
  namespaces, 39–49
  root hints, 78–81
  whois services, 42
Firewall Toolkit (Network Associates), 335
firewalls, 333–336, 348
first-level domains, 16
forests
  application partitions, 153
  domains, 147

formatting
  DNS messages, 247
  zone datafiles, 75–77
forward mapping for IPv6 addresses, 234
forwarders, 336
forwarding servers, 229–232
FQDNs (fully qualified domain names), 12
fully qualified domain names (FQDNs), 12

G

gateways, 334
generic top-level domains (see gTLDs)
geographic domain names, 19
  choosing, 40
  list of, 376
Gizmonic Institute, 45
glue records, 196
gov domain, 18
gTLDs (generic top-level domains), 18, 44

H

Header section (DNS messages), 247
Hesiod (HS) class, 16
history
  of DNS, 1
  of Microsoft DNS Server, 8
homogeneity of multiple name servers, 167
hostnames, mapping, ix
hosts, 15
  adding/deleting, 317
  aliases
    determining, 331
    searching, 331
  bastion, 350
  DNS suffixes, 107
  domains, 15
    names, 6
  errors in, 325
  mail exchangers, 97
  remote, 327
  RP records, 134
HOSTS.TXT file, 3
  outages and, 183
HS (Hesiod) class, 16

I

ignoretc option (nslookup), 241
in-addr.arpa domain, 32, 49, 198–206
  delegating, 197
  internal roots and, 342
  misconfigured servers, 207
  reverse-mapping, 67
  secondary zone creation and, 89
  zones, 131
incremental zone transfers (see IXFR)
incrementing serial numbers, 313
indexes, subdomains as, 6

installing Microsoft DNS Servers, 51, 262
 batch scripts, 278
 executing, 262–265
int domain, 18
integrating Active Directory, 171
interfaces
 Perl/VBScript, 284–289
 WMI, 282–284
Interfaces tab, Server Properties window (DNS
  console), 93
interior nodes, CNAME records, 329–332
internal name servers, configuring, 346
internal root name servers, 340
 internal name servers and, 347
internationalization, 18
 list of, 376
Internet
 connections, 10
 dial-up connections, 351
 domain namespaces, 17–21
 firewalls, 333–336, 348
 overview of, 2
 split namespaces, 348–351
Internet Protocol (IP), finding addresses (see IP)
Internet service providers (ISPs), 46
Internet Software Consortium, 9
internets
 classes of, 16
 overview of, 2
InterNIC, 46
interoperability, troubleshooting, 324
inverse queries, 248
IP (Internet Protocol), 31
 finding addresses, 38
ip6.int namespace, 234
ipconfig, 279
IPv6 addresses, mapping for, 234
ISPs (Internet service providers), 46
iterative (nonrecursive) queries, 29
IXFR (incremental zone transfer), 222
 nslookup and, 242

J

JEEVES, 8

K

KB (Microsoft Knowledge Base), xiv
Kerberos authentication, 161

L

labels, text, 4
lame delegation, 177
LANs (local area networks), 10
 traffic, 169
life cycle of parents, 214
limitations of MX records, 333

lists
 name server properties, 295
 search, 112–115
 zones, 303
load, 3
load sharing, 234
local
 addresses, 325
 domain, in MX records, 103
 name servers, 125
 names, 84, 325
 networks, 169
 nslookup and, 244
local area networks (see LANs)
location, selecting for name servers, 165
logging, 129
 Event Viewer, 138
 overworked name servers, 169
 queries, 128
logical disks, enumerating, 286
loopback address, 77
loops, 102–104
ls command (nslookup), 251
lserver command (nslookup), 244

M

mail addr field, 42
mail exchangers, 97, 102
mailing lists, 37
 namedroppers, 38
maintenance
 aging, 141–145
 disaster planning, 180–184
 Event Viewer, 138
 scavenging, 141–145
 servers, 57
 zone datafile controls, 136–145
management
 delegation, 210
 filesystems, 7
 primary master name servers, 59
 resource records, 275–277
 servers, 57, 265–277
 subdomains, 7, 212–214
 WMI, 282–284
  scripting, 284–289
 zones, 269–273
manual configuration
 resource records, 130–132
 search lists, 114
manual searches, nslookup, 238
mapping
 addresses, 31–33, 234
 hostnames, ix
 reverse, 67, 78
master file formats, 355–364
master server, 86

MB records, 42
MD records, 97
memory, 167
   resource records, 71
messages, 138, 365–370
   Event Viewer, 138
MF records, 97
MG records, 42
Microsoft DNS Server, x
   aging and scavenging, enabling, 141
   batch scripts, 278
   classes, 289–299
   converting BIND name server to, 372
   executing, 262–265
   forwarding, 229
   from command line, 83
   history of, 8
   incremental zone transfer, 222
   installing, 262
   interoperability with BIND, 324
   managing, 265–277
   monitoring, 299
   resources for, 38
   restarting, 263, 296, 375
   security, 215
   selecting, 36–39
   starting/stopping, 82
   troubleshooting, 308
      checking caches, 309
   version control, 336
   zone transfers, 223
Microsoft Exchange Server, 104
Microsoft Knowledge Base (KB), xiv
Microsoft Management Console (MMC), 55
Microsoft web site, support, 38
MicrosoftDNS_ResourceRecord class, 304
MicrosoftDNS_Server class, 289
MicrosoftDNS_Statistic class, 299
MicrosoftDNS_Zone class, 299
mil domain, 18
minimum TTL, 180
mirroring servers, 234
MMC (Microsoft Management Console), 55
MNAME field (DNS console), 65
mnemonics, CLASS, 364
Mockapetris, Paul, 4, 8
models, domain, 148
modification
   computer names, 109
   DNS suffixes, 109
monitoring performance, 299
moving files, 374
multiple domains, 147
multiple name servers, 164–170
   nslookup, 238
   registering, 174–177
multiple networks, 2
MX records, 97–99, 359
   adding, 99
   limitation of, 333
   routing loops, 102–104

N
Name Server Modification window (DNS
      console), 196
name servers, x, 4, 22
   accessing, 26
   adding, 59, 174
   BIND, converting to Microsoft DNS
      Server, 372
   caching-only, 176
   capacity of, 167
   closest known, 29
   configuring, 296
   conventions, 373
   deleting, 60
   forwarders, 229
   forwarding servers, 229–232
   homogeneity, 167
   internal roots and, 347
   listing properties, 295
   local, 125
   looking up, 320
   losing manual changes, 314
   master, 86
   Microsoft DNS, x
   misconfigured, in-addr.arpa domain, 207
   nonrecursive, 235
   NOTIFY protocol, 218
   NS records and, 66
   nslookup, 237–239
   off-site, 164
   primary, 25
   properties of, 93
   querying, 116–118, 244
   records, 133–135
   recursion, 28
   registering, 174–177
   remote, 124
   root, 27, 183, 235, 242, 340
   secondary, 86
   security, 234–236
   selecting, 36–39
   selecting number of, 164–170
   troubleshooting, 235, 297
   types of, 25
   viewing statistics, 141
   zones, 22–31
namedroppers mailing list, 38
names, ix
   address mapping, 31–33
   caching, 33–35
   children, 187–188
   CNAME records, 329–332
   collisions, 3
   domains, 5
      Active Directory, 147–152
      aliases, 6
      disjoint/private, 151
      root domains, 149
      selecting, 39–49
      as subtrees, 13

names *(continued)*
    local, 325
    modifying, 109
    NetBIOS, 238
    relative, 5
    resolution, 26, 31
    split namespaces, 348–351
    suffixes, 112–115
    troubleshooting, 318
    WINS, 10
namespaces
    directories, 13
    domains, 11–17
        Internet, 17–21
        name servers, 22–31
    finding, 39–49
    ip6.int, 234
    split, 348
    visibility of, 350
name-to-address mapping for IPv6 addresses, 234
negative caching, 33
net domain, 18
NetBIOS, 238
netdiag, 280
Network Associates Firewall Toolkit, 335
Network Information Center (see NIC)
Network Information Service (see NIS)
Network Solutions, Inc., 40, 45
networks
    CIDR, 47
    DNS, 4–8
    history of DNS, 1
    Internet, 2
    internets, 2
    LANs, 10, 169
    loopback, 77
    registering, 46
    servers, 51
    subnetting, 200
    TCP/IP, 10
    troubleshooting, 319
New Delegation Wizard, 194
New Host window (DNS console), 68
New Zone Wizard, 203
    DNS console, 61
newsgroups, 37
NIC (Network Information Center), 321
    whois service, 42, 49
NIS (Network Information Service), 10, 15
nod2 option (nslookup), 241, 246
nodebug option (nslookup), 240, 246
nodefname option (nslookup), 241
nodes, 4, 11
    domains, 13
    sibling, 12
noignoretc option (nslookup), 241
nonauthoritative nslookup answers, 244
nonexistent domain error (nslookup), 254
nonoctet boundaries, subnetting on, 200
nonrecursive queries, 29, 230
norecurse option (nslookup), 241, 249

no-refresh interval, 142
nosearch option (nslookup), 241, 249
NOTIFY protocol, 218
    requests and responses, 219
novc option (nslookup), 241
NS records, 66, 359
    adding, 89, 318
NSFNET traffic reports, 169
nslookup program, xi, 38, 237–239, 279, 308
    aliases, 331
    CNAME records, 330
    customizing, 239–242
    delegation, 322
    domain setup, testing, 84
    host configuration errors, checking, 325
    mimicking, 248
    name servers, 320
    queries, tracing, 246
    querying other servers, 244
    searching, 242–252
    troubleshooting, 240, 252–256
    using dig utility instead of, 256
    zone transfers, 251
number of domains, configuring, 147–152
numbers, ARIN registry, 46

O

objects
    enumerating, 286
    modifying, 129
    referencing, 284
    searching, 287
octets, 32
    subnetting on/off octet boundaries, 199
off-site name server, 164
opcodes, 247
optimizing zones, 223
options
    dig, 260
    nslookup, 239–242
org domain, 18
origin, zone datafile, 76
outages, 181, 183

P

packet-filtering firewalls, 334
packets, truncated, 241
parents, 186
    aliases, 213
    children, 187
    configuring, 188–198
    delegating, 206–212
    delegation, 206
    domains, 5
    life cycles, 214
    naming, 187
    of in-addr.arpa domains, 198
    parent-level aliases, 213
    suffixes, 113
partial-secondary name servers, 173

partitions
  application, 153
  dnscmd commands, 273
pathnames, 4
peak periods of activity, 168
performance
  capacity planning, 167
  mail exchangers, 101
  monitoring, 299
  SOA values, 90
  troubleshooting, 328
Perl, 284–289
port option (nslookup), 241
power outages, 181
preference values (MX records), 97
primary master name server, 25, 59–60
  configuring, 194
  DNS console and, 59
  NOTIFY, 218
  registering, 174–177
  running, 82
  signals, 314
  zones
    creation and, 65
    transfers and, 218
prioritization of subnets, 119
private domain names, 151
programming
  configuration check script, 297
  WMI, 282–284
    Perl/VBScript, 284–289
promoting domain controllers, 159
properties, name servers, 295
Properties selection (DNS console), 92
protocols
  DHCP, 229
  NOTIFY, 218
  TCP/IP, 1
PTR records, 360
  missing, 317
  multiple, 71
  stale, 141
Public Interest Registry, 40

Q

quad A records, 234
queries
  caching and, 33
  dig, 256–260
  inverse, 248
  iterative (nonrecursive), 29
  logging, 128
  name servers, 116–118
  nonauthoritative nslookup answers, 244
  nonrecursive, 230
  nslookup, 237–239
    customizing, 239–242
    implementing, 242–252

mimicking servers with, 248
troubleshooting, 252–256
recursive, 28, 230, 235
refused, 255
trace of, 246
troubleshooting, 235
volume of, 168
WQL, 287
querytype option (nslookup), 241, 243
Question section (DNS messages), 248

R

rcodes (response codes), 247
RDATA field, troubleshooting, 318
records
  AAAA ipv6-address, 363
  classes, 304–307
  CNAME, 329–332
  deleting, 141
  incremental zone transfers, 222
  MX, 97–99, 359
    adding, 99
    limitations, 333
    routing loops, 102–104
  name servers, 133–135
  NS, 359
  PTR, 360
    troubleshooting, 317
  refreshing, 141
  resource
    classes, 364
    creating, 306
    data, 371
    dnscmd commands, 275
    modifying, 130–132
    types, 357
    wildcards, 332
  round robin, 232
  RP, 134, 362
  searching, 305
  SOA, 41, 65, 90, 360
    modifying, 179
    serial numbers, 132
  SRV, 156, 363
  stale, 141–145
  TXT, 134, 362
recurse option (nslookup), 241
recursion, 28, 235
  caching and, 33
  disabling, 235
  queries, 230
  resolution, 28
references, objects, 284
refresh interval, 91, 218
  no-refresh interval, 142
  records, 141
  secondary servers, 172
refused queries, 255

regional Internet registries (RIRs), 46
registrars, 40
   selecting, 45
registration, 40
   name servers, 174–177
   networks, 46
   zones, 48
registries, 40
   RIRs, 46
Registry
   maximum TTL, 118
   modifying, 375
relative names, 5
remote hostnames, 85, 327
remote management
   filesystems, 7
   subdomains, 7
remote name servers, 124
replication
   AD-integrated zones, 153
   application partitions, 153
resolution, 26
   caching and, 33–35
   iterative (nonrecursive), 29
   names, 31
   root name servers, 27
   roundtrip time, 30
resolvers, 4, 26, 106
   caching, 118
   configuring, 107–118, 124–126, 193
   nslookup versus, 238, 239
   stub, 26
   subnet prioritization, 119
   TTL, 118
   Windows 2000, 106–120
   Windows 95, 120
   Windows 98, 122
   Windows NT 4.0, 122
   Windows Server 2003, 106–120
   Windows XP, 106–120
resource records, 16
   Active Directory, 159
   case sensitivity, 75
   classes, 304–307, 364
   CNAMEs in, 330
   creating, 306
   data, 371
   dnscmd commands, 275
   domain names in, 75
   modifying, 130–132
   properties of, 93
   scavenging, 141
   stale, 141
   storing, 71
   TTL, 177–180
   types, 357
   wildcards, 332
   zones, 305
resources, 37
response codes (rcodes), 247

responses
   inconsistent, 327
   time for, 328
   tracing, 246
Responsible Person records (see RP)
restarting servers, 127, 263, 296, 375
restrictions
   forwarding servers, 231
   servers, 230
retry interval, 91, 179, 242
reverse mapping, 67, 78
   for IPv6 addresses, 234
   zones, 67
RIPE Network Coordination Centre, 47
RIRs (regional Internet registries), 46
root command (nslookup), 242
root domains, 11
   naming, 149
root hints, searching, 78–81
root name servers, 27, 235, 340
   caching, 375
   hints file, 78
   setting with nslookup, 242
root.dns file, 343
round robin, 234
roundtrip time, 30
routing
   CIDR, 47
   loops, 102–104
   MX records, 97–99
RP (Responsible Person) records, 134, 362

S

scalability, forwarding and, 340
scavenging, 141–145
scripting
   configuration check, 297
   WMI, 282–284
      Perl/VBScript, 284–289
search option (nslookup), 241
searching
   CNAME records, 330
   configuring, 114
   DNS suffixes, 107
   domain controllers, 158
   domains, 238
   hosts, 331
   IP addresses, 38
   names, 325
   namespaces, 39–49
   nslookup, 242–252
   resource records, 305
   root hints, 78–81
   RP records, 134
   SRV records, 156
   suffixes, 112–115
   turning off, 242
   whois services, 42
   wildcards, 332

WQL, 287
(see also finding)
secondary name servers, 25, 86
  adding, 174, 198
  automating, 278
  configuring, 194
  expired zones, 315
  loading from other secondaries, 171
  NOTIFY protocol, 218
  partial-secondary servers, 173
  registering, 174–177
  running, 86
  zone transfers and, 218
second-level domains, 16
security, 215, 234–236
  DHCP, 229
  dynamic updates, 154, 216–224
  encryption, 216
  firewalls, 333–336, 348
  forwarders, 336
  forwarding servers, 229–232
  load sharing, 234
  multiple name servers, 166
  root name servers, 340
  split namespaces, 348–351
  transaction signatures, 216
  WMI, 288
selection
  of children, 186
  of domain names, 39–49
  of name servers, 36–39, 164–170
  of registrars, 45
sendmail program, 99
serial numbers
  incrementing, 313
  nslookup and, 238
  zones, 132–133
server command (nslookup), 244
Server Properties window (Microsoft DNS
      Server), 93
ServerName parameter, 265
servers
  adding, 59
  batch scripts, 278
  BIND, 372–375
  cache.dns file, 135
  caching, 375
  classes, 289–299
  DNS console, 99
  dumping, 128
  Event Viewer, 138
  executing, 262–265
  forwarding, 229–232
  installing, 51, 262
  load sharing, 234
  logging, 129
  managing, 57, 265–277
  Microsoft DNS Server, 8
  Microsoft Exchange Server, 104
  monitoring, 299
  name, 4

  capacity of, 167
  configuring, 296
  conventions, 373
  listing properties, 295
  local, 125
  losing manual changes, 314
  querying, 116–118
  records, 133–135
  remote, 124
  selecting, 36–39
  troubleshooting, 297
  types of, 25
  viewing statistics, 141
  zones, 22–31
NOTIFY protocol, 218
nslookup, 237–239
  customizing, 239–242
  searching, 242–252
  troubleshooting, 252–256
primary master name, 82–86
restarting, 127, 263, 296, 375
secondary name, 86–92
security, 216, 234–236
signals, 127–129
troubleshooting, 308,
    checking caches, 309
whois, 42
  searching, 42
WINS, 229
zones
  adding, 92
  adding resource records, 68–71
  creating, 60–67
  formatting loopback addresses, 77
  formatting zone datafiles, 75–77
  listing, 303
  mapping, 67
  searching root hints, 78–81
  storing resource records, 71
  viewing zone datafiles, 72–74
SERVFAIL errors, 315
service location broker, 155
service location records (see SRV records)
services
  batch scripts, 278
  executing, 262–265
  managing, 265–277
  restarting, 296
  whois, 42
    searching, 42
  WINS, 229
set all command (nslookup), 326
set command (nslookup), 240
shadow namespaces, 348
sibling nodes, 12
signals, 127–129
  troubleshooting, 314
signals to primary name server,
          troubleshooting, 314
simple dial-up connections, 352
Simple Mail Transfer Protocol (SMTP), 97

sites, Active Directory, 162
SMTP (Simple Mail Transfer Protocol), 97
SOA (start of authority), 41, 360
    records, 65, 90, 179
    serial numbers, 132
software, x
    firewall, 334
    multiple name servers, 166
    name servers, 36–39
    nslookup, 38
split namespaces, 348–351
srchlist option (nslookup), 242
SRV (service location) records, 156, 363
stale records, troubleshooting, 141–145
start of authority (see SOA)
starting/stopping DNS server, 82
    from DOS command line, 83, 262–265
StartService method, 296
state-level domains, 19
statistics, name servers, 141
StopService method, 296
storage, Active Directory zones, 152–155,
        161–163
stub resolvers, 26
stub zones
    delegation, 211
    troubleshooting, 340
subdirectories, 5
subdomains, 4, 6, 16, 151
    choosing, 40
    delegation, 21, 23, 190, 206–212
        troubleshooting, 322
    determining, 16
    in-addr.arpa domains, 198–206
    life cycles, 214
    non-U.S., 19
    parents, 186
        configuring, 188–198
        naming children, 187
    reading, 20
    remote management, 7
    size, 186
    SOA records, 41
    transitions, 212–214
    troubleshooting, 321
    (see also domains)
subnetting networks
    Class A and B, 200
    Class C, 201
    on/off octet boundaries, 199
    prioritization, 119
subtrees, 4
    domains, 13
suffixes, 107
    modifying, 109
    searching, 112–115
support, Microsoft web site, 38

T

TCP (Transmission Control Protocol), 335
    virtual circuits, 241
TCP/IP (Transmission Control Protocol/Internet
        Protocol), 1, 10
    nslookup and, 241
temporary root servers, 183
testing
    delegation, 206–212
    domain setups, 84
text labels, 4
TeXT records (see TXT records)
TextRepresentation method, 305
time to live (see TTL)
timeouts
    nslookup, 238, 242
    troubleshooting, 254
TIS Firewall Toolkit, 335
TLDs (top-level domains), 16
    choosing, 40
    generic (gTLDs), 44
    Internet, 17
    list of, 376
    naming subdomains as, 188
    registries and, 40
    root name servers, 27
tools
    command-line, 279–281
    dig, 256–260
    DNS console, 57
    DNSLint, 206–212, 311–313
    Firewall Toolkit, 335
    nslookup, 237–239
        customizing, 239–242
        searching, 242–252
        troubleshooting, 252–256
top-level domains (see TLDs)
tracert utility, 321
tracing queries and responses, 246
traffic, 3, 33, 168
    dial-on-demand and, 352
    root name servers, 27
trailing dot (.), 76
    in domain names, 12
transaction signatures (TSIGs), 216
transfers
    incremental zone, 222
    zones
        nslookup, 251
        unauthorized, 235
transitions, subdomains, 212–214
translation
    caching, 118
    configuring, 107–118, 124–126
    resolvers, 106
    subnet prioritization, 119
    Windows 95, 120
    Windows 98, 122
    Windows NT 4.0, 122

Transmission Control Protocol (see TCP)
Transmission Control Protocol/Internet Protocol
    (see TCP/IP)
trees, 4
    domain namespaces, 11–17
        Internet, 17–21
    domains, 147
troubleshooting
    aging, 141–145
    command-line tools, 279–281
    configuration check script, 297
    connections, 319
    delegation, checking, 206
    dial-up connections, 351–353
    dig, 257
    disasters, 180–184
    DNS, 308
    DNSLint, 311–313
    Event Viewer, 138
    files, 128
    host configuration errors, 325
    inconsistent responses, 327
    interoperability, 324
    manual changes, 314
    Microsoft support, 38
    name servers, 297
    nslookup, 237–239, 252–256
    preventive measures, 182
    PTR records, 317
    recursion, 235
    scavenging, 141–145
    serial numbers, 313
    servers, 57, 308
        checking caches, 309
    signals, 314
    stub zones, 340
    subdomains, 321
        delegation, 322
    unauthorized zone transfers, 235
    WINS reverse lookup and, 229
    zones, 223, 315
truncated packets, 241
TSIGs (transaction signatures), 216
TTL (time to live), 91
    changing, 177
    master file formats, 357
    minimum, 180
    modifying, 177–180
    resolvers, 118
TXT (TeXT) records, 134, 362
types
    of addresses, 17
    of name servers, 25
    of resource records, 357

U

UDP response packets, 174, 241
unauthorized zone transfers, 235
uninterruptible power system (UPS), 182

Update Server Data Files command (DNS
    console), 72
updating
    cache.dns file, 135
    dynamic updates, 154
    glue records, 196
    security, 216–224
    SOA records, 132
    zones, 129–136
UPS (uninterruptible power system), 182
us domain, registering under, 43
USC Information Sciences Institute, 4
Usenet newsgroups, 37
utilities
    DNS console, 57
    using, 256
    (see also tools)

V

values, CLASS, 364
VBScript, 284–289
vc option (nslookup), 241
VeriSign registrar/registry, 40, 49
version control, 336
View menu (DNS console), 57
    Filter option, 57
viewing
    name server statistics, 141
    zone datafiles, 72–74
virtual circuits, 241

W

wantrecursion string, 247
whois databases, 48
whois service, 42, 49
    network registration, checking, 48
    searching, 42
wildcards, 332
Windows 2000 resolver, 106–120
Windows 95 resolver, 120
Windows 98 resolver, 122
Windows filesystems, 4
Windows Internet Naming Service (see WINS)
Windows Management Instrumentation (see
    WMI)
Windows NT 4.0 resolvers, 122
Windows Server 2003 resolver, 106–120
Windows XP resolver, 106–120
WINS (Windows Internet Naming Service), 10,
    229
    lookup, 225
    records, 324
    reverse lookup, 227
wizards
    Configure Your Server, 53
    New Delegation, 194
    New Zone, 203
WMI DNS Provider, 283
WMI Query Language (WQL), 287

WMI (Windows Management
        Instrumentation), 282–284
   scripting, 284–289
WQL (WMI Query Language), 287
writing debugging information, 128

Z

Zone Properties window (Microsoft DNS
        Server), 93
zones, x, 5, 22, 26
   Active Directory, 152–155, 161–163
   application partitions, 153
   BIND, 324
   classes, 299–304
   CNAME records, 329–332
   configuration, 10
   creating, 60, 87, 302
   datafiles, 26
      controls, 136–145
      domains, 76
      manual changes to, 315
   dnscmd commands, 269
   domains, 22
      selecting, 39–49
   expired, 315
   in-addr.arpa, 131
   incremental transfers, 222

   listing, 303
   MX records, 100
   name servers, 22–31
      selecting, 36–39
   naming conventions, 373
   NOTIFY, 218
   nslookup, 237–239
   parents, 189
   properties of, 93
   registering, 48
   resource records, 305
   reverse-mapping, 67
   secondary name servers, 174
   serial numbers, 132
   SOA records, 41
   split namespaces, 348–351
   stale resource records and, 141
   stub zones
      managing delegation, 211
      troubleshooting, 340
   subdomains, 151
   transfers, 25, 86, 218
      nslookup, 251
      optimizing, 223
      unauthorized, 235
   updating, 129–136
   WINS lookup, 225

About the Authors

Matt Larson works for VeriSign's Naming and Directory Services division, the folks who maintain the database of all *.com* and *.net* domain names and run the name servers for those two zones, along with other pieces of the Internet's critical DNS infrastructure. In 1997 he started Acme Byte & Wire with Cricket Liu. Before being acquired by VeriSign in 2000, Acme Byte & Wire counted many large companies as its customers, including 10 of the Fortune 100. Matt's first job out of college was with Hewlett-Packard, first as Cricket's successor as *hp.com* hostmaster, then as a consultant in HP's Professional Services Organization.

Matt graduated from Northwestern University with degrees in computer science and music. He lives in the Washington, D.C. area with his wife Sonja, son Christian, and their two pugs. In his spare time, he enjoys playing the 10-rank pipe organ in his house.

Cricket Liu matriculated at the University of California's Berkeley campus, that great bastion of free speech, unencumbered Unix, and cheap pizza. He joined Hewlett-Packard after graduation and worked for Hewlett-Packard for nine years. Cricket began managing the *hp.com* zone after the Loma Prieta earthquake forcibly transferred the zone's management from HP Labs to HP's corporate offices (by cracking a sprinkler main and flooding the Labs' computer room). Cricket was *hostmaster@hp.com* for over three years, and then joined HP's Professional Services Organization to cofound HP's Internet Consulting Program.

Cricket left HP in 1997 to form Acme Byte & Wire, a DNS consulting and training company, with his friend and coauthor Matt Larson. Network Solutions acquired Acme in June 2000 and later the same day merged with VeriSign.

Cricket is currently an executive vice president at Infoblox, a maker of appliances that support network infrastructure services, including DNS. Cricket, his wife Paige, and their son Walt live in California with two Siberian Huskies, Dakota and Annie.

Robbie Allen (*www.rallenhome.com*) is a Member of Technical Staff at Cisco Systems, where he has worked since 1997. He was instrumental in the deployment and automation of DNS, DHCP, and Active Directory at Cisco. Robbie is the author of several articles and books, including O'Reilly's best-selling *Windows 2000 Active Directory*, Second Edition, and *Active Directory Cookbook*.

Colophon

Our look is the result of reader comments, our own experimentation, and feedback from distribution channels. Distinctive covers complement our distinctive approach to technical topics, breathing personality and life into potentially dry subjects.

The animal on the cover of *DNS on Windows Server 2003* is an African white-necked raven (*Corvus albicollis*), a subspecies of raven, the largest of the crow-like birds at about 24 inches long. The sexes look alike; the female is slightly smaller. Perceived as spirited or even impudent, the raven has a distinctive hoarse carrying call. They are excellent flyers, hovering and gliding, and are safe in flight from predators. Ravens are scavengers and eat carrion and small live animals, as well as some plants. They sometimes hide and store excess food, and will occasionally carry food in their feet.

African raven nests, built in niches in rocks, are crafted of an underlying stick structure, covered by grass, dirt, and rocks, then smaller twigs with soft materials such as moss or rags, and finally a layer of grass or similar plant material. Ravens lay 3 to 6 mottled grayish-green eggs, and the young hatch after 18 to 20 days of incubation. Both parents (a pair mated for life) will change the nest lining materials to adjust for changes in temperature and climate.

The raven is a popular figure, both profane and sacred, in many legends. Ravens, along with their relatives, jays and crows, have long been considered omens of evil in folklore, possibly due to the supposed annual tribute in feathers paid to the Devil; this legend is probably based on the molting of feathers every summer, during which the raven stays relatively well hidden—only this and nothing more. The Old Testament lists ravens among "unclean" birds; ravens also fed Elijah by the brook. Other ancient and medieval cultures considered the raven a symbol of virility or wisdom. An ancient Norse saga describes the use of ravens by ocean navigators as guides to land, and Norse mythology describes ravens as scouts for Odin. Native American folklore tells that the raven created the world and its creatures.

Because it preys on locusts, mice, and rats, the white-necked raven is generally welcomed in Africa (despite the occasional theft of domestic fowl). Like that of many other wild animals, the raven's habitat is dwindling with expansion of the human population.

Matt Hutchinson was the production editor for *DNS on Windows Server 2003*. Octal Publishing, Inc. provided production services. Sarah Sherman, Reg Aubry, and Claire Cloutier provided quality control.

Edie Freedman designed the cover of this book, based on her series design. The cover image is a 19th-century engraving from the Dover Pictorial Archive. Emma Colby produced the cover layout with QuarkXPress 4.1 using Adobe's ITC Garamond font.

David Futato designed the interior layout. This book was converted by Julie Hawks to FrameMaker 5.5.6 with a format conversion tool created by Erik Ray, Jason McIntosh, Neil Walls, and Mike Sierra that uses Perl and XML technologies. The text font is Linotype Birka; the heading font is Adobe Myriad Condensed; and the code font is LucasFont's TheSans Mono Condensed. The illustrations that appear in the book were produced by Robert Romano and Jessamyn Read using Macromedia FreeHand 9 and Adobe Photoshop 6. The tip and warning icons were drawn by Christopher Bing. This colophon was written by Nancy Kotary.